Contents

Preface   ix
Acronyms and abbreviations   xi

1 Introduction   1

2 The housing situation in Europe   7

The demographic background   8
Relative standards of living   10
The housing stock   11
Tenure   16
Conclusion   22

3 Housing policy in France   23

Tenure   26
Owner occupation   26
The private rented sector   30
The social rented sector   35
Housing allowances   41
The costs of the policy   42
Conclusion   43

4 Housing policy in Germany   45

Tenure   48
Subsidies to investment   51
The owner occupied sector   53
The private rented sector   58
The social rented sector   61
Housing allowances   68
The costs of the policy   70
Conclusion   72

5 Housing policy in the Netherlands   75

Tenure   78
The owner occupied sector   80
The private rented sector   83
The social rented sector   86
Housing allowances   91
The costs of the policy   92
Conclusion   94

6 Housing policy in Spain   96

Owner occupation   98
The rented sectors   112
The costs of housing policy   115
Conclusion   116

7 Housing policy in Sweden   118

Owner occupation   121
Co-operative housing   126
The private rented sector   129
The public rented sector   132
Housing allowances   135
The costs of the policy   136
Conclusion   137

8 Housing policy in Britain   139

Tenure   142
The owner occupied sector   143
The private rented sector   151
The social rented sector   155
Housing allowances   171
The costs of the policy   174
Conclusion   176

9 The Single Market and European integration   179

A European housing policy?   180
European funds   184
Conclusion   188

Housing policy
in Britain and Europe

Gavin McCrone
Mark Stephens

UCL
PRESS

First published in 1995 by UCL Press

UCL Press Limited
University College London
Gower Street
London WC1E 6BT

The name of University College London (UCL) is a registered
trade mark used by UCL Press with the consent of the owner.

ISBNs: 1-85728-410-0 HB
       1-85728-411-9 PB

British Library Cataloguing-in-Publication Data
A CIP catalogue record for this book is available from the British Library.

Library of Congress Cataloging-in-Publication Data are available

Typeset in Plantin and Optima.
Printed and bound by
Page Bros (Norwich) Ltd, England.

10 A single market in mortgage finance? 190

The economics of the Single Market 190
Implementing the Single Market 196
The Single Market in operation 208
Conclusions 218

11 Housing and labour mobility 221

The British housing market and population movement 222
Housing, planning and regional policy 226
The European Union and population movement 228
Conclusion 233

12 The economics of European integration 234

Housing policy and public expenditure 234
The structure of housing debt 240
Housing finance and macroeconomic policy 243
Conclusion 250

13 The future of British housing policy 251

The objectives 251
The policies 253
Financing the policy 268
Conclusion 272
Summary of proposals 273

References 275
Index 285

Preface

The work for this book was made possible by generous financial support from the Joseph Rowntree Foundation. Our first debt of gratitude is therefore to the Foundation and to the Steering Group – Sir Donald Barron, Richard Best, Christopher Johnson and Duncan Maclennan – whose comments at various stages of the work were of great value to us. We would also like to thank Neil Menzies and Nigel Campbell who kindly offered to read the whole text and gave us many helpful points of detail.

For the country chapters we are greatly indebted for help and advice to a large number of experts both from universities and from government departments in the countries concerned. All were ready to give generously of their time to discuss their countries' policies with us and to provide critical and constructive comments on our drafts. While, of course, they bear no responsibility for any errors that remain, their painstaking assistance has enabled us to remove many inaccuracies and to take account of the latest changes in policy. In particular we would like to thank: Anne-Marie Fribourg, Gilles Horenfeld, Elizabeth Devlin and Hervé Huntzinger in France; Franz Hubert, Eugen Dick and Dr Wiek in Germany; Hugo Priemus and Matthé van Oostrom in the Netherlands; Lennart Lundqvist, Lars Johan Waldén, Kristina Swärd, Bo Bengtsson and Ian MacArthur in Sweden; Baralides Alberdi, Luis Furones and Luis Orgaz in Spain; and Alan Holmans, David Middleton and Kenneth Gibb in the United Kingdom. Diane Miles of Woolwich Europe also provided invaluable information concerning Spain.

For the chapters in the second half of the book we were assisted by discussions at the European Commission, in particular with Paolo Clarotti, Ruud van Wensen and Sybren Singlesma. We also received much help from Grant Baird of Scotland Europa and we are grateful to him, Richard Grover of Oxford Brookes University, and to Richard Quinn of the Bank of England and of the Office of the United Kingdom Permanent Representative to the European Union for comments on the chapter on mortgage finance in the Single Market. This chapter relies heavily on discussions we had with banks, building societies and other financial institutions. Space does not allow us to mention all of those who kindly set aside their time to see us, but we would particularly like to record our thanks to David Jenkins, Robert Browning and their colleagues at the Bank of Scotland, Frank Kirwan and Ian Finlayson at The Royal Bank of Scotland, Iain Tweedie and Mike Jones at

ix

Lloyds Bank, David Smith at the Dunfermline Building Society, David Gilchrist and Ian Lumsden at the Halifax, Trevor Thornhill at Bradford and Bingley, David Parry at Nationwide, David Small at the Woolwich, Mark Paine at Abbey National, Christopher Head and Anthony Ward at Mortgage Trust, Guy Knight and Stephanie le Saux at Crédit Agricole and Norman Dijance and Bill Champion at the Building Societies Commission. Once again, however, the responsibility for the conclusions we have drawn from these discussions is ours alone.

Finally, Fiona Tomkinson assisted us with translation. The tasks of typing our drafts, producing order out of a chaos of computer disks and preparing charts and diagrams were undertaken by Julie Morgan, Stella Cowan and Margaret Keoghan. To them too we express our thanks.

Gavin McCrone   October 1994
Mark Stephens

Acronyms and abbreviations

AL *allocation de logement* (personal housing allowance) (France)
ALF *allocation de logement familiale* (type of AL for families) (France)
ALS *allocation de logement sociale* (type of AL for elderly, handicapped and unemployed) (France)
ANAH *Agence Nationale pour l'Amélioration de l'Habitat* (provides assistance for house improvement) (France)
APL *aide personalisée au logement* (personal housing allowance tied to housing) (France)

BES Business Expansion Scheme (Britain)
BIC Banque Immobilier de Crédit (France)
BKN Swedish National Housing Credit Guarantee Board
BLS Besluit Lokatiegebonden Subsidies (location tied subsidies) (Netherlands)
BSA Building Societies Association (Britain)
BSC Building Societies Commission (Britain)
BWS Besluit Woninggebonden Subsidies (housing tied subsidies) (Netherlands)

C&G Cheltenham and Gloucester Building Society (Britain)
CDC *Caisse des Dépôts et des Consignations* (funding body for HLM organizations) (France)
CDU Christian Democratic Union (Germany)
CEC Commission of the European Communities
CECODHAS European Liaison Committee for Social Housing
CEL *Comptes d'epargne-logement* (housing savings scheme; see also PEL) (France)
CFF Crédit Foncier de France
CGT Capital Gains Tax

DOE Department of the Environment (Britain)
DC desired level of capital (Britain)

xi

ECSC European Coal and Steel Community
ECU European Currency Unit
EEIG European Economic Interest Group
EFTA European Free Trade Association
EGFI European Group of Financial Institutions
EMU economic and monetary union
ERDF European Regional Development Fund
ERM Exchange Rate Mechanism (of the European Monetary System)
ESF European Social Fund
EU European Union

GDR German Democratic Republic
GRO Grant for Rent and Ownership (Scotland)

HAG Housing Association Grant (Britain)
HAT Housing Action Trust (Britain)
HBK Antwerp Savings Bank (Belgium)
HBM *habitations à bon marché* (housing associations for social housing; predecessors to HLMs) (France)
HIP Housing Investment Programme (England)
HLM *habitations à loyer modéré* (social housing at a moderate rent – housing associations) (France)
HLM-OP (*office public*) and HLM-OPAC (*office public d'aménagement et de construction*) housing associations set up by local authorities, *départements* or regions (France)
HLM-SA (*société anomyme*) HLM associations set up by companies, public corporations and other independent interests (France)
HRA Housing Revenue Account (Britain)
HSB Tenants' Savings Bank and Housing Association (Sweden)

IBOS Inter-Bank On-Line System

LCHO low cost home ownership (Britain)
LIBOR London Inter-Bank Offer Rate
LSVT large-scale voluntary transfer (Britain)
LTV loan to value ratio

MAC minimum acceptable capital (Britain)
MBS mortgage backed security
MHC municipal housing company
MITR mortgage interest tax relief
MMC Monopolies and Mergers Commission (Britain)

PAH   *prime à l'amélioration de l'habitat* (grant for house improvement, France)

PALULOS   *prime à l'amélioration de logement à usage locatif et à occupation sociale* (grant for house improvement in the social sector, France)

PAP   *prêt d'accession à la propriété* (low interest loans for purchasers of new owner-occupied housing, France)

PC   *prêt conventionné* (regulated or contract loans for house purchasers, France)

PEL   *Plans d'epargne-logement* (housing savings scheme) (France)

PIBS   Permanent Interest Bearing Shares (Britain)

PLA   *prêt locatif aidé* (subsidized loans mainly for social rented, but available for some private rented housing, France)

PLI   *prêt locatif intermédiare* (alternative name for PLS, France)

PLS   *prêt locatif social* (subsidized loans (less subsidized than PLA) for private rented and social rented housing, France)

RFC   Rate Fund Contribution (Britain)

RTB   right to buy (Britain)

RTM   rents to mortgage (Britain)

SA   *Société Anonyme* (a limited liability company, France)

SABO   Sveriges Allmännyttiga Bostadsföretag (Swedish Association of Municipal Housing Companies)

SAGA   Municipal Housing Company in Hamburg

SBAB   Statens Bostadsfinanslertingsaktiebolag (State-owned mortgage finance agency, Sweden)

SCIC   *Société Civile Immobilière de la Caisse des Dépôts* (property arm of the *Caisse des Dépôts et des Consignations*

SEM   *Sociétés d'Economie Mixte* (public–private partnership landlords, France)

SKB   Stockholm Tenant Housing Cooperative Association

SPD   Social Democratic Party (Germany)

SSHA   Scottish Special Housing Association

UNFO-HLM   Union Nationale des Fédérations d'Organismes HLM (National Federation of Social Housing Organizations, France)

UPP   Urban Pilot Project

VAT   Value Added Tax

VROM   The Netherlands Ministry of Housing, Physical Planning and Environment

CHAPTER 1
Introduction

There are few matters that affect the quality of life for the bulk of the population so much as the condition of housing. It is therefore a subject of concern to all democratic governments. Nevertheless, the shape of housing policy differs greatly from one country to another; although all countries of the European Union have found it necessary to subsidize housing by one means or another, this has been done in a wide variety of ways. Some provide support to each of the tenures, and in certain cases it is an objective of policy to be tenure neutral. Others have concentrated support on one or two tenures, with no attempt at equality of treatment. There is a choice too between subsidizing the buildings (this is generally referred to as bricks and mortar subsidy), and support to individuals in the form of personal housing allowances (known in Britain as Housing Benefit). Most countries provide a mix of both types of support, although, as later chapters show, the balance over time has tended to move towards the latter. Most countries also have a social rented sector, in which subsidies are applied to enable rents to be below their economic cost. But again the sector varies widely between countries, not only as regards the extent to which rents are subsidized but also the chosen institutional arrangements. The size of this sector obviously depends on several factors, not least the extent to which other sectors are subsidized and therefore able to cater for the less well off.

In Britain there has never been any attempt at tenure neutrality in policy and the three main tenures have therefore been treated quite separately. In the social rented sector, by far the largest part of the stock has been in the direct ownership and management of local authorities and various agencies of central government. Although the proportion of such stock is reduced today, it is still a feature of the British housing scene that is all but absent in most other western European countries. Britain has also assisted the owner occupied sector and now has one of the highest proportions of owner occupied housing in Europe. By contrast, the private rented sector has been largely unassisted, subject to a very long period of rent control and regulation, and is now extremely small; yet in the early years of the century it accounted for about 90 % of the housing stock in the UK, and it still plays a major part in Germany and many other European countries.

In all countries, regardless of the average standard of living, there is a large section of the population that cannot afford the full economic cost of what would

1

generally be regarded as an adequate or tolerable standard of housing. This is a feature of the economics of housing. As a result, in Britain in the nineteenth century, and in many poorer countries today, a substantial part of the population has to live in accommodation that is seriously substandard, such as shanty towns or slums. But as economic advance has provided the means to improve social conditions, so by one means or another the State has assumed responsibility for ensuring that the population is adequately housed. In most western European countries, in the absence of such intervention, something of the order of a quarter to a third of the total population would be unable to pay the full economic cost of the housing it occupies.

It might be thought that such a problem would cure itself as a country becomes richer and the general standard of living rises. No doubt the proportion of the population unable to afford an "adequate" standard of housing is now less than it was, say, at the beginning of the century. But perceptions of an adequate standard have also risen. There is therefore no European country, no matter how advanced, where it is considered that housing can be left completely to the free market without State subvention in some form; and it would be unwise to assume that this will change with rising living standards. It may be that the reason for this is that housing costs tend to rise faster than those of many other goods in the economy. Housebuilding is a labour intensive industry and, as an economy advances, the output of labour intensive industries becomes relatively more expensive, because the rise in wage rates is not fully matched by the rates of productivity increase available in some other sectors. In addition, building materials have risen more rapidly in price than many other goods, at least in recent years, and the scarcity of prime sites, coupled with planning constraints, ensures escalating land prices. The result is that, although in the countries of the European Union average incomes are many times higher than they were at the end of the Second World War, public subventions are still necessary if affordable housing of an adequate and acceptable standard is to be provided for all sections of the community.

Although there is much variation in the detailed measures applied across Europe, there is a good deal of common ground in the choice of principal instruments. In the owner occupied sector, most countries have made wide use of tax reliefs: mortgage interest tax relief or depreciation allowances, exemption from capital gains tax, and exemption from owner occupier's imputed rent that would balance the tax paid on rent by landlords. In some countries there has also been widespread use of grants for investment and low interest loans.

In the private rented sector, there has also been some use of tax reliefs, grants and subsidized loans, although the incidence has varied greatly from one country to another. There has been widespread use of rent control and rent regulation, commonly adopted in time of war to prevent unscrupulous profiteering from the ensuing shortage of accommodation, but which usually turns into a forced subsidy from landlord to tenant, with severe implications for the supply of rented dwellings. In some countries, apart from Britain, there have also been subsidies to this sector to enable it to cater for the less well off tenant and which therefore blur the distinction between this sector and the social rented sector proper.

The social rented sector is usually, but not always, distinguished by non-profit making landlords, whose purpose is to provide rented accommodation below the economic cost and who receive a subsidy to enable them to do so. Such a subsidy may be in the form of either a one-off capital grant or low interest loan, to meet part of the cost of the investment, or as a recurrent subsidy that may be adjusted year by year to achieve an acceptable level of rent. In this sector, the effects of inflation can be particularly important: even where social landlords appear to receive no subsidy at all, rents can be far from economic levels, in the sense of covering costs and providing a return on capital in real terms, because outstanding debt has been eroded by rising prices.

Finally, there are housing allowances, now available in most countries for individuals whose incomes are not sufficient to enable them to pay their current housing costs. Such allowances may apply to all sectors or be restricted to rented accommodation only. Unlike the other subsidies, they are targeted on at individuals and are related to both to their means and their housing needs, rather than being tied to a particular house. For the government there may be a "trade-off" between the two kinds of support: with given levels of income, lower subsidies to bricks and mortar require greater expenditure on housing allowances, and *vice versa*. But support through personal allowances is more sharply focused on those in need and would therefore not normally cost as much as general subsidies to bricks and mortar. There will always be some in receipt of a subsidy on their house, who in its absence would not qualify for a personal allowance.

The contributions made by governments, and therefore by taxpayers, are very large in the European countries. The cost of support ranges between 1% and just over 4% of GDP, but it is difficult for at least two main reasons to calculate the true cost of all the various types of intervention accurately. First, the scale of housing assistance depends at least in part on the generosity of other forms of social provision. The better pensions and unemployment relief are, the less need there is for housing subsidies. Secondly, an accurate assessment would require a comparison to be made with a hypothetical situation in a free market. Because of such factors as the erosion of housing debt through inflation and the effects of rent control and regulation, the expenditure by central and local government is not necessarily a complete measure of the extent to which housing costs to the individual differ from their economic level. Nevertheless, housing policy is a major item of expenditure for all governments in western Europe. In Britain it cost about £20000 million in 1992/3, well in excess of the expenditure on roads or on industry, but less than is spent on defence, education, health or social security.

However, in few European countries could it be said that the expenditure is well targeted to achieve value for money, if the objective is to achieve an adequate standard of housing for all sections of the community. Policies have developed over a long period, and in most countries they contain an inheritance

3

of measures, whose purpose may have relatively little to do with the central objective of housing policy but which are politically difficult to change. Sometimes governments have themselves applied measures to meet secondary political objectives and have tended to lose sight of what housing policy is really for. In addition, some countries for many years deliberately adopted a policy that made support general and non-discriminatory, as it was for other social services, rather than related to the circumstances of the individual. As a result, tax relief or, in some cases, grants and subsidized loans have been received by many people who could well afford the economic cost of housing. The costs of such an approach are making these policies increasingly difficult to sustain, and the effect of such general intervention may at least partly feed through into higher house prices. If so, it may do little for those most in need. The rationale for the various measures therefore needs to be properly thought through, even if changes do require political courage.

This book is concerned with the instruments of housing policy, the measures employed by governments, and their respective merits in achieving their objectives. Its focus is economic rather than social and therefore it does not attempt to cover such problems as deprivation and social exclusion. Nor is it a study of housing conditions, a subject that requires detailed local knowledge and which has been tackled by other authors (e.g. Emms 1990, Power 1993). Its purpose is twofold: to compare Britain's housing policy with that of other European countries and to consider how far the increased economic integration stemming from the Single European Act, and from the movement towards economic and monetary union, will require changes. Will the present widely differing national policies be able to continue or will there be pressure for some kind of convergence? Will member States, learning from the experience of others, see advantage in adopting similar policies, even if they are not obliged to by the process of integration?

Housing policy is not formally within the competence of the Commission or the Council under the treaties, and at first sight it might seem to be a good example of a subject that can be left to the unfettered discretion of national governments. But even in policy areas where the Commission does not have competence, the process of economic integration can have implications. It is the contention of this book that this will be the case with housing. There are a variety of ways in which this may arise:

- the effect of liberalization of capital movements and the attempt to achieve a single financial market on the provision of mortgage finance
- fiscal and monetary harmonization, and the attempt to meet the convergence criteria for economic and monetary union set at Maastricht, will have implications for public expenditure, including expenditure on housing policy
- freedom of movement of labour and the need to attract investment, while avoiding inflationary pressures, require a housing market that is flexible, and policies that facilitate mobility

- in the European market, instability in the housing market may adversely affect economic prospects if it contributes to the destabilization of the economy. There is clear evidence that this has been a feature of Britain in the recent economic cycle.

There are therefore several issues related to housing policy that need to be considered, some of which may affect the operations of the economy in a more closely integrated European market. But there are also lessons to be learnt from the policies pursued in other European countries, which may enable British policy to be improved. Even if there is no case for a European housing policy and everything to be said for continuing with policies that most closely meet national circumstances, the increasing dialogue on economic policies generally requires greater awareness of policies pursued in other member States. It would be surprising if States could not learn from each other in the housing field as much as in other aspects of social and economic policy.

The chapters that follow in Part 1 set out the national housing policies in Britain and a selection of five other European countries. Some explanation is necessary for the way in which Britain has been handled. Most books on housing policy in Britain or the UK concentrate on policy in England, since that is by far the largest constituent country, and they leave the reader to assume that policies in the other three countries of the UK are broadly similar. But this is far from correct, as there are considerable variations. The present study makes no attempt to describe policy in Northern Ireland, where the differences both in circumstances and policy are greatest. For this reason it is described as a study of policy in Britain rather than the United Kingdom, which would include Northern Ireland. Occasionally, however, the UK is referred to, mainly for statistical purposes. Nor does the book deal explicitly with Wales, where the policy is very similar to that followed in England. But it does attempt to describe policy in Scotland as well as England, since there are some important distinctive features in Scottish housing policy that are of interest in a comparison with other countries. The other five countries include: France and Germany, because of their importance in the European Union and also because there are aspects of their policies that are of particular interest in Britain; the Netherlands, because its policy has been strongly socially orientated and it has also built a high proportion of its housing stock since the war; one Scandinavian country, Sweden, which has had a policy both strongly socially orientated and closer to being tenure neutral than in any other country; and one Mediterranean country, Spain, which is also among the four less well off member States in the Union. An effort has been made to follow the same layout for each country chapter, so that measures can be compared and, where appropriate, the differences highlighted.

But the perspective of the book is British, as is the experience of the authors. This will be particularly evident in the discussion of the European issues in Part 2. Some important conclusions for the other countries arise from these chapters and, where they do, every effort is made to draw them out; but it is with the lessons for Britain that the book is mainly concerned. Although major changes have taken place in British policy over the past 15 years, the authors' view is that it cannot yet be said to be achieving the objective either of a well housed population or of assisting rather than hindering the performance of the economy in an increasingly integrated Europe.

CHAPTER 2
The housing situation in Europe

A wide variety of factors play a part in shaping housing policies, notably population growth and migration, levels of income, climate, and of course the political objectives of governments. The purpose of this chapter is to set out this background using available statistical material to draw contrasts across western Europe as a whole, but concentrating particularly on the six countries chosen for more detailed study in the rest of the book. The chapter starts by setting out factors that influence housing demand: population, including growth and migration, and comparative standards of living. This is followed by the national characteristics of housing supply: the size of the housing stock, its age, quality, composition and cost. The second half of the chapter contrasts the national patterns of housing tenure, a particularly important aspect of housing supply which has been much influenced by the policy measures described in the subsequent country chapters.

Statistical material on housing in Europe is collected by national governments for their own purposes and is therefore not always on a comparable basis. However, in 1991 the Dutch Ministry of Housing, Planning and the Environment published housing statistics covering the 12 member States of the European Union for the meetings of European housing ministers, and in 1993 this work was undertaken for the first time by the European Commission and extended to include Sweden and Austria (VROM 1992, CEC 1993). Comparative statistics on this subject are therefore still at an early stage of development; and, as always with such material, it is difficult to take adequate account of definitional or qualitative differences between the countries. This is especially important when trying to analyze the quality of the housing stock. Some factors can only be judged subjectively and these are often as important as those that can be statistically measured, so that, even if the statistical material were better than it is, it would still be an imperfect guide. In the paragraphs that follow, care is therefore taken to avoid pushing such comparisons too far, but caution must nevertheless be exercised in interpreting some of the results.

The demographic background

The population of the countries is set out in Table 2.1. Although in absolute terms the populations vary greatly in size, the feature of greatest interest and of most relevance to housing policy (because it affects the construction effort required) is the difference in growth in the period since the Second World War. In France, the former West Germany and Spain, the growth has been very similar, at around 45%; the Netherlands, perhaps surprisingly, has had by far the largest growth in its population over this period (over 60%), while the Swedish population has grown by under 30%. Of the six countries, the UK's population growth has been by far the lowest: at 16%, not much more than half the rate for Sweden; and, within the UK, Scotland had a 1991 population that was slightly below that of 1945.

Table 2.1 The demographic background.

	Population, 1991 (000)	Population as % of 1945	Population/ km²	Persons per household
Belgium	10022	144.5	334	2.5
Denmark	5129	126.8	119	2.2
Germany	79984	–	225	2.3
former FRG		143.9		
former GDR		92.2		
Greece	10200	126.7	77	3.1
Spain	38872	145.5	77	3.3
France	56634	144.3	104	2.6
Ireland	3526	119.4	50	3.3
Italy	57746	122.6	192	2.8
Luxembourg	384	135.7	148	2.6
Netherlands	15060	161.3	442	2.4
Portugal	10400	118.4	113	3.1
United Kingdom	57800	116.4	235	2.5
England	47055	119.5	364	
Scotland	5100	98.3	65	
Austria	7796	114.7	93	2.5
Sweden	8644	129.0	19	2.1
Finland	5029	130.0	15	2.6

Source: CEC, Demographic statistics; CEC, Statistics on housing in the European Community.

Population growth is a product of both natural population increase and net migration, the contribution of these two components to population growth for 1985–91 is shown in Figure 2.1. Rates of natural increase have tended to come down throughout Europe during the 1980s. But a net inflow of migrants has been a particularly important feature of West Germany, especially up to 1961, when the Berlin wall was built, and again since 1989. However, since much of the migration was from East to West Germany, it became internal after unification. Migration has also affected the Netherlands. By contrast net immigration to the UK has been very low, and to Scotland negative. The birth rate in Ireland has been well above the EU average, but its effects on the Irish population have been

Errata

p. 79, Figure 5.1
Corrected version below:

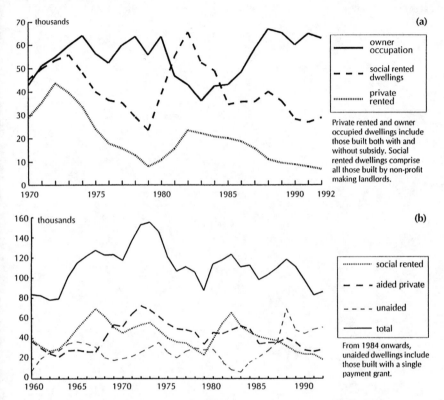

Figure 5.1 Dwellings completed (% of total): (a) by tenure, (b) by type of financing (*Source: Statistical yearbook of the Netherlands*).

p. 173, Figure 8.2
Source: Wilcox 1993.

p. 275, Figure 12.4
Source: HM Treasury.

p. 276, Figure 12.5
The numerical values on the vertical axis should range from 80 to 150, with the value for 1985 being 100.

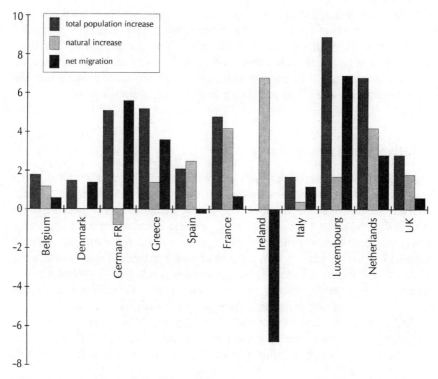

Figure 2.1 The composition of population growth (*Source:* Eurostat 1993b).

counteracted by high and continuing rates of net emigration. There are many non-nationals in residence in the various countries (a subject that is discussed further in Ch. 11); some of these are nationals of other EU States, but many are "guest workers" from Turkey, North Africa and other States outside the Union.

Population density is of less immediate concern for housing policy, although it is likely to affect the price of land and may thereby have an influence on both the cost and form of housing. The most densely populated countries are the Netherlands (442 persons per km²), Belgium (334), the UK (235) and Germany (225), and the least being Sweden (19), Ireland, (50), Spain, (77). However, there are substantial differences within the UK itself. England, with 364 persons per km², has a density that is second only to the Netherlands. This is principally because of the large population in the South East, where the density is 641, comparable with North Holland (645), and the smaller population but even greater density in the North West (871), which compares with South Holland (964), and Ile de France (890). In contrast, Scotland (65) has a population density comparable with Ireland or Spain (Eurostat 1993a).

Persons per household differ relatively little among the wealthier States, ranging between 2.1 and 2.6 in five of the six countries studied. The figure is higher in the poorer countries, of which Spain and Ireland provide examples (both with

3.3). In all countries, the number of persons per household has come down over the past 20 years as a result of lower birth rates, later marriage, increased divorce rates, the trend towards single-parent families, and an ageing population. The growth of households therefore exceeds the rate of population increase, so that continuing growth in housing demand can be expected, even in circumstances where the size of the population is more or less static.

Relative standards of living

Figure 2.2 shows the relative levels of gross domestic product per head in the member States of the European Union, with the addition of Sweden and of Switzerland, the latter, although outside the Union, being of interest because of its very high level of GDP per head. The figures are calculated using purchasing-power parities, which is the most appropriate method for estimating relative standards of living, since it takes account of cost differences between countries, These are sometimes substantial and are not always reflected in exchange rates. Rather different results, usually less favourable to the UK, are obtained if conversion of national GDP per head is done using current exchange rates.

The chart shows that Switzerland, Luxembourg, France and, in 1989, the former West Germany, are clearly ahead of the other countries. However, the re-unification of Germany means that the 1993 figure, which includes the five

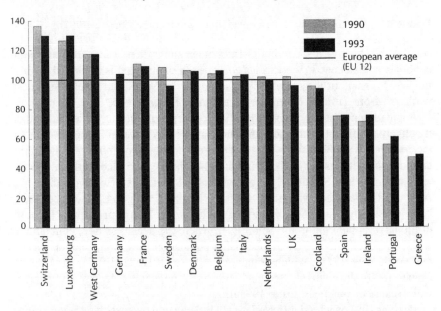

Figure 2.2 GDP per head in purchasing power parities (*Source:* CEC European economy, 56, 1994; OECD Main economic indicators, March 1994, Scottish economic bulletin, 48, Winter 1994/5.)

eastern *Länder* from the former German Democratic Republic (GDR), is just above the EU average. There is then a group of countries, including the Netherlands, Sweden and the UK, that all have GDP per head around the EU average. However, the 1993 figures show the UK and Scotland in a less favourable position than those for 1989, the UK's GDP per head falling from 2% above to 4% below the EU average. This is because of the very poor rates of growth in the early 1990s, as a result of the UK's recession being earlier and deeper than in the other countries. It remains to be seen how far the gap will be closed again by the more rapid rate of growth in 1994. Scotland was about 5% below the EU average in 1989 and, although suffering less severely from the 1990s recession than the rest of the UK, was about 6% below by 1993. The remaining four countries are significantly less well off, although Spain and Ireland, with GDP per head around 75–77% of the EU average, are ahead of the other two. Apart from Greece, these countries have had above average rates of growth and have therefore been catching up.

Over a long period, the UK's relative position and has deteriorated in comparison with the other countries as a result of lower rates of economic growth. This was especially true in the 1960s and 1970s, when it lost what had been in the 1950s a pre-eminent position (Gilbert & Associates 1958), with GDP per head higher than in any of the other 11 States of the pre-1995 EU; it has applied again in the early 1990s, when the UK suffered a deeper and more prolonged recession than most of the other countries. But in the 1980s the UK's relative position marginally improved, as growth rates in the other countries were sharply reduced compared with earlier decades. Sweden, which along with Switzerland was one of the two countries in Europe to have a higher GDP per head than the UK in the 1950s, has also had rates of economic growth below the average and it too was particularly affected by the recession of the early 1990s.

The housing stock

The housing stock for each country is set out in Table 2.2. When expressed as dwellings per thousand inhabitants, the figures are fairly close for all six countries in the study, with Sweden the highest at 475, followed by France at 463; the UK had 411 and the Netherlands the lowest proportion of the six at 393.

However, it is important to be aware of the shortcomings of these figures if any attempt is to be made to draw conclusions from them about the adequacy of supply. In the first place, requirements depend not so much on crude numbers of population as on actual and potential households. In countries where families are large, the number of people per house will be larger than in those where they are small, without this necessarily implying anything about the adequacy of provision. The figures for average size of household (Table 2.1) give no information on whether these are the desired sizes or whether relatives and friends are sharing accommodation simply because they have nowhere else to go.

11

Table 2.2 Housing stock.

	Total stock, 1991 (000)	Dwellings per 1000 persons, 1991	Second homes as % of stock	Useful floorspace per dwelling of existing stock (m^2) 1992	Unfit, lacking amenities or in serious disrepair (%)	% of stock with bath/ shower	Expenditure on housing as % of total private consumption 1989
Belgium	3748	395	–	86.3	32	88	16.7
Denmark	2375	465	8	106.9	13	90	27.4
Germany:							
former FRG	27139	421	–	86.6	–	96[4]	18.4[1]
former GDR	7033	445	–	64.4	–	82[1]	11.5
Greece	4690	457	–	–	34	84[5]	13.1[2]
Spain	17154	441	15	83.6	51	94[1]	18.9
France	26237[1]	463[1]	9[1]	85.4	9	95	10.9[5]
Ireland	1039	286	–	95.0	13	90[6]	12.5[1]
Italy	23232[2]	404[2]	–	92.0	49	86[6]	20.0
Luxembourg	135	404[2]	–	107.0	49	86[6]	18.6
Netherlands	5965	393	–	98.6	20	99[1]	–
Portugal	41811	424	9	–	23	84	19.5
United Kingdom	23750	411	1	79.7	14	99	17.9[2]
Austria	3393	435	6	85.0	16	84	20.0[2]
Sweden	4106	475	15	92.0	–	–	–

Notes: 1: 1990; 2: 1989; 3: 1982/83 for those lacking amenities; 4: 1987; 5: 1988; 6: 1981; 7: 1991.
Source: CEC, *Statistics on housing in the European Community*. Brussels.

Secondly, in several countries a sizeable proportion of the stock is either vacant or second homes. Second homes are particularly important in Spain and Sweden, in both of which they amount to about 15% of the stock, but they are also significant in France. For Spain this may explain why what seems to be a more generous level of provision in dwellings per thousand inhabitants than, for example, in the UK, is combined with an average household size of 3.3, the largest in the EU. And, where population has shifted rapidly from rural areas to towns, the average may reflect a surplus in the former (probably of rather run-down stock), combined with a serious shortage in urban areas.

Of the other countries, Denmark, like Sweden, has a high ratio of housing to population and a low average size of household. Greece also has a remarkably high ratio but, like Spain, a relatively large household size, so that a significant proportion must be second homes or standing empty. But the most striking figure is that of Ireland: at 286 dwellings per thousand population, by far the lowest proportion of all the countries. This is, not surprisingly, combined with a household size of 3.3, equal to that of Spain, reflecting a high birth rate and above-average number of children.

The scale of housing investment is shown in Table 2.3. In all countries it is much reduced from the high levels that were required by the major programmes of new house building in the post-war years and which continued up to the early 1970s. Such investment is a response not only to a need to accommodate a growing number of households, and therefore dependent on the rate of population growth, but also to the requirements of renovation and replacement. As the table

Table 2.3   Housing investment, 1992.

	As a % of gross investment	New dwellings completed (000s)	New dwellings per 1000 existing stock	Flats as % of all dwellings	Stock built since 1945 (%)
Belgium	21[1]	47	12.4	27[2]	50[5]
Denmark	20	17	7.2	38	54[5]
Germany	26	375	10.9	50	67
former GDR	–	–	–	69[4]	–
Greece	23[2]	–	–	57[3]	23
Spain	20	223	13.0	63[1]	73
France	25	277	10.6	42[1]	58
Ireland	22[1]	23	22.1	–	54[5]
Italy	26[1]	292	12.6	–	70
Luxembourg	20[1]	3[1]	22.2	32[4]	38[5]
Netherlands	23	86	14.4	30[1]	75
Portugal	17	66[1]	15.8	40[1]	55[5]
United Kingdom	18	174	7.3	19[2]	54
Scotland	–			45	59
Austria	19[1]	41	12.1	37[1]	67[5]
Sweden	27[1]	57	13.9	54	72

Source: CEC, Statistics on housing in the European Community, 1993; Lebègue Report; Swärd 1993.
1. 1990; 2. 1991; 3. 1988; 4. 1981; 5. 1945–81.

shows, the UK now spends less of its gross investment on housing than any of the other EU countries except Portugal; and, since UK gross investment as a proportion of GDP is below the EU average (16.7%, compared with 20.3 in 1991), this measure understates the difference.

The figures for new dwellings completed are consistent with this picture. Completions in the UK fell from 242000 a year in 1980 to 174000 in 1992, a drop of nearly 30%. At this level only seven dwellings were completed for every thousand of existing stock, which compares with 14.4 in the Netherlands, 10.9 in Germany and 10.6 in France. This lower level of new housebuilding effort in the UK does partly reflect a lower rate of population growth; it is also partly a response to the collapse of the boom in the owner occupied sector and the government's restraint on new building by local authorities (see Ch. 8). Nevertheless, it is striking in comparison with the other countries and it raises questions as to whether current housing investment in the UK is adequate for the longer term.

As to the character of the housing stock, a striking feature is the low proportion of flats in the UK: only 19%, compared with 50% or more in Germany, Sweden and Spain, 42% in France and 30% in the Netherlands. However, this is chiefly a characteristic of England and Wales, the Scottish stock being some 45% in flats and therefore similar in composition to the other countries.

It is difficult to form a reliable impression of the state and condition of the housing stock from published statistics, because so many aspects of quality, such as those that affect the environment of a housing area, cannot be measured. Even where there are statistical measurements, it is not clear that basic amenities and unfit dwellings mean the same thing in different countries. Even within the UK, the statutory definitions of "tolerable" standard in Scotland and the "fitness" standard in England are slightly different.[1] Generally, however, the UK scores well on such assessments, with only a few dwellings lacking basic amenities or classified as unfit, and 86% classified as "good" (i.e. neither lacking basic amenities, classified as unfit or in serious disrepair); 99% are equipped with a bath or shower and 82% with central heating, higher proportions than for most other countries (Table 2.2). However, these figures do not adequately cover problems such as dampness, which at best can only be assessed subjectively, and which are important in northern Europe. (For example, in Scotland, where for reasons of climate this is a serious problem, the "tolerable standard" does not cover dampness arising from condensation, but only rising damp and dampness as a result of exterior penetration). In addition, there is no officially required minimum floorspace standard for new dwellings in the UK, as there is in most other countries and, perhaps because of this, UK dwellings have a lower average floorspace than those of the other countries.

Table 2.3 also shows the proportion of the dwelling stock built since 1945. The Netherlands, as might be expected with its large population growth, has built the greatest part of its housing stock (75%) since 1945, and the UK with 54% has

---

1. See Housing Act (1985: Section 604) and Housing (Scotland) Act (1987: Section 86).

built the least. The British housing stock is, therefore, on average older than that of other countries. But it is more surprising that Spain, with much the same population growth as Germany and France, should have built a higher proportion of its present stock than either since 1945, especially in view of the amount of wartime destruction in Germany. But this figure may well be a result of the construction for second homes and also the movement from rural to urban areas, as the country became industrialized. The Swedish figure is also striking – 72% – and, since Sweden has the second lowest population growth after the UK, this illustrates the amount of replacement, particularly through urban renewal, that has taken place. The same explanation applies to Scotland, which, despite having a virtually static population, has a younger housing stock than the UK as a whole, with 59% built since 1945.

Costs and prices

Information on the costs of housing on a basis that permits a cross country comparison is fragmentary and it is therefore difficult to draw valid conclusions. Policy in some countries aims to keep costs for the less well off, especially in the social rented sector, below some predetermined proportion of income, usually 20 or 25%. But rents vary widely, in Britain usually from one local authority area to another, depending on its financial circumstances, and in other countries more commonly in relation to the age of the building. Averages, even if obtainable, are therefore not particularly useful.

The Commission estimates expenditure on housing of all types, including fuel and power, as a proportion of private consumption expenditure (Table 2.2). These figures vary considerably, from 20% for Sweden to 13.1% for Spain. The figures for the three large countries are very similar: Germany 18.4, France 18.9 and the UK 19.5. In general there seems to be some tendency for the figures for Scandinavian countries to be higher, and for southern Europe lower, which may be attributable to the inclusion of fuel and the need in northern Europe for more expensive accommodation for climatic reasons.

Better information is available on the cost of owner occupied housing, where there are considerable differences in house prices. A study by the Woolwich Building Society carried out in 1990 is reproduced in (Fig. 2.3). Although there are some reservations about comparability, which make it unwise to attach significance to small differences, the striking feature is that the average cost of an owner occupied house in Western Germany was £140000, more than double the cost in the Britain (£60317), which is itself higher than any of the other countries apart from Italy. As the figure shows, the differences between the other countries are not remarkable, especially as prices within a country vary substantially from one area to another. In the UK, for example, average house prices ranged from £37775 in Northern Ireland and £48347 in the northern region of England to £78254 in London and £74347 in the rest of the South East (Wilcox 1993: 98–

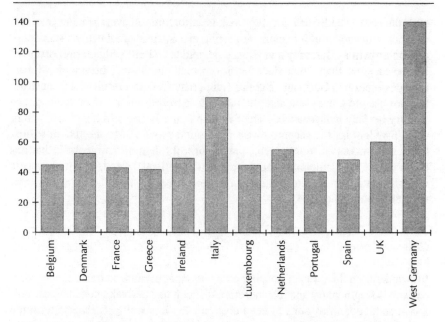

Figure 2.3 Average house prices (*Source:* Woolwich Survey, December 1990).

9). Indeed, if London and the South East were excluded, average UK house prices for the rest of the country would be similar to those in other countries.

The German case is therefore exceptional. There are several possible explanations: the very high standards set by building regulations in Germany; the much greater reliance on rented accommodation in the early years of married life, so that first-time buyers are on average ten years older than their counterparts in the UK and therefore likely to be better off; and the absence of "starter homes", with a tendency to buy a home for life rather than with a view to trading up-market in a few years' time.

Tenure

In most countries the proportion of stock in home ownership has increased substantially during the past 50 years, and this is commonly thought to be related to the improvement in living standards. On the face of it, this would appear to be a plausible view. Surveys in many countries show that most people aspire to own their own homes eventually, and as they become well enough off, they will seek to do so. At the same time, the better off people are, the less need one might expect there to be for a subsidized social rented sector. Private rented accommodation might then be regarded as an intermediate category: a tenure that meets the needs of those who are not yet settled in their careers, who have difficulty in

16

making a substantial down-payment and look for something at less than the full cost of home ownership.

Although this may partly explain the changing tenure pattern in favour of home ownership in individual countries, which is explored more fully in subsequent chapters, Table 2.4 shows that there are substantial differences between the countries and that these bear little or no relation to differences in standards of living, as already shown in Figure 2.1.

The table shows that the UK's share of home ownership is now exceptionally high by the standards of northern Europe. Belgium comes close to the UK share, but the only three countries where the share of owner occupation is higher than in the UK are among the four poorest: Ireland, Spain and Greece. And although in many countries the private rented sector has declined significantly since 1945, in no other country of western Europe is it as small as it has become in the UK.

On the other hand, Germany (excluding the five eastern *Länder* of the former Democratic Republic), although one of the wealthier nations in Europe, still has a very strong private rented sector, slightly larger even than the home ownership sector; and the latter at 38% in 1987 (the most recent census year) is substantially smaller than in Scotland, let alone England. The proportion of the stock in owner occupation in Sweden, Denmark, the Netherlands, and France ranges between 43% and 54%, slightly higher than in Germany. Switzerland, with the highest GDP per head in Europe has only 30% of its housing stock in home ownership, and at 66% the share of private rented accommodation is much the highest.

The size of the social rented sector bears no more relation than owner occupation to levels of income and wealth. In Germany and France it accounts for some 15–17% of the total stock, compared with about 23% in England and about 40% in Scotland. Only the Netherlands has a social sector of a size anywhere near that of Scotland, although it is very different in form. Sweden also has a large social rented sector and a significant co-operative "tenant ownership" movement, which was originally intermediate in status but has become increasingly close to a form of ownership. In Switzerland, with its high standard of living, the social rented sector accounts for only 4% of the stock, but it is even smaller in Spain, one of the four poorest countries, at about 2%.

The contrasts are perhaps most striking in the case of Belgium and the Netherlands, countries of similar size, economic characteristics and income levels, yet their patterns of housing tenure are totally different. Belgium's home ownership sector is among the largest, whereas in the Netherlands it is fairly small; and, whereas the Netherlands has the largest social rented sector (apart from Scotland), in Belgium it accounts for only 6% of the total stock.

Table 2.4 Housing tenure in western Europe (% of total stock).

	Denmark 1990	Sweden 1990	Norway 1988	W. Germany 1987	Neth. 1990	Belgium 1991	France 1988	Switz. 1990	Austria 1990	Spain 1990	Greece 1990	UK 1992	England 1992	Scotland 1992
Owner-occupied	52	43	60	38[a]	45	65	54	30	50	78	77	66	67	54
Privately rented	18	21	18	43	17	28	20	66	18	18	23	9	10	6
Non profit or social rented	17	21	4	15	36	6	17	4	21	2	–	24	23	40
Co-ownership or ownership co-operatives	7	15	18	–	–	–	–	–	–	–	–	–	–	–
Other	6	–	–	4	1	1	9	–	11	2	–	–	–	–

Source: CEC, Statistics on housing in the European Community 1993, Brussels; Boverket, 1992, Stockholm; Geindre, 1993 Paris; DoE et al., Housing and construction statistics 1993. London: HMSO.

a. Includes about 3% of stock in condominiums.

The causes of differences in the tenure pattern

The respective size of the three sectors is therefore more dependent upon the policies adopted in the various countries than their stage of economic development. These may not always be explicitly housing policies. In Ireland, for example, the Anglo-Irish landowners were bought out at the turn of the century with the help of the British government, largely for political reasons, leaving the former tenantry with the freehold of their agricultural holdings (Kee 1980: 142–5). The policy of the Catholic Church favours home ownership and this is given as a reason for the high percentage in Belgium (Boelhouwer & van der Heijden 1992: 86).

In many countries the proportion of home ownership in urban areas is much smaller than in small towns or in the countryside, so that degree of urbanization can be a factor. So is the predominant house form. The proportions of single houses (including semi-detached and terraced) and flats vary greatly from one country to another, even between England and Scotland. Flats, whether in tenements or in multi-floored apartment blocks, present greater, although not insurmountable, problems for housing management when ownership is fragmented.

The development of mortgage finance for home owners is certainly a key factor in the change in tenure pattern over time, and it accounts also for some of the present inter-country differences. Relatively few people can afford to buy their houses outright, even with today's living standards. Historically, before mortgage arrangements were as developed as they are now, this was a principle reason for the very low percentages of home ownership and the large size of the private rented sector. The development of the various forms of mortgage finance has enabled people to commit *future* savings to the *present* purchase of a house, given that for most earners investment demand exceeds saving in the early part of their careers, whereas saving exceeds investment later on. The system also permits, through a bank or building society, those with savings to invest to finance the housing investment of others. Given the widely expressed preference for home ownership, it is therefore only to be expected that, as housing finance has become more efficient and sophisticated, a shift from private renting to ownership would occur, even in the absence of other factors.

Other aspects of policy are also important. Most countries have encouraged home ownership, either with subsidies in the form of grants or low interest loans, or with various kinds of taxation incentive, of which relief against income tax liability on mortgage interest costs is the most important. In many countries, such incentives (in particular the subsidies) were originally intended to encourage private investment in housing in the face either of rapid population and household growth or to help overcome an acute housing shortage. Where this was the primary objective, efforts were sometimes made to ensure that such incentives were as far as possible tenure neutral, by providing comparable support for the rented sector. Elsewhere, incentives have been explicitly intended to encourage the share of home ownership to be larger than it would otherwise be.

19

Tenure neutrality has been a feature of the policies in Sweden and Germany, in particular, but has never been an objective in Spain, or in Britain, where ownership has been particularly strongly encouraged since 1979.

The size of the private rented sector has been greatly affected by rent control, wherever it has been applied, as it has been for long periods with varying degrees of rigidity in most of the countries. Rent control has been widely condemned for its pernicious effects on the housing market (e.g. Minford et al.: 22). But it is important to recognize that the private rented sector in many countries was associated with overcrowding and slum conditions in the nineteenth and early twentieth centuries. And although these problems may be more correctly attributed to poverty than to the system of tenure, public perception was not helped by the unscrupulous practices often applied to obtain increased rents from near-destitute tenants (e.g. Glasser 1986: ch. 6).

Apart from the historical legacy and the attitudes resulting from it, there were more pragmatic reasons for rent control in many countries. Supply and demand in the housing market take a long time to adjust to any sudden shock that disturbs the system's equilibrium. With any commodity where this is so, price movements are likely to be large; and, in the case of housing rent levels in a free market, where there is a shortage, could rise to very high levels indeed. In a war, when supply is less elastic than normal, even if not actually reduced, rent rises in the absence of control would transfer income from tenants to landlords, which could have serious social and economic consequences. Such rises are part of the mechanism of adjustment, but that does not make them any more palatable to or affordable by the large section of the population affected. Political pressures are imposed that force action by government. In some countries this has been reinforced by an ideological antipathy to a system that provides at a profit an item so essential as rented living accommodation.

The problem is that, once adopted, rent control becomes politically difficult to abandon, even when its adverse consequences are widely apparent. It has therefore existed in many countries for much of this century, but the rigour of the control has varied greatly from one country to another and this offers one of the main explanations for the widely differing size of the private rented sector. There is now a widespread movement towards removing control, but this is fairly recent in some countries and, in many, restrictions of various kinds still apply.

If controls had simply moderated the more extreme swings in rent, their effect might not have been so serious. They might have impeded the adjustment of the market to a prevailing shortage, but need not have affected the part played by the rented tenure in the long run. However, in most countries the period since 1945 has been one of continuing, and at times high, inflation. In such a situation, rent control prevents rents from keeping pace with the general rise in prices, and causes them to fall progressively further behind their free-market level. The disequilibrium that this produces has serious effects. The market value of tenanted property falls well below the vacant possession value. Security of tenure, with which rent control is normally combined to make it effective, prevents landlords from releasing the cash value of their assets, and makes their role even less attractive. Landlords therefore sell whenever the departure of a tenant gives them the opportunity, and the supply of accommodation is continually reduced. The low cost to the tenant causes the stock to be less efficiently used and alternative rented accommodation becomes hard to find; tenants are thereby encouraged to stay put rather than look for something more suitable to their needs, but probably more expensive, so that shortage is exacerbated. Stock is not properly maintained, so that the tenure becomes unpopular, and dilapidation may lead either to demolition or to take over by the public authorities. The upshot is that the tenure goes into long-term decline and, in the extreme case as exemplified by the UK, housing stock that could be of value to the nation may be lost.

A further important reason for this sector's decline is found in the differing effects of inflation on rents and mortgage finance, especially where (as in the UK) the bulk of mortgage borrowing is on short-term or variable rates. Unless long-term fixed rate mortgages are used, the burden of interest rates on loans is likely to prove much more volatile than income from rents, with the consequence that, where property is financed by debt, periods of high interest rates may leave landlords with expenditure exceeding their rental income. In several Continental countries, long-term fixed rate borrowing remains the norm for both the rented and owner occupied sectors. But where it is not available on suitable terms, if landlords are to avoid the risk of insolvency, rented accommodation has to be financed by equity funding, which may be practical for institutions, but takes it beyond the means of all but very wealthy individuals (A. E. Holmans 1987).

The differences in the size of the social rented sector among the European countries are plainly a product of policy. Since the rationale of this sector is to provide a decent standard of accommodation for those who cannot afford the full economic cost, the need for it is affected by the level of incomes and particularly income distribution. The scale of provision that is necessary is much affected by other support for the less well off, such as the level of pensions and various forms of social security. More direct aspects of policy are also relevant: for example, views may differ on whether to subsidize housing directly or to assist through personal housing allowances those individuals with inadequate means. In some countries, eligibility for entry to the social sector is means tested, whereas in others it is not. In some Scandinavian countries and in the Netherlands, not only is there is no means test but policy has encouraged a wide range of population of differing means to enter social rented housing in order to avoid social segregation.

The size of the social rented sector is also a product of the policies adopted for the other sectors. Most obviously where the private rented sector is large, where it is aided and where adequate housing allowances or benefits are available, the social rented sector can be smaller than would otherwise be possible. Policies for owner occupation affect it too. The more generous the assistance to this sector, the more people can afford it. In several countries, assistance is targeted on the less well off in the form of grants or low interest loans to enable them to become home owners, thereby creating a social sector within home ownership.

The widely differing size of the three sectors therefore is partly a product of history and of social and economic conditions, but above all is a result of the policies pursued. There is no one pattern of housing tenure that is right, and towards which Europe should be moving. However, it is worth remembering that the three sectors serve different functions and that they therefore each have a part to play. Home ownership is the tenure most people aspire to; it gives them a stake in property, greater control over their environment, and unlocks constructive effort that brings investment and improvement to a part of the nation's capital stock. Private renting is the most flexible tenure, which most readily promotes mobility of population and labour, and caters for those not yet ready to assume the responsibilities and burdens of ownership. The social rented sector plays an important part in ensuring that those unable to pay the economic cost of housing have a decent standard of accommodation. There are also hybrid tenures, combining elements of more than one of the above, as the chapter on Sweden will illustrate, and there are many types of landlord in both the private and social rented sectors. But the functions of the three sectors remain essentially the same in all countries.

No country is completely without one of the sectors, although in Britain the private rented sector is now very small, and in several countries, including Spain, the social rented sector is very small indeed. This means that the functions to which that sector is particularly suited have to be carried out by others and possibly done less well or at greater cost.

Conclusion

The chapters that follow show that, although there is much common ground in the policy measures followed by the six countries, there are also some important differences. Generally, the policies followed in the Continental countries, with the exception of Spain, have more in common with each other than they do with Britain; Spanish policy, like British, has changed radically since the 1970s, but is in other respects very different. Many of the differences are of political origin, the strength of social democracy in Scandinavia and the Netherlands being one example, the inheritance from the dictatorship in Spain being another. They are also the result of the different circumstances each country had to face: differing rates of population and household growth, migration, relative wealth, and the nature and state of the housing stock. The pattern of tenure is an inheritance from the past, a consequence of attitudes to different types of housing and the outcome of policies followed.

CHAPTER 3
Housing policy in France[1]

French housing policy has undergone considerable changes in recent years, but the process has been more evolutionary than the abrupt changes of direction that have characterized the UK.[2] Although there have been some noticeable shifts in emphasis with different French governments, generally there has been a substantial measure of cross-party agreement on the priorities of housing policy. As in other countries, the impetus for many of the changes since the mid-1970s has been the need to contain costs and to target the measures more effectively. Recently, changes to the financial institutions have also become a factor, as a result of the closer integration of the European market.

France emerged from the Second World War with a serious housing shortage and a legacy of bad housing conditions. This was a consequence not only of war-time destruction and the absence of new building during the war, but also of a grossly inadequate amount of housing investment in the inter-war period. In part this appears to have been caused by the imposition of strict rent control in 1914, which was maintained throughout the inter-war period and affected adversely investment in what was then the dominant housing tenure. But it was also a consequence of the social rented sector remaining very small between the wars and therefore not able to play the expansionist role that it did in Britain. It is estimated that in 1945 France had a cumulative deficit of some 2 million dwellings from the inter-war period, a further 450000 destroyed during the war and nearly 1.5 million damaged (Duclaud-Williams 1978: 15; Heugas-Darraspen 1985: 5; Emms 1990: 61).

The post-war period saw a substantial increase in the birth rate and, coupled with immigration, this led to a growth in population of 16 million to 56 million, a 40% increase, between 1946 and 1990. Even more important, given the much higher proportion of rural population in France at this time, was the substantial

---

1. A description of French housing policy requires greater use of acronyms and abbreviations than for other countries. Since they are used in official documents and have a precise meaning, there is no way of avoiding them without giving scope for misunderstanding. Each is explained on the first occasion it is used, but readers new to the subject may find them confusing and are therefore advised to make use of the explanatory list at the front of the book.
2. For a discussion of the evolution of French housing policy since the Second World War, see Duclaud-Williams (1978: 15–27), Emms (1990: 61ff) and Boucher (1988: 292–5).

movement off the land; the result was that the urban population grew from 53% to 75% of the total French population between 1946 and 1990 (Heugas-Darraspen: 1985 5; Emms 1990: 61).

It is perhaps surprising, therefore, that a major housebuilding programme did not really get under way until the 1950s. This was in part because the social rented sector, which was in the van of developments in other countries, was too small to make an impact, and local authorities were much less directly involved than elsewhere. An increased building programme was therefore largely a matter of inducing private sector investment into housing, not only into owner occupation but particularly into the private rented sector. The latter could occur only if there was a substantial upward movement in rents. (Rent control had reduced the proportion of family income devoted to housing from 16% to 1.6% between 1914 and 1948 (Satsangi 1993: 2).) A major purpose of the 1948 Rent Act was therefore to bring about a managed increase in rents, nearer to market levels, an objective in which it was not wholly successful, and to cushion the effect for tenants through the introduction of a personal housing allowance. In addition, over the years, a complex variety of investment incentives were introduced for both the owner occupied and the rented sectors; and from the 1950s onwards, a major expansion of the social rented sector began to take place. As a result of all these measures, a large building programme got under way, which reached a peak annual construction rate of over 500000 dwellings in the early 1970s, before falling back to about half this level in the mid-1980s (Fig. 3.1). Despite its late start, a slightly larger proportion of the housing stock has been built since 1945 than in Britain, although not as much as in the other four countries in this study (see Ch. 2).

As supply caught up with demand and the costs of the policy became increasingly burdensome, it was felt that the support was not sufficiently targeted on those who most needed it. The 1975 Barre Report, which recommended a shift from bricks and mortar subsidies to support for the individual through housing allowances, and the subsequent legislation of January 1977, therefore marked a watershed in the development of French housing policy (Barre 1976). Up to this time the incentives were relatively indiscriminate. All sectors were aided, although this was subject to a means test, and applied only to new construction and rehabilitation. Since then there has been a gradual but marked reduction in assistance to bricks and mortar through subsidized loans, in both real and nominal terms, and a switch to personal housing allowances. These reductions have been particularly evident in assistance to the owner occupied sector, although the volume of construction in this sector, having fallen in the first half of the 1980s, has nevertheless increased sharply since then. In the private rented sector, both the assistance and the level of construction declined, and in the social rented sector there was a more gradual fall in the amount of support: the level of activity fell from 1974 onwards, until by 1980 it was about half its previous level. But it has been rather more stable in the 1980s and showed some modest recovery in 1992, with some 63000 dwellings built, much the same number as in 1985, and 23% of the total number of dwellings constructed (Lebègue 1991: 10–19;

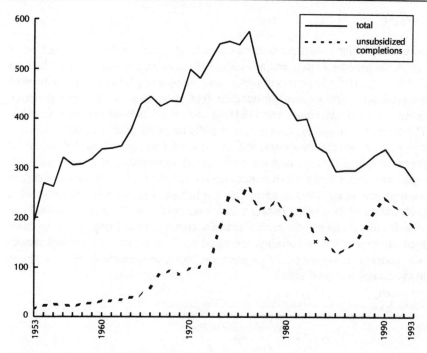

Figure 3.1 French housing starts, 1953–92 (thousands) (*Source:* Heugas-Darraspen (1985), Geindre (1993)).

Geindre 1993: 22f). However, despite the reductions in bricks and mortar subsidies, the costs of housing policy have continued to escalate as a result of the increased proportion of relatively poor people, the larger number of retired, and increased rates of unemployment.

By the early 1990s there was also concern about the growing pressure of demand on the stock in the social rented sector. Supply having caught up with demand in the 1970s, by the 1990s a shortage was once again emerging that was increasingly regarded as a crisis. The waiting list for social rented accommodation had lengthened to two and a half years on average, and was much worse in some cities. Some 200000 people were said to be homeless, more than 600000 in temporary accommodation or mobile homes, and 1.4 million were in dwellings that were below normal health and sanitation standards. Over 2 million people were therefore housed in unsatisfactory conditions, some 3% of the total population (Geindre 1993: 22).

With a new government assuming office in 1993, French housing policy was therefore at an interesting juncture. The impact of closer European integration on financial institutions and the market for housing finance, the need to decide on the future roles of the private rented and social rented sectors, and a widespread concern that the level to which house building has fallen would result in a growing deficit – all called for urgent consideration.

25

Tenure

As in most other countries, the proportion of the housing stock in owner occupation has gradually risen, and at 54% in 1988 comprised more than half the total (Table 3.1). The private rented sector has consequently fallen as a proportion of the total stock and in absolute numbers (but only since the late 1970s). From being the dominant tenure after 1945, it comprised 20% of the stock in 1988. The social rented sector, having risen rapidly up to the middle of the 1970s, has continued to advance modestly, but not on a scale to compensate for the fall in private renting. There is now some concern in France that, if these trends continue, not only will the social rented sector overtake the private rented sector in the next few years, but something like the British situation may emerge, with a polarization of the market between owner occupation and the social rented sectors. Further decline in the private rented sector is seen as likely to lead to problems of reduced labour mobility, increased pressure on the social rented sector, with consequent higher public expenditure, and a de-stabilizing effect on prices in the owner occupied sector.

Table 3.1 French dwelling stock according to tenure.

	As a percentage of total stock			
	1961	1978	1988	1990
Owner occupiers	39.4	47.2	54.3	54.4
Private rented	33.2	25.9	19.7	} 39.6
Social rented	5.4	15.1	17.1	
Other*	7.6	2.9	9.0	6.0

	As a percentage of 1961		
	1961	1978	1988
Owner occupiers	100	154	197
Private rented	100	101	85
Social rented	100	360	452

* Mostly provided free.
Source: L. Ghékiere, op. cit. 1991; CEC, *Statistics on housing in the European Community 1993*, Geindre Report op. cit.; *Annuaire Statistique de la France*.

Owner occupation

Housing finance

Approximately half of the owner occupiers in France are paying a mortgage, the remainder owning their houses outright (Schaefer 1990). The expansion of the sector has been encouraged by a wide range of subsidized loans, to the extent that in the 1960s and 1970s the majority of new building was assisted in this way. Since 1977 the forms of assistance have been rationalized into three main schemes:

- PAP loans (*prêts aidés pour l'accession à la propriété*)
- PC loans (*prêts conventionnés*)
- PEL (*plans d'epargne-logement*), a subsidized housing savings scheme.

In addition there are grants to assist with house improvement, and a limited scheme of mortgage interest tax relief.

PAP loans can be provided both for new building and to assist with the costs of improvements to existing dwellings. They are subsidized by the State and administered as well as provided, principally, but not exclusively, by *Crédit Foncier de France* (CFF), a State-controlled institution that raises funds in the private market. They are available only in so far as resources allow and are limited to households whose means fall below a certain level, allowing for the number of dependants and with some regional variation. The interest rate has usually been about 2% below the free-market rate, and in 1994 was 6.95%. Loans are at fixed rates, and the length of the annuity is normally 20 years, but can vary. The maximum loan may be up to 90% of cost, subject to certain standards of space and cost per metre (Ghékiere 1991: 144). In 1982 37% of lending on new housebuilding was under the PAP scheme, with a much more modest proportion on older buildings where only improvements qualify; but recently the importance of these loans has been sharply reduced as a result of deliberate policy. This has been achieved by maintaining the income ceiling without adjustment, despite inflation and the rise in incomes, and without uprating the eligible size of house (Ghékiere 1991: 139; Lebègue 1991: 18; Diamond & Lea 1992: 54). For a single person, this ceiling is FF9000 per month, and for a family of four with two salary/wage earners FF18200 (approximately £13000 and £26300 a year respectively). Between 1986 and 1990, the result was a reduction of 63% in loans granted. In the latter year PAP loans financed only 5% of new housing loans to individuals (Lebègue 1991: 18; Diamond & Lea 1992: 54). Recently the proportion has been somewhat higher, but only because total lending has been reduced during the recession.

The importance of PAP loans is that they have made possible a social element in the owner occupied sector, thereby enabling people to move into this sector who would otherwise have been unable to afford it. There has been some speculation that, having fallen to such a low level, PAP loans would eventually be phased out altogether. With the advent of the new government in 1993, for the time being this trend is reversed; interest rates have been lowered and income thresholds raised. But in the longer term the decline of PAP loans is expected to continue and, if they were to disappear, this would leave the movement into owner occupation to be assisted mainly by tax relief and housing allowances.

PC loans, or regulated loans, accounted for about 30% of the loans to individuals on new housing at their peak in 1985; and like PAP loans they have declined, but by a lesser amount, a reduction of some 25% since 1987 (Lebègue 1991: 18). These loans are regulated rather than subsidized; but rates of interest, although

27

now fairly close to market rates, have in the past been significantly lower. This is because of the privileged access the institutions have had to low-cost finance, in particular current accounts (on which interest payment is prohibited in France) and the funds generated by the housing savings scheme, which involve an indirect subsidy and tax relief (see below). PC loans can be offered by any institution that has signed an agreement with the government, and their rates of interest vary depending on time and circumstances. They may cover up to 90% of the purchase price and are normally on a fixed interest basis, with a term of 10–20 years. PC loans were originally available only for new dwellings and for improvements to older buildings, both of which are subject to conditions on floorspace and cost limits; but recently they have been extended to the purchase of older buildings, without major improvements being undertaken. Unlike PAP loans, PC loans carry no income restriction on eligibility. However, like the PAP loans, they carry an entitlement to the APL (*aide personalisée au logement*) system of housing allowances, described below.

France has a well developed housing savings system, not unlike the system operating in Germany, described in the next chapter, which attracts both a State bonus and tax exemption on interest received (Diamond & Lea 1992: 73–7; Papa 1992: 128). In 1990 there were nearly 18 million account holders: approximately one third of the citizens of France. The scheme has great flexibility: proceeds of the accounts can be used to finance second houses as well as principal dwellings, and may be transferred to relatives. The system is operated by designated banks, of which Crédit Agricole has the largest share. Two schemes are in operation: PEL (*plans d'epargne-logement*), which is for larger amounts and to receive the bonus deposits has to be maintained for a minimum of five years; and CEL (*comptes d'epargne-logement*) for smaller deposits at a lower rate of interest, which have to be maintained for 18 months for the benefit to be available. The maximum period of loan under these schemes is 15 years, at a fixed rate of interest subject to periodic revision. They are a straight commercial operation for the institutions concerned, since the low interest on loans is matched by that on deposits. The attraction for those who use the schemes is in the bonus provided by the State and the tax exemption, both of which are a form of subsidy. However, as the European financial market becomes more liberalized and integrated, other competing uses are becoming available for savings at much higher rates of interest, which may outweigh these advantages. It is not surprising, therefore, that in real terms there has been some reduction in the flow of funds into contract savings schemes. This has given rise to concern that this gradual decline will continue in future with important implications for housing finance.

As the assisted and regulated loans (PAP and PC) have declined, free-market loans, provided by banks and principal financial institutions, have expanded considerably, so that they now comprise almost half of the home lending to individuals. The banks fund most of this lending through retail deposits and the majority of it is on a fixed interest basis; since 1986, however, variable rate lending has been encouraged and on new lending it now comprises about 20% of the total.

Because no interest may be paid on current accounts or certain types of deposit accounts, the banks can offer mortgage rates that are frequently lower than those for government borrowing. The terms of these free-market loans are not subject to control by the public authorities; but there is no insurance scheme and they are generally limited to a maximum loan-to-value ratio of 80% of the total purchase price. However, since security in housing assets is much more difficult to implement in France than in Britain, and repossessions are less common, greater importance is attached to the ratio of mortgage payments to income. The institutions generally set this ratio at a maximum of 33%.

In addition to these loans and mortgage arrangements, owner occupied housing may also be assisted by the employers' so-called "1% levy". This scheme requires all those who employ more than ten people to pay a percentage of their salary bill, currently reduced from 1% to 0.45%, to assist with housing costs. Most of this levy goes to finance the social rented sector, as described below, but employers may make loans available to staff to help them with the costs of house purchase.

Home improvement is assisted in France by a system of grants. For owner occupiers this is known as PAH (*prime à l'amélioration de l'habitat*) and it is available only for dwellings that are at least 20 years old. Like PAP, this assistance is subject to an income ceiling. It also forms the basis of a contract and, therefore, like PAP and PC, entitles the owner to the special APL system of housing allowances. The schemes for improvement are subject to approval on standards and the level of costs involved; grants are at a maximum rate of 20%, subject to a ceiling.

Taxation

Mortgage interest tax relief is only available on a very restricted basis, and is therefore less important than in the UK, at least before the changes made to the British system in 1993. A house purchaser may obtain a tax credit equivalent to 25% of mortgage interest costs; this may then be deducted from the tax bill for up to five years. This benefit is subject to an income ceiling that in 1992 was FF210000 (about £25300) for single persons and FF410000 (£49400) for married couples. The maximum annual credit has been increased steadily over the past ten years and is presently FF40000 (£4,800), with additional amounts for each child in the family (Lebègue 1991; Papa 1992: 129).

There are other aspects of the taxation system that affect owner occupiers (Diamond & Lea 1992: 43). Registration fees and sales taxes are levied at rates of 0.6% and 4.2% of purchase price for both new and existing dwellings, so long as the property is destined for at least three years' owner occupancy. For all other property the registration fee is substantially higher. Value added tax is payable on new property at 18.6%; but where construction is undertaken using PAP or PC loans, it is VAT exempt. Residential property is subject to capital gains tax on

29

sale, but only where the market value is above FF4.13 million (about £500000) with allowance for deduction of outstanding loans, and even then, where only one property is owned, it is exempt. Together these provisions exclude all but a few very expensive houses. No tax is levied on imputed rental income for owner occupiers; but this notional income is used as the basis for France's land tax system, which is a source of local government revenue. However, new dwellings are exempt from this tax for two years and, where they have been financed by PAP, for four years.

The private rented sector

Although declining, the private rented sector, is still the second largest in France, with 20% of the total housing stock, slightly ahead of the social rented sector. Many landlords own only one property, which they let and which was originally seen as an investment providing a steady income in retirement. There is a long history of rent control and regulation, and, although this gave rents more flexibility than in the UK for much of the post-war period, it has undoubtedly had a major influence on trends in the sector.

Rent control and regulation

As in the UK, rent control was imposed in 1914 to avoid war-time profiteering and to prevent social unrest when living standards were necessarily depressed by the war effort (Duclaud-Williams 1978: 31; Boucher 1988: 294). The control was maintained by a series of short-term expedients throughout the inter-war period, although it did not apply to new building. This was a period when France suffered from some inflation, unlike the deflationary conditions that applied in the UK throughout much of the 1920s and 1930s. Largely in consequence of this and of the further inflation during and immediately after the Second World War, rent control had a drastic effect on landlords' rate of return, and reduced the average cost of housing as a proportion of income to very low levels, as already described. This tight rent control is widely regarded as responsible for the low level of housebuilding activity in the inter-war period, which led to a severe shortage of supply by 1939, and also for a serious deterioration in the quality of the housing stock, which it did not pay landlords to maintain properly. The fact that rent control did not apply to new building led to some wide differences in rental levels, but does not seem to have prevented the growing shortage, no doubt because landlords feared that at any moment the control might be extended.

In the immediate post-war period there was widespread recognition that tackling the housing problem involved action on rents to restore them to a level that would make new investment viable. The 1948 Rent Act, while maintaining control and necessarily being based on a series of compromises, therefore aimed to raise rents gradually to near market levels. To make this acceptable, a housing allowance (AL: *allocation de logement*) was introduced. Low interest loans for new construction were also made available to encourage investment. Unlike Britain, substantial new building did take place in this sector, although over the period as a whole it has not compensated for the number of previously rented dwellings being sold into owner occupation. In the event, because of inflation, the objectives of the 1948 Act in raising rents to market levels were never properly attained and, even if they had been, the aim of market-level rents appears to have been based on a rate of return of only 1%. However, by degrees, major categories of dwellings were freed from control altogether, greatly reducing the number to which the control still applies. Those that remain subject to the 1948 Act are now predominantly but not exclusively in Paris and they constitute only 2% of the total housing stock; the rents charged are still significantly below those for other privately rented property (Boucher 1988: 298; Satsangi 1993: 3).

Other privately rented housing is not caught by this control, but is subject to regulation (Satsangi 1993: 4–6).[3] The degree of regulation has varied depending on the political complexion of the government. The 1982 Rent Act brought rent levels and rent increases for newly let dwellings within the jurisdiction of a national consultative body consisting of tenants, landlords and government representatives, as well as limiting the circumstances in which a landlord could refuse to renew a tenancy. This resulted in some reduction in the supply of rented accommodation and the 1986 Act attempted to find a new balance. Rents for newly let properties were to be fixed by agreement between landlord and tenant; and tenants were to be offered a three-year contract. Annual increases at the rate of inflation of construction costs were allowed only as stipulated in the contract. Landlords were under no obligation to renew a lease. The Act of 1989 introduced further changes. Under the *loi Malandrain*, leases were to be offered for six years, and only rents for newly let and vacant property were to be freely set. Rents for renewed leases would be set by reference to comparable dwellings, and would generally be raised only by the rate of increase in construction costs. (Lebègue 1991: 54).

These measures generally provide a substantial degree of security of tenure and also limit rent increases to inflationary indices, regardless of market circumstances. But in addition there was a long series of government interventions during the 1970s and 1980s that imposed either temporary rent freezes or limitations on the rate of increase, as part of the policy aimed at controlling inflation.

---

3. Lebègue (1991) gives a useful summary in Annex 9 of the long series of government interventions on rent levels.

Finance for private rented housing

However, throughout the post-war period the sector has been assisted by loans at reduced rates of interest for new construction and rehabilitation, which are designed to increase investment. At present these are available in three forms:

- PLA (*prêt locatif aidé*) or assisted loans for rented housing
- PLS (*prêt locatif social*) or social loans for rented housing, and
- as for the owner occupied sector, PC (*prêt conventionné*) or regulated loans.

PLA loans, which are aided by the State to enable the interest rate to be below market levels, are the main form of assistance available to the social sector; but they may also be made available to private landlords through *Credit Foncier de France*, which receives a subsidy from the State. They are provided on some-what less generous terms than to non-profit social landlords and for housing with slightly higher rents. The loans are subject to an income ceiling on the part of the tenants and to agreement on rent levels. These loans are available up to 55% of cost, a lower proportion than for social landlords, and the rate of interest at 6.5% in 1994 is higher, although well below market rates. There is a ceiling on acquisition and development costs, and rent increases are tied to inflation of the construction cost index. The loan is normally for 30 years. The effect of this sub-sidy would typically be to reduce combined capital and interest payments by 12–20% (Satsangi 1993: 10). Only a small part of the private rented sector has made use of these loans; in recent years the number of new dwellings started averaged 10000 a year.

PLS loans were formerly known as PLI (*prêt locatif intermédiare*) and, con-fusingly, under the new Balladur government are to resume this name. Their purpose is to encourage investment in rented housing for tenants who have higher incomes and are consequently able to make higher rental payments than those in accommodation assisted by PLA. These loans were discontinued in 1990 and 1991, but have been re-started in 1992. They are available to non-profit social landlords as well as to the private sector. A landlord must agree to keep property let for at least nine years and the loan may be for up to 15 years, at a variable interest rate. As with PLA, rents, which are subject to agreement, can be increased only at the rate of increase of the index of construction costs. How-ever, unlike PLA, the use of a PLS loan does not entitle the tenant to draw the APL form of housing allowance, although other forms are available as explained below.

The PLA and PLS loans are financed in part through the use of funds from the *Livret A* accounts of savings banks. These are accounts on which depositors receive a relatively low rate of interest but are exempt from tax; they therefore offer a cheap form of finance as a result of this indirect subsidy. This source of funds was formerly used for the PAP loans in the owner occupied sector as well as for PLA, but alternative more highly remunerated investment opportunities have constrained the amount of savings going into *Livret A*. They are now therefore reserved exclusively for PLA loans and to a limited extent for PLS (Satsangi 1993: 12).[4]

PC loans may be obtained from the banks on the same basis as for the owner occupied sector. As for that sector, they have in the past been at rates of interest significantly below market levels; but the gap has narrowed in recent years and is now very small. No restriction on the income of tenants applies, but the use of a PC loan to finance a rented house does carry the advantage that it entitles the tenant to the APL form of housing allowance (Ghékiere 1991: 144).

Improvement and refurbishment of private rented property, including schemes for energy saving, may also be eligible for assistance under a grant scheme operated by ANAH (*Agence Nationale pour l'Amélioration de l'Habitat*). This is the counterpart of the PAH scheme for owner occupiers, but it is of generally greater importance. In this case it is partially financed by the proceeds of the tax on letting contracts.

Private landlords can of course also obtain finance from banks and other private sector institutions. There is a very widespread use of fixed interest long-term mortgages in France, which are much better suited to financing rented accommodation than are variable rate loans, especially in circumstances where rents are regulated in the way described. Housing allowances are available to tenants of accommodation financed in this way, but not the special APL type of allowance described later in this chapter, and which is limited to those who have financed their rented property under one of the contract schemes (PLA, PC) or in the case of refurbishment with grant from ANAH.

Taxation

Private sector investors in rented accommodation are also entitled to tax benefits in addition to subsidies, although not on the same generous scale available to owner occupiers. A private sector landlord may obtain a tax credit equal to 10% of the interest paid on a mortgage, which may be deducted from his tax bill for two years, up to a ceiling of FF60000 (about £7000) (Satsangi 1993: 9). This contrasts with the owner occupier's tax credit of 25% over five years. The dwelling must continue to be let for at least six years. However, there are also tax credits available to assist with the cost of repair and improvement, particularly for the cleaning and repair of facades, pointing and plasterwork.

In further contrast to the owner occupied sector, where imputed rent is not taxed, the rent received by private landlords from tenants is taxed as part of the landlord's income after appropriate expenses have been deducted. This includes capital depreciation on the value of the asset, which is not a deductible charge for tax purposes in Britain. Purchasers of rented accommodation are liable to registration fees and sales taxes, the former being levied at 15.4%, compared

---

4. Lebègue (1991: 58) shows the gradual decline of Livret A deposits since 1980.

with 0.6% for owner occupiers. Capital gains tax may also, in theory, be levied on rented property, but only if the value is in excess of FF4.13 million, as for the owner occupied sector. This effectively excludes most rented accommodation. As for the owner occupied sector, new dwellings are exempt from land tax for two years, but where they are financed by PLA loans this exemption is extended to 15 years.

These arrangements have resulted in the private rented sector in France being more generously treated than it is in the UK. Limited mortgage tax relief, no capital gains tax (except on extremely expensive properties), deduction of depreciation from taxable income, and low interest loans – are all benefits that do not apply in Britain. Rent control has also generally been less tight than in Britain for much of the post-war period.

Nevertheless, the sector is certainly less generously treated than owner occupation. Returns on investment have also been low, lower than on alternative investments, whether in property or in shares. The Lebègue Commission found that over a 30-year period the real return on investment in rented housing lay well below that on other personal investments; and for institutional investors the return, whether on new or older houses, was well below that which could be obtained on offices over a similar period (Lebègue 1991: 47). The large scale of the investment necessary and the lack of liquidity, which results from security of tenure, also make private renting less attractive than alternative investments. In these circumstances it is not surprising that landlords have been selling their property to owner occupiers and the sector has been in long-term decline.

The issue for France, therefore, is whether to let the private rented sector continue to decline, following the example of the UK, or to attempt to arrest the trend. It is recognized that further decline is likely to result in an increased need for expansion in the social rented sector and is likely to affect labour mobility adversely. The Lebègue Commission and the Geindre Report therefore both recommended remedial action. A rise in rents would unbalance the demand between the private rented and social rented sectors, and also increase the cost of housing allowances, and is not seen as the principal need. The *loi Malandrain*, already referred to, is seen as providing a satisfactory rent-fixing system so long as there are no further changes; in fact, it is based on much the same principles as the "assured tenancy" system in Britain. The prevailing view consequently favours more generous tax allowances, in particular greater equality in treatment with the owner occupied sector and possibly entitlement to deduct expenses, including depreciation, from income from whatever source, not simply from letting. This is a provision that applies in Germany and has attracted some interest in France.

The social rented sector

As noted earlier, the development of a social rented housing sector of significant size occurred much later in France than in the UK or in Germany. Even by 1961, it accounted for only 5.4% of the stock (784000 dwellings). However, in the following years it grew rapidly, the level of new construction reaching a peak in the early 1970s. By 1988 it accounted for 17% of the total stock, with more than 3.5 million dwellings (Emms 1990: 67; Lebègue 1991: 10). It is now almost as large as the private rented sector and, given the continuing decline of the latter, it may soon exceed it. The sector is larger than its counterpart in Germany, but still considerably smaller than in the UK and the Netherlands.

Landlord organizations

French local authorities do not have the same direct responsibility for housing as do their counterparts in the UK, and none of the stock is in their direct ownership. By far the largest part of the social rented housing stock – 89% or 3.3 million dwellings – is owned by non-profit making associations known as HLMs (*habitations à loyer modéré*) (Ghékiere 1991: 140). The remainder, nearly 400000 dwellings, is owned either by private/public partnerships, known as *sociétés d'economie mixte* (SEM) or by private sector landlords who, as has been seen in the previous section, may let housing at social rents in return for assisted loans. Social landlords have been encouraged to build for sale as well as to rent, in order to help into ownership those who would otherwise be unable to afford it. Since 1945, approximately 1.3 million dwellings have been sold in this way (CECODHAS 1993: 63; UNFO-HLM 1993).

Despite the late growth in this sector, the HLM organizations have their origins as far back as 1894, when the Siegfried Act of that year made it possible to set up non-profit making organizations to provide cheap housing. In 1912 they were established under the title of *habitations à bon marché* (HBMs) (Boucher 1988: 293; Heugas-Darraspen 1985: 8–9). Subsequent legislation made it possible for the sector to be assisted by local authorities. Despite this, up to the Second World War the scale of the operation remained small; and, although the organizations were re-established in 1947 and renamed HLMs, the building programme between 1945 and 1950 amounted to only 12000 dwellings. It was therefore not until the 1950s that the HLMs became a major source of rented housing, with completions of 97000 between 1951 and 1955, rising to 324000 in the following five years and peaking at 682000 in the five years 1971–5. As shortages were overcome, the volume of construction fell to less than half this level by the end of the 1980s, but the reappearance of shortages is now causing it to increase again.

The HLMs are best described as a form of housing association. There are some 1000 affiliated organizations, but this includes financial institutions who own no houses, and 167 co-operatives who own only a few. There are 707 associations building and owning dwellings. These vary greatly in size from very small to very large, but the average number of dwellings is just over 4,500 each, much smaller than the average stock for a typical local authority in the Britain but very much larger than the average for British housing associations. HLM associations build housing for sale to low-income buyers as well as housing to rent; by 1991 they had built 3.3 million dwellings to rent and 1.3 million for first-time buyers, since the first social housing was started. The average rent on an HLM dwelling is approximately 40% below unsubsidized private sector rents (UNFO-HLM 1993).

There are two main types of HLM organization: those formed at the instigation of local authorities and those formed as non-profit making companies. The latter are usually sponsored by private sector firms or public enterprises (both as employers) and are intended to cater for their own employees, among others. There is also the small co-operative sector, referred to above, which has both allocation rights in HLM estates and some dwellings of its own to rent, but it has never really taken off in France and it accounts for only 4,500 dwellings.

The HLMs founded at the instigation of local authorities account for rather less than half the total number, but nearly 60% of the HLM stock. The largest number (293) are known as *Offices Publics* (HLM-OP), and are formed by communes, municipalities and *départements* under legislation that goes back to the years before the First World War (Emms 1990: 72;. UNFO-HLM 1993). But there are also 54 larger HLM organizations known as *Offices Publics d'Aménagement et Construction* (HLM-OPAC), which are established under an Act of 16 July 1971. Many of these have been formed by the transfer of previously existing HLM-OPs. Both types of organization are geographically based and, although the OPACs may be larger, this is not always so.

The main difference between HLM-OPs and OPACs is in the statute setting them up, the 1971 Act providing for greater flexibility of operation and structure than the earlier legislation. HLM-OPs are managed by boards of 15 members, of which five are appointed by the local authorities, five by the *Préfet* of the *département* acting for central government, three by the tenants, and the remaining two by financial institutions that support the HLM organizations. Local authority representatives are therefore clearly in the minority, but those of central and local government together comprise two thirds of the board. The boards for HLM-OPACs are larger, with 21 members (seven each appointed by the local authority and by the *Préfet*, three by the tenants, two by financial institutions and two by trades unions); they are less rigidly determined by statute and are intended to be more independent.

The second type of HLM organizations, which are founded as non-profit making limited-liability companies or *Sociétés Anonymes* (HLM-SAS), number 360 and have some 43% of the total stock. Their present legal status derives from an Act of 24 July 1966 and a Decree of March 1967. This limits any one shareholder's rights, so as to avoid dominance on the board. Boards must have at least five members and not more than 12; for those with fewer than seven, there must be one tenant representative, and for others two. The HLM-SAs also vary greatly in size but are generally smaller than the OPs and the OPACs. Since an HLM-SA does not relate to any particular local authority area, it may also be geographically much more dispersed, although this will depend on the firm or organization that founded it.

In addition to the HLMs, there is the huge *Société Civile Immobilière de la Caisse des Dépôts* (SCIC) the property arm of *Caisse des Depôts et des Consignations* (CDC). This organization, originally set up in 1954, built much of the housing for HLMs in the 1950s and 1960s, and now owns and manages some 180000 socially rented dwellings throughout France, of which 100000 are in the Paris area (Devlin 1993: 4). SCIC is one of the largest social landlords in western Europe, comparable in size only to the former *Neue Heimat* in Germany or to Glasgow District Council in Britain.[5] In terms of structure, the only British housing body in any way comparable to the SCIC was the former Scottish Special Housing Association, now part of Scottish Homes (see Ch. 8). SSHA was of course very much smaller, but both bodies were set up to provide housing at social rents in supplement of the efforts of other agencies and without regard to local authority boundaries. However, whereas SSHA was an agency of central government, SCIC is a subsidiary of a public financial institution.

The other landlord organizations in the social rented sector, the *Sociétés d'Economie Mixte* (SEMs) and private companies and individuals, generally cater for a higher standard of provision than the HLMs, and housing is normally offered at higher rents. The *Sociétés d'Economie Mixte* are essentially private companies, but with a high level of municipal sponsorship; the accommodation they provide is intended for tenants whose incomes, although modest, are too high to qualify them for the HLM sector.

Finance for social housing

Social landlord organizations are funded by a variety of low interest loans, channelled through the medium of the *Caisse de Depôts et des Consignations* (CDC), a public sector institution that forms the counterpart of the CFF for this sector. These include the two types of loan already referred to in the section on the private sector, PLA (*prêt locatif aidé*) and PLS (*prêt locatif social*), both of which are available only for new construction. In addition PALULOS (*prime à l'amélioration des logements à usage locatif et à occupation sociale*) is a grant available to finance the improvement of existing stock.

The rate of interest on PLA loans for HLM landlords is the most heavily subsidized of all the assisted housing loans in France. For example, in 1994 the rate

5. The Northern Ireland Housing Executive is also of comparable size in number of dwellings, but it has a near monopoly of social rented housing in the province.

was 5.8%, compared with 6.5% for PLS loans and 6.95% for PAP loans for owner occupiers, the last being about 2% below the free-market rate. Moreover, the HLMs can obtain loans to cover up to 95% of their total costs, substantially more than is available to other landlords. Landlord organizations receiving PLA loans are required to meet certain minimum standards of space and amenity. Rents have to be set at approved levels that are intended to cover costs. Access to this accommodation is limited to those whose incomes fall below a ceiling set by the State; but if the incomes of existing tenants rise above this level, the landlord organizations have the option of levying an excess rent as an alternative to requiring the tenant to give up the accommodation.

PLS loans (or PLI, as they are now being renamed), as was seen in the section on the private rented sector, are really a variant of PLA intended for higher-quality housing and tenants with higher incomes. They are used more extensively by the SEMs and private landlords than by HLMs. The PALULOS grants for house improvement are payable in conjunction with a loan at market rates to encourage renovation. Eligibility depends on the level of income of the tenant or prospective tenant. Dwellings financed by PLA or PALULOS, but not by PLS, entitle the tenants to the APL system of housing benefits (described below).

In addition to direct assistance from the State, which in the case of PLA amounts to some 12% of the sum lent, the CDC in providing low interest loans also draws on funds from the savings banks' *Livret A* accounts, already described. These funds, which were formerly used more widely for the financing of local authorities and for the PAP loans to owner occupiers, have been reserved for PLA and PLS since 1990. In recent years they have been supplemented by the *Livret Bleu* accounts of *Crédit Mutuel*, which operate on a similar tax-exempt basis (Ghékiere 1991: 144). Even with the addition of *Livret Bleu* and the ending of other claims on *Livret A*, the funds available are not enough to fund social housing without recourse to the market. This is because, despite the tax advantages, savings accounts of this type have become less attractive to depositors in the face of higher-yielding investments. But, of course, the more that CDC has to borrow on the market, the less able it is to lend at below market rates.

The HLM-SAs also benefit substantially from funds available through the employers' "1% levy" described earlier. Since most of the HLMs of this type are set up by employers, they are seen as the most obvious use for these funds, which provide a relatively secure source of finance and can meet a substantial part of the costs.

To a British observer, this system of funding may seem extremely complex, perhaps unnecessarily so. But it does have interesting features as a means of bringing private sector investment into the provision of social rented housing. The tax exemption of the *Livret A* accounts may be regarded as simply an alternative to providing a higher level of grant to the CDC to enable loans to be made available at a particular subsidized rate of interest. This indirect mechanism, however, means that the cost is lower in terms of public expenditure. Not only does it provide a strong incentive for private sector savings to be channelled into housing investment at relatively low cost to the State, but tax exemption, although affecting the government's public sector deficit, does not score as public expenditure. In marked contrast to the system in Britain, the only public expenditure cost involved in the French social rented sector is the modest direct subsidy of 12% to PLA loans, rather less to PLS, and the expenditure on PALULOS grants.

In other respects the system of providing social housing in France has both advantages and disadvantages when compared with the British system. In the first place, many of the same problems exist. As in Britain there has been a legacy of hard-to-let estates. There is also much problematic system-built housing; only 9.1% of HLM dwellings are houses, the remainder being flats, often in highrise buildings (Emms 1990). Peripheral estates often lack local shopping and social facilities and may become unpopular. A reputation for problems and deprivation is often compounded by anti-social behaviour, as it is in Britain. The social and ethnic problems arising from a large immigrant population (mainly from North Africa), which tends to be concentrated in such areas, only serve to exacerbate these difficulties. Since the Balladur government came to power in 1993, tackling these problems has featured as one of the most important issues to be addressed in housing and urban renewal.

The growing housing shortage of recent years means that vacancies in the HLM stock are not a serious problem at the moment; indeed the vacancy rate has fallen from 3.6% in 1986 to the very low level of 1.9% in 1991 (Geindre 1993: 23). But where vacancies have arisen in the past in hard-to-let estates, this has undermined the financial position of HLMs in a way that could not happen with a British local authority landlord. Since the rent regime is controlled under the terms of the assisted loan system, rent increases do not offer a simple way out and would require the agreement of the State, which is in turn concerned about the knock-on effect on housing allowances. According to one estimate, in the late 1980s approximately half of the HLM tenants were drawing housing allowances and only 18% of any rent increase was borne by the tenants. Many HLMs have therefore resorted to selling land and, where appropriate, housing, in order to try to restore their finances. But in some cases the result has also been an inadequate level of maintenance expenditure, which only exacerbates the situation further in problem estates.

A consequence of these aspects of the French system is that it appears less able than the British to tackle the provision of accommodation for problem tenants and for the homeless. Although French local authorities and the *Préfets* have nomination rights in the HLM-OPs and OPACs, French local authorities have neither the means nor the obligation that their British counterparts have to provide accommodation for the homeless. Some HLMs, particularly HLM-SAs, tend in so far as they can, to exercise a selective system in choosing tenants so as to avoid those likely to give rise to problems. In view of the way in which they are financed, tenants who do not pay their rent or who cause the desirability of a particular estate to deteriorate, thereby giving rise to vacancies, can have serious financial implications for the HLM as a whole. Largely to counteract this, a variant of the PLA scheme, known as *PLA d'insertion*, has been introduced. This scheme is aimed at such disadvantaged groups and it carries lower rates of interest than normal PLA.

The system of finance prevents rent pooling on the scale that applies in the UK. Since rents are approved for a particular building programme as a consequence of receiving a subsidized loan, it is not open to a landlord to increase rents for older housing, on which loans are still outstanding, so as to reduce high rents on newer stock. This contract system on loans means that rents are likely to bear a much closer relation to historic costs than they do in Britain.

On the other hand, the French system seems to have a clear advantage over the British in the size of the landlord organizations and the greater scope for competition. Although the size varies considerably, in general the smaller scale will make it possible for the management of HLMs to be closer and more sensitive to the needs of their tenants. Furthermore, although the HLM-OPs and OPACs are sponsored by local authorities, there may be several of them within a single local authority area and some HLM-SAs as well. Rents will vary between them, reflecting not only the age and quality of the housing but the financial circumstances of the landlord organization; all of this provides the tenants with a range of choice, as well as providing the landlords with a spur to efficiency and quality, which has been much less marked in Britain, at least until the recent development of housing associations.

Finally, the system is less financially constrained by government funding than its British counterpart, because of the use made of private sector investment through the CDC. This makes it possible to avoid the rigid controls that apply to public expenditure approval for housing investment in Britain. British housing authorities would certainly find this flexibility enviable. On the other hand, French social landlords are more exposed to movements in interest rates than British local authority landlords, who are protected by recurrent annual subsidy. Although subsidized PLA loans and the bulk of the money raised on the market will be at fixed long-term rates, during times of high interest rates HLMs may be reluctant to borrow funds for new building if it means that rents will be higher than for existing tenants. High interest rates would therefore cause a tightening in the funding for social housing to a greater extent than in Britain, unless the subsidy on PLA loans were increased. This may be why both the Lebègue and Geindre reports attach considerable importance to the continuation of bricks and mortar subsidies as an incentive to investment in new housing (Lebègue 1991: 45f; Geindre 1993: 49f).

Housing allowances

France has various schemes that provide personal housing allowances, or benefit, to those on low incomes (Ghékiere 1991: 137; Heugas-Darraspen 1985: 57). The most important of these now is APL (*aide personalisée au logement*), which was introduced in 1977, along with other changes to rationalize housing subsidies. APL is available both to owner occupiers for mortgage payments and to tenants in the private and social sectors. The scheme is partly financed by the 1% levy and partly by the budget. It is based on what is considered to be an appropriate level of rent or mortgage payments, and does not necessarily cover the whole cost; assistance is available up to a certain level of household incomes adjusted for size of household and location. However, the critical feature of APL is that it is available only to those whose housing has been assisted under one of the qualifying loan schemes. These include PAP loans (owner occupiers), PC (owner occupier and rented sector) and PLA loans (social sector); it can also be made available to those occupying dwellings subject to the various improvement grants (PAH, ANAH and PALULOS). The logic for tying housing allowances to aided housing in this way is to encourage new housing investment in the knowledge that mortgage and rental payments will be paid. In the case of rented dwellings, only allowances under the APL system are paid direct to landlords, other types of housing allowance being paid to the tenant.

An older system of allowances stemming from the legislation of 1948 is known as AL (*allocation de logement*). This now takes two forms:

- ALF (*allocation de logement familiale*) dating from 1948, which is paid to families with dependent children or elderly dependent adults, and to childless couples who have been married for up to five years, and
- ALS (*allocation de logement sociale*), which dates from 1971, and is targeted on persons over 65, employed persons under 25, handicapped people, the long-term unemployed who receive insurance based benefits, and those who receive a minimum income benefit.

The scheme has been extended to students, but the resulting costs are very high. These allowances are most commonly paid to tenants in the private rented sector, whose houses are of mainly older stock and have not benefited from assisted loans, to tenants in the social sector whose houses pre-date the 1977 introduction of PLA, and to owner occupiers whose dwellings have not benefited from PAP or PC. In all cases these benefits are paid direct to the occupier. As with APL, they are based on standardized eligible rent payments, which vary according to household type, size and location, and include a service charge. In general the ceilings for APL payments are more generous than those for the AL system and it seems that this difference in cost prevents the French government from taking the obvious and rational step of amalgamating the APL and AL systems.

The costs of the policy

The shift in the costs of French housing policy from direct bricks and mortar subsidies to housing allowances is very evident from the figures in Table 3.2. From 1981 to 1991, bricks and mortar subsidies had risen only some 20% in current values and at FF16000 million (£1900 million) had fallen considerably from the peak figure of FF26000 million (£3100 million) in 1985. The fall in real terms is of course much more substantial. Tax relief was also substantially reduced.

On the other hand, subsidies under the housing savings scheme had risen by about 70% and housing allowances at FF55000 million (£6600 million) had risen from only FF16000 million (£1900 million) in 1981. The increase in the cost of allowances is no doubt attributable in part to the economic and demographic trends that increased the numbers of both unemployed and pensioners; but it is also a direct consequence of the changed emphasis of policy after 1977, the introduction of APL and the fact that, unlike Britain, allowances are available to owner occupiers as well as tenants. Indeed, it is a striking feature of the situation in France that, since their introduction, the APL housing allowances paid to owner occupiers have exceeded those paid for tenants (Heugas-Darraspen 1985: 64; Papa 1992: 121).

Table 3.2 The cost of French housing policy (000 million francs, at current prices).

	1978	1981	1985	1991	1993[a]
Aid to bricks & mortar	10.8	15.2	25.7	16.3	16.0
Aid to savings schemes	1.3	5.3	3.4	9.1	7.9
Land tax exemption (State)	2.4	3.6	3.7	2.8	1.5
Allowances:	8.6	16.1	34.5	54.7	61.9
of which:					
APL	0.0	2.8	13.9	29.7	32.1
ALS	2.4	4.3	7.5	10.4	14.2
ALF	6.1	8.8	12.3	12.8	13.8
"1% levy"	3.9	5.7	8.5	7.7	7.2
Tax reliefs:	11.2	17.7	21.6	36.0	37.1
of which:					
Owner occupier	2.9	5.5	6.6	10.7	11.7
Landlords	2.6	4.2	4.8	6.1	7.2
Savings schemes	1.4	2.7	3.7	9.0	8.0
Livret A	0.9	1.6	2.7	3.4	3.7
Land tax exemption (local authorities)	1.4	2.2	1.9	4.0	3.8
TOTAL	38.2	63.7	97.4	126.6	131.5
As a % of GDP	1.8	2.0	2.1	1.9	1.8

a. Estimate.
Source: Lebègue report (1991: 114); Geindre report (1993: 37).

Despite the 1977 changes, which introduced a more direct income related policy, the total costs have continued to rise (Table 3.2). However, these figures are in current prices, and in constant price terms (as estimated in the Geindre report) the total cost stabilized in 1989 and fell slightly in 1992. As a proportion of GDP, the cost was 1.8% in 1993, which compared with over 3% for the UK (see Table 8.5) (Lebègue 1991: 24–5; Geindre 1993: 37).

Conclusion

The major post-war housebuilding programme in France started a good deal later than in the Britain, but when it did get under way, it peaked at higher levels of output. Partly in consequence, there is a legacy of much high-rise system-built housing, especially in the social sector, some of which exhibits the same problems as housing of similar vintage in Britain.

The owner occupied sector, although now accounting for more than half the total stock and benefiting from a policy of encouragement, is still significantly smaller than in Britain. The bulk of the mortgage lending is in the form of fixed interest long-term loans; and, although it is now much less important, in the past a substantial part of finance for new house purchase was provided through the subsidized loan system. The house savings scheme remains important. There was a fall in Parisian house prices of some 20% or more between the peak of 1988 and 1991, not unlike the housing slump in Britain (Compagnie Bancaire 1993: 2). But the French system, can be expected to give more stability to the housing market than in Britain and in particular to result in less distress through negative equity.[6] Personal loan debt is not so high and there is less danger of destabilizing effects on the management of the economy.

The sector is likely to continue to grow as a proportion of the total housing stock, but the integration of European financial markets could have far-reaching implications for French mortgage finance. If competition leads to higher interest rates being offered for savings and the relaxation of the rule that no interest is paid on current and short-term savings accounts, mortgage borrowing would inevitably become more expensive. The house savings scheme could also lose its attractions.

The private rented sector is still much more significant than in the UK, but the trend is one of long-term decline. This has accelerated as a result of the higher interest rates in the 1980s, which reduced landlords' profit when rents could not readily be adjusted. But the decline must also be partly attributable to the long history of rent regulation. If it is to be reversed, or even stabilized, rent and tenancy regulation needs a period of tranquillity based on the *loi Malandrain,*

---

6. The term "negative equity" is used to describe the situation were resale house value falls below the value of the outstanding mortgage. It is discussed at greater length in Chapters 8 and 12.

which is broadly comparable to the "assured tenancies" system in Britain. But the fiscal arrangements would also need to be made more comparable in generosity to those for the owner occupied sector. Several commentators see advantage in the German system, which permits eligible expenses (including depreciation) to be deducted from income generally, rather than simply income from letting (Geindre 1993: 56). As it is, the French fiscal arrangements are much more generous than those that apply to this sector in Britain.

The social sector is of particular interest because of the form of the landlord organizations: the HLMs. In principle these would appear to have advantages of tenant involvement, competition and choice, and greater freedom from public expenditure constraints when compared with British local authorities as landlords. In fact, they have encountered many similar problems with difficult estates, which simply shows that not all problems of British local authority housing can be laid at the door of the ownership structure. But the French system, or variants of it, would appear to be worth consideration at a time when the British social sector has been undergoing considerable change.

The motives for the 1977 changes in France were partly the rapidly growing cost of housing policy and partly the need to target it better on those of limited means. Despite the more selective approach, the cost has continued to increase, largely because of rising numbers of unemployed and elderly people. The fact that it appears to cost less than UK housing policy in recent years may not be very significant, given some of the hidden costs in the system of finance (e.g. the non-interest bearing bank accounts) and the difference in the social security system. But a substantial part of the higher cost in Britain must be accounted for by the more indiscriminate mortgage interest tax relief scheme and the predominance of variable rate mortgages, which increased the cost of relief when short-term interest rates were high. In France, attempts to contain costs by restraining the rise of rents in the social sector seem to have had an adverse effect on the quality and maintenance of the stock.

For the future, although the volume of new house construction in France has remained well above the levels in Britain in recent years, there is concern that housing investment is inadequate in relation to future demand. This is the main issue addressed by the Lebègue and Geindre reports, and both recommend measures to encourage it more directly. If a worsening housing shortage is to be avoided, action is needed to halt the declining trends in the private rented sector, to maintain assistance for the less well-off who move into ownership, and to increase resources for the social rented sector, so that it can both upgrade existing stock and undertake a larger expansion.

CHAPTER 4
Housing policy in Germany

The former West Germany had a housing policy that relied heavily on working with the market; indeed, it was probably the most market based policy followed by any of the six countries covered in this study. Although the scale of the housing crisis immediately after the war greatly exceeded the problems faced by the other countries, by the 1980s shortages had disappeared and the standard of provision was generally good. The State had, therefore, been gradually withdrawing from direct intervention in the housing market, until the problems of re-unification raised a need once again for a more active policy. In the enlarged Germany the very different circumstances and problems of the five *Länder* that formed the German Democratic Republic (GDR) have now to be tackled. This has profoundly changed the housing situation in the West as well, because of the large amount of population movement, but the indications are that the underlying philosophy and the shape of the policy measures are remaining unchanged.

As in France, policy in Germany has undergone considerable changes over the years, but there has been much greater continuity than in the UK. Housing policy has been less affected by political divisions and there would seem to be a wide measure of agreement on both aims and measures. There has, nevertheless, been some difference in emphasis between the parties, notably on rent policy and the role of the social sector. When in office, the Social Democratic Party (SPD) legislated to provide tenant protection and to moderate the unrestricted rental market; the SPD also sees a continuing need for a subsidized social sector. On the other hand, the Christian Democrat/Free Democrat coalition has shifted the emphasis of policy to housing allowances, and some of their members appear to favour the gradual but eventually complete ending of all subsidies to bricks and mortar, apart from taxation allowances.

However, the federal constitution requires a degree of joint responsibility between the three major parties that does not apply in any of the other major countries of the European Union. This is not only because the Federal government is normally a coalition of at least two parties, but also because housing policy is a joint responsibility between several levels of government, which may be under the control of different political parties. The first and second Housing Construction Acts (*Wohnungsbaugesetz*) of 1950 and 1956, which are the basis of postwar German housing policy, laid a duty on the Federal and *Länder* governments,

45

the communes and associations of communes to promote the construction of housing of a standard suitable for the broad mass of the population. There is a sharp contrast here with the situation in France, where policy is uniquely a central government responsibility, and also in Britain, where, despite the major part played by local authorities, especially in the decades after 1945, central government takes responsibility for policy and to a large extent for funding.

Although the structure of German housing policy is determined by the *Bund* (Federal government), its implementation is largely the responsibility of the 16 *Länder* (States) and there is also a significant role for the *Gemeinden* (local authorities). The *Länder* are not simply agents of central government policy in the way that local authorities have increasingly tended to be in Britain; the constitution gives them a substantial measure of sovereignty of their own. As a result, there are differences in the application of the policy from one *Länd* to another and some supplement the measures laid down by the Federal government with measures of their own (Jaedicke & Wollmann 1990: 133; Boelhouwer & van der Heijden 1992: 105–7). Funding is a joint responsibility of the *Bund* and *Länder*; for some measures the costs are shared between them, whereas for others the responsibility may lie primarily with one or the other. Local authorities are responsible for planning, including planning in relation to housing, and also have powers to top up the schemes of assistance for housing investment. All of this means that there is more policy variation than in other countries, in some ways not unlike the UK (see Ch. 8), where there are differences of both legislation and application between the constituent countries.

At the end of the Second World War, the Federal Republic faced a housing crisis on a scale that was much more severe than that of any of the other belligerent countries. Although there was no legacy of accumulated pre-war shortage, unlike France, a large amount of stock had been destroyed by Allied bombing, especially in the major cities. One estimate puts the loss of dwellings at 2.3 million out of a total of 10.5 million, whereas in the worst affected cities, such as Cologne and Hamburg, nearly 50% of the total stock was destroyed (Duvigneau & Schönefeldt 1989: 9, 48; Jaedicke & Wollman 1990: 128–9).

In addition to the obvious problem that this destruction created, there was a huge inflow of refugees from the east, not only from the GDR but also from the former German territories beyond the Oder–Neisse line, which formed the new eastern boundary, and from the Sudetenland in Czechoslovakia. The combination of the destruction and this population inflow produced an acute shortage of housing stock, which is variously estimated at 4.8–6 million dwellings (Leutner & Jensen 1988: 147; Jaedicke & Wollmann 1990: 128). The population inflow was a particularly acute problem in the years immediately after the war; but immigration continued until the erection of the Berlin wall in 1961 and then resumed again on a large scale at the end of the 1980s and in the early 1990s. In addition, as a result of the outstandingly successful growth of the German economy, there was a large inflow of foreign workers (*Gastarbeiter*), which amounted to some 4.4 million by the end of the 1980s (Duvigneau & Schönefeldt

1989: 9). And as a result of these movements, combined with natural population increase, the population of the territory comprising the Federal Republic, which had been 40 million in 1939 and 44 million in 1945, rose to 54 million in 1961 and reached 61 million by the late 1980s before reunification.

Despite the challenge that this situation posed, an immense investment in housebuilding transformed the severe shortages of the years after the war into an approximate market balance and even an overall surplus by the early 1970s.[1] This surplus was more pronounced in the heavily industrialized north than in the more rapidly growing south; but for some years, with the ending of large-scale immigration and a sharp fall in the natural increase of the population, a declining population seemed to be in prospect and became a matter of comment and concern. It was only in the late 1980s that a serious shortage returned, particularly after the fall of the Berlin wall, when a huge inflow from the former GDR and from the other countries of eastern Europe resumed.

To cope so successfully with the post-war shortage, obviously the scale of housebuilding effort had to be very large. As was seen in Chapter 2, two thirds of today's stock has been constructed since the war, compared with just over half in the UK and 58% in France. This amounts to some 18.6 million dwellings (Boelhouwer & van der Heijden 1992: 57, 64). At its peak in 1973 the construction output rose to a total of 714000 dwellings, compared with 536000 in France and 294000 in the UK in the same year. However, this burst of activity was short lived (Lebègue 1991: 32);[2] it coincided with the move into surplus and thereafter the housebuilding effort declined rapidly, so that it was down 400000 by the late 1970s and to 208000 dwellings per annum by the end of the 1980s, still substantially more than in Britain. As a result of the events since 1989, the volume of construction rose again; the figure for reunited Germany was 374000 in 1992 (Fig. 4.1).

In the five eastern *Länder*, which comprised the former GDR, in contrast to the market based policy of the West, the housing sector was subject to government allocation, which resulted in major imbalances. The stock is relatively old, with 40% pre-1919 and 60% dating from before the Second World War. Only 30% of the pre-war stock has been upgraded and low rents have led to a problem of urban decay, with severe lack of maintenance. Approximately half of the multi-apartment housing is below standard and according to some estimates 9–21% of the stock is unusable. Perhaps surprisingly in view of the high average age of the stock and the comparatively low volume of housebuilding activity since the war, the number of dwellings per 1000 inhabitants is even higher than West Germany: 426 compared to 415. But this is at least in part a consequence

1. Hallett (1977: 11) has a graph illustrating the move from shortage to surplus by the 1970s, whereas Boelhouwer & van der Heijden (1992) speak of an overall surplus of 100000 units in the 1970s.
2. However, construction did fall sharply after 1973, see Boelhouwer & van der Heijden (1992: 123), where a chart is given.

47

Figure 4.1 West German housing completions (*Source:* Duvigneau & Schönefeldt (1989); CEC *statistics on housing in the European Community* (1993b)).

of demographic outflow. Although at the time of reunification there was a sub-stantial waiting list, this was more a list of those anxious to move, and who were prevented under the rigidities of the communist system from doing so than a record of those who did not have accommodation. The average size of dwelling in the East is $64\,m^2$ compared with $84\,m^2$ in the West.[3]

Tenure

Perhaps the most striking contrast between the German housing situation and that of the UK is in the pattern of tenure. There is some difficulty in obtaining reliable up-to-date figures for housing tenure in Germany and the most satisfactory for West Germany are those from the 1987 census. As was seen already in Chapter 2 and as Table 4.1 shows, in 1987 38% of the West German stock was in owner occupation (of which 3% was in condominiums, a form of owner co-operative or co-ownership), 43% was privately rented and 15% was socially rented. In the five eastern *Länder* in 1988, 24% was in owner occupation, 17% was privately

3. *Statistisches Jahrbuch* 1992.

rented, 18% was rented by co-operatives and 41% by the State.[4] (Under the communist system all rents, both public and private, were held so low that a social rented sector in the West German sense cannot properly be distinguished.)

Table 4.1   Housing tenure in Germany (% of total stock).

	West Germany		E. Länder
	1978	1987	1988
Owner occupied	38	38	24
Private rented	45	43	17
Social rented	18	15	59*
Others	–	4	–

* 18% co-operatives and 18% owned by the State.
Source: Hubert (1993), Ghékier (1992), Tomann (1992).

Compared with the other countries in this study, the former West Germany therefore had an owner occupied sector that was proportionately not very much smaller than in the Netherlands or Sweden, but much smaller than in the UK, even in Scotland, and significantly smaller than in France. The private rented sector, on the other hand, was very large by the standards of the rest of Europe and particularly in comparison with the UK. Remarkably, even in the eastern *Länder* that comprised the former GDR, the private rented sector is proportionately larger than in the UK and much larger than in Scotland. But in West Germany perhaps even more significant than the size of this sector was its relative stability as a proportion of total stock over almost 20 years. Despite government policy that aimed to encourage the owner occupied sector and to increase its share to 50% of the stock, it too has changed little. The share of the socially rented sector has diminished slightly since the 1970s, but the general picture is one of stability in tenure shares, which contrasts with the experience of other European countries.

However, it is one of the more notable features of the German situation that the distinction between the three tenures is more blurred than elsewhere. The reason is that the social sector depends less on ownership than on whether the landlord has received subsidized finance to provide a dwelling on social market terms. The complexities of this situation are considerable and are illustrated in Figure 4.2.

The diagram shows that, of a West German stock of 26 million dwellings in

4. The West German figures are taken from the 1987 census as being the most reliable, but some more recent sources show the share of owner occupation as high as 40%. The figures for East Germany are even less satisfactory and show quite wide differences between sources. All agree however that, at the time of reunification, the public rented sector was very large – in the region of 60%, if not higher – and that there was still a significant private rented sector. See Tomann (1992: 4) and VROM (1991, 1992).

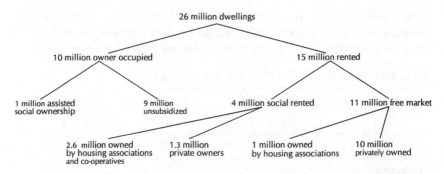

Figure 4.2 Housing stock in west Germany (after Jaedicke & Wollman (1990), with updated figures; information compiled by Woolwich Building Society from various sources and not appropriate for comparisons, except of broad orders of magnitude).

1987, 10 million were in the owner occupied sector. But, as in France, some of these, amounting to over 1 million had been subsidized for those on low incomes and should be regarded as part of the social sector. Of about 15 million rented dwellings, about 4 million were subsidized social housing units and over 11 million were unsubsidized. But since the same aids are available to all landlords, whether private, commercial or non-profit making associations, in return for a contract to provide their dwellings at social rents, the pattern of ownership does not necessarily correspond with the terms on which the housing is provided for rent.

The situation of the housing associations in Germany is particularly complicated, since, apart from those that are co-operatives, they have lost their tax exempt status since 1990 and are now regarded as private sector landlords. These associations have traditionally been the main vehicle for social rented housing and they let the bulk of their stock in this sector, but they also provide over a million dwellings at uncontrolled rents. On the other hand, normal private and commercial landlords who rent the bulk of their stock in the unsubsidized sector also provide over 1 million dwellings at social rents.

Furthermore, a feature unique to Germany is that the provision of housing at social rents in return for a subsidized loan may cease when the loan is repaid; on average this is after 35 years, but may be sooner if the landlord decides to pay it off. Although the private rented sector may therefore lose dwellings from sales into owner occupation, in the same way as in other countries, it also gains from those that transfer out of social renting; the social rented sector is therefore the one that in the absence of new building would be most threatened by decline. Indeed, it was declining up to the end of the 1980s; and of the mid-1980s social rented stock in West Germany up to a half is expected to have become private rented housing by the mid-1990s, as repayment of subsidized loans becomes due. The inclusion of the former GDR, with its large social rented stock, alters this tenure balance considerably, although it is unlikely to affect the trend, since social housing in the five new *Länder* has been reorganized to accord with the system in the rest of the country. For the enlarged country the social sector is now approximately twice the size that it was for West Germany alone, with the addition of a further 3.5 million dwellings.

Subsidies to investment

The subsidies for new construction and for rehabilitation and improvement are not tenure specific and it is appropriate, therefore, to describe them before discussing the individual tenures. Because of this and also because of greater equality in tax treatment, German policy can claim to be much more nearly tenure neutral than that of either Britain or France. The 1950 and 1956 Housing Acts (*Wohnungsbaugesetz*), which remain the basis of the subsidy system to bricks and mortar, extended assistance to all sectors in the belief that this was necessary if the acute West German housing crisis was to be overcome. There are at present three promotion or incentive schemes under which aid may be granted:

- First Incentive Scheme (*Erster Förderungsweg*) This may take the form of either an interest free loan repayable over a long period or of an interest subsidy, decreasing over 15 years, to enable rents to be kept to an agreed level. The tendency has increasingly been to prefer the latter method, because of the advantage in public expenditure terms, in particular because it avoids the high initial cost. The assistance is given only for dwellings allocated to households with income below a ceiling that is adjusted for the number of persons in the household, and for handicapped persons, young married couples, migrants, refugees, and so on. Assistance under this scheme may be given to housing associations or private investors, and has also been given to owner occupiers. However, the largest part has been granted to rented accommodation on the condition that it is then let at agreed social market rents.
- Second Incentive Scheme (*Zweiter Förderungsweg*) This scheme is for those with higher incomes, which are not more than 40% above the ceiling for the first scheme. Assistance takes the form of an interest subsidy on loans and is intended mainly but not exclusively for the owner occupied sector.
- Third Incentive Scheme (*Dritter Förderungsweg*) This scheme is more recent than the other two, having been introduced only in 1989. It provides a more flexible system with regard to the amount of subsidy and is intended mainly to assist the private rented sector, where it caters for groups of the population with intermediate incomes. The scheme is at the discretion of the *Länder*, and only some of these have so far adopted it. The intention is to match assistance more closely to requirements, thereby making the best use of the public expenditure. The length of the contract on this assistance is shorter than for the other two schemes, being seven to ten years compared with about 35. Loans are therefore paid back earlier and rents are then free to return to market levels.

51

Over the years, some significant trends are evident in the application and costs of these schemes (Table 4.2). In the first place the total number of new dwellings approved under the schemes has fallen substantially. In 1960, when social housing was a major element in reconstruction, 326000 social housing units were built, some 51% of all dwellings in that year; by 1975 there were about half this number, 154000, which comprised 35% of completions; and in 1988 only 39000, or 19%. Thereafter, there was an increase as a result of the effects of reunification. The fall in the number of rental dwellings was much greater than those for owner occupation approved under the schemes. In 1960 71% of the dwellings were for rent; this share came down to 53% in 1975, and by 1988 only 34% of the dwellings approved under the subsidy schemes were to rent. Under the second scheme the number of houses approved for rent by the end of the 1980s had become almost negligible (Duvigneau & Schönefeldt 1989: 14–15). But in the most recent period, following the collapse of communism and the consequences of reunification, net inward migration rose to over 600000 a year and, in response to this, the proportion of assisted rented dwellings has risen again.

In the financing of the schemes, the balance between the Federal government and the *Länder* had also changed. The former stopped making contributions to rental housing under the second scheme from 1982, although continuing assist-

Table 4.2 Assisted housing as a proportion of German housing completions.*

	Total housing completions (000)	Assisted housing completions (000)	Assisted housing (% of column1)	Rental as % of assisted housing
1960	574	326	57	71
1965	592	209	35	69
1970	478	165	35	69
1973	714	126	18	na
1975	436	154	35	53
1980	389	91	23	41
1985	312	69	22	44
1988	208	39	19	34
1990	257	59	23	70
1991	314	94	30	66
1992	374	82	22	na

*W. Germany, 1960–90; including eastern Länder 1991 and 1992.
Source: Jaedicke & Wollman (1990), Duvigneau & Schönefeldt (1989), CEC Statistics on housing in the European Community (1993b).

ance for owner occupied housing, and from 1986 the financing of all rental housing was left to the *Länder*, many of which also reduced their funding. This illustrates not only the withdrawal from intervention already referred to, but also that owner occupation has always had an important part, and latterly the major part, in German social housing policy. Only the events at the end of the decade, including reunification, caused both levels of government to take a more active part again and to increase funding.

The owner occupied sector

As has been noted already, the owner occupied sector is relatively small in Germany, despite government efforts to promote it. There appear to be several reasons for this. In the first place, much of the total housing stock in Germany is in the form of flats and these are usually rented. Detached houses tend to be owner occupied, but, as was seen in Chapter 2, are usually much more expensive than in the UK or France. This is partly because building regulations impose very high specifications, higher certainly than in the Netherlands, France or Britain, and this involves substantial costs (Hallett 1977: 72). But it is also because the system of housing finance, which is described below, gives encouragement for owner occupation to be delayed until the purchaser is well established in a career. At that stage, the demand is likely to be for a high-quality house and, once established, the average length of stay is 28 years. Home owners are, therefore, much less likely to move than their counterparts in the UK (Fannae Mae 1991: 33).

House purchase later in life is a much more viable option in Germany than it is in Britain. This is because the large private rented sector offers an alternative that has considerable advantages for young people with as yet slender means and the prospect of having to move between jobs. Furthermore, investment in a house has never been seen in Germany as superior to other investments, either in providing a hedge against inflation or as the best way of achieving a high long-term growth in accumulated wealth. This has been one of the main motives for early house purchase in the UK and, despite the fall in prices in the latest recession, it has been borne out by experience over the longer term. House prices in all countries fluctuate, and calculations therefore depend on the years taken, but a study by Holmans (1991b: para. 16) finds that, in real terms between 1972 and 1989, house prices rose by an average of 0.4% a year in Germany compared with a rise in Britain of 2.2% over the 40 year period up to 1988. Whereas the British real price increase was approximately in step with the rise in disposable income, the rise in German house prices fell well short of it . The only exceptions to this were some of the cities in the southern part of West Germany, where economic growth has been particularly strong and caused a more rapid escalation in house prices.

As well as normal owner occupation, Germany has a small co-ownership or condominium subsector. This is somewhat similar to "tenant/owner" co-operatives in Sweden (see Ch. 7), but on a very much smaller scale, and German condominiums comprise both ownership and renting, the latter now being the larger share. Owner-occupied condominiums account for some 3% of the stock, or just under 1 million dwellings. This tenure form, which provides common ownership of the external fabric and service areas but enables the flats to be individually owned, is particularly appropriate for apartments. It provides a means of ensuring the maintenance and upkeep of common areas and fabric, since all who purchase apartments have to agree the arrangements for this at the time of purchase. However, although condominiums as a special tenure undoubtedly have these very real advantages, their recent growth in Germany is also seen partly as a means of getting around the restrictions on rent and security of tenure that apply in the rented sector. This aspect, which is a matter of some concern, is explained more fully later in this chapter.

Housing finance for owner occupation

The system of housing finance remains much more tightly regulated than in Britain and is probably the most regulated and most difficult for outside institutions to penetrate of any in the European Union. There is a diversity of institutions and in some of them there is a large amount of *Länder* and local authority involvement. But there is also a wide cross-ownership and a high degree of vertical integration between them. Almost invariably, therefore, the house purchaser in Germany has to draw on finance from several different sources. To a British observer the system will seem extremely complex; but it does provide a degree of stability in the housing market that contrasts with the much more competitive but more volatile British situation.

First mortgage loans may be obtained from mortgage banks (*Hypotheken-banken*), savings banks (*Sparkassen*), credit co-operatives, or from the commercial banks. Of the 24 mortgage banks, 17 have commercial banks as their largest shareholders and the three largest are owned by the three large commercial banks (*Grossbanken*).

Only approved mortgage banks can issue mortgage bonds, known as *Pfand-briefe*, for which the collateral loans must be made on German real estate. Like all first mortgages in Germany, these are restricted by law to a loan to value ratio of not more than 60%, unless guaranteed by a public co-operative or institution. Loans provided by the mortgage banks are at fixed rates, normally for 20–25 years but subject to renegotiation of the interest rate within the first ten years. In general these banks, which also finance commercial property, concentrate on wealthier clients purchasing the more expensive dwellings, and leave the less well off to the savings banks. In 1992, for example, clients taking out loans with the Association of German Mortgage Banks had an average net family income per month of DM5731 (£28000 a year) in north Germany and DM7108 (£34000 a year) in the south.[5]

The 586 savings banks, which are publicly owned, provide loans at either fixed or variable rates, the latter being less common but on the increase. They are not entitled to issue mortgage bonds and, where fixed-rate loans are offered, they would normally be for five or a maximum of ten years. The co-operative bank sector, which consists of many small agricultural and urban co-operatives, offers all types of banking services but concentrates on making short and medium-term loans.

---

5. Information Supplied by the Association of German Mortgage Banks.

The commercial banks, of which Germany has some 300 (a very large number compared with Britain) also provide housing finance, and their share has tended to grow at the expense of the specialist institutions. But the sector is dominated by the three major clearing banks – Deutsche Bank, Dresdner Bank and Commerzbank, known as the *Grossbanken* – which account for about half the total number of branches. No doubt it is because these banks have a substantial stake in the specialist mortgage institutions that they do not have a larger direct share of the mortgage business themselves. Although their share is significant, much of it is in the form of unsecured loans, either to top up mortgage loans or to provide funds that are paid back when loans from the contract savings scheme become available.

In addition to this first mortgage, a particularly important part in the German housing finance system is played by the contract savings scheme, which provides part of the finance for three out of four newly constructed owner occupied houses (Diamond & Lea 1992: 107). This scheme is in some ways similar to its counterpart in France, but, unlike the French scheme, its operation is restricted to the specialist group of housing savings banks, the 34 *Bausparkassen*. Some of these, known as *Landsbausparkassen*, are specific to particular regions and are publicly owned, but the remainder are private, have strong links with the other financial institutions (many being owned by commercial banks) and operate throughout the country.

The system is entirely closed and is therefore little influenced by market interest rates. Depositors contract for a desired amount of loan (the *Bausparsumme*). They receive a low rate of interest on their savings and when 40–50% of this sum has been saved, depending on the contract, they can obtain the full loan. The loan is also at a low and fixed rate of interest, which is normally some 2% above the deposit rate. Since both the savings deposited and the loan attract low rates of interest, the system would not provide any special advantage over normal market investments and loans at commercial rates, were it not for the tax relief and bonus provided by the government.

Savings deposited are eligible for a tax credit, and interest on savings deposited with the *Bausparkassen* is also likely to be tax exempt. The latter is not a major benefit, since interest accruing to individuals from any source is subject to tax only if in total it exceeds DM6000 (£2500). The tax credit, however, amounts to 10% of savings deposited, with a maximum exclusion of DM936 from taxable income per year. The credit is part of a general allowance for precautionary expenditure, which covers the premiums on most insurance policies as well, and therefore ceases to be available if the overall limit is breached. This limit, which is presently DM9500 for single persons and DM13000 for couples, has not been increased since the 1970s and is therefore much less generous than it was originally (ibid.: 109–110).

The bonus, which is aimed at the less well off, who cannot take full advantage of the tax credit, is subject to an income eligibility ceiling. Although this ceiling was raised in 1990, the bonus has also been significantly reduced during the

55

1980s, having been cut in two stages from 18% of annual savings before 1982 to 10% since 1989. These cuts clearly reduce the advantages of savings with the *Bausparkasse*, but this form of saving remains popular and there is no suggestion that it will cease to be a central element in private housing finance (Council of Mortgage Lenders 1990: 7–13).

There is a disincentive under this system for purchasers to buy their houses before their savings have reached at least 40–50% of the sum they have contracted to save with the *Bausparkasse*. If they do so, they will normally have to take out a short-term loan at very much higher rates of interest, until the entitlement for a *Bausparkasse* loan matures. Although such arrangements are quite common, and are likely to become increasingly so, the costs can be quite high. Moreover, to qualify for the benefits of having an account with a *Bausparkasse*, the purchaser will have to continue to build up savings in the meantime; and, once eligible, the provision of a loan will depend upon the availability of finance, so that queueing may be necessary and a delay of over a year may be involved. Therefore, although this system certainly provides a powerful incentive to encourage personal savings for house purchase and gives great stability to the housing market, the delay that it entails provides a major reason for the habit of relatively late house purchase in Germany.

The first mortgage, together with a *Bausparkasse* loan, cannot provide more than 80% of the cost of house purchase, leaving purchasers to find the remaining 20% from their own resources. In addition to funding from these financial institutions, purchasers of new dwellings with lower incomes may also be entitled to an assisted State loan to finance construction under one of the systems already described. This would be either at a reduced rate of interest or interest free for a period of years. This corresponds to the PAP loans in France and is a form of social housing targeted at those who would not otherwise be able to afford owner occupation.

However, even when all these systems are put together, potential purchasers are likely to have to find a significant part of the purchase price either from their own resources or in the form of a personal loan which, lacking the security of a mortgage, would probably be at higher rates. This contrasts with the very high loan-to-value ratios (LTV) offered on housing loans in the UK in recent years and in Germany too one might expect deregulation and greater competition when the Single Market takes effect in European finance. But although the present German system may result in fewer less well off purchasers moving into owner occupation, it also leads to greater stability in the housing market. The combination of relatively late house purchase, the provision of finance that is much less subject to fluctuations in short-term interest rates, and the conservative loan to value ratios make German house-owners much less vulnerable to repossessions and the phenomenon of negative equity. There is therefore likely to be some resistance to following the British example.

Taxation and fiscal relief

The principal incentive to housing investment in the owner occupied sector, apart from the provisions of the contract savings scheme, is provided by a depreciation allowance. This permits the owner occupier to deduct from his *taxable income* depreciation on the value of his house and on 50% of the value of the land for a total period of eight years, once in the owner's lifetime. The depreciation rate is 6% per annum for four years and 4% for the remaining four, subject to a maximum of DM19800 (about £7920) a year. The system applies regardless of the way in which the house purchase is funded and is therefore not tied to a mortgage. Married couples can use this facility twice, but not simultaneously and not for the same dwelling. Deductions can also be made from taxable income for various expenditures related to the dwelling, including loan interest while the building was being constructed, costs of renovation before moving in, and various forms of upkeep expenditure in the first three years after acquisition, provided these do not exceed 20% of the purchase price. This is clearly a powerful incentive for the eight years of its operation. However, it is regressive, giving more assistance to the better off, since the relief is at the individual's marginal rate of tax. Because of this, and even more because it is a once-for-all benefit, it too encourages house purchasers to wait until they can afford a reasonably expensive house, rather than use it up on something of relatively low value.

In addition to this major incentive, there are special tax exemptions for investments such as the installation of energy-saving equipment and for renovation and purchase costs in urban renewal areas. There is also a *tax credit* for each child (*Baukindergeld)* of DM1000. There is no longer any tax on imputed rents for owner occupiers, nor is there a capital gains tax on owner occupied housing or on other personal financial assets held for at least two years.

Limited mortgage interest tax relief has also been available in Germany at various times in the past. It was phased out in 1984 but was reintroduced in late 1991 for new construction of owner occupied housing. It applies only for the first three years after construction, is limited to a maximum of DM12000 (about £4800) per annum and is available only until the end of 1994.

Two other taxes apply to housing, regardless of tenure. The *Grundsteuer* or local property tax (equivalent to the old British "Rates") is based on rateable value or *Einheitswert*. It is used to finance local authorities, but now accounts for less than 5% of their revenue, since rateable values have not been updated and have therefore become greatly under-assessed, in many cases valuing the property at less than a tenth of its market value. Since any mortgage can be deducted at its nominal value, housing assets are effectively exempt from this tax. Land Acquisition Tax or *Grunderwerbesteuer* is levied at a flat rate of 2% (Hallett 1988: 34–5; Hubert 1993b: 20).

The private rented sector

The German private rented sector is of particular interest from a British stand-point, because it provides such a marked contrast with this sector in Britain. While Britain has the smallest private rented sector, Germany has the largest of the countries in this study (although not as large as Switzerland); and while the British private rented sector has been declining rapidly, its German counterpart has been remarkably stable. Indeed, it is the only one of the six countries where there has not been a marked decline. At 43% of the total stock, there are more dwellings privately rented in Germany than in owner occupation.

In large part this must be attributable to a much more neutral application of subsidy and fiscal measures between the sectors; indeed, in contrast to most other countries, the fiscal arrangements for this sector are probably more favour-able than they are for owner occupation and they strongly encourage investment. But it is also a consequence of the unusual nature of the social rented sector, which results in dwellings reverting to the free market once their subsidized loans have been paid off.

Rent control

Rent control has been a major factor in the decline of the private rented sector in many European countries, but it has been of much less significance in Ger-many. In the circumstances of extreme shortage that existed after the war, it was inevitable that the pre-war system of general rent control should be extended. However, because of the currency reform of 1948 and the low inflation rate dur-ing the 1950s, this did not produce such a sharp fall in landlords' real income as in Britain and in France. Moreover, as in France and in contrast to Britain, peri-odic increases were allowed. The government nevertheless considered that rent control was incompatible with the "social market economy", which it was their aim to create, and in 1960 an Act was passed that provided for the control to be dismantled. This was to be undertaken gradually, district by district, as calcula-tions of the extent of the housing shortage showed that it had fallen below 3% of the total stock in the area. During the 1960s, therefore, rent control was gradu-ally abolished (except in West Berlin, Hamburg and Munich, where exceptional pressure on housing continued) and, for a time, a system of more or less un-restricted market forces applied. By the end of the 1980s only Berlin remained subject to control and it too is scheduled to be lifted in 1994 (Hubert 1993b: 9).

A substantial escalation in rents took place following the abolition of control and there was some feeling that the increases were excessive. Hallett has argued that this was not so in real terms, the increases being no more than one would expect in a period of increased inflation (Hallett 1977: 27–33). But in 1971 the Social Democrat government passed a Tenancy Protection Act (*Wohnraum-kündigungsschutzgesetz),* which, although not re-imposing control, established a system for regulating rents. The aim of this Act was to find a system that would protect tenants from abrupt changes in rent levels, while enabling rents to reflect market conditions. In this it is very similar to the "assured tenancy" system adopted in Britain with the 1988 Housing Act. For new lettings, landlords and tenants continued to negotiate rents freely; but, for a renewal of a let to an existing tenant, the Act made provision for rent arbitration based on comparable rents (*Vergleichsmiete*) for similar property in the area.

This system of rent regulation continues, but the conservative bias, to which it may be expected to give rise, was modified in 1982. The comparator used in rent setting for relets was altered to rents set in the area in the previous three years, rather than the average for all comparable accommodation (Hubert 1993a: 14; 1993b: 12). Where a disagreement between a landlord and tenant arises, under the present arrangements the parties may choose to have it resolved by arbitration in one of three ways:

- evidence of rents fixed for three comparable dwellings over the past three years
- evidence from an expert surveyor, or
- a rent survey undertaken by the local authority.

Rent increases are capped at a maximum of 30% within three years. But where improvements have been carried out, to enable landlords to recover the cost of their investment, rent may be raised by 11% per annum of the cost without regard to this ceiling.

Despite these changes to the arrangements for assessing comparability, there is clear evidence that rents for new lettings adjust much more sharply to market conditions than relets. Rents for relets are normally some 20–30% below rents that are freely negotiated for new lets on comparable dwellings. Hubert has shown that, in the face of the growing market scarcity in the late 1980s and early 1990s, rents set under new contracts rose sharply, whereas those for the remainder were very little affected (Hubert 1993b: 25–6). This suggests that regulation still prevents rents from adjusting fully to market conditions. But it is thought that this is not simply a consequence of in-built inertia in the rent setting system, but may also be attributable to a desire on the part of landlords to retain good tenants rather than going for the maximum return.

The same Tenancy Protection Act increased security of tenure by defining the conditions in which a tenant could be evicted. These are:

- where the landlord needs the property for his own use or that of his close family
- where the tenant has failed to pay rent
- in certain limited circumstances where improvement, redevelopment or demolition of the property is required.

Unlike the situation in Britain following the 1988 Housing Act, fixed-term leases are not available in Germany, and tenants therefore have virtually indefinite security of tenure.

This situation has led to two quite significant problems. The first is that, since new lets tend to command substantially higher rents than relets, tenants are reluctant to move to smaller accommodation when their needs change, for fear that they will have to pay a substantially higher rent for a smaller flat. This is likely to result in less than optimal utilization of available stock, a matter that becomes serious when there is a shortage. The second is the conversion of rented property to condominiums, as those who are unable to find rented accommodation to suit their requirements buy tenanted property from a landlord and, to take possession, use their rights as owners needing the accommodation for themselves. In these circumstances, tenants have special rights that prevent termination of their contracts for some years, but the situation became sufficiently serious for some large cities to try to block condominium conversions in the late 1980s. With the pressure that has built up in the German housing market since the late 1980s, these problems are of course amplified; and if policy were to change in response to the political pressure that is presently strong both in the CDU and SPD in favour of tighter rent regulation, it is likely that they would get worse.

Finance and fiscal incentives

Housing finance for individual owners, who still account for by far the largest part of the privately rented sector, follows broadly the same pattern as in the owner occupied sector, except that the *Bausparkassen* loans will not normally be available. However, fixed interest loans from the mortgage banks are very appropriate for rented accommodation, since they avoid the difficulties created by variable rate mortgages in circumstances where rents are difficult to adjust to changes in interest rates. Commercial companies that own property will raise their funding from a variety of ordinary market sources, including both equity finance and long-term fixed-rate loans, and will therefore also be able to withstand movements in interest rates.

Fiscal incentives to encourage investment and taxation arrangements parallel those that are available to owner occupiers. Housing is treated as an investment good and the main incentive is therefore the depreciation allowance, which is set at an accelerated rate. In contrast to the position of owner occupiers, landlords are entitled to the depreciation allowance at the maximum rate only for new construction or for housing bought within one year of construction. But the allowance is not limited to an entitlement of eight years, as it is for owner occupiers. Instead it can be claimed at a reducing rate for the lifetime of the asset. Since 1989, in consequence of the increased need for housing investment, these depreciation rates have been raised and are now 7% for the first four years, 5% for the next six years, 2% for a further six, and 1.25% for the remaining 24. For a new rented dwelling, therefore, the allowance is now higher than for one in owner occupation, as well as escaping the eight-year limit, and is clearly a very powerful incentive for investment (Hubert 1993b.: 20–21).

Furthermore, purchasers of older accommodation can claim a depreciation allowance on its repurchase price, regardless of the allowances claimed by previous owners. For buildings constructed before 1925, there is a linear depreciation rate of 2.5% and for more recent buildings 2%, if they are bought two or more years after completion. The full depreciation period then starts afresh for a new owner from the date of purchase. In this way, provided the asset is durable, the depreciation may continue well beyond its original assumed life and be uprated as a result of rising house prices.

Landlords are subject to tax on the rental income they receive, whereas owner occupiers are not taxed on imputed rent. But this liability may be significantly offset by the depreciation allowance. Moreover, an important feature of the German system, which does not apply in France, is that housing depreciation allowances may be deducted (along with other relevant costs) from taxable income from any source, not simply income from house letting. This makes the depreciation allowance a very powerful incentive and one that makes housing investment attractive to companies and individuals with other sources of income.

As for owner occupied housing, property taxes, are a very modest burden, being based on rateable values that undervalue the property. Land Acquisition Tax is again at 2%. Like owner occupiers, private owners of rented accommodation pay no capital gains tax, provided that the assets are held for a minimum of two years; nor is tax payable on the difference between the written-down value of a dwelling after depreciation allowance and its resale value, although for other investments, for example industrial machinery, this difference would be taxable.

The unusual nature of the incentives to provide socially rented accommodation, however, must also be one of the factors that encourages private investors. If they accept a State loan under one of the three schemes already outlined, rents will be controlled during the period that the loan is outstanding; but, as will be seen in the next section, the social rent regime provides for a 4% return on capital. Although this may not seem a very generous return, it is a sure one, and it has been estimated that, for many investors, capital appreciation and the tax offsets have the effect of raising the controlled 4% return to around 6 or 7%. Furthermore, the investor has the prospect, when the loan is repaid, of raising the rent to ordinary market rates or of selling the property and realizing its full capital value. If, for whatever reason, the owner cannot wait for the end of the controlled period, s/he has the option of either selling the property as occupied with its outstanding loan or of paying the loan off early, although in that case the obligation to charge social rents will continue for eight years.

The social rented sector

One of the key features of the former West Germany, as has been seen, is that the social sector does not equate with a particular type of landlord, but depends on the contract entered into for assistance received and on the consequent obligation to let at agreed social rents, rather than whether the landlord is a private individual, a company or some form of non-profit making body. On this basis, as was seen earlier, some 4.0 million dwellings, or 15% of the stock, comprised the social rented sector in 1987. Of this, about 2.6 million were owned by housing associations and slightly over one million by private owners. In East Germany under communism the rents of all dwellings were extremely low, regardless of landlord, and therefore fell well short of a commercial return. But if the social sector is taken to equate with the co-operatives and the former publicly owned stock, it is proportionately very much larger, accounting for nearly 60% of the total stock (Tomann 1992: 4; CECODHAS 1993: 53).

In both parts of Germany the social sector has played a major part in construction since the war, but whereas in the West it has been one element in a massive investment programme, in the East public sector building has been overwhelmingly dominant. From 1950 to the later 1980s, over 7 million dwellings out of 18 million constructed in West Germany (43%) were built with government assistance and therefore comprised the social sector broadly defined, including dwellings built for home ownership with subsidies (Duvigneau & Schönefeldt 1989: 27). In East Germany the housebuilding programme approached its peak much more slowly than in the West and, although an element of private building always continued, some 90% of construction (virtually all rented housing) was undertaken either by agencies of the State or by co-operatives (Power 1993: 152).

Landlords

In West Germany, for the part of the social rented stock that is privately owned (rather less than a quarter), the predominant landlords by far are individuals, but there is also some stock owned by commercial companies. However, for the remainder, ownership is in the hands of housing associations. These include both municipal companies and co-operatives. Until the legislative change that took effect in 1990, all of these were classified as non-profit making landlords; now this status applies only to the co-operatives. These bodies have a history in Germany that extends back to the nineteenth century, especially in the case of co-operatives, and social housing built by them made a much more substantial contribution in the inter-war period than was made by their counterparts in France (Hallett 1977: 6–7). Indeed, the vigour of the social sector, which was further boosted after it was commandeered by the Nazis, was a major factor in enabling Germany to avoid the inter-war housing deficit experienced by France.

The German housing associations are members of an umbrella organization that acts on their behalf in negotiations and discussions with government. Since 1990, when the charitable non-profit making status of those associations that were not co-operatives was ended and the associations in the former East Germany joined, this has been known as *Gesamtverband der Wohnungswirtschaft*

(*GdW*). In 1993, there were 1812 associations in the former West Germany, comprising 1165 co-operatives, 622 companies or foundations, and 25 others of differing legal form. Although the members of both groups vary greatly in size, the co-operatives are generally smaller than the companies, with an average of slightly more than 920 dwellings each, compared with around 4000 for the companies, a figure very similar to the average HLM in France. In 1993, the associations owned about 3.4 million dwellings, of which slightly fewer than 1.1 million belonged to the co-operatives and 2.4 million to the companies. However, only 59% of this stock (or just over 2 million dwellings) was receiving subsidy in 1993 and therefore was subject to social rent.[6] This was significantly less than at the time of the tenure census in 1987 (Fig. 4.2). The remainder were free to be let without restriction, either because they were not financed by subsidy or because the assisted loans originally used to finance them had been paid off, making them no longer subject to agreed social rents.

The co-operatives are owned by their members, who have to subscribe a modest fee on joining; but, before gaining access to a dwelling, they have to put down a much more significant sum, which is a refundable charge equivalent to 5% of total cost (Emms 1990: 128-9). Co-operative members must therefore have significant resources. This effectively imposes a self-selection process and, together with their small size, makes it not surprising that co-operatives have had relatively little trouble with their tenancies.

The companies may be formed by a variety of interests, including employers, trade unions, churches or local authorities (*Gemeinden*) and *Länder*. Traditionally, employers have played an important part in Germany, where company housing was an early feature of the rebuilding programme after the Second World War, especially in the years of shortage. But housing companies in the ownership of the local authorities and *Länder* comprise about half the stock and, unlike the situation in France with the HLM-OPs, the German local authorities' interest can be a controlling one or, indeed, outright ownership. Thus, although these companies differ from local authority housing in the UK, in that they have an arm's length relationship with their local authority, draw funding from the market as well as from subsidized public sources, and have to be financially viable, the local authority does have a major interest in their successful operation.

Although the average amount of stock managed by a West German housing company is modest by the standards of a British local authority, some of the companies are very large indeed. For example, the municipal company SAGA in Hamburg has 100000 dwellings, which is large by any UK standards, equivalent to the public sector stock of the City of Birmingham, the largest social landlord in England, and exceeded in size only by Glasgow District Council in Scotland and SCIC in France.[7] The former company, *Neue Heimat*, which was sponsored

---

6. Gesamtverband der Wohnungswirtschaft, *Daten und Facten 1993*, Cologne.
7. The Northern Ireland Housing Executive (the largest landlord in the UK) is also larger, with 153000 dwellings.

by the trade unions and went bankrupt in the 1980s, was even larger, with a total of more than 300000 dwellings throughout West Germany, making it at the time the largest landlord in western Europe (Emms 1990: 130; Hallett 1977: 65; Power 1993: 143–4). Although the collapse of *Neue Heimat* was regarded as a scandal in Germany, because is was brought about by a combination of incompetence and corruption, the experience is nevertheless salutary in a UK context, since it demonstrates that in the last analysis there is a discipline of financial viability applied to social landlords in Germany, which is lacking from the local authority sector in Britain.

It was the scandal associated with *Neue Heimat* and to a lesser extent similar problems with other companies, combined with a general feeling that there was too much bureaucracy and incompetence, that led the government to change their status in 1990 (Tomann 1990: 922; Power 1993: 143–4). The aim was to put these companies on the same footing as private landlords, so that they would face competition and be subject to the same disciplines. In fact "non-profit making" had always been something of a misnomer for their previous status, since, unlike British housing associations, shareholders' capital was a feature of these bodies. The legislation under which they were set up did not prohibit profit but limited distributed dividends to 4% of shareholders' capital, where such capital was up to 15% of total funding, and to 6.5% for amounts above 15%. Any surplus above these figures had to be reinvested. It also restricted their activities to the provision of "non-profit" housing (Tomann 1990: 922; Hallett 1977: 62–72). With their new status since 1990, the restriction on distribution of dividends is lifted and profits may be freely distributed to shareholders, as in any other company; they are also free to engage in other activities. Like normal private companies they are now subject to tax; but, since the taxation arrangements are very favourable to private rented housing in Germany and the companies are expected to have significant provision for allowances, their tax burden is likely to be very small for a considerable time to come.

These changes only affect the companies; the co-operatives retain their special tax-exempt status, together with the limits on profit distribution. Even for tenants of the companies, the immediate effect of the change is likely to be small, as rents remain governed by the conditions of the existing contracts on which assistance was granted. But the longer-term implications could be substantial, as the freedom to distribute greater profits will give companies an incentive to raise rent to free-market levels on stock for which subsidized loans have been paid off. Against this it should be borne in mind that these companies were set up on a social rather than a profit-making basis. For most of the housing companies, and certainly those owned by municipalities, this will not change, and it is therefore unlikely that they will pursue a goal of profit maximization.

In the five former GDR *Länder*, the co-operatives survived both the Nazi and Communist periods, although during the latter they were heavily controlled and influenced by the State (Power 1993: 150–4). They have now been put on the same basis as co-operatives in the rest of the country. However, the largest component in the East German stock was housing built and owned directly by agencies of the State. Under the re-unification treaty, this was transferred to local government and has now in turn been passed to municipal housing companies set up on the basis of the former local housing administrative units. These are similar to the municipal companies in the West and therefore now also operate as private sector bodies.

However, the problems inherited by these bodies (both co-operatives and companies) in the eastern *Länder* are substantial. The stock is a combination of inadequately maintained and unmodernized older dwellings, and unattractive and badly constructed system-building. Massive investment is required. Yet the legacy of long years of very low rents was an encumbrance of debt that was converted into Deutschmarks at the 1 for 2 ratio agreed under monetary union. Although this halved the debt, the normal conversion rate being 1 for 1, interest rates more than doubled. Even with substantial increases in rents, therefore, a severe solvency problem arose, both for the co-operatives and the new companies. This not only threatened the viability of their operations, but made investment in stock improvement virtually impossible (Tomann 1992: 18–27). In 1993 this problem was the subject of an agreement between the Federal government and the *Länder*, under which the housing companies and co-operatives will receive relief from their debt burden, provided that they sell 15% of their stock to either private occupiers or investors. Part of the proceeds are to be handed over to the government.

Allocation and rents

Local authorities handle the applications for social housing. Since income level is a criterion for eligibility, they have to certify prospective tenants as within the maximum qualifying level. They also have nomination rights, although landlords may still find grounds to refuse the nomination of a particular tenant. However, if local authorities have topped up the loans provided to social landlords, this gives them "special nomination rights" that enable them to nominate three possible tenants for a property, out of which the landlord is obliged to choose one.

Central to the rent setting arrangements is the notion of a cost-covering rent. This is inclusive of a 4% return on equity capital and it is what the landlord receives over the period of the outstanding loan that financed the project. The level of rent needed to cover costs is based on the landlord's or developer's estimates of cost at the time the project was approved, and, if the estimates are exceeded, the authorities may refuse to make adjustments.

The social rent paid by the tenant will be subsidized so that it is below this cost-based rent, thereby bringing it down to a level that prospective tenants in this sector can afford. The scale of subsidy needed to bridge the gap between social rent and cost rent will depend on whether low interest State loans, or loans at market rates, have been used to finance the project. The latter are now more common as explained earlier in this chapter, and, where they are used, the cost-covering rent will obviously be higher than with a subsidized loan. But in either case the subsidy will be a reducing one over time in recognition of the heavily front-loaded nature of housing costs and in the expectation that, as the loan is repaid, the combination of inflation and rising incomes will make it possible for tenants to pay a higher proportion of costs. At some point, depending on the original financing arrangements, the subsidy is likely to be eliminated, so that social rent becomes equal to the cost-based rent. The tenant's payments and the landlord's receipts are then both based on the cost-based rent for the remainder of the period of the outstanding loan. These arrangements have been illustrated graphically by Hubert (Fig. 4.3). Cost rent, represented by AB, rises over time as a result of inflation, but not as sharply as social rent, EF, and the subsidy is shown by the triangle AFE.

A free-market rent for a similar project is illustrated by the line CD in the

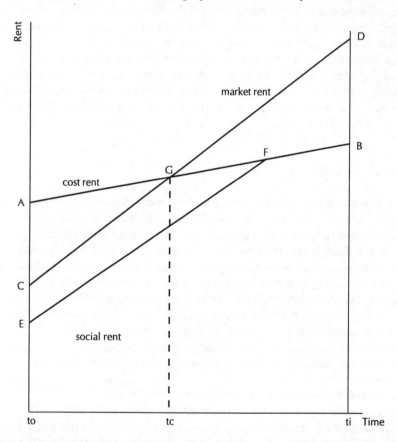

Figure 4.3 Market, cost and social rent in Germany. to: time at which dwelling first let; ti: length of period for which the loan is contracted; tc: point at which market rent rises above cost rent. (*Source:* Hubert 1992).

diagram. It is assumed that it too is likely to be below cost rent in the early years, although not by as much as social rent. This is because competition from older dwellings, built when costs were lower and on which loans are largely paid off, will keep rents below the level that would produce a satisfactory return on new investment. But the private investor assumes he will make up for this later on, partly as a result of appreciation in the value of his asset but also through the erosion of debt and the ability to raise rents, both as a result of inflation.

Whether over the longer term the free-market landlord can get a better return from his investment than the social landlord depends on the market and is by no means a foregone conclusion. What is clear is that the social landlord's return is more certain: the costs are fully covered from the start so long as they have been estimated correctly; and the landlord has the prospect of moving into the free market, when the loan contract has expired, with a debt-free asset at a value that will almost certainly have appreciated.

Both landlords face a risk of an unexpectedly high level of vacancies, for whatever reason. The social landlord is perhaps more likely to be affected by rent arrears from tenants who are unwilling or cannot afford to pay and who are perhaps inadequately protected by housing allowances. Depending on how much equity the landlord has in the project, either of these problems could threaten solvency. For this reason, despite the local authorities' power of nomination, difficulties can arise in trying to place problem tenants, especially if they are thought likely to make the estate less attractive for others. This has led to some feeling among the municipal companies that they are regarded as the landlords of last resort and are left with the largest share of such tenants. The co-operatives largely escape this problem, because of the financial hurdle that membership entails.

The use of controlled social rents set at the outset of a project means that there is no rent pooling. Rents differ widely across the sector, depending not only on the condition of the housing but also its age. This can produce anomalous results, with older housing of good-quality costing less to rent than modern stock, which may be inferior, in a worse location or less desirable. Had it not been for the low rates of inflation that have existed in Germany, these anomalies would probably be much greater than they are. As it is, some tenants may be paying much less for their houses than they are really worth or than they could afford, whereas new building will require a high subsidy or personal housing allowance if it is to be let. But the anomalies, although different, are probably no greater than exist in the UK, where rent pooling tends to result in similar rents within one housing authority, regardless of the quality or location, and with no additional rent paid for improvements. However, there is concern in Germany, as in other countries, that the assistance given to the social sector is not adequately targeted. Apart from the question of low rents on older housing, there is a tendency for a significant proportion of tenants to have incomes that exceed the limits that qualify them for social housing. This is because, although they were initially qualified by low incomes, incomes may rise as people become established in a job. The

Länder are therefore empowered to collect a supplementary rental charge (*Fehl-belegungsabgabe*). Some but not all of the *Länder* have availed themselves of this scheme, and the proceeds (which are substantial) are used to finance other aspects of their housing expenditure.

Housing allowances

Personal housing allowances were first introduced in Germany in 1965, later than in France, which instituted an allowance in 1948 (see Ch. 3). This was a time when rent control was being progressively removed, and adjustments to free-market rent levels were taking place. Since that time, expenditure on housing allowances has steadily grown in the same way as it has in other countries (Table 4.3). This reflects a deliberate shift in German policy from bricks and mortar subsidies to personal allowances, in the belief that such assistance is better targeted on those who need it.

Table 4.3 West German housing allowances.

	Expenditure (DM millions)	Recipients (000)	Tenants (%)
1965	148	395	na
1970	600	908	na
1975	1655	1849	na
1980	1830	1622	94.7
1985	2469	1572	93.9
1988	3697	1858	92.7
1990	3618	1774	93.2
1991	3810	1759	na

Source: *Statistisches Jahrbuch* 1992. *Wirstschaft und Statistik*, January 1994. *Wohngeld and Mietenbericht* 1991, Bundesministerium für Raumordnung, Bauwesen und Städtebau.

The German housing allowance (*Wohngeld*) is the responsibility of the housing department in government and is not (as in Britain) seen as social security. It is paid jointly by the Federal government and the *Länder*, with the former paying rather more than half. It is available both to tenants of all forms of rented accommodation and to owner occupiers. It is therefore provided regardless of tenure, like the French system and unlike the British; but in contrast to the French system it is a single scheme. In practice, and also in contrast to the French system, very few of the recipients are owner occupiers, 93% being tenants. This is not because of any bias in the system, but is most probably the result of the German tendency for prospective owners to delay house purchase until they are well established in their careers. In 1990 roughly 6% of the population – 10% of tenants and 1.2% of home owners – received housing allowances, and recipients' income was on average only about a third of that for the population as a whole. It is believed that the numbers taking up housing allowances are much fewer than those who are entitled, possibly because some stigma is attached to doing so.

A third of the recipients were also on social benefit and, where this is so, the housing allowance to which the recipient is entitled is paid in part reimbursement to the authorities responsible for social security. In such cases, but not otherwise, the full allowable housing costs may be met up to 100% by the social benefit system. Although the German system is based on actual housing costs, so long as they fall within the allowable limits, rather than some system of standardized costs as in the Netherlands, there is no "upmarketing" problem as in Britain, where tenants are fully covered for changes in rent level. Since the system is not intended to meet the whole of housing costs, the assumption being that part at least will always be paid out of other income or benefits, it does not normally cover more than two thirds of a rent increase, and often much less.

The aim of the German system is to reduce housing costs to 15–25% of the recipient's income. For this purpose, income after tax (or "disposable income") is expressed as "family income" after adjustment to reflect the number of dependants. Eligible housing costs for tenants are rent (excluding any element of heating or furnishing costs) or interest payments, plus an allowance for maintenance for owner occupiers. A ceiling is set on allowable housing costs, based on space standards in relation to family size and with variation to reflect regional differences. Periodic adjustment is made to this ceiling to reflect the effect of inflation, since the figures are in nominal price terms. But this adjustment is not automatic and is usually done at only three- to five-year intervals. This means that there is a substantial impact on those who are near the maximum rent figure; indeed, in the period before the 1985 adjustment, the proportion of those whose rent was above the upper limit had risen from 31% to 53% of all recipients and it fell back to 31% afterwards (Tomann 1990: 928). Where the rent is above the maximum, the allowance is still payable, but it does not reflect the full housing costs paid by the tenant or owner occupier.

A further problem with the German system is the difficulty of covering the wide dispersion of rent levels, even in the social rented sector. Because social rents are set historically and there is no rent pooling, wide differences exist, which do not necessarily reflect quality of accommodation. The result is that, for reasons unrelated to quality, a significant proportion of the stock may be at rents that are above the maximum for *Wohngeld*; and in consequence even low-income tenants may find that not all of their housing costs qualify. Alternatively they may be limited to older private stock or to social stock that comes within the limits but which, for that very reason, is subject to low turnover and therefore is very difficult to obtain. Because of these problems, the objective of the German allowance of limiting housing costs to around 25% of recipient's income cannot always be attained. In this respect, therefore, it is not necessarily superior to the British system, where at some levels of income the proportion spent on housing costs can rise to over 30%.

In part to deal with this problem, and also because of the infrequent uprating of the *Wohngeld* system, some of the *Länder* have devised their own supplementary schemes of housing allowances. The *Härteausgleich* scheme of North-Rhine–Westphalia is an example. This may be claimed by tenants whose rent is above the maximum for *Wohngeld* and is also available to those whose income is up to 20% above the limit for social housing. In 1989 120000 tenants in North-Rhine–Westphalia were assisted by this scheme (Papa 1992: 56).

The problem with all systems of housing allowances is that loss of benefit plus increasing taxation, amounting to high implied "taxation" rates for those can create a poverty trap. In the German case, however, this appears to be much less serious than it is at present in Britain. For those on full social security, rental payments may be met in full, and it is therefore difficult to avoid very high implied rates of taxation of around 90% as income rises. But for those not in receipt of social security and who draw housing allowance, the effective marginal rate of benefit withdrawal is 25% on average, compared with 65% in Britain. The actual marginal rate is affected by rent levels, but even for the worst cases it is well below a third (Hills et al. 1989: 29–33). This means that there are in effect two "tapers" (i.e. the rate at which benefit is cut as income rises), a steep one at low levels of income for those on social security as well as housing allowance, and a much more gradual one for those on housing allowance alone.

Compared with housing allowance systems in other countries, the relatively modest cost and proportion of households drawing benefit is notable, especially when one reflects that rents in the social sector are generally higher and nearer to market rents than the British equivalents. The greater prosperity of West Germany and the low levels of unemployment before reunification may largely account for this; costs are likely to have escalated with the onset of recession that began to affect Germany in 1992–3 and with the addition of large numbers claiming benefit in the former East Germany. But it is also a reflection of the system of social security, which is one of the more generous in Europe. Indeed, it is striking that, although there has been some fluctuation in the numbers drawing *Wohngeld* over the years (which may reflect the delay in uprating the scheme as much as anything else), the number of West German claimants in 1991 was actually less than in 1975 (Table 4.3). And, although the number of unemployed who draw housing allowances has risen sharply over the years, this is to a considerable extent compensated for by the fall in the number of pensioners, as a result of the increasingly generous pension provisions, even though the proportion of elderly people was rising.

The costs of the policy

It is particularly difficult to obtain adequate information on the costs of German housing policy. Not only are the costs split between the Federal government, the

Länder and to some degree the local authorities, but there are also policy differences between the *Länder*. Some of the measures give them a substantial degree of discretion, and the claw-back on those tenants who are above the income limit for social housing (*Fehlbelegungsabgabe*) is not operated by all of them. In addition, there is the difficulty that some of the assistance under the Incentive Schemes is financed by interest free or low interest loans and some by recurrent grants.

However, estimates for past years have been made by several authors and, for 1990, both by Ulbrich & Wullkopf and the authors of the Lebègue report.[8] For 1991, as obtained from official sources, they are set out in Table 4.4. The earlier authors show that the total cost of the policy measures in West Germany at current prices, but excluding landlords' depreciation allowances on rented housing, had risen from about DM13000 million in 1974 to DM21–23000 million in 1990. For 1991, as a result of the pressures following reunification, the cost appears to have risen substantially, to at least DM26000 million for the former West Germany alone. The Lebègue Report estimates the value of landlords' accelerated depreciation at approximately DM10000 million in 1990, which, assuming a similar figure for 1991, would give a total of over DM36000 million (approximately £12000 million at the rate of exchange then prevailing). There is a view that since tax relief can be claimed from any income source, not only housing income, and since there are other tax reliefs apart from depreciation, this figure substantially underestimates the true value of the tax relief to landlords. However, estimates of other forms of tax relief, such as freedom from capital gains tax and from tax on imputed income for owner occupiers, have not been included in other chapters.

Table 4.4   The cost of West German housing policy (DM 000 million).

	1990	1991
1. Social housing	8.3	10.2
2. Housing allowances	3.8	3.8
3. Tax relief for owner occupiers	7.6	10.0
4. Bausparkassen premium and tax relief	0.9	0.8
5. Subsidies for energy saving investment	} 0.8	0.5
6. Modernization assistance (*Länder*)		1.5
7. Other	2.2	na
SUBTOTAL	23.6	26.8
8. Landlords' accelerated depreciation	9.8	[10.0]
TOTAL	33.4	36.8

Source: Wohngeld & Mietenbericht (1992); Ulbricht & Wullkopf in Hallett (1993); Lebègue Report (1991); for 1991 information supplied by Dr Eugen Dick.

If the cost of policy in West Germany is taken at about DM36000 million, it amounted to 1.4% of GNP, slightly less than in France and less than half the level

---

8. See, for example, Duvigneau & Schönefeldt 1989: 18–23; Jaedicke & Wollmann 1990: 136; Lebègue 1991: 40; Papa 1992: 70–71; and the chapter by Ulbrich & Wullkopf 1993: 107)

in the UK. But the inclusion of East Germany, on which information is still incomplete, will increase the cost considerably and raise it as a proportion of GNP, as major housebuilding programmes there get under way.

Conclusion

There are several features in German housing policy that contrast interestingly with that of other countries, in particular with the Britain:

- The policy has worked with the grain of the market, probably to a greater degree than that of any other country and yet there are measures to ensure that hardship is avoided and the disadvantaged are catered for.
- The building programme involved a proportionately greater effort than in Britain or France, especially up to the early 1970s; and although the quality of provision is a subjective matter, it seems to be fairly widely accepted that standards in the west (although not of course in the east) are at least as good and, in the opinion of some commentators, better than in other countries (Emms 1990: 183–4).
- The owner occupied sector is relatively small and has grown slowly. This appears to be attributable to the high cost of housing, the financing arrangements (particularly the house savings scheme, which encourages prospective owners to delay purchase), the high proportion of apartments, the availability of good private rented accommodation, and finally to the absence of the British perception that owner occupation is better than other forms of investment, both in its overall performance and as a hedge against inflation.
- Long-term fixed interest loans, especially those based on the *Pfandbriefe* of the mortgage banks and the low interest loans of the *Bausparkassen*, still play a large part in financing the owner occupied sector, although variable rate loans are growing in importance. In the case of the mortgage banks and some of the other institutions, this reflects a healthy long-term bond market in Germany that scarcely exists in Britain. When this is combined with maximum loan-to-value ratios of 80% and the tendency of Germans to put off house purchase until they are established in a career, it is not surprising that the market is much less subject than its British counterpart to repossessions, negative equity and equity withdrawal.
- The strength and stability of the private rented sector contrasts with all the other countries, but especially with Britain and Spain, and for this the structure of incentives must be largely responsible. West Germany started to decontrol rents early, but the system of regulation and security of tenure, which now gives more indefinite security than the British system of assured tenancies, does appear to make rents on relets much less responsive to the market than rents on new tenancies. The pressure on the Ger-

man housing market that has developed since the late 1980s seems more likely to result in these restrictions being strengthened than reduced.

- The depreciation allowance has several advantages over mortgage interest tax relief: it is not dependent on a particular form of funding for investment, it is not affected by movements in interest rates, and it is applied, although at different rates, to both the owner occupied and the rented sectors. German landlords' ability to deduct depreciation costs from pre-tax income from whatever source greatly adds to the value of this incentive, but increases its cost in lost public revenue.

- The social rented sector is much less related to a particular type of landlord than in other countries, especially since the change in status of the former "non-profit making" companies or associations. Dissatisfaction with the performance of these companies appears to be a principal reason for this change.

- The unique feature of the social rented sector in Germany is the transfer of stock to a free-market regime as assisted loans are paid off. In the absence of an equivalent amount of new construction, this causes the sector to shrink over time.

- Social rents, being historically determined, vary considerably in a way that does not necessarily reflect the quality of the accommodation and which can inhibit movement.

- The *Wohngeld* system of housing allowances covers all tenures; and, with the exception of those on full social benefit, the poverty trap is largely avoided, as is the situation where changes in rent level are fully covered by benefit. The taper on the housing allowance depends on rent levels, but even in the worst case is well below one third, in contrast to 65% in Britain. But difficulties can arise as a result of the relatively infrequent uprating of *Wohngeld* to take account of inflation and the wide spread of rent levels that causes the rent on some quite standard accommodation to exceed the *Wohngeld* ceiling.

For the future, the country faces greater challenges than any other in western Europe. The inflow of population to the former West Germany since 1989, and the legacy of major problems in the eastern *Länder*, have already resulted in a substantial increase in expenditure and a return to a more interventionist policy. It seems certain that a larger scale of effort, more comparable to the 1960s and 1970s, will be required for a considerable time, especially but not exclusively in the eastern *Länder*. This has already resulted in political pressure for tighter rent restrictions on the private rented sector, a policy that if adopted could well be self-defeating. It also raises important questions about the future of the social rented sector. If the 1980s trend of decline were to continue as a result of stock transferring to the private sector, more weight would fall on housing allowances than the system as presently constructed seems able to bear. If substantial hardship is to be avoided for the poorer sections of the population, either *Wohngeld* would need reform to ensure more regular uprating and coverage of more expen-

73

sive property, or a more substantial building programme of social rented housing will need to continue for some time.

CHAPTER 5

Housing policy in the Netherlands

Dutch housing policy since 1945 has been one of the most comprehensively interventionist in western Europe; indeed, among the countries in this study, only in Sweden can the emphasis given to the social objectives of policy be considered equally strong. The Netherlands is Europe's most densely populated country (see Table 2.1); and, whether for this reason or simply by tradition, it is a country typified by well ordered development. Both physical and economic planning have been accorded an importance seldom matched elsewhere, and the influence of the State on the housing market has been both substantial and widely accepted.

The need for State intervention in the housing market was accepted as long ago as the Housing Act (*Woningwet*) of 1901. This legislation has been subject to revision and a series of amendments since the Second World War, but the 1901 Act remains the cornerstone of Dutch housing policy. Dwellings in the social sector are still known from this Act as Housing Act dwellings; and developments in policy over the past 50 years can be seen as a process of evolution commanding a wide measure of cross-party support. Housing policy has therefore not been a contentious issue in party political terms and it has enjoyed a degree of continuity throughout most of this long period, which is quite remarkable when compared with Britain. Since 1988, however, there has been an important change of direction in Dutch housing policy, which has demonstrated that it is not immune from the pressures affecting other countries. In particular, the escalating cost and the need to contain public expenditure are important issues for the Dutch government in the context of closer economic integration in Europe, especially in the light of the country's high rates of outstanding public debt to GDP.[1]

The change in direction of Dutch policy was set out in the government White Paper of 1989, *Nota Volkshuisvesting in de jaren Negentig* (Policy Document on Housing in the 1990s).[2] This important document is also known by the name of

---

1. See Chapter 12, where the issue of debt is discussed in greater detail.
2. Originally published in 1989; English summary 1992; see VROM (1992).

the housing minister responsible for it as the *Heerma Memorandum* and is referred to by this name in the rest of this chapter. The principles set out in the Memorandum include a more selective policy more closely targeted on the needy, greater reliance on the market and on private capital, reduced controls on rent, and decentralization in the administration of policy. These principles had in some cases already begun to be adopted, but from the early 1990s they have featured in a series of policy changes and in proposals not yet fully implemented.

Apart from the central government, there are two other levels of government in the Netherlands: the provinces, and the local authorities or municipalities. There are 12 provinces, but, like Scottish regions and English shire counties, these have little responsibility for housing, with the important exceptions of physical planning matters and where for some reason a local authority is unable to discharge its functions.

The main responsibility for housing policy is therefore divided between central government and the local authorities. Central government's role is to set and control the framework of housing policy, and to administer some schemes, such as housing allowances and fiscal measures. In sharp contrast to Britain, the emphasis (which is not only confirmed but further stressed in the Heerma Memorandum) is on transferring responsibility where possible from central to local government. The administration and implementation of the policy lies mainly with the local authorities, of which there are some 646. Considering the size of the Netherlands, this is a very large number in comparison with Britain and, in consequence, many of them are very small. But as well as operating many of the schemes of assistance to housing providers, for which they are funded by central government, they are responsible for regulating the housing associations, a role broadly comparable to that of the Housing Corporation in England or Scottish Homes in Scotland. In some cases Dutch local authorities, especially the larger municipalities, also provide social housing directly at their own hand; but this role was never as important as in Britain and has declined considerably since the post-war years. In addition, under urban renewal legislation, they have considerable flexibility to assist housing through schemes of their own devising.

A striking feature of the housing situation in the Netherlands is the amount of housebuilding activity that has taken place since 1945. Indeed, of the countries in this study, the Netherlands has the highest proportion of its total stock (75%) built since 1945 (see p. 14). Like France and Germany, the level of housebuilding activity in the Netherlands built up more slowly after the war than in Britain, the peak being reached only in 1972 and 1973, when the annual rate of construction exceeded 150000; but although the level of activity has fallen since that time, it remains relatively high at around 80–90000 a year in the early 1990s (Table 5.1) (Ymkers & Kroes 1988: 190; Emms 1990: 187; VROM 1993b).

Like the other countries affected by the war, The Netherlands suffered destruction resulting in loss or serious damage to 120000 dwellings (Emms 1990: 188). Combined with the lack of building activity in the war years, this meant there was much catching up to be done. The result was a housing shortage

Table 5.1   Housing completions in the Netherlands (annual average in thousands).

	1970–4	1975–9	1980–5	1985–90	1991
Owner occupied: non-subsidized or					
with single payment grant*	25.1	25.9	18.1	33.8	38.2
Owner occupied: subsidized	29.5	31.7	30.1	23.3	15.7
Private rented: non-subsidized or with					
single payment grant*	2.0	0.8	1.4	3.7	2.5
Private rented: subsidized	34.3	15.0	17.3	10.3	4.0
Social rented	50.5	32.9	52.3	35.1	22.9
TOTAL	121.5	106.4	115.7	106.4	82.9

*Note: Single payment grant of FL5000.
Source: Boelhouwer & van der Heijden Volkshuisvesting in Cijfers (1992).

estimated at 250000 dwellings in 1945, and which by 1948 had risen to 300000, partly as a result of immigration from Indonesia (Ymkers & Kroes 1988: 190). But the high rate of housebuilding soon dwarfed this deficiency and it owes much more to the remarkably high rate of population growth. As Chapter 2 showed The Dutch population, although occupying Europe's most densely populated country, has grown more rapidly in the period since the war than that of any other country in this study. The 1945 population of 9.3 million had risen to 15 million in 1991, an increase of 61% (see Table 2.1). In part this is accounted for by a birth rate above the European average, but it is also a consequence of very high immigration from former Dutch territories, and both immigrants and guest workers from Southern Europe and Turkey, as in Germany.

This substantial rate of population increase was expected to diminish in the 1990s, with greatly reduced birth rates. But recently revised predictions on immigration, which suggest much larger numbers coming from eastern Europe particularly, but also from the Mediterranean, now make this less likely. In addition, as in other countries, there is a trend towards single-parent families and much smaller households, with the result that the number of households is expected to continue to grow, at least until the year 2030. The latest official estimates suggest a need for a further 936000 dwellings between 1990 and 2000, an increase of 16% on the 1990 stock of 5.8 million. This rapid growth in housing needs has had a major effect on Dutch housing policy since the war. The difficulty of accommodating it in an already densely populated country may account, at least in part, for the emphasis that the Dutch put on planning. It is no doubt also a reason for the extensive use of subsidies to new construction, which, in the form of either direct grants to private building or aid to the social sector, applied to 90% of dwellings built, even in the early 1980s. It may be that this rapid population growth, especially the many immigrants, combined with the general political orientation of many of the Dutch governments also helps to account for the exceptionally large size of the social rented sector.

Tenure

As Table 5.2 shows, 47% of the Dutch housing stock is in owner occupation, a low proportion by comparison with the Britain, or even with Scotland, but fairly similar to the proportion of owner occupied stock in Sweden, and substantially more than in Germany. In other respects the Dutch tenure pattern is quite unlike Germany; the social rented sector at 36% of total stock is the largest among the countries in this study, apart from Scotland. (On some definitions the Dutch percentage of social rented housing is actually higher than this, but since 1990 only organizations eligible for government subsidies on new construction are included, other non-profit landlords being now classified as private sector.) The private rented sector, superficially at least, bears some similarities to the situation in Britain. After Britain, it is the smallest among the countries studied, and it has been falling rapidly during the post-war years as a proportion of the total stock and also, although less dramatically, in absolute numbers (Table 5.2). But in other respects, especially the composition of the landlords and the amount of new construction, there are important differences.

Table 5.2 Housing tenure in the Netherlands (% of total stock).

	1950	1960	1970	1980	1990	1992
Owner occupied	28	33	35	42	45	47
Privately rented	47	41	34	24	17	17
Social rented	24	26	31	34	36	36

Source: European Community, *Statistics on housing in the European Community*, Ghékiere op cit., VROM, Volkhuisvesting in Cijfers 1992.

Murie & Priemus have shown that for many years the pattern of housing tenure in the Netherlands moved very closely in step with that of Britain (Murie & Priemus 1994: 2). In 1920, home ownership in the UK was 10% and in the Netherlands 17%. By 1950 in the UK it was 29% and the Netherlands 28%, and the social rented sector 18% and 24% respectively. By 1960 the gap in home ownership was beginning to widen, with the UK at 42% and the Netherlands at 33%, but the shares of the social rented sector were virtually identical at 26%. In the 1970s and especially the 1980s trends in the two countries started to diverge. This was not because incentives for owner occupation were any less generous in the Netherlands than in Britain (as is shown below, the reverse is the case), but mainly because the Netherlands kept up the pace of building in the social rented sector. There were substantial increases to the stock in this sector during both the 1970s and 1980s. In contrast, the 1970s were when Britain first began to reduce local authority housebuilding effort, as shortages were overcome, and then, in the 1980s, following a major shift in policy, virtually ended construction by local authorities and promoted schemes to encourage stock transfer to owner occupation.

Another feature of past Dutch housing policy, which accords with the country's approach to economic planning but also stands in sharp contrast to the UK, was the use made of intervention by the government to counteract the effects of the economic cycle. In the second half of the 1970s the Netherlands experienced a remarkable house-price inflation, with average house prices rising by 94% between 1975 and 1978, greatly outstripping the rate of inflation (Boelhouwer & van der Heijden 1992: 57, 64). This was followed by a fall of some 30% between 1978 and 1982, thereafter holding fairly steady, before rising modestly in the late 1980s. Not surprisingly, the volume of private house construction fell substantially in the early 1980s from 76000 dwellings in 1978 (nearly 70% of construction in that year) to 58000 in 1982. But, as Figure 5.1 shows, the 1982 level of construction was actually higher than in 1978 as a result of a deliberate expansion of the social rented building programme, which more than doubled during these years. It then reverted gradually to its earlier level, as the private sector recovered in the second half of the 1980s. Although this was certainly of benefit to the construction industry and it enabled a considerable advance in social rented housing to be made, it proved a costly intervention and it is unlikely to be repeated if similar circumstances were to recur.

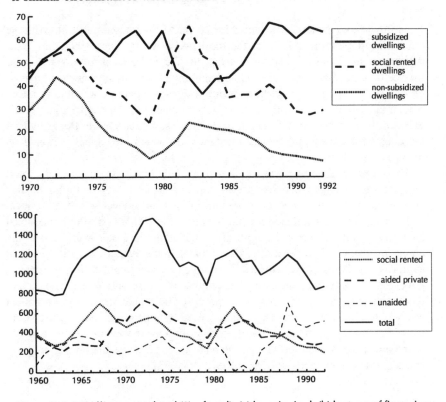

Figure 5.1 Dwellings completed (% of total): (a) by principal, (b) by type of financing.

The owner occupied sector

Despite the relatively small size of the owner occupied sector as a proportion of the total stock, its expansion has been an explicit objective of successive Dutch governments. The sector is assisted by tax allowances, which are now more generous than those available in any of the other countries in this study, apart from Spain. There have also been various grant schemes for new construction, but apart from grants to meet special circumstances, these are expected to end in 1995.

Mortgage finance

Finance for owner occupiers is provided by a variety of institutions. The specialist mortgage banks provide over 20% of the total funding, insurance companies and pensions funds a similar amount, but the largest share (over half) is provided by banks, a sector dominated by the large *Rabobank*, the product of a merger between several co-operatives originally of agricultural origin (Ghékiere 1991: 259).

Mortgages are generally provided for 30 years and at fixed rates, but with the rate renegotiable after five or at the most twelve years (Papa 1992: 23). This adjustment mechanism makes it possible for the financial institutions to raise finance on a medium-term basis but to lend long. There are a variety of types of mortgage. The largest proportion, about 46%, are repaid on an annuity basis; but, in the same way as in Britain, the tax arrangements favour keeping up the value of the loan for the full length of its life, and this has led to the growth of mortgages backed by endowment insurance, on which the capital is repaid on maturity.

Purchasers of existing stock are limited to a 70% maximum loan to value ratio on mortgages, except when they are covered against default by a mortgage guarantee. There is a well developed system of such insurance provided by local authorities, subject to a maximum house value of FL250000 (£89000). The local authority obtains advice on the application, including the credit worthiness of the applicant, from an independent advisory body. In the event of default, the local authority stands surety for any loss the mortgage lender might suffer, but central government covers half the cost. The number of house purchasers who cannot meet their mortgage obligations is about 600–700 a year, involving an annual cost of FL22 million (about £8 million). With the guarantee, house purchasers can obtain mortgages up to 100% of house value and, in view of the reduced risk to the lender, it is common for the interest rate to be lower than for an unguaranteed loan (Ghékiere 1991: 159; VROM 1993a: 32).

Grants

Grants to owner occupiers to assist new construction have been subject to a variety of changes over the years. Sharp escalation in the costs, especially in the early 1980s, has led to the schemes being made more restricted and less open ended, in the sense that, instead of being demand related, there are now specific budgetary allocations. From January 1995 a change will be made that will restrict them further.

At present the arrangements, which apply to the other tenures as well, provide assistance under two statutory instruments, the Housing Tied Subsidies Decree BWS *(Besluit Woninggebonden Subsidies)* and the Location Tied Subsidies Decree BLS *(Besluit Lokatiegebonden Subsidies)*. In both cases, budgetary allocations are made to local authorities and, although they contain generous carry forward provisions amounting to 50% of the annual allocation, the authorities have to work within the totals allocated. The allocations are made under four main schemes.

The first scheme is the main form of assistance for both the owner occupied and rented sectors. In the owner occupied sector it is designed to help potential purchasers on the margin of being able to afford owner occupation. Although a grant rather than a loan, this subsidy may be seen as the parallel to PAP loans in France or the assistance for owner occupiers in Germany. The grant is provided on an annual basis to meet a proportion of mortgage costs; eligibility depends on the income level of the recipient not exceeding FL61500 (£22000), subject to five yearly review, and is subject to a maximum dwelling cost of around FL140000 (£50000). The grant is paid at the rate of 10% a year and the average total payment is substantial, FL36100 (£12900) (VROM 1993a: 254).

The second scheme is intended more to encourage construction than to assist a particular class of owner, and is paid only in urban regions. It provides for a single payment grant of FL5000 (approximately £1700) and only dwellings not exceeding FL162000 (£58000) in cost are eligible. It is paid regardless of the owner's income. The remaining two schemes provide for assistance in specific locations, mainly urban areas, and are intended to encourage the building of higher-quality dwellings in such areas. The amount of assistance is at the discretion of local authorities.

After January 1995 these general schemes are to be replaced with a single allocation to local authorities. This will still contain provision to assist cheap and medium-level owner occupied and rented dwellings, to provide a premium to encourage construction and to assist affordability, particularly in specific locations. Local authorities will have greater freedom than with the present separate allocations, but the amounts available are likely to be reduced, and assistance consequently much more tightly restricted.

Taxation and fiscal relief

The fiscal arrangements treat housing as an investment good and, on this basis, permit mortgage interest to be deducted in full from pre-tax income without either limiting the total sum that may be claimed or the eligible period. The relief is at the claimant's marginal rate of tax and is therefore regressive in so far as it gives more benefit to the better off. It is not restricted to a single property. This provision is therefore similar to the situation in Britain in the 1960s, before housing loans became the only type of loan on which individuals could claim tax relief and before the £25000 limit was introduced. The present Dutch arrangements are very much more generous than comparable provisions in the other countries in this study; even Spain, which also has a generous system of mortgage tax relief, imposes a ceiling. And despite the reforms aimed at reducing expenditure in other areas of Dutch housing policy, there are no proposals to limit mortgage interest tax relief either in scope or amount.

To conform with the philosophy of regarding housing as an investment good, this relief is offset (although only partially) by owner occupiers' liability for tax on imputed rent. The Netherlands is the only country among those in this study where this tax remains, although it did formerly exist in some of the others, usually at an undervalued rate. In Britain and France it disappeared in the 1960s. Under the Dutch system the imputed rent is calculated according to a formula that must be regarded as generous to the owner, although, as a result of recent increases, less so than it was. The value of a dwelling in an occupied state is taken to be 60% of its vacant possession value, no doubt reflecting the fact that tenanted property, being subject to rent regulation and security of tenure, sells for less than untenanted. Taxable income from imputed rent is expressed as a percentage of this value. The amount of tax raised can be varied by adjusting this percentage and in 1994 it was 3.1% (Papa 1992: 24). This means that on a dwelling worth FL150000 (approximately £50000) sold with vacant possession, the occupied value would amount to FL90000 (£32000) and the income assessed for tax would be FL2790 or about £1000. The revenue from this tax amounted to FL1250 million (£450 million) in 1990, compared with FL5700 million (£2000 million), which is the value of the mortgage interest tax relief (VROM 1993b: 83–6).

Other taxes borne by owner occupiers include: VAT of 17.5% on newly constructed dwellings, or dwellings sold within two years of construction, and on repair and maintenance; transfer tax at 6% on sales transactions, but only where VAT is not levied; and property tax, a local authority tax that varies considerably from one authority to another and is levied separately on owners and occupiers, with owner occupiers paying both parts. The sale of dwellings is not subject to capital gains tax, whether owned or tenanted, a principal residence or a second home.

The private rented sector

The Dutch private rented sector falls into two quite distinct parts, that owned by private individuals as landlords, who in many cases only have one property to let, and the part owned by institutions. The former tends to be older property, frequently dating from before the Second World War and in need of modernization; typically it is in the centre of towns and is often the cheapest property available, with rents lower than in the social rented sector. As in Germany, this type of property ownership was originally seen as a good investment, providing an income to supplement resources in retirement. But the combination of rent control and security of tenure, the growth of pension schemes and the availability of other more profitable and less troublesome investments have resulted in this type of investment ceasing to be attractive to individuals. To this should be added a steady process of conversion of such dwellings to condominiums (as in Germany) and purchase by public authorities, mainly as a result of urban renewal schemes. The consequence has been a sharp drop in this type of accommodation, which in turn mainly accounts for the rapid fall in the private rented sector (Ghékiere 1992: 243; Boelhouwer & van der Heijden 1992: 50).

In contrast to ownership by individuals, the role of companies and institutions as landlords has declined very little and now accounts for the greater part of the private rented sector. In general the type of housing owned by these landlords is of higher quality and is more expensive than that owned by individuals (Boelhouwer & van der Heijden 1992: 51). In contrast to the latter, it has been built mostly since 1960. It also tends to be concentrated in areas where demand is high and is seen by the institutional owners, who may ultimately be pension funds or insurance companies, as a straight commercial investment. Management is usually delegated to factoring agents.

Despite the fall in the proportionate and absolute size of the sector, there has been a continuing volume of new construction, mainly by institutional owners. Over the 20 years 1970–90, 372000 subsidized dwellings were built in this sector and 44000 either without subsidy or in receipt of a single one-off grant (ibid.: 48). Together this represents approximately 18% of total completions during this period. But the volume of construction in the sector was not steady, falling sharply in the second half of the 1970s, then recovering, although not to its previous level, and falling again to about 14000 dwellings a year in the late 1980s and to only 6500 in 1991 (Table 5.1).

Rent control and regulation

There is a long history of rent control and regulation in the Netherlands. Although this permitted annual rent adjustment, it remained extremely comprehensive until the recommendations of the Heerma Memorandum began to take effect. Before 1979 it seems that the way in which the control was operated was a major factor in the decline of the sector, but since that time rents have been allowed to rise much more rapidly than the rate of inflation (Table 5.3).

Table 5.3   Housing rents in the Netherlands, 1970–91 (1980 = 100).

	Price index	Rents	Building costs
1970	51.2	54.9	40.5
1975	73.3	67.7	66.1
1980	100.0	100.0	100.0
1985	122.3	136.6	98.0
1990	128.0	160.1	112.0
1991	133.2	166.7	115.0

Source: Volkshuisvesting in Cijfers (1992).

The Netherlands was not involved in the First World War, so that, unlike other countries, it did not introduce rent control in 1914. But rent freezes and security of tenure were introduced immediately after that war in the climate of shortages then prevailing and, from 1925 onwards, rents were fixed on a basis of cost prices rather than market prices. In 1940, rents were frozen for the duration of the Second World War, and security of tenure was introduced. After the war, under the 1947 Housing Distribution Act and the Rent and Reconstruction Acts of 1950, rent control, security of tenure, allocation policy and control of building prices were all maintained, coupled with State housing subsidies. Rents were held at their 1940 level until 1951, when an increase of 15% was permitted, far less than the inflation in the intervening 11 years (Ymkers & Kroes 1988: 191). Although this was followed by further increases, a gap developed between the rents of older and more recently built properties. To rationalize the situation, a scheme was introduced that assessed the quality of a dwelling on the basis of a points system (*Woningwaarderingsstelsel*). This system remained the basis of Dutch rent policy for many years and it still exists. There was a move towards liberalization in areas of housing surplus in the 1960s, but growing shortages in the 1970s caused this trend to be reversed.

Under the 1979 Housing Rent Act, Parliament set yearly a permitted rate of increase, which was applied if the old rent accorded with the level appropriate to the quality standard under the points system. Where this was not so, there was room for some negotiation between landlord and tenant, but using the points system as the basis for establishing the new level. Although this system was very highly regulated and might therefore seem likely to deter investment, the trend rate of increase in rents set by Parliament was substantially in excess of inflation (Table 5.3). Although rents rose rather less than the cost of living index or building costs during the 1970s, from 1980 to 1991 they rose by 67%, twice as much as inflation and four times as fast as building costs. It is claimed that this resulted in rents that were in many cases no longer below their economic level and in some cases above, as evidenced by the difficulty in filling vacancies.

Since the publication of the Heerma Memorandum, there has been substantial liberalization of private rents. Under the system now operating, rents for new dwellings are determined by the free market, without restriction. For new tenancies in existing rented dwellings, rents are also set freely, if the rent level is above the maximum for housing allowances. Where rents are below this level, a statutory rent adjustment system still applies (*Huusombedadering*). This replaces the earlier fixed-trend increase, with a band within which the landlord may vary the rent. Rents may not be increased by more than 6% per annum per dwelling, and the points valuation system continues to exist so that a maximum reasonable rent can be set. However, the aim, even for these dwellings, where the rent is within the housing allowance level, is to achieve a level of rents in the longer run that covers costs and enables the buildings to be managed and maintained without direct government subsidy.

Subsidies and finance

Where rented dwellings have been built with State subsidy, rents have in the past been more tightly controlled than for those where there was no such support. The system of subsidies was the same as for the social rented sector. Before 1989, this involved the complicated "dynamic cost rent" system, which is described below and which aimed at the amortization of costs over 50 years. Although this system protected the investor against loss, it also ensured that there were no substantial surpluses, and capital gains were effectively prevented. Since 1989 this system has been replaced with a simpler scheme of annual grants, but the control of rents on subsidized dwellings remains until 1995. In many respects it may be appropriate to regard this part of the private rented sector in the Netherlands as equivalent to German privately owned rented housing, which is let on social rent terms and therefore more strictly part of the social rented sector. However, if the sector were redefined in this way, the private rented sector proper would be substantially smaller than the figures already given suggest.

Landlords will normally finance private rented housing from their own resources. This is especially so with institutional landlords, who have been responsible for virtually all of the new construction in the sector, and who may either have retained profits or be in a position to raise equity. Where they do decide to borrow, this will generally be in the form of long-term fixed-rate loans. For such loans, they are able to make use of the mortgage interest insurance arrangements already described in the section on owner occupation.

Private rented housing may qualify for grants, under the BWS scheme, which also apply to owner occupiers and have been described above. Following the replacement of the "dynamic cost rent" system, annual subsidies for a fixed period of years may be provided for agreed contract costs. Eligibility depends upon rent falling below a maximum of FL690 (about £250) a month. Responsibility for determining, as well as paying, these grants lies with local authorities. Alternatively, rented housing may qualify for single-payment grants to encourage construction. The amount of grant is FL10000, twice the level for owner occupied dwellings.

Taxation

Companies and institutional owners of private rented housing are subject to corporation tax on rent and on subsidies received. There are no special fiscal incentives for this sector, but, since housing is regarded as an investment activity, interest on borrowings and depreciation are expenses deductible from taxable income. As in Germany, these expenses may be deducted from pre-tax income from whatever source, not only from letting, but there is no special provision for depreciation at an accelerated rate. Investment in residential property is generally treated in the same way for tax purposes as investment in commercial property. But sales of dwellings are not liable for capital gains tax. VAT and transfer tax are levied in the same way as for the owner occupied sector. Property taxes are split between landlords and tenants.

Despite the fall in the sector to its now relatively small size, and the history of comprehensive rent regulation and control (at least until 1989), the feature that contrasts with the UK is that there has been a surprisingly large volume of new construction. This has been carried out mainly by institutional investors of a kind that many people would like to see attracted into the British private rented market. Admittedly, the volume of new construction has fallen, but the fact that it is continuing on a significant scale at all suggests that subsidies and more generous tax provisions than in Britain have been sufficiently positive to counteract, at least partially, whatever negative effects there were from rent control. The changes introduced following the Heerma Memorandum are intended generally to bring to an end assistance in the form of recurrent subsidies; but they are also freeing a large part of the private rented sector from rent control and introducing greater flexibility to the remainder. It will be interesting to see whether this increases or diminishes the volume of construction in the sector.

The social rented sector

The Dutch social rented sector, like that of Britain, France and Germany, has its origins in the social reform movements of the nineteenth century. But the Housing Act of 1901 established the principle of State assistance to the sector. "Housing Act housing" began to be of significance in the inter-war period and, like social housing in other countries it played a dominant part in the period of reconstruction after the Second World War. Over 75% of the sector's stock has been built since 1945; and, according to surveys, all of the stock is in good condition, including that built pre-war. Although the owner occupied sector increasingly played a larger part after the immediate post-war years, the momentum of construction in the social rented sector has held up to a greater extent than in Britain, Germany or France. Between 1960 and 1990, some 39% of the dwellings completed have been in this sector. This gives an yearly average over the period of 43000, but both in absolute numbers and as a proportion the contribution of the sector tended to be largest in the years 1965–75 and had fallen to its lowest levels in the early 1990s.

Landlord organizations

The Dutch social rented sector is divided between three types of landlord: housing associations, local authorities and other non-profit institutions. By far the greater part, some 2.1 million dwellings, are owned by non-profit–making housing associations (*Woningcorporaties*). In 1991 there were 864 associations, which gives an average stock of 2486 dwellings; and as in other countries the size of the individual associations varies greatly, with only 24 having a stock in excess of 10000 (VROM 1993a: 102). The local authorities are responsible for registering and monitoring the associations, and in order to acquire registered status the associations have to be not only non-profit–making, but must restrict their activities to housing. Registration is tightly controlled and is subject to the approval of the Minister of Housing. The Dutch arrangements make it more difficult than in Britain to run associations as co-operatives, and only ten co-operatives exist (Ymkers & Kroes 1988: 206). The local authorities largely determine the construction programme of the associations and until 1989 they were also responsible for allocating the funding, most of which came from central government. The associations are grouped under two umbrella organizations, *Nationale Woningraad* (the National Housing Council) and *Nederlands Christelijk Instituut voor Volkshuisvesting* (Netherlands Christian Housing Institute), that carry out regular consultation with central government.

Dutch local authorities own some 295000 rented dwellings themselves (Murie & Priemus 1994: 4). But this does not bear much resemblance to the position of local authority stock in Britain. In the first place, the balance between association and local authority ownership is almost exactly the reverse of the British situation. And secondly, relatively little of the local authority stock is managed directly by housing departments in the local authorities that own municipal housing; for the most part it is run by local authority housing companies, of which there are no less than 214. This means that the average holding is very small – only about 1300 dwellings – a figure that compares with only the smallest British housing authorities. The Dutch companies therefore have a closer similarity to the municipal housing companies of Sweden or Germany, where these are in 100% local authority ownership. They are much more closely associated with their parent local authority than are the HLMs in France.

As part of government policy, over time there has been a deliberate switch in favour of the independent associations. Although the municipal companies were never the dominant form of landlord in this sector, they were responsible for the larger part of the construction effort in the immediate post-war years. However, since 1970 preference has been given to the associations, and in 1990 they completed 25000 new dwellings as compared with 2367 by the municipal companies (Murie & Priemus: 5). The percentage of housing in direct local authority ownership has therefore fallen. As a result of this, local authority stock is on average older than that of the associations, it is often cheaper, and it tends to accommodate tenants on lower incomes. Under the recommendations of the Heerma Memorandum, the separate role of the municipal companies will now disappear altogether with the proposal that they be converted into housing associations. However, even with this change, the very close relationship between housing associations and local authorities under the Dutch system means that the authorities will continue to have a key role in the provision of social rented housing, although more an enabling role than that of direct housing providers.

The third category of social landlord, the "other non-profit–making institutions", generally cater for tenants with special needs, such as the elderly and students. Most of these institutions are foundations and are treated like housing associations. They are included with them for most statistical purposes. From 1990 they have been obliged to turn themselves into housing associations, or to merge with an existing association, if they want to continue building for rent. The result of this is that, although some of these bodies may retain their existing status for the management of dwellings already built, in future for any new construction there will only be one type of social housing landlord: the housing associations.

Finance for social rented housing

Loan finance for social rented housing used to be provided exclusively by central government through local authorities, except for a very small part, around 10%, of the association stock, which was intended for better-off tenants and was privately funded. Government finance was at normal unsubsidized rates, although because of the security offered, interest was generally lower than on private market loans. As in the UK, such funds counted towards the government's public sector borrowing requirement and were therefore regarded as public expenditure. But the Dutch government never attempted to control borrowing for housing investment in the way that British governments have done, especially since the late 1970s.

Before 1989 the proportion of funding provided by local authorities had already started to decline. However, following the Heerma Memorandum, public loan funding has been abolished and associations now raise their funds for investment directly from private institutions or from the market. A Social Rented Sector Guarantee Fund (*Waarborgfonds Sociale Huursector*) has been set up jointly by central government, local authorities and the associations, to cover both interest payments and loan repayments in case of insolvency of an association. This typically enables such borrowing to be at about 1% below normal market rates. Since the former local authority funding was on the basis of fixed-rate loans, the change has meant not only that new requirements have been met from the market since 1989, but, as interest rates fell, associations paid off much of their public borrowing early, in order to refinance their requirements with cheaper loans from the market. Such market loans are typically of between 10 and 20 years duration and are normally at fixed rates adjustable after 10 years, although variable rate loans are also possible.

The system of subsidies for new construction and renovation has been subject to many changes, which it would be confusing to describe at length, and details are available elsewhere. But, because it has left a legacy of financial problems, the system of "dynamic cost renting" that applied between 1975 and 1989 needs some explanation. It is tempting to see this as an example of Dutch rationality and planning that was carried too far and went wrong. The dynamic cost system was designed to overcome the defect of previous systems that were thought to be needlessly expensive. This was because, under the Dutch system where there is no rent pooling, subsidies had been required to meet in full the difference between social rent and costs in the early years after construction, although a cost-covering rent might fall below what a tenant might reasonably be expected to pay in later years, particularly if high rates of inflation had eroded the value of the outstanding debt. Unlike the system in Germany (described on p. 65–7), where cost rent then becomes the social rent, a surplus would then be generated.

Dynamic cost rent was an attempt to ensure that costs were fully covered without unnecessary costs and surpluses being generated. Inclusive of subsidy, the scheme was based on a recovery of costs over 50 years. This meant that subsidy would be substantially less in the early years than under previous systems; income from social rents plus subsidy would therefore be insufficient to remunerate the loan funding fully, with the result that borrowing would initially increase. But as rents rose over time, partly because of inflation, interest payments could increasingly be met in full, and by the end of the 50 years the loans paid off. The trouble with this ingenious scheme, and what caused it to be abandoned, was that future levels of rents and inflation could not be forecast with the accuracy that the scheme required. In the event, the scheme led to ballooning deficits that would take many years to pay off and which threatened financial disaster (Conijn 1994: 6–8).

The Heerma Memorandum of 1989 instituted a much simpler system. Subsidies are now paid by local authorities under the BWS scheme (already referred to) to cover major renovation of existing social housing stock as well as new construction. Payment is made at the rate of 10% a year and the total contribution averages FL28000 (£10000), compared with FL36000 for owner occupiers (VROM 1993a: 27). If the cost of interest payments rises, the term of the subsidies may be increased, but not the annual payment. Instead of rents being set under contract with the central government, they can now be adjusted to cover varying costs, and some limited rent pooling will be possible. In consequence, the associations, rather like British housing associations with post-1988 HAG, will bear a larger part of the risk and are under greater pressure to avoid cost overruns.

The financial management of the housing associations is therefore under increased pressure and, in recognition of this, a Central Housing Fund (*Centraal Fonds*) was established in 1989 in addition to the Guarantee Fund (VROM 1993a: 14–15). The new Fund is managed by a Board drawn from the associations and membership is obligatory. It is funded by charges to the associations based on their capital and it is intended to provide for the reorganization of financially weak associations. Insolvency is much more than a theoretical possibility; indeed the local authority companies (especially the larger ones) have in some cases been in financial difficulty, partly as a result of no new building. On the other hand, the position of the associations is generally strong; but, with rents levels being set by the central government under the system that applied until the Heerma recommendations took effect, there was little scope for landlords to raise revenue to cover higher than expected costs.

Part of the background to the Heerma Memorandum is the need to contain the public expenditure costs of housing policy; and, with such a large social rented sector in a relatively affluent country, this points to more careful targeting. Considerable attention is therefore being given to the problem of mismatch. The 1985 Housing Needs Survey revealed that almost one third of the cheaper rented housing was occupied by households with above average income. There is no system, such as the German *Fehlbelegungsabgabe*, which empowers landlords to collect a supplementary rental charge from those on higher incomes, but the Heerma Memorandum set a clear aim of reducing substantially the number of those who could afford to pay more for their accommodation.

Also with the aim of improved targeting, "Special Attention Groups" were proposed in the Heerma Memorandum for preferential treatment in the sector. They included households with income up to FL30000 a year (£10700) and single persons with income up to FL22000 (£8000). The Memorandum states that more than half of the Dutch population fell into this category in 1988, and 75% of tenants. The Dutch Parliament has also encouraged the sale of social rented dwellings to their tenants and has suggested an annual sale of 15000–20000 dwellings. In fact, sales have so far been very modest, averaging around 3000–5000 a year, but the government assumes that this latter figure might be doubled by the mid-1990s (Boelhouwer & van der Heijden 1992: 61). Approval by local authorities for any sale of social housing, even if it was not owned by them, had been a necessary condition in the past and this is now ended. But there is no question of introducing the British type of Right to Buy, with its huge discounts, or of ending the need to secure the landlord's consent to sale. Furthermore, in contrast to the position in England, receipts generated by such sales would be retained for expenditure within the housing sector.

The most radical proposal, and one that at the time of writing is still being discussed (although with the expectation that it will be implemented), involves a swap under which the outstanding loan debt of social housing landlords would be paid off in return for the cancellation of future subsidy obligations. This debt amounts to some FL35000 million (£12500 million). Because of the ballooning deficits inherited from the dynamic cost rent system, the obligation on central government to pay continuing subsidies is also very high. The discounted value of these future obligations has been estimated at some FL40000 million (£14300 million). The reforms that have already been implemented will reduce the cost of future commitments, but not those inherited from the past. The obligations flowing from the dynamic cost rent scheme account for 30% of the entire housing budget of the ministry in 1993 and are therefore a major burden. Moreover, as already noted, the Netherlands has a high ratio of accumulated public debt to GDP and, despite sound finances in other respects, therefore fails to meet the convergence criteria set under the Maastricht Treaty for European Monetary Union.

Each housing association has an opportunity to vote on the proposed scheme and, in recognition that circumstances vary between them, a FL2000 million fund is proposed to assist those that are particularly affected by dynamic cost rents. If this scheme is introduced, the effects are at present difficult to predict. On the one hand, for those that do not embark on major programmes of new building, costs will be limited to management and maintenance, and it may be that they will find themselves able to keep rents at a low level, just as some British local authorities with low levels of outstanding debt have been able to do. For those that do engage in major construction, the cost of servicing new loans at market rates will come through into rents, except in so far as a measure of rent pooling with the debt-free stock enables them to be reduced. Over time, the advantages of the debt cancellation would diminish. But it seems that the effect of meeting the full cost of new build through rents is not thought to be a major problem, as a result of the rent increases that have taken place in recent years.

Housing allowances

Housing allowances were introduced in the Netherlands in 1970; the system is operated by the Ministry of Housing, not (as in Britain) the ministry responsible for social security. As in other countries, allowances were seen as a means of targeting assistance more closely on those who needed it, and were originally part of a strategy intended to reduce direct intervention in the housing market (van Weesep 1986: 64; Emms 1990: 207–8; Papa 1992: 15). During the first five years, the expenditure was modest, but since July 1975, when the scheme was revised, it has been much more substantial. From that date to 1990, the number of persons assisted has grown by 2.7 times and the expenditure in current prices has increased more than fivefold (Table 5.4). In 1990/1, 29% of tenants received an allowance, 35% of whom were elderly (VROM 1993a : 30f).

91

Table 5.4   Housing allowances in the Netherlands.

	Number of claimants (000)	Cost in FL (millions)
1975/6	348	339
1980/1	456	629
1984/85	715	1271
1986/7	830	1467
1988/89	918	1661
1989/90	949	1698
1990/91	953	1779

Source: Netherlands statistical yearbook (1992), Volkshuisvesting in Cijfers (1992).

Unlike France, Germany and Sweden, but like the UK, the system of housing allowances in the Netherlands is available only to tenants; it is paid regardless of the form of tenancy, whether private or social renting. The main criteria for eligibility are household incomes and the rent level, both of which are subject to annually specified maxima. The system is based on a table of rent norms for each income bracket, with appropriate adjustments, depending on whether the applicant is single, married, or has children (Papa 1992: 14–15). The rent norm is what a tenant might be expected to pay on a given income, and the aim of the allowance is to limit housing costs to 11.6–22% of income (Ghékiere 1991: 251). The actual rent paid may of course differ from the norm and, where it is higher, the State *may* meet the difference; but whether it will do so, either in whole or in part, will depend on the circumstances. Clearly, if the accommodation is thought to be either unnecessarily large or luxurious, this difference will not be met, or be met only in part.

As in other countries, the mix of applicants for housing allowances has undergone considerable change over the period since 1975. Growing unemployment is no doubt a factor in this change, as it has been in other countries, but so is the growth of single-parent families and the earlier age at which young people leave home. In fact, when unemployment fell during the 1980s the number of applicants for housing allowances was not reduced.

The costs of the policy

Dutch housing policy is undoubtedly expensive. The extensive nature of the subsidies, not only in the social rented sector but also in the owner occupied sector, coupled with the unrestricted tax concessions for home owners, ensure that this is so (Table 5.5).

The figures are affected by the treatment accorded to mortgage interest tax relief and tax on home owners' imputed rent. Some people in the Netherlands argue that, since housing is treated as an investment good, mortgage interest tax

Table 5.5   The cost of housing policy in the Netherlands (FL millions).

	1990	1993
Property subsidies and loans	8950	7822
Housing allowances	1817	2220
Urban renewal	1179	1234
Total public expenditure	11940	11276
Less loans	906	523
SUBTOTAL	11040	11799
Tax relief for owner occupiers	5720	na
TOTAL	16760	na

Tax revenue from housing (FL million)	1990
Tax on imputed rent	1256
Transfer tax	1190
VAT	3200
	5646

Source: VROM (1993b).

relief should not be treated as a subsidy at all; and, in some estimates, tax on imputed rent is deducted from the cost of mortgage tax relief to give a net subsidy figure. Views can legitimately vary on how housing expenditure should be regarded, and the arguments for treating it as an investment good, a consumption good or the purchase of a financial asset are dealt with elsewhere in this book. For other countries, mortgage interest tax relief has been treated as a subsidy and that is how most governments regard it. Consistency requires that the same be is done for the Netherlands if a valid comparison is to be made. As for the revenue from tax on imputed rent, it should not automatically be assumed that any tax raised, even on housing, is an offset against any particular subsidy; or that in the absence of the subsidy the tax would also be discontinued. The same argument applies to other taxes on housing.

In 1990 the total housing budget of the Ministry was FL12249 million. If administrative expenses and loans on which market rates of interest were paid are excluded, the expenditure on housing policy was FL11040 in 1990 and FL11799 in 1993. To this should be added the cost of mortgage interest tax relief of FL5720 million (figures only available for 1990) giving a combined total of FL16716 million (about £6000 million), which is about 9% of the national budget expenditure and about 3.2% of gross domestic product. By this measurement, Dutch housing policy is comparable in cost to that of the UK.

Within this total, housing allowances account for about 11% in 1990 and bricks and mortar subsidies amounted to 48%. Over the period since 1975 there has been a substantial increase in all three components of the cost of Dutch housing policy, but although housing allowances have increased substantially more than the other two, they still account for a smaller part of the total cost than in several of the other countries.

Conclusion

Dutch housing is heavily subsidized and involves a degree of market intervention that compares only with that of Sweden among the countries in this study. However, in other respects it is unlike Sweden: there is little if any attempt at neutrality in the measures, and the private rented sector has declined more rapidly in the Netherlands. The exceptionally large social rented sector distinguishes it from the other countries (apart from Scotland).

The owner occupied sector, despite being one of the smallest, has been more generously assisted than in any of the other countries, with both tax allowances and grants for new housing to those with low incomes. Grants are being reduced and, against a climate in which costs are being cut and policy made more selective, there seems no good argument for leaving the unrestricted mortgage interest tax relief unreformed, despite the continued existence of tax on imputed rent. But even the reforming ministry of Mr Heerma seems to have regarded this as politically too difficult.

The size of the private rented sector has been falling rapidly in proportionate terms and also, although less significantly, in absolute number of dwellings. This is mainly attributable to the withdrawal of individual landlords from the sector; the institutional landlords continue to see rented housing as a worthwhile investment. The sector differs from its counterpart in the UK not only in the importance of the role played by these landlords but also in the scale of new construction. But even with subsidies and a much more favourable fiscal regime than in Britain, new development has not been sufficient to counteract the transfer of dwellings out of the sector through sales and demolitions. It remains to be seen whether the new climate of reduced subsidy and reduced rent regulation will permit the sector to be stabilized, or whether it will continue to decline to something like British levels.

The social rented sector is of particular interest because of its size in a relatively affluent country. Housing associations are the dominant form of landlord; municipal housing companies have played an important role in the past but are of diminishing importance and are being converted into housing associations. The regulatory role of local authorities gives them an important position in the provision of social housing, even where they do not directly own housing stock. This contrasts with Britain, where associations are regulated by agencies of central government, and are often seen as a means of transferring the housing function from local government.

The proposals presently being considered for a simultaneous cancellation of the associations' housing debt and outstanding future subsidy obligations are among the most radical in any country. They would leave the social rented sector with a substantial debt-free asset base and, coupled with the reduction in bricks and mortar subsidies to the owner occupied sector, would greatly reduce subsidies to housing in the Netherlands. Support would then be mainly limited to tax relief and housing allowances.

Personal housing allowances, which are of relatively recent origin, are based on standard costs rather than actual rents (as in Britain). They therefore give greater scope for the market, but they risk leaving some poorly off people unable to afford the rent of the only accommodation available. How serious this is depends on how well the standard costs take account of local variations and on the adequacy of general social security. There would appear to be the same case as in Britain for extending the allowances to the owner occupied sector; but, because it is smaller and there is greater scope for those of limited means in the rented sector, problems of hardship are less likely to arise.

Unrestricted tax allowances, the grants to the owner occupied and private rented sectors and the large size of the social rented sector all make Dutch policy expensive. It has in the past been less targeted than elsewhere, as is shown by the high proportion of cost devoted to bricks and mortar subsidies and the small share spent on housing allowances.

But the policy changes since the publication of the Heerma Memorandum have brought about a major change. Like Sweden, which has also undertaken a sharp change of direction since 1990, the Netherlands seems to have realized that, in the present fiscal climate, a policy on the scale of the past cannot be sustained. If the radical proposals for the social rented sector are implemented, together with the measures already in train, Dutch policy could become one of the least costly among the countries in this study, instead of being one of the most expensive.

CHAPTER 6

Housing policy in Spain

With a population of 39.4 million, Spain is the fifth largest country in the European Union. Population rose by about 1% a year in the 1960s and 1970s, but its growth rate was more than halved during the 1980s. Although Spain was not a combatant in the Second World War, it suffered destruction from the 1936–9 Civil War and was slow to recover thereafter, partly because it was isolated politically until the 1950s and received no Marshall Aid. Spain's migration trends have been somewhat different from countries such as the UK, France and Germany. Between 1960 and 1973, when the oil crisis substantially reduced economic growth in western Europe, Spain experienced large-scale emigration for economic reasons to western Europe and to France in particular. Official figures of 2.3 million emigrants probably underestimate its true extent (Harrison 1993: 31–2). However, since the mid-1970s, the pattern has reversed and Spain has experienced net immigration, much of it from North Africa. Of great importance to Spanish housing policy were the huge internal population movements that resulted from urbanization. It is estimated that 2.3 million workers and their families left the countryside for the urbanizing areas in the 1950s and 1960s (ibid.: 31). Between 1940 and 1981, the proportion of the population living in cities of more than 100000 inhabitants rose from 19% to 42% (ibid.: 33).

Spain's housing stock has some outstanding features. It has a very high level of second homes and vacant dwellings, each making up 15% of the total stock.[1] Of the stock of primary dwellings, three-quarters has been built since the Civil War.[2] Owner occupation is the dominant tenure, accounting for 78% of first homes, among the highest levels in the European Union. The rented sector is made up almost exclusively of private rented dwellings; a distinguishing feature of Spanish housing policy is the virtual absence of a social rented sector. The rented sector is of poorer quality and is older than the stock of owner occupied dwellings. These features give clues as to the nature of Spanish housing policy.

The growth of owner occupation from some half of primary dwellings in 1960 to 78% in 1991 (Table 6.1) is partly accounted for by the absolute decline of the

---

1. Census of Population and Housing 1991. Information provided by the Public Works Ministry.
2. Public Works Ministry Household Survey 1990. Information provided by the Public Works Ministry.

Table 6.1   Tenure of primary dwellings in Spain.

	1960	1970	1981	1991
Owner occupied	50.6	63.4	73.1	77.5
Rented	42.5	30.4	20.8	14.9
Other	6.9	6.5	6.1	7.6

Source: Census information in *Nota* 1 (1993: Table 7).

private rented sector under the pressure of strict rent control, which continued until recently, and the failure of any significant social rented sector to emerge after the Civil War. The existing stock of private rented dwellings declined in numbers, and, even when the government's housing programmes were not aimed at any particular tenure, the effect was to support owner occupation. Consequently, owner occupation has been the principal focus of State expenditure on housing.

Under the dictatorship of General Franco (1939–75), Spain was a highly centralized unitary State, so local authorities and the regions had little autonomy. When democracy was restored, housing policy was formally devolved to 17 Autonomous Communities, or regions. However, this has had relatively little impact on housing policy, because the Autonomous Communities have virtually no stock of social rented dwellings that they own and manage (as in the UK), or over which they have influence (as in France and Germany). In practice the Autonomous Communities administer parts of the government's housing policies, principally the personal aid system, according to rules laid down by the government. They can supplement these schemes from their own funds, so they have more autonomy over the personal aid system than do UK local authorities when administering Housing Benefit, on behalf of the government. Recently, some Autonomous Communities have provided cheaper land for housing development.

Housing policy has evolved under democracy rather than changed radically, but the result has been a substantial shift in emphasis over the past twenty years. A distinctive feature of Franco's housing policy was the subsidizing of developers to build housing, usually for sale. This policy was supported by a highly regulated finance system, under which private institutions were obliged to provide credit for particular projects at submarket rates of interest ("official credit"). From the late 1960s, the emphasis of subsidies shifted away from developers and towards individual purchasers. This pattern was reinforced in the 1980s when subsidies became increasingly related to individuals' incomes and family circumstances. In the 1980s and 1990s, the focus of policy also moved away from an exclusive concern with building new houses and towards providing subsidies for rehabilitation and the purchase of second-hand dwellings.

The financial system was deregulated in the 1980s, and within the space of a decade Spain moved from having one of the most regulated financial systems in Europe to one of the least regulated. The official credit system was phased out, and there was a large increase in the volume of mortgage credit. A house price boom followed, so creating acute affordability problems. The government's response has been to revive various forms of subsidies for owner occupiers, especially middle-income households. It is not yet clear whether this is more than a temporary interruption to the withdrawal of the government from housing policy. Attempts to revive the rented sector have focused on the deregulation of new tenancies after 1985 and, in 1992, the introduction of more generous subsidies for the development of housing for rent than for owner occupation.

Owner occupation

Post-war housing policy has been characterized by a series of Housing Plans with targets for housing output. Until the late 1960s these plans concentrated solely on encouraging developers to build new housing, but since then, and particularly in the 1980s, the emphasis of housing policy has shifted towards lowering the cost of loans for buyers in relation to their incomes and family circumstances. Over the period, the contribution of public sector developers has declined markedly and is no longer important. Only comparatively recently has aid been extended to the renovation of poor quality housing and to purchasers of second-hand housing. In the 1980s the availability of subsidized mortgages declined greatly, marking a significant withdrawal of the government from housing policy. The 1992-5 Housing Plan, which was a response to high house prices, signified some revival of government activity, at least in intent.

Subsidies to developers

Both the public and private sectors of the construction industry are able to obtain subsidies for housebuilding. The private sector is fragmented and its companies are small by international standards. Ownership structures are sometimes complex, links with banks, property development companies and suppliers of building materials being common. There are also thousands of small firms, many of which operate in the informal economy (Salmon 1991: 163). In the late 1980s a co-operative sector, sponsored by the largest trade union, UGT, emerged in response to high house prices. The co-operative, Planificación Social de la Vivienda (PSV), attracted 20000-50000 members, but collapsed in December 1993, prompting comparisons with Neue Heimat in Germany (Bruce 1993).

The public sector has developed since 1939, when the Instituto Nacional de la Vivienda (INV) was established as a public sector holding company (Wright 1977: 92). This and its successor, the Instituto para la Promoción Publica de la Vivienda (IPPV), formed in 1980, held the capital in public sector construction companies (Tamames 1986: 136). These were transferred to the Autonomous Communities in 1985. There are also a few public sector construction companies that are owned by communes and savings banks. The public sector has tended to specialize in cheaper housing, sometimes referred to as being "outside the market". The price of owner occupied housing built by public sector construction companies is very low (because of cost limits). Its allocation has a reputation as being something of a lottery.[3]

The choice of directing housing subsidies towards developers reflected the severe housing shortage that resulted from the Civil War and the absence of any existing administrative mechanism to direct subsidies towards individuals. The 1950 Census identified a housing shortage of one million homes, which had scarcely been touched by the 1940–50 Housing Plan (Tamames 1986: 136). Subsidies took the form of grants, loans and tax exemptions, and were directed through State organizations such as the Instituto Nacional de la Vivienda (INV) and the Banco de Crédito a la Construcción (Davies 1963: 400). The total production of subsidized housing exceeded 200000 in 1951–5, and rose to a total of 465000 over the 1956–60 Housing Plan (ibid.: table 19.1). Perhaps a further 65000–100000 houses were built over the decade, without government assistance. Housing production became heavily concentrated in the public sector, which accounted for 90% of all housing output by 1960 (Wright 1976: 176).

Despite the significant levels of housing output achieved in the 1950s, internal migration from the rural areas to the cities and coastal areas became a major cause of continued housing shortages. A new Housing Plan was adopted for 1961–76, but it was divided into four-year periods and, during each of these, total housing output rose, from an annual average of 190000 units in 1961–4 to 350000 in 1973–6 (Tamames 1986: table 4.5). Subsidies were cut after 1965, but this was the era of rapid economic growth that exceeded 7% between 1960 and 1973, as Franco's Spain was integrated into the Western economy. Subsidized housing still accounted for 190000 units built in 1971 and even rose a little to 196000 in 1975, but its share of total output fell to 60% in 1971 and to 52% in 1975, as unsubsidized output grew. The private sector became dominant and in 1975 accounted for 91% of subsidized and 95% of total housing output (Banco Bilbao Vizcaya 1992: 77).

While the direction of housing subsidies towards developers was associated with high output levels, the policy encountered distinct problems and limitations:

- *Poor targeting of subsidies* Although the purpose of subsidizing housing production was to increase the supply of affordable homes, cost controls were weak and builders were often free to build for higher-income households and so gain higher profits (Wright 1976: 95). The problem was particularly acute in rural areas where, in the early 1960s, "thousands of families still live[d] in primitive caves and shacks" (Davies 1963: 402).
- *Empty dwellings* The number of registered empty homes more than tripled from 350000 in 1960 to 1.1 million a decade later, far exceeding the general growth in stock, and despite housing shortages (Wright 1976:

3. Interview with Baralides Alberdi, 22 September 1993.

176). The problem of vacant properties has been attributed to the lack of cost controls causing developers to price themselves out of the market, and also by the failure to anticipate the extent of population migration, leading to development occurring where it was not needed, particularly in rural areas.

- *Incomplete dwellings* Poor co-ordination between government agencies and the construction industry, the fragmented structure of the construction industry itself, and the frequent failure to provide essential infrastructure (such as water supplies, sewerage and access roads) caused hundreds of thousands of dwellings to remain incomplete (Davies 1963: 401).

- *Falling quality and low planning standards* Perhaps given the extent of the housing shortage and its highly visible manifestation in the form of the shanty towns that grew up around Madrid and Barcelona, it was inevitable that housing quality would suffer. Many of the high-rise developments that were aimed at tackling the housing shortages in the urban areas were of low quality and with few amenities. Indeed, between 1958 and 1965 the average size of new housing fell from $75.8\,m^2$ to $63.9\,m^2$, when the European average was $73.2\,m^2$ (Wright 1976: 95).

In response to the inefficient targeting of subsidies, the 1969–72 Housing Plan introduced subsidies that could be paid directly to the purchaser, rather than to the developer. Since 1978 four Housing Plans have been completed and a fifth (1992–5) is under way. These schemes introduced the concept of "officially protected housing" (VPO) and are based on lowering interest rates for house purchasers, either directly or indirectly through developers. It is described in more detail in the following section. When VPO is applied to developers, they act as intermediaries between financial institutions and house purchasers. The developer gets a scheme approved by the government at its outset and becomes eligible for a short-term loan at a submarket interest rate. Developers also administered the selection of purchasers entitled to subsidized mortgages, an arrangement that left the scheme wide open to fraud. As the financial system has been deregulated and the State mortgage bank has become more commercialized, banks now vet all applicants before they receive subsidized mortgages, so further personalizing the system.[4] During the house price boom in the late 1980s, many developers abandoned building VPO, partly because cost limits failed to keep pace with inflation, but also because greater profits were obtainable in the free-market sector. However, since the housing market entered recession, private developers have renewed their interest in building protected housing.[5]

The 1988–91 Housing Plan introduced a new type of protected housing, known as the "special regime", which introduced greater subsidies for lower-income purchasers. The less generous scheme then became known as the "general regime". During the 1988–91 Housing Plan, only public sector developers

4. Interview with Baralides Alberdi, op. cit.
5. Interview with Baralides Alberdi, op. cit.

could participate in the special regime, but the 1992–5 Housing Plan has permitted private sector developers to participate in the special regime too (Pareja & Riera, 1993: table 1).[6]

The types of investment eligible for help under the VPO programmes have widened over the years. Originally, only new dwellings were eligible. In recognition of the poor quality of much of the housing stock, housing rehabilitation work became eligible for subsidy under the VPO programme in 1984. In this programme, subsidized loans for rehabilitation were based on 40% of costs, repayable over seven years (ibid.). The 1992–5 Housing Plan extended the scope of subsidy to two further categories. First, second-hand dwellings became eligible, which is of great importance (although not directly to developers). Secondly, subsidies became available for the purchase and development of land to be used for protected housing.[7] The last measure represents a response to the problem of developments failing to meet cost limits during the house price boom.

Subsidies to borrowers

Since the late 1960s, and particularly since 1978, housing subsidies have shifted away from developers and towards purchasers. Among purchasers, subsidies have been refined in an attempt to match the circumstances of individual families. Until 1992, there was also a marked decline in the total numbers of subsidized loans under the protected housing (VPO) programmes (Table 6.2).

Table 6.2 Protected and free-market housing starts by housing programme (000 units).

Programme	Protected	Free market	Total
1978–80			
Total	402.5	418.1	820.6
Annual average	134.2	139.4	273.5
%	49.0	51.0	100.0
1981–3			
Total	420.8	285.8	706.6
Annual average	140.3	95.3	235.5
%	59.6	40.4	100.0
1984–7			
Total	484.3	404.2	888.5
Annual average	121.1	101.0	222.1
%	54.5	45.5	100.0
1988–91			
Total	221.7	774.3	996.0
Annual average	54.4	193.6	249.0
%	22.3	77.7	100.0

Source: Banco Hipotecario.

6. This paper is now published in Bartlett & Bramley (1994), but without the useful table 1.
7. Information provided by the Public Works Ministry.

There are now three ways in which purchasers may qualify for subsidies under the 1992–5 Housing Plan. These are through the "general regime" of the VPO programme, the "special regime" of the VPO programme, and the new programme of housing under controlled prices, *Vivienda a Precio Tasado* (VPT). In addition to these explicit subsidies, owner occupiers benefit from the generous tax treatment of housing.

VPO general regime

The General Regime was the original and sole component of the VPO programme. The 1978–80 Housing Programme established the basic qualifying criteria for a mortgage under the general regime. Space and price limits, based on an annually adjusted module that varied between regions, were imposed on eligible properties. These had to be newly built. Originally, there was provision for neither housing renovations nor the purchase of second-hand housing. There are three types of subsidy available to households that qualify for assistance under this scheme:

- *Agreed rate mortgages* Each year the financial institutions agree with the public works ministry the interest rate that will be applied to general regime loans. The interest rate is fixed at slightly below expected market rates; in some respects these mortgages are comparable to the French *prêts conventionnés*. The financial institutions bear the subsidy on these loans, with the likely consequence that the cost of other loans is raised to compensate. In 1992, the agreed mortgage rate was 12.25%, that is 2.25% below the market rate of 14.5% (Pareja & Riera 1993: 9). However, in 1993, a general fall in interest rates and competition in the mortgage market actually reduced the market rate to below the agreed mortgage rate. Consequently, the authorities covered the agreed rate.[8]

  To qualify for a mortgage with an agreed mortgage rate, a purchaser's income must not exceed 5.5 times the minimum wage, which varies according to region and family structure. In 1992, the basic minimum wage for a single person was Ptas886253 (about £4400) in the urban areas and Ptas804759 (about £4000) elsewhere. However, for a family of two earners with three children, the minimum wage rises to Ptas1.15 million (about £5750) in the urban areas and Ptas1 million (about £5200) elsewhere.[9] Thus, the income criteria for a mortgage at agreed rates is very generous, with single people earning the equivalent of £25000 or families with incomes exceeding the equivalent of £30000 qualifying for these loans.

- *Personal aid system* The personal aid system was introduced in the 1981–3 Housing Plan, with the intention of targeting interest subsidies on lower-income groups. It was developed in subsequent programmes,

---

8. Interview with Baralides Alberdi, op. cit.; interview with Diane Miles, 3 March 1994.
9. Calculated from Pareja & Riera (1993: table 9).

becoming more closely related to household income over time. There are now four categories of additional interest subsidy within the general regime, with first-time buyers whose income does not exceed the minimum wage by more than 3.5 times being entitled to the loans at the lowest interest rates. Such first-time buyers qualified for mortgages at 6.5% in 1992, which was 1% lower than the entitlement for all other qualifying borrowers in the same income category. Households with incomes no more than 3.5–4.5 times greater than the minimum wage were entitled to mortgages at 9.5%; and those with incomes in the 4.5–5.5 times the minimum wage range were entitled to mortgages at 11%. Mortgages under the personal aid system are repayable over 15 years. Interest rates remain fixed for five years, at which time they are reviewed. Adjustments are made according to changes in income over the previous two years, and according to changes in the concessionary interest rates (Pareja & Riera 1993: table 4).

The administration of the personal aid system was devolved to the Autonomous Communities in 1984. Applications are now made by individuals to the Autonomous Community, but they have to be confirmed by the government. Successful applicants are issued with a certificate to present to a financial institution, which issues the loan at the concessionary rate and claims the subsidy from the Autonomous Community (Pareja & Riera 1993: 14).[10] The cost of the scheme is effectively borne by central government, which allocates funding to each Autonomous Community through the interregional grant system, but financial institutions also incur costs by operating the personal aid system. These arise from the delays in claiming the interest subsidy. Claims are made in blocks at set points in each year and there is a further delay while these claims are administered.[11]

- *Grants for deposits*   Grants for deposits were introduced in 1984, but these are restricted to households whose incomes do not exceed 3.5 times the minimum wage. The level of aid is substantial for qualifying households. They receive 5% of the purchase price. First-time buyers receive 10% if they have participated in a housing-savings scheme (Pareja & Riera 1993: table 5). Some Autonomous Communities provide additional aid, which they pay for from their own resources.

VPO special regime

The "special regime" was introduced by the 1988–91 Housing Plan and represented a further targeting of subsidies according to income, thereby reinforcing the trends within the general regime. The special regime is aimed at lower-income groups, and has a lower maximum qualifying income of 2.5 times the minimum income (compared with 3.5 to 5.5 under the general regime). This

---

10. Interview with Baralides Alberdi, op. cit.
11. Interview with Diane Miles, op. cit.

works out at Ptas2–2.2 million for single person depending on the whether they live in an urban or other area (about £10000–11000); or Ptas1–1.15 million for a dual-earning couple with three children, again depending on where they live (about £12500–14375).[12]

Households that qualify for a subsidized mortgage under the special regime enjoy more favourable terms than those qualifying under the general regime. In 1992, the interest rate was 5%, that is 1.5% lower than the lowest interest rate obtained by someone qualifying for the most generous assistance under the personal aid scheme of the general regime (for this reason, the personal aid system is redundant for households that qualify under the special regime), a full 9.5% below the market rate of interest, and was a real rate of interest of just 0.4%. Loans under the special regime are repaid over 20 years, compared to 15 under the general regime. Purchasers under the special regime also qualify for grants for 10% of the purchase price to be paid for by the government. A more generous grant of 15% is payable if the purchaser has participated in a housing-savings scheme (ibid.: tables 4 and 5).

Although the level of assistance under the special regime may appear generous, the viability of owner occupation for some of the low-income groups who qualify for assistance must be questioned. Indeed, the levels of loan default are high, and little is done to retrieve bad debts (Ghékiere 1991: ch. 7).

Housing under controlled prices (VPT)

The VPT programme is similar to VPO, but the maximum price of qualifying housing is higher under VPT, which was introduced under the 1992–5 Housing Plan in response to the affordability problems faced by middle-income groups following the house price boom. The VPT scheme is applicable to both new and second-hand housing, providing that prices fall within specified limits, which vary to reflect differences in costs between regions. Assisted loans can be granted up to 70% of prices, or 80% if the dwelling was built under a VPO scheme. Interest rates vary according to income and to the size of the property. There is a direct relationship between the maximum size of qualifying property and income, so higher-income households are permitted to live in larger dwellings and still qualify for subsidized mortgages. The maximum qualifying size for first-time buyers with incomes under 3.5 times the minimum wage is $70m^2$, rising to $120m^2$ for those outside the first-time buyers' scheme with incomes up to the maximum qualifying level of 5.5 times the minimum wage. The mortgage interest rate is adjusted so that it rises with income, ranging between 6.5%, for first-time buyers whose incomes do not exceed 3.5 times the minimum wage, to 11% for those whose incomes do not exceed 5.5 times the minimum wage. However, unlike the personal aid system, there is some flexibility over interest rate and maximum property sizes. Thus, people with incomes up to 3.5 times the

---

12. Calculated from Pareja & Riera (1993: tables 4 and 9).

minimum wage are eligible to mortgages at 7.5% on properties no larger than 90 m^2 or 11% on properties not exceeding 120 m^2 (Pareja & Riera 1993: table 7).

The interest rates under the VPT scheme are very similar to those under the personal aid system with the VPO general regime, but the price limits are higher than under VPO. As under the special and general VPO regimes, borrowers under the VPT scheme can qualify for grants as deposits (ibid.: 14).

Taxation of owner occupied housing

Owner occupied principal dwellings attract some of the most generous tax advantages anywhere in the European Union. The structure of the tax subsidies makes them worth very much more to higher-income householders, although their sheer scale helps to explain why owner occupation is open to very low-income households.

Mortgage interest payments are deductible from taxable income, so tax relief is worth more as income rises and crosses through the 17 tax bands. Interest payments above Ptas800000 (about £4000) for single people (Ptas1 million, or about £5000, for couples) are not deductible. This tax deduction is counterbalanced to some extent by a tax on imputed income (the *cadastral*) by which 2% of the value of the property is added to taxable income. The value of the property used to be self-assessed, so was obviously subject to underestimation. However, official valuations are now being carried out that will reduce evasion, although values will become outdated, depending on the frequency of revaluation.[13]

Owner Occupiers may also deduct capital allowances from their tax liability (as opposed to taxable income). Up to 15% of all investment in housing may be set against income tax liability, so long as it does not exceed 30% of income. For these purposes, housing investment includes:

- money invested in a housing-savings account
- a deposit put down when a house is purchased (money that first passed through a housing-savings account can thus be deducted from tax liability twice)
- transaction costs, such as legal fees
- all capital repayments (so the repayment of mortgages is encouraged; this might account for the preponderance of repayment mortgages, the relatively short terms of mortgages, and the calculation of interest payments at frequent (monthly) "rests")
- housing improvements.[14]

Capital gains tax is payable even on principal dwellings, but in two ways its impact is very much reduced. First, roll-over relief is provided, so households that move are exempt. Secondly, annual allowances are provided that accumulate over time, so greatly diminishing liability when an owner occupier might wish to sell up and trade down into rented accommodation during retirement.[15] The

---

13. Interview with Diane Miles, op. cit.
14. Ibid.

tax seems to be aimed at only the most obvious types of housing speculation.

VAT on new owner occupied housing is charged at concessionary rates: 6% in cases other than the VPO special regime housing, which is taxed at 3%; the standard rate is 15% (Ghékiere 1991: ch. 7).

Financial deregulation and the free-market sector

Since the introduction of the VPO schemes, free-market mortgages have always made up a significant proportion of housing loans. During the 1978–80, 1981–3 and 1984–7 Housing Plans, 40–51% of new mortgages were financed by the free-market sector. This proportion rose rapidly in the 1988–91 Housing Plan to 78% of the total. The rise of the free-market sector reflected not only the decline in the protected sector, but also the vibrancy of the private market under the coincidence of economic growth and financial deregulation.

Until the 1980s, Spain had one of the most regulated financial systems in Europe, as the State attempted to direct financial investments of both public and private sectors through a system called "official credit". This enabled the State to promote certain activities at the expense of the private sector. At the centre of this system lay the Official Credit Institute (ICO), which had five dependent banking institutions beneath it. Specialist institutions existed for agriculture, industry, local government and export finance, as well as for housing that was organized through the State mortgage bank, Banco Hipotecario de España (BHE) (Salmon 1991: 148–9).

The ICO raised finance for State-sanctioned projects through a system of compulsory investment ratios, known as *coeficientes*, which were applied to private as well as public sector banking institutions (ibid.: 148). The *coeficientes* worked in two ways. Either financial institutions invested in low-yielding bonds issued by the Treasury on behalf of the ICO, which were then distributed among the five State banking institutions, or they invested directly in an approved programme at a controlled interest rate. With finance for housing, private banks preferred the first route, but savings banks were willing to lend directly (Alberdi 1992: 5).[16]

From around 1970, but especially in the 1980s, the highly regulated financial system was deregulated in four principal areas:

The abolition of coeficientes

The system of compulsory investment ratios, or *coeficientes*, has now been abolished. The ratios were reduced first reduced in 1974, but further reductions in 1977 formed part of a wider reform of the financial system that continued until 1987 when the ratios were cut dramatically from 13% to 1% of liabilities

---

15. Ibid.
16. Interview with Baralides Alberdi op. cit. Alberdi (1992) is now published in Turner & White-head (1993).

(although outstanding commitments left the effective ratio at 6%). The following year, the obligation to refinance official credit loans was abolished, and the remainder of the system was phased out altogether in 1993 (OECD 1988: 56; Caminal et al. 1990: 267).

With the abolition of official credit, the institutions that were dependencies of the ICO were merged in 1991 into a single banking group called Argentaria. The Caja Postal, although not a dependency of the ICO, was also added to Argentaria, which became the third largest banking group in Spain (in terms of assets). Argentaria was initially wholly owned by the government, but nevertheless developed along commercial lines. In 1993, half of Argentaria was sold off to the private sector (in two tranches). The ICO still exists, but undertakes very little new lending. On its formation, the viability of Argentaria was enhanced by the transfer of historic bad debts to the ICO from its predecessor institutions.[17]

Financial institutions continue to subsidize loans through the agreed rate mortgage system within the VPO scheme. However, private banks have now largely withdrawn from it. They provided one quarter of new protected mortgages during the 1981–3 Housing Plan, but just 1.7% in 1988–91. The savings banks and Banco Hipotecario remain the largest participants in the 1992–5 Housing Plan. In 1992 Banco Hipotecario supplied nearly 30% of the finance and the savings banks just over 60%. In the first half of 1993, Banco Hipotecario's share fell to 12.6%, whereas the savings banks supplied almost 78% of the total.[18]

Reduction in other banking ratios

Other banking ratios were reformed and brought more in line with the levels prevalent in other EU countries. This reform represented an important step towards regulatory convergence between the private banks and the savings banks (in favour of the savings banks), whereas the replacement of minimum reserve requirements (which took the form of low-yielding deposits at the Bank of Spain) with much lower cash reserves (which are non-interest–bearing) increased the liquidity of the financial system (OECD 1991: 37).

Deregulation of interest rates

Interest rates on deposits were deregulated between 1974 and 1987. In 1974, control over deposits and loans with maturities over two years were removed. Those with maturities over one year were lifted in 1977. In 1981 all loan rates were deregulated, regardless of maturity. Finally, in 1987 all controls over interest rates (including those on instant access accounts) and service charges were removed (OECD 1988: 55).

---

17. Interview with Baralides Alberdi, op. cit.
18. Information provided by Banco Hipotecario.

Competition for wholesale funds

Greater competition was also created in the wholesale markets when reforms were introduced with the initial objective of creating sources of long-term finance. Three funding instruments were created by the 1981 Act on Mortgage Regulation, by far the most important of which being the *cedulas hipotecarias*. Initially, these bonds had a minimum maturity of three years, and received several regulatory privileges that greatly enhanced their attraction. They did not count towards assets liable for official credit, and investors were encouraged to buy them by the tax concession that enabled them to deduct 15% of the bonds' value from their tax liability. As these bonds became established, these privileges were withdrawn. In 1984, they began to count towards investment ratios, but, by then, official credit was fast disappearing in any case. In 1987 the tax concession was withdrawn too (Alberdi 1992: 7–9).

Initially, only Banco Hipotecario and the savings banks were allowed to issue *cedulas hipotecarias*. Thus, savings banks were given access to a funding source not enjoyed by their counterparts in Continental Europe. However, private banks responded to their exclusion from the mortgage bond market by creating a particular type of subsidiary, the mortgage credit company (SCH), which was authorized to issue *cedulas hipotecarias*. In 1988 the private banks were allowed to issue *cedulas hipotecarias* in their own right, but an effective barrier remained because institutions that issued these bonds had to hold 30% of their assets as mortgages. Thus, banks did not significantly increase their issues of mortgage bonds until 1991, when this restriction was removed (ibid.).

Freedom of branching

Competition in banking has been limited by restrictions placed on the branching activities of savings banks and foreign banks, but since the 1970s these restrictions have been gradually dismantled. Until then, savings banks were confined to operating within their own locality, and foreign banks were not permitted to open full branches anywhere. In 1977, the two largest savings banks were allowed to open branches in each of the five largest cities, and in 1989 all geographical restrictions on savings bank activity were removed (Salmon 1991: 153–4). Foreign banks were allowed to open three full branches in 1978 and this restriction remained in place until 1993, when the European Union's Second Banking Directive swept aside such restrictions (ibid.: 157). Although not a function of regulation, it is noteworthy that the formation of Argentaria has given Banco Hipotecario access to an extensive nationwide branch network. Banco Hipotecario has 25 branches of its own, but now it can originate loans through the 500 branches of the Caja Postal. Indeed, there is some speculation that Banco Hipotecario and Caja Postal might form a natural grouping on their own.[19]

Financial market deregulation allowed a large expansion in mortgage credit availability. The quantities of outstanding mortgage credit rose by 450%

---

19. Interview with Baralides Alberdi, op. cit.

between 1982 and 1992, from Ptas2200 million to Ptas12200 million (Table 6.3). Most of this increase took place in the second half of this period. Even taking account of inflation, these figures represent a very large credit expansion.

Table 6.3 Share of mortgage market[a] in Spain, 1982–92 (Ptas 000 million and %).

Year	Total	Private banks	Savings banks	ICO[b]	BHE[c]	SCH[d]
1982						
Amount	2184.3	169.7	1283.3	728.5	498.3	2.8
%		7.8	58.8	33.4	22.8	0.1
1986						
Amount	3952.0	392.2	2008.2	1423.9	960.6	127.7
%		9.9	50.8	36.0	24.3	3.2
1990						
Amount	9534.1	2421.9	4811.4	1716.1	1313.5	584.7
%		24.5	50.5	18.0	13.8	6.1
1992						
Amount	12197.9	3866.9	6196.7	1412.4	1384.2	721.9
%		31.9	50.8	11.6	11.3	5.9

a. Share of outstanding loans.
b. Official Credit Institute.
c. BHE (Banco Hipotecario de España) is a subtotal of ICO.
d. Mortgage credit companies.
Source: Banco Hipotecario.

The expansion of mortgage credit followed on from increased competition between financial institutions, particularly when the private banks entered the mortgage market and increased their market share from 7.6% in 1985 to 32% in 1992. However, the savings banks retain the largest share of the mortgage market and have consistently held about 50% of it since the mid-1980s. The main loser of market share was the ICO, reflecting the winding down and abolition of official credit. From a peak of 39.2% in 1985, the ICO's market share fell away to almost nothing by 1992. Banco Hipotecario's market share fell from about 25% in the mid-1980s to 11.3% in 1992. The private bank mortgage credit subsidiaries (SCHs) have never had a great impact. Their share rose to 5% in 1987 and it has remained in the 5–6.6% range since then.

Competition in the mortgage market had clear implications for the type of mortgage products offered to borrowers in the free-market sector. Maximum loan to value ratios rose from 50–60% in the 1970s to 80% in the 1980s. Moreover, valuations in the 1980s were based on the full market value of properties, whereas those conducted in the 1970s were based on less than the market value (Alberdi 1992: 1). Maximum repayment periods lengthened from 8–10 years in the 1970s to 15–20 years in the 1980s, although many mortgages are still repaid over relatively short periods, such as 10–12 years (ibid.).[20] The typical mortgage in the 1970s was at a fixed rate of interest, but in the 1980s the variable-rate mortgage came to dominate the market (although a 12-year fixed rate product

20. Interview with Diane Miles, op. cit.

was launched in 1993) (ibid.: 1; Burns 1993). Spain's dependence on variable-rate mortgages, at least in the free-market sector, is shared with Britain, but not with the other countries included in this study.

Competition in the savings and mortgage markets has manifested itself by successive "deposit wars" (started in 1989 when one bank launched so-called "super accounts" with competitive interest rates) and "lending wars" (begun in 1993 when mortgage rates were cut) (OECD 1991).[21]

Affordability and the house price boom

As in the UK, the deregulation of the mortgage market was accompanied by a house price boom. In both cases, deregulation was a necessary facilitator of boom conditions, although not necessarily the direct cause. Some of the cyclical conditions that contributed to the house price boom in the UK and Spain were similar, such as a buoyant economy and increased levels of household formation. Other similarities are noteworthy, such as inelastic land supply and the distorted tenure structures of both countries. But it is important not to exaggerate the similarities, because other conditions were different. In the case of Spain, it is widely believed that entry into the European Union started the speculative boom in house prices. It is well known that membership brought new investment into Spain; it is less well known that some foreign investment was targeted at the housing market and was attracted by the unusually low levels (by international standards) of property prices. It is also believed that investment from the informal economy found its way into speculative housing investment.[22]

The house price boom lasted from 1985 to 1990 (Table 6.4). According to an index of new house prices, nominal house prices rose by almost 250% in this period, and real house prices by almost 80%. Nominal house prices rose by more

Table 6.4   House price inflation in Spain, 1986–90 (%).[a]

Year	All Spain (nominal)	Madrid (nominal)	All Spain (real)	Madrid (real)
1986	21.0	43.0	12.2	34.2
1987	23.1	33.6	17.9	28.4
1988	22.8	29.8	18.0	25.0
1989	23.0	22.6	16.2	15.8
1990	10.2	8.6	3.5	1.9

a. House prices based on valuations of new houses.
Source: Public Works Ministry.

21. Interview with Baralides Alberdi, op. cit.
22. Interview with Luis Furones, 23 September 1993; interview with Luis Orgaz, 23 September 1993.

than 20% in each year between 1985 and 1989; real house prices rose by 16–18% in the three years 1987–9. As in the UK, the house price boom was not spread evenly. In Madrid, real house prices rose by 159% between 1985 and 1990. House prices here were also more volatile than the average, real prices rising by 34% in 1986 and by just 1.9% in 1990.

Although Spanish real house prices have fallen, the general fall in nominal house prices experienced in England has not occurred. However, there have been falls in nominal house prices in some areas of Spain (particularly where the boom had been greatest). Nevertheless, wide difference in house prices remain. House prices are highest in Madrid, averaging almost Ptas15 million (about £75000) in 1993, which is about twice the level of average house prices in the lowest cost Autonomous Community, Valenciana. In 1993, house prices in Spain as a whole averaged Ptas10.7 million (about £54000), about five times the average income. In terms of affordability, housing was slightly cheaper in 1993 than in 1991, because interest rates had fallen, but more than half of the average income is required to finance a mortgage on the average priced house. In the highest-cost areas, Madrid and Catelonia, the price to income ratio of free-market housing was almost 6:1. In these areas the proportion of average income needed to finance a mortgage on an average-price house was 56.6% in 1993, compared to 32.9% in the lowest cost area, La Rioja.[23]

The impacts of the VPO General Regime can be measured against these figures for free-market housing. VPO General Regime housing is cheaper than free-market housing, with prices averaging Ptas7.1 million in 1993, two thirds of the price of free-market housing. This reduced the price:income ratio to 3.3:1. Interest subsidies through the personal aid system could reduce to just under 19% the proportion of income required to finance a mortgage (ibid.: table 8).

The availability of protected housing is clearly an important component of a housing policy that aims to tackle the affordability crisis. In the first three of the VPO Housing Plans, the average annual production of protected housing ran at 120000–140000 units. This slumped to an average of 55000 during the 1988–91 Housing Plan, as cost limits became impossible to meet and private developers found more profitable investment opportunities elsewhere. The 1992–5 Housing Plan responded to the affordability problem by supplementing the VPO special and general regimes with the VPT scheme and subsidies aimed at land development. So, although scarcely no increase in VPO outputs was planned for 1992, the addition of the new schemes would take the total up to over 100000 units. However, in the event the VPO general regime was oversubscribed, and each of the other schemes fell well below target levels, so only 74% of the overall target was met.[24] Unless the plan is more successful, it is unlikely to prove to be a satisfactory response to the affordability crisis.

---

23. Banco Hipotecario, *Nota* 1993, Número 7, Table 9.
24. Banco Hipotecario, *Nota* 1993, Número 1, Table 1.

The rented sectors

The rented sector in Spain has declined from 42.5% of principal dwellings in 1960 to 14.9% in 1991 (Table 6.1). There has been an absolute fall in the number of rented dwellings from almost 3 million in 1960 to 1.76 million in 1991. One survey, conducted in 1989, placed the rented sector at just 11.7% of the stock of principal dwellings, but the basis of the survey was different from the census information, so it is not clear whether the rented sector ever became that small, or indeed whether it has since revived (Table 6.5).

Table 6.5   Size of the rented sector in Spain, 1970–91.[a]

Year	Total stock	Rented stock	Rented (%)
1970	8504332	2555116	30.0
1981	10430895	2168661	20.8
1985	10531444	1734978	16.5
1989	11670000	1365814	11.7
1991	11824849	1757172	14.9

a. Measurements are not on a consistent basis, so are not strictly comparable.
Source: Census (1970 and 1981), Survey of family budgets (1985), Public Works Ministry household survey (1989) – all in Massieu (c. 1990); Census (1991) in Nota 1 (1993: Table 8).

The social rented sector has never been a significant tenure in Spain, whereas the private rented sector has been strictly regulated. Since the mid-1980s, attempts have been made to revive the private rented sector by deregulating new tenancies and by offering additional subsidies to developers of rented housing.

The social rented sector

The 1989 household survey estimated that the total stock of social rented dwellings scarcely exceeded 100000 units, that is 7.6% of the rented stock and less than 1% of the total stock of principal dwellings (Ghékiere 1991: ch. 7).

The stock of social rented housing was largely built in the 1950s and 1960s, as is indicated by its above-average age. It was often constructed using cheap materials to low standards, as part of large-scale schemes aimed at facilitating slum clearance programmes. The vast majority (70%) of social rented housing is owned by government agencies. Originally, this meant central government, through the INV, but in 1984 it was transferred to the Autonomous Communities (and sometimes the municipalities). Spain is unusual among the countries in this survey in having rented housing in direct government ownership, although compared to the UK the size of this sector is tiny. Partly to avoid the cost of repairs and renovation, there is an active policy to sell this housing to its tenants at low prices. The remainder of the social rented housing stock is managed by non-profit–making independent organizations that nevertheless retain links with the Autonomous Communities and municipalities. Rents in social rented housing are fixed administratively at below market levels, although further subsidies are available to those tenants who are particularly poor. These latter subsidies are as close as Spain comes to having a housing allowance (ibid.).

The social rented sector has always been small and is in further decline. It has not featured in any of the policy initiatives taken in recent years in response to the affordability crisis that arose from the house price boom.

The private rented sector

The private rented sector has been a focus of government intervention in the housing market since 1920, when rent control was introduced into the large towns. In 1931 it was extended to the rest of the country (Wright 1976: 92). The regulation of tenancies covered the level of initial rent that could be charged, the revision of rents, security of tenure, and succession. The rules relating to these matters were changed in 1946, 1955 and 1964, but the level of regulation has remained high. In an attempt to revive the rented sector, new tenancies were deregulated after 1985. To simplify a complex situation, there are now three main types of private tenant:[25]

- Pre-1964 tenants have the greatest degree of protection. Their rents were frozen at the point of registration, they enjoy complete security of tenure, and the tenure can be inherited twice. When these tenancies eventually lapse, the property can be relet at market rents.
- 1964–85 tenants had their rents set administratively at the start of their tenancies. However, the rents are uprated annually, according to inflation. These tenants enjoy a high degree of security.
- Post-1985 tenants have the least protection. The initial rent is set by the market and there are no restrictions on its uprating. There is no security outside the terms of the contract.

Tenancies agreed after 1985 were deregulated by the Boyer Decree (named after the responsible minister) in response to the house price boom. It was believed that deregulation would encourage owners of properties that had been bought for speculative reasons (and kept empty) would be attracted to the short-term rental market if tenancies could be terminated to allow such properties to be sold with vacant possession. It is not possible to say whether deregulation has been successful in reducing or reversing the decline of the private rented sector. Critics suggest that the measure succeeded only in hiking rents and shortening contracts (Massieu, c. 1990). Surveys conducted in 1985 and 1989 suggested that deregulation failed to halt the decline in the private rented sector. Others argue that rising rents reflected the general property boom and were not, strictly

---

25. Interview with Baralides Alberdi, op. cit.

speaking, caused by deregulation (although it must have been a necessary pre-condition).[26] Further, the 1991 census shows a rise in the proportion of rented dwellings compared with the 1989 survey. However, the 1985, 1989 and 1991 estimates of tenure composition are not part of the same series, so do not provide a definitive answer to this question.

Nevertheless, some of the impacts of the Boyer Decree are known. Three-quarters of tenancies remain under the strictest form of rent control, that is with rents frozen and with security and succession rights. However, 138000 tenancies were created between 1986 and 1990, representing 8% of the 1985 total (Ghék-iere 1991: ch. 7). This is a significant number of new tenancies, but they are, as the legislation allows, overwhelmingly short-term in nature. Only 35% of dereg-ulated tenancies are for more than twelve months, the clear majority (63.5%) being for 6–12 months (ibid.). As one would expect, rents vary enormously across the sector as a whole, according to the date at which they were agreed. The overall average rent is Ptas16700 per month (about £83.50). Rents agreed before 1980 are on average less than this; those agreed after 1980 more. Rents agreed since deregulation are 38% higher than those agreed between 1981 and 1985 (OECD 1992: table 15). There is also considerable variation in deregulated rents, according to length of contract. In particular, rents on very short-term leases (less than six months) are particularly high, being 1.5 times the average (Ghékiere 1991: ch. 7). Only a part of this difference is likely to be explained by variations in the quality of the stock.

The high level of rents on short-term leases contributed to pressure for some kind of re-regulation and, in 1994, legislation was approved that introduced a minimum length of tenancy of four years. Clearly, this would greatly reduce the liquidity of rented housing as an asset and is likely to deter potential landlords, as well as those tenants who wish to have short-term tenancies of less than one year, the minimum commitment required under the new legislation.

The same legislation will also liberalize the vast majority of tenancies that pre-date 1985. Rents on these dwellings will be deregulated over a decade and the right of succession will be severely restricted. Loopholes arising from the transfer of tenancies in anticipation of the legislation have been closed.[27] This policy is likely to bring many tenancies to an end, but will not necessarily feed through into new deregulated tenancies. Landlords might take the opportunity to sell the dwellings and, given the extent of house price inflation since these ten-ancies were agreed, they would certainly make a handsome capital gain.

The deregulation of new tenancies was effectively the only measure taken to revive the rented sector in the 1980s. No housing allowance remains for private tenants, which some regard as necessary to support economically viable rents, although a token tax allowance has been introduced for private tenants. It is token because hardly anyone qualifies for it, such are the unlikely coincidences

26. Interview with Baralides Alberdi, op. cit.; interview with Luis Orgaz, op. cit.
27. Interview with Diane Miles, op. cit.

of income and rent requirements.[28] Under the 1992–5 Housing Plan, tenants became eligible for grants towards rental deposits. Under the VPO General Regime, qualifying households can claim 10% of their deposit, or 15% if the property was smaller than 70m². Under the Special Regime, the grants for deposits are more generous: 15%, or 25% if the property is under 70m².[29]

The private rented sector is predominantly owned by individuals. Only 5% is owned by institutions, and deregulation has not enticed institutions into renting. Indeed, institutions account for just over 1% of deregulated tenancies (Ghékiere 1991: ch. 7). This may reflect the greater gains that could be made in the late 1980s in the commercial property sector and even in forms of investment such as long-term government bonds.

The 1992–5 Housing Plan established subsidized loan rates for rented housing under the VPO special and general regimes (4% and 5% respectively) that are generally lower than those available for owner occupied housing. It remains to be seen whether these subsidies will attract institutional investment into rented housing. The 1992–5 Housing Plan also sets explicit targets for rented housing under the VPO regimes. It envisages an additional 30000 units of rented housing to become available through subsidized programmes. If the target is met, then it will represent an addition of 17% to the 1991 rented stock. It is intended that two-thirds of the anticipated expansion of rented housing through the Housing Plan will be concentrated within the special regime, where it will account for 35.5% of the special regime's planned output.[30] The concentration of VPO subsidies for rented housing within the special regime suggests that rented housing is being treated for the first time as a more appropriate tenure for lower-income groups.

The costs of housing policy

Compared with the UK, Spain spends a smaller proportion of its GDP on support for housing, allowing for tax relief about 1% compared to 3%. The proportion fell slightly from 1.09% in 1987 to 0.98% in 1989 and 1990. However, in real terms, housing expenditure in Spain kept pace with inflation in the late 1980s and grew somewhat in 1990. In 1990 the total cost of housing policy was Ptas490000 million (about £2500 million). Then, only 43% was accounted for by direct government expenditure, almost half by tax concessions, but almost 10% was met by financial institutions, not by the government (Leal 1992: table 24). It is not surprising that the cost of housing policy in Spain should be relatively low, since there is hardly any social rented sector and no housing allowance system.

28. Interview with Baralides Alberdi, op. cit.
29. Information provided by Woolwich Europe Ltd.
30. Information provided by the Public Works Ministry.

Conclusion

The unusual features of Spanish housing policy are the focus of subsidies on owner occupied housing and the virtual absence of a social rented sector. Nevertheless, within this context, the pattern of housing policy in Spain has been similar to that followed by other European countries.

The imposition of rent control on the private rented sector occurred at roughly the same time as in other countries. Its rigidity in recent decades is more reminiscent of the UK than of other countries. The form of rent deregulation after 1985 was very similar to that followed by the UK from 1989, in that existing tenancies remained regulated, whereas new ones were deregulated. However, unlike most other countries (including the UK from 1989), Spain has not separated rent regulation from security of tenure, so has moved from the extensive regulation of both to the extensive deregulation of both.

Although subsidies were focused on the owner occupied sector, the same shift from producer to consumer subsidies occurred, as it has done elsewhere, but in Spain's case the producers were developers, as opposed to public sector landlords or housing agencies such as housing associations. As in other countries, this change in policy reflected changing concerns away from housing output to tackle crude housing shortages and towards equity issues in a climate of lower economic growth.

Perhaps the most striking similarity with the UK concerns the deregulation of the financial system in the 1980s and the coincidence of a house price boom. Certainly, deregulation in the UK and Spain was quicker and more extensive than in France and, particularly, Germany. But it is important to note differences as well as similarities in the experiences of Spain and the UK. Spain had the additional factor of inward investment in housing for speculative purposes, but the same direct connection between increased housing wealth and unsustainable consumer expenditure using equity withdrawal instruments has not been made in Spain. However, even without equity withdrawal instruments, one would expect increased wealth to contribute to a lowering of the personal savings ratio, which indeed fell from 5.2% in 1985 to 1.4% in 1988 (OECD 1991: 65–8). Although there have been some falls in nominal house prices in some parts of Spain, these have been much more limited than in the UK. Negative equity is not a problem, partly because loan to value ratios rarely exceed 80%.

The tax advantages of owner occupation remain substantial in Spain and there has been little attempt to limit mortgage interest tax relief, which is still available at the owner's own marginal tax rate. There appear to be no plans to reduce this subsidy, which is recognized to have a regressive impact on income distribution.

Like other countries, Spain faces many housing problems. Shanty towns have reappeared, now inhabited largely by gypsies and immigrants from North Africa.[31] The affordability problem remains acute, as is indicated by the age at

---

31. Interview with Baralides Alberdi, op. cit.

which young people leave the parental home. This rose throughout the 1980s, and in 1993 was almost 28.[32] Mortgage default has increased. Among mortgages made by private banks, default has risen from 2.5% of outstanding loans in 1988 to 6.8% by 1993.[33] Possessions by lenders are limited only by the lengthy foreclosure process. There is no provision for housing allowances, not even among the 20% of the workforce who are unemployed. Even the duration of unemployment benefits was reduced under the pressure of the Maastricht convergence criteria. It is questionable whether a housing policy that still concentrates subsidies on owner occupation can ever be sufficiently responsive to the needs of households with low or insecure incomes; but as Spain's neighbours find that they can no longer afford the large programmes of social rented housing they undertook after 1945, it is most unlikely that Spain can now create a significant social rented sector, even if its policy-makers wished to do so.

32. Letter from Jesus Leal, 5 January 1994.
33. Interview with Baralides Alberdi, op. cit.

CHAPTER 7

Housing policy in Sweden

Housing policy in Sweden has traditionally been more regulated and more interventionist than in the other countries in this book. In common with the other Scandinavian countries, the economy has been accustomed to a high taxation, high public expenditure regime, and this, together with other aspects of policy, owes much to the fact that for most of the past half century the Social Democratic Party has formed the government.

However, the present situation is one of change. In the 1980s there was a growing recognition that a major change in the direction of policy was necessary. Sweden's economic performance in the late 1980s and early 1990s has been disappointing, with low rates of growth and deteriorating public finances. At the time of writing, the government budget deficit was still larger than for any of the other countries in this book and plainly insupportable in the longer term (see Ch. 12). High taxation has increasingly been seen as having an adverse effect on incentives, on investment and on the country's competitive position. With freedom of capital movements, and particularly now that Sweden has become a member of the European Union, rates of taxation substantially out of line with those in other European countries will be increasingly difficult to sustain. However, any change involves reductions in public expenditure, including the containment or reduction in public finance for housing. These trends were given added impetus by the policies of the Centre/Right government, the so-called "Bourgeois Coalition", that held office from 1991 until the autumn of 1994 when a Social Democrat government returned to power.

However, although the policies followed have undoubtedly been expensive, they have given Sweden a high standard of housing provision. The nation is one of the best housed in Europe, with good space standards and very little unmodernized stock. Despite sustaining no wartime damage, there was a substantial housing shortage in Sweden in the post-war years. The stock, which was 2.1 million dwellings in 1945, had approximately doubled to 4 million by 1990. This means that, allowing for demolitions (which seem to have been extensive, as there is much redevelopment in Swedish towns), over 70% of the present stock, almost as much as in the Netherlands, has been built since the war (Lundqvist 1988b: 59; Boelhouwer & van der Heijden 1992: 246–7; Swärd 1993: 4). A large part of this increase is accounted for by the "one million programme",

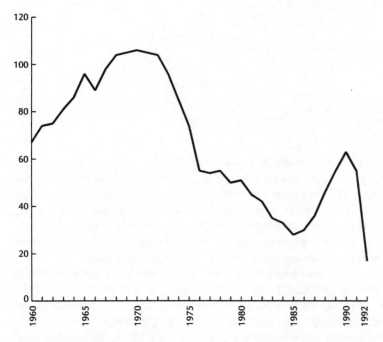

Figure 7.1 Housebuilding completions in Sweden.

which took place between 1965 and 1974. The number of dwellings completed peaked at 110000 in 1970 and then fell sharply to fewer than 30000 in the mid-1980s. Thereafter there was a recovery, before falling to the present very low level of fewer than 20000 a year (Fig. 7.1).

A major reason for this large housebuilding programme, apart from the post-war shortage, has been the movement of population from rural areas to the towns. Sweden industrialized later than the UK, and in 1945 there was still a substantial rural population dependent on agricultural activities. Rural housing was often of poor quality and lacking basic amenities. Much of it was built of wood, as else-where in Scandinavia. Today, despite the huge land area of the country, 80% of the population now live in urban areas (Boelhouwer & van der Heijden 1992: 233).

The share of home ownership in the total stock is fairly small, at 43% (Table 7.1) comparable in size to Germany and the Netherlands; there is an important co-operative/co-ownership sector, accounting for 16%; and the shares of public and private renting are 22% and 17% respectively. These shares have remained remarkably stable over the past twenty years. More than in any other country in this book, the division between detached housing, which comprised 46% of the stock in 1990 and multi-apartment dwellings (54%), corresponds with the divi-sion between owner occupation and various forms of renting. This is because in Sweden the law does not permit the sale of apartments into owner occupation (Lundqvist 1988a: 111–13; 1988b: 64).

119

Table 7.1   Housing tenure in Sweden (% of total stock).

	1975	1980	1985	1990
Owner occupation	39	42	42	43
"Tenant owner" co-operatives	14	16	16	16
Private rented	23	19	18	17
Municipal housing companies	20	20	21	22
Central and local government	4	3	2	1

Source: Statistisk Årsbok (1993), Swärd (1993), Lundqvist (1988a).

There is also, in consequence, a clear predominance of owner occupation in rural areas, where single houses are typical, comprising 95% of the stock, and of other tenures in urban areas where multi-apartment dwellings greatly exceed single houses. These features help to explain the success of co-operative housing in Sweden and in several of the other Scandinavian countries. This form of tenure, which is in effect a hybrid between owner occupation and renting, is an important feature of Sweden and it forms a fourth housing sector.

The changes in housing policy that are now taking place in the 1990s are largely driven, as already indicated, by the need to reduce the tax burden, in particular income tax. This tax, which is levied by both central and local government and therefore differs slightly from one local authority area to another, was at a combined top marginal rate of about 80% at one stage in the 1970s. It was still around 72%, depending on the area, until it was reduced in the major tax reform of 1991, which was the most radical restructuring of the Swedish tax system for many years (Ministry of Finance 1991). Now the maximum rate is around 50%, but the majority of taxpayers, whose income does not bring them into the higher tax bands, pay only the local income tax of 30%. A substantial part of the tax burden has been shifted to VAT; this tax was extended for the first time to some items that were previously exempt, rates were raised for other items that previously had low VAT rates, and the general rate was raised to 25%. But it has also been necessary to constrain public expenditure tightly and, as part of this, major changes in housing policy are taking place. There has already been a sharp reduction in fiscal relief for owner occupiers, and the further changes, which took effect from 1993, will not only cut by stages the very high cost of Swedish housing policy but shift the balance from virtually universal bricks and mortar subsidies to a much greater reliance on income-related housing allowances.

These changes mark something of a watershed in Swedish housing policy. The country will move away from a general housing subsidy, applicable to all tenures and under which almost all new construction and refurbishment was assisted by low interest loans, to a policy that is much more tightly targeted. But it is not intended to abandon the principles that have set Swedish housing policy apart from that of other countries. These are that the policy should be as far as possible tenure neutral, that housing costs should be approximately the same for comparable accommodation regardless of tenure, and that social segregation should be avoided.

The distinction between the social sector and the other sectors has therefore been less apparent than elsewhere, since all are subsidized more or less equally. Indeed, it may be argued either that Sweden has had no social sector or that all housing is in the social sector, since all sectors are treated in the same way. People of all levels of income move from one sector to another at different times in their lives. No means test is applied to any particular type of housing and even the publicly rented sector is open to everyone (Lundqvist 1988a). A major issue for Swedish housing policy in the years ahead is therefore whether the changes now being introduced will indeed be compatible with the retention of these principles.

In the sections that follow it was felt necessary to describe the policy as it existed up to the end of 1992 and also the changes that have been introduced since. Inevitably this makes the description rather cumbersome and perhaps confusing. But it is necessary to a proper understanding of the policy. The transition, which has now been embarked upon, is even more radical than that undertaken in the Netherlands and, although very different in purpose, may be compared with the UK in the years after 1979 under the Conservative government.

Owner occupation

Mortgage finance

Under the system that prevailed up to January 1993, all sectors of the housing market, including the owner occupied sector, have been entitled to loans at reduced rates of interest for new construction and rehabilitation. There was a cost limit, but almost all owner occupied housing was eligible, only a few extremely expensive dwellings being above the qualifying level. But applicants had to abide by certain rules. These included a requirement to seek alternative tenders, and the assistance was based on a system of controlled costs, which could fall some way below the actual costs of construction (Boelhouwer & van der Heijden 1992: 261).

For owner occupiers this low interest mortgage finance was combined with tax relief and this was taken account of in the attempt to achieve tenure neutrality. A purchaser of a new house took out a first mortgage for 40 years at fixed rates from a mortgage finance institution, the major lenders being the commercial banks, insurance companies, and the National Pension Fund. Mortgage bonds are widely used to finance such lending. This could cover up to 70% of the cost. The purchaser could then apply for a second mortgage covering up to 25% of cost, making 95% in all; originally this second mortgage was obtained directly from the State, but from 1985 onwards from SBAB (*Statens Bostadsfinansleringsaktiebolag*), a State-owned mortgage finance agency. The balance of 5% had to be found by the owner, as either cash or a loan at market rates. If the

121

cost of the house was above the maximum cost limit for a subsidized loan, an additional private sector loan could be taken out at market rates for the balance.

A successful application for the second mortgage entitled the borrower to a guaranteed pegged rate of interest of 4.9%, which was then applied to the first mortgage as well. The pegged interest rates then escalated by 0.5% a year until the level of market interest rates was reached. The State met the difference between this guaranteed rate and market rates, which of course varied but could be substantial. In some years, market rates for mortgages were as high as 15%, and for most of the period 1980–92 exceeded 12% (see Fig. 7.2). This system applied only to new house construction and to the costs of rehabilitation on older properties to which the availability of second mortgages was limited; and on rehabilitation the pegged interest rate was higher, 10% in the latest year. Both the pegged rate and the escalation were higher for owner occupied dwellings than for other tenures to take account of the benefit that owner occupiers derived from tax relief.

Both the pegged interest rate and the escalation arrangements could of course be adjusted by government at any time. In practice, changes to the pegged rate were infrequent in this sector, but the possibility of changes in the escalation could give rise to considerable uncertainty. The much greater stability of the pegged rates than market rates of interest resulted in a government subsidy that was not only substantial but fluctuating and open ended. No doubt the scale of subsidy eventually entailed by this system was unexpected when it started. In the early years, when market rates were low, the gap between the two rates was small and the system was probably intended more to give stability than a subsidy; but in the high interest climate of the 1980s the subsidy became very substantial and a heavy burden on public expenditure (Fig. 7.2).

The changes introduced in January 1993 were intended both to phase out the interest subsidy by stages and in the meantime to reduce the government's open-ended liability (Fig. 7.3). In place of a pegged interest rate on loans of 4.9% for new construction, which left the government to pay the whole balance between that rate and market rates, whatever they may be, the new system provided a subsidy for owner occupiers of 42.67% of market rates in 1993. This fell to 36% on new loans in 1994 and is thereafter reduced by 5.5% each year until the subsidy is eliminated altogether by the year 2000. The calculation of the subsidy is based on fixed production costs and the subsidy therefore will not rise if actual costs exceed this. This is expected to be a tighter system than the old one, which was based on "controlled" actual production costs; the consequence is therefore likely to be that a larger proportion of houses will have actual costs above those used for calculation of the subsidy. There is a ceiling on the payment of subsidy in relation to the size of dwelling. Above $35\,m^2$ the subsidy per square metre is reduced, and no subsidy is paid for building in excess of $120\,m^2$.

There are also changes in the mortgage arrangements. The distinction between first mortgages of 70% from private institutions and 25% State mortgages was abolished in 1992. All mortgages now have to be taken from private

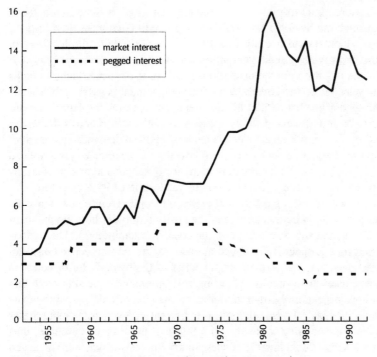

Figure 7.2 Market interest rate and pegged rate in Sweden.

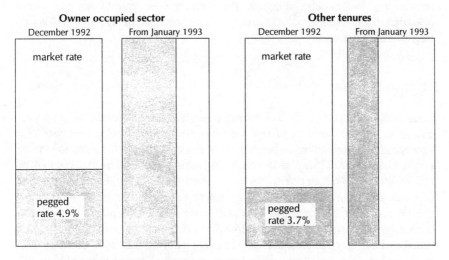

Figure 7.3 Interest rate subsidies in Sweden.

sector institutions, but, in place of the second mortgage, a State guarantee is available through the Swedish National Housing Credit Guarantee Board (BKN). This Board, which started operating in 1992, is responsible to the Ministry of Finance and it provides credit guarantees for all housing development; it is financed by fee income from the institutions to which it gives guarantees, and its debt is underwritten by the government. The arrangement is essentially a guarantee to the lender against default by his client, but requires the latter's creditworthiness to be fully assessed. In the event of default, BKN requires the lender to sell the property, and it takes over the lenders' right to demand repayment of losses from the client. For owner occupied housing the guarantees are provided for the last 25% of a loan, corresponding to the former second mortgage, thereby enabling the total mortgage to reach a loan to value ratio of 95% as before.

In Sweden there is a sharp distinction between the aid given to new construction, which is broadly tenure neutral, and the position of older housing that benefits from no interest subsidy, except on the costs of rehabilitation. The logic is that this assistance is specifically aimed at encouraging investment in construction and improvement, rather than simply relief to the owner. But of course a subsidy that reduces the cost of new housing will automatically feed through into the cost of housing generally, thereby reducing the cost of older housing below what it would otherwise be. In addition, it is normal in Sweden for a purchaser to take over an outstanding mortgage on a house at the time of purchase, thus preserving the terms, including the concessionary interest, which were arranged for the original sale. In this way, a mortgage attaches to a house, unlike the system in Britain; and the terms that provided an incentive for the original construction transfer to the new owner for whatever length of time the mortgage may still have to run. In this case, of course, the purchase price paid by the new owner may differ from the original cost and, if it is higher, a supplementary loan would be at commercial rates.

Taxation and fiscal relief

Deduction of mortgage interest payments against tax on income is allowable, but, as in Britain, the value of this relief has come down. The government have been steadily reducing the *proportion* of interest costs that may be applied for tax relief. First, in 1982 it was reduced to 50%, then in 1990 it was lowered to 40% and in 1991 to 30% (Lundqvist 1988b: 78; Papa 1992: 151). There is also a limit to which this figure applies: where the interest costs exceed SKr100000 (about £8300) *per taxpayer* in a family (SKr200000 for married couples) the applicable percentage comes down to 21%. Unlike the system in Britain this claimable percentage of mortgage interest cost may be deducted from the owner occupier's *tax liability* as a tax credit; it therefore has greater value than a comparable deduction from his *taxable income*. Apart from the changes that have reduced the value of mortgage interest tax relief, the pegged rate of interest on finance for new building and rehabilitation means that at present its greatest significance is for the purchaser of existing housing, on which the pegged rate of mortgage interest does not apply. However, as the subsidized loans are phased out, interest payments will become more substantial and tax relief will assume greater importance.

Other aspects of the fiscal system that apply to housing include VAT on new building at 25% and a national real estate tax at 1.5% of rateable value for houses and 2.5% for apartment buildings (rateable value being set at 75% of the estimated market price). Unlike most of the other countries, Sweden also levies capital gains tax on sales of all dwellings. This has been revised several times in recent years, but since the autumn of 1993 is levied on half the nominal gain at 30% (to be reduced to 25% in 1995) (Ministry of Finance 1991: 33–4; and information supplied by Kristina Swärd). This is defined as the sales price net of the acquisition price, with deductions for selling costs, estate agents fees etc., and with an allowance for value increasing refurbishment. On gains exceeding SKr50000 (£4160) there is roll-over exemption if the seller buys another house.[1] Prior to 1991 there was inflation adjustment of gains, but this no longer applies. The tax would appear to be the most severe of any capital gains tax on residential property in the six countries, since most of the others exempt at least main residences and some exempt housing altogether. The 1993 changes seem to have been intended to reduce the tax burden, compared with the regime that had existed since 1991 and on which there was no roll-over relief; but, even with its reintroduction, the tax may still discourage house movement if a change from ownership to renting is envisaged.

The Swedish housing market has, like the British, been subject to considerable fluctuations. Deregulation and the liberalization of credit in 1986 led to a boom, which saw production costs of new housing rise by 30% between 1987 and 1991. Thereafter, the financial sector was beset by difficulties. Combined with the government's policy of reducing subsidies to housing, this precipitated a slump, with the result that between 1990 and 1993 prices fell in real terms by 30%. Since the Swedish mortgage arrangements permit very high loan to value ratios, the result when prices fell was widespread negative equity. Turner estimates that in 1993 as many as 3% of home owners in Stockholm had negative equity, and 6.5% in the country as a whole (Turner 1993, Bengtsson 1994). Sweden has a high ratio of available housing to population, as has been seen in Chapter 2, and the years of subsidy, coupled with the 1980s boom, appear to have led to an over-provision that will take many years to absorb. This weakness of the market affects the other sectors, as well as owner occupation.

---

1. Roll-over exemption means that, if the proceeds are invested in a new property, the capital gain transfers with purchase, and tax liability is deferred until a property is sold without the proceeds being re-invested in housing.

Co-operative housing

Housing co-operatives or schemes for co-ownership have an important place in the housing market in Scandinavia, and the form varies between the countries. In Sweden the co-operative housing movement now accounts for 16% of the total housing stock, having increased rapidly from less than 5% in 1945. It is mainly, but not exclusively, confined to multi-apartment dwellings, where it is well suited to cope with the problems of common management and maintenance. No doubt the growth of the movement is strongly encouraged by the fact that owner occupation of flats in multi-apartment dwellings is not permissible under Swedish law, but the tenure also offers particular advantages. Although the form of co-operative varies, the predominant type can be seen as intermediate between owner occupation and rented accommodation.

The movement has its origins in the nineteenth century, but the number of co-operatives was very limited before the First World War. The first significant development was the formation of the Stockholm Tenant Housing Co-operative Association (SKB) in 1916, a "par-value" co-operative similar in form (but not in size) to such co-operatives in the UK. The co-operative members are tenants rather than owners. They cannot buy or sell their rights in the company, and any increased value in the company's assets remains within the company itself. SKB, which still exists, now has just over 6000 dwellings.

SKB is therefore very much larger than typical British co-operatives. It also differs in other respects. Members have to pay to join, although the fee which is equivalent to only a few pounds is extremely modest. They are also expected to put forward a loan to the society of SKr950 (about £90) to secure a place on the allocation list and a further loan when they are allocated an apartment. This typically amounts to SKr6000 (about £550) for a three-room apartment. This type of co-operative is popular in Sweden and is of interest as a form of tenants' co-operative, as opposed to the so-called "tenant/owner" co-operatives, which are the more general form and are described below. But SKB is at present the only one of its kind in Sweden. Its form conflicts with the provisions of the Co-operative Housing Act of the early 1970s and an explicit exception was made so that it could continue.

The dominant role in the Swedish co-operative movement is played by two large organizations, the Tenants' Savings Bank and Housing Association (HSB) formed in Stockholm in 1923 and expanded into a national organization in 1927, and *Riksbyggen*, which was founded in 1940 by trade unions in the construction industry. Essentially these are umbrella organizations to which local co-operative associations may be affiliated. There are about 9000 associations, altogether owning some 600000 apartments, and more than half of these dwellings were owned by societies affiliated to the two large national organizations. HSB is the larger of the two, having about 4000 associated societies, compared with *Riksbyggen's* 1900[2].

The rights of co-operative members are regulated under the Co-operative

Housing Act of 1972. This Act specifies that co-operative dwellings must be restricted by societies to members, and the societies themselves must be registered with the State Regional Board, which approves the financial plan of the society. A member who is granted a right to a dwelling must pay an initial fee to acquire a share in the co-operative.

Once the member has obtained the dwelling, there is full security of tenure without limit of time, so long as the member abides by the society's basic rules. If the member decides to leave, the right to occupy the dwelling is sold for the market price, as if it were a house in normal ownership; the purchaser then takes over the apartment and replaces the former member in the co-operative. For new buildings in the ownership of co-operatives that are municipally audited and not promoted by a developer, the initial fee is a minimum of 1% of the cost of the loan raised for the building and is therefore quite modest. For private co-operatives the minimum fee is 5%. However, it is open to the management of the co-operative to decide how much of the cost of a new building to finance by loan. They may decide to cover a significant part of the building cost in a cash payment raised from members, in which case their contribution will be substantially in excess of 1%. In deciding this, the management will be influenced by the cost of raising the loan and the burden of annual charges it would impose; they would also bear in mind the cost of finance to a member and the tax relief he or she would obtain.

For existing co-operative dwellings the price is determined by demand and supply in the market; and for locations that are in high demand, especially in cities, the price can be substantial. The co-operative member may, if desired, take out a loan to finance the entrance fee or the purchase of rights in an existing co-operative. The most natural source would be a bank house savings scheme, where a loan three times larger than the amount saved can normally be obtained. The right to the dwelling can be used as security for this loan and the member is entitled to claim tax relief on interest in the same way as on an owner occupier's mortgage. Since the price at which rights to a dwelling in an existing co-operative can be bought tends to be much higher than the entrance fee for a new one, there are substantial capital gains to be made by members, and these are subject to capital gains tax in the same way as the capital gains of owner occupiers.

In addition to the entrance fee, the co-operative member is also obliged to make regular payments to the society to cover repairs, maintenance, common services provided (such as water, electricity and heating), interest and repayment of loans and depreciation. These payments correspond to the rent paid by a tenant in a property that is let, and have tended to be rather less for comparable dwellings (Lundqvist 1988b: 71). This is partly, but it seems not wholly, accounted for by the co-operative members' obligation to meet the cost of repairs internal to the property, which in the case of rented accommodation would be met by the landlord and allowed for in setting rent payments.

2. For a fuller description of the co-operatives, see Clapham & Miller (1985: 28–30) and Lundqvist (1988a: 39–60). Latest figures (1994) supplied by Kristina Swärd.

Finance for new construction

Having agreed production costs with the Regional Housing Board, a co-operative society wishing to finance new construction raises loans on the amount, up to 99%, which is not covered by member fees. As with owner occupation, the system up to 1993 was that the first 70% of this was financed from a fixed interest long-term mortgage from a private sector institution, and the remaining 29% (compared with 25% for owner occupiers) from SBAB. This distinction is now abolished, with all mortgages coming from private sector institutions; and a State guarantee from BKN for the last 29% of the loan, corresponding to the former second mortgage, makes it possible to borrow up to 99% of funding requirements (compared with 95% for owner occupiers). The interest subsidy, which extends to both loans, is also more generous than for owner occupiers. In this case the pegged interest payment for loans on new construction was 3.7% in 1992 and on rehabilitation 5.1%, rising in both cases by 0.375% annually until market rates were reached. Under the system introduced in 1993 this pegged interest rate was replaced by a subsidy of 57% for 1993, reducing by 4% in 1994 and each subsequent year to 25% by the year 2000. It is then expected to remain at this level, rather than being phased out completely, to compensate for the benefit of mortgage interest tax relief to an owner occupier.

In return for the scale of subsidy they receive, most co-operative societies are subject to municipal control. This is exercised through municipal membership of society boards and auditors appointed by the municipalities. However, there are also private co-operatives not subject to these controls, and these have a somewhat less generous financial regime with the maximum mortgage, totalling 95% of cost and the minimum entrance fee the remaining 5% (Lundqvist 1988b).

Advantages of the Swedish co-operatives

For a British observer the Swedish co-operative system has two features of particular interest. First, it offers an efficient way of managing large blocks of multi-apartment housing. In Britain owner occupation is the only alternative to tenancy in these circumstances, but it gives rise to problems over provision of common services and expenditure on maintenance where several owners are involved. These have proved surmountable, with certain difficulties, in a typical Scottish tenement, where the owners of up to eight, or even ten, apartments share a common stairway and are jointly responsible for maintenance of the roof and other parts of the external fabric. But the difficulties are much greater in a multi-apartment tower. Undoubtedly, this has been an inhibiting factor in transferring such stock from the British local authority sector to owner occupation. The Swedish type of co-operative, which has many of the attributes of owner occupation, could be an interesting way of dealing with this. But it would work in Britain only if, as in Sweden, it were given fiscal incentives that enabled it to compete on equal terms with other tenures.

The second feature of interest is that, because the Swedish co-operative is a hybrid between the owner occupied and rented sectors, it combines some of the merits of both. Unlike co-operatives in Britain, which are in reality simply a form of housing association, the Swedish co-operatives involve an ownership stake and an investment, which is likely to appreciate with house values generally. This form of tenure is therefore quite distinct from the social rented sector, and it may provide a bridge between renting and ownership for those who want a stake in their house but are not able to assume the full burdens and obligations of owner occupation. This remains true, although over the years there seems to have been a tendency for co-operatives to become closer to owner occupation and less like renting. Up to 1969 resale of rights to a dwelling involved transferring the apartment back to the co-operative at a controlled price; but, since that time, rights have been sold on the open market at considerably higher prices. 1969 is therefore seen as something of a turning point, when the co-operative tenure shifted from a character that was closer to renting to one that was closer to ownership.

This balance also depends on the circumstances of the particular co-operative, in particular whether a new or existing building is involved, its location and its age. These factors are likely to affect the relative importance of the entrance fee, or the cost of buying the rights, and the annual payments to the society for interest, management and maintenance. In a new co-operative, where the entrance fee is low and the capital borrowed by the society substantial, annual charges are likely to be quite large, although held down by the interest rate subsidy. This may therefore seem more like renting. But many co-operatives now ask for a much larger cash-down entry fee than 1%, so as to reduce the amount that has to be borrowed and to keep annual charges down. In an older co-operative in a desirable location that has scarcity value, the cost of buying the rights may be high, more akin to the cost of home ownership, and the annual charge may be relatively small, especially if the original loan has been paid off.

Co-operatives are popular in Sweden, and the sector has grown rapidly to the point at which there are signs of oversupply. Although this growth must be in part because owner occupation is not permitted in multi-apartment housing, it is also greatly encouraged by the prospect of capital appreciation and the belief that rights in a co-operative are a good investment.

The private rented sector

Private renting used to be the dominant form of tenure in Swedish multi-apartment housing, but it has declined considerably since the Second World War. Rent control, which was introduced in 1942 and lasted until 1968, may well have been responsible for part of the decline; and, even after rent control was removed, the sector was subject to a managed rental regime, similar to the public housing companies described below. This managed regime lasted until the early 1990s. There have been sales from the sector into private co-operatives set up by the tenants themselves; but the decline of the sector might have been considerably faster if direct sales had been possible to sitting tenants or with vacant possession to owner occupiers. Although some new building has continued, the pace of new development has not been sufficient to prevent the sector from declining slowly in absolute number of dwellings, as well as relatively to other tenures.

Because of these trends, as in many other countries the private rented stock tends to be older than the stock in other tenures. More than 75% was built before 1950, and a large proportion dates from before the Second World War (Lundqvist 1988b: 103). Many of the landlords are private individuals, usually elderly and retired, owning small amounts of stock in tenements; but, at the other extreme, 1% of the landlords own 33% of all private rented dwellings.

Mortgage finance for private renting

The financial regime is similar to the tenures already described. Like them, private rented accommodation was formerly funded by a 70% first mortgage at a fixed rate from a private sector financial institution, and a second mortgage from the State agency SBAB up to 25%, making 95% in all. Under the new system this is replaced by a single private sector mortgage up to a maximum of 95%, backed by a State guarantee from BKN on the top 25% of loan, in the same way as for the other tenures. This is the same percentage as is available to a private housing co-operative and an owner occupier. Interest was formerly guaranteed at 3.7% on new construction and 5.1% on rehabilitation, rising by 0.375% a year until the market rate was reached. This was replaced in 1993 by a 57% mortgage subsidy, and with the percentage on new mortgages falling by 4% a year in each subsequent year to 25% by the year 2000, at which level it is expected to remain to preserve neutrality with the owner occupied sector. This is the same as for co-operative housing.

Taxation and allowances

Private landlords cannot claim mortgage tax relief, and they pay tax under the rules for business income, if the income exceeds SKr4000 (£330). But they are entitled to deduct expenses, including interest payments, depreciation and operating costs from pre-tax income. If this results in a negative net figure, landlords can deduct this from their other taxable income. Capital gains are treated as income from capital and taxed at 30%. As for other apartment dwellings, the real estate tax is 2.5% of rateable value, compared with 1.5% for owner occupied houses. In other respects the fiscal arrangements are the same as for owner occupiers.

Rent regulation

Rent paid by tenants is not now subject to control, the setting of rent and the annual increase being for negotiation between landlord and tenant. However, until the most recent changes introduced by the Coalition government, the market had been highly regulated. The Rent Negotiations Act gave the National Tenants' Association, and other recognized tenant bodies, a special role in negotiating rental levels with the public and private landlords' organizations. The intention was that public and private sector rents should be broadly in line for equivalent "use value". If a landlord gave notice of wanting to change a tenancy agreement, for example by increasing rent, the tenant could ask for the case to be heard by a Rent Tribunal. The Tribunal would determine a "fair rent" based on the level of municipal housing company rents for accommodation with equivalent use value in his locality. Appeals over what constituted a fair rent could be taken to the Housing Court.

This system, from which it may seem that the British fair rents were copied, was likely to entail a degree of conservative bias, especially in periods of inflation. It was not the intention of the system that rents should reflect any short-run market shortage, but instead be related to long-run equilibrium, a concept that is hard to define. Moreover, if rents were intended to be similar to those in the non-profit making public sector, it would not be surprising if they failed to provide the private investor with a return comparable to other forms of investment. On the other hand, in Sweden, unlike Britain, with subsidy concentrated on the cost of borrowing, the clear intention has always been that rents should fully cover the landlord's costs in running the housing business, whether a private or a public landlord. Furthermore, it was argued that, since the private sector stock is in general older than that of the public sector, rent levels that only covered costs in the latter could still yield a profit in the former.

Nevertheless, it does not seem surprising that the private rented sector has declined. The inadequacy of significant opportunity for profit and the highly regulated nature of the system can scarcely have made it attractive for the private landlord continue his or her role, when other opportunities for investment were available offering a potential return subject to no such constraint. In a free market, if the stock were comparable, one might expect private rents to settle at a level slightly above rents for dwellings owned by public non-profit making bodies. In fact, according to Lundqvist, the reverse seems to be the case, with private sector rents somewhere below those of the public rented sector but still above the annual payments of co-operative members (Lundqvist 1988b: 105). This may in part be accounted for by the respective age of the dwellings, but the system has clearly under-rewarded private landlords in comparison with alternative investment opportunities. Lundqvist found that the rate of return on owner capital, excluding capital appreciation, ranged between 0% and 2% between 1975 and 1982 and only rose to between 3% and 4% in 1983.

Under the new policy introduced by the "Bourgeois Coalition" government, it is possible that the decline in the private rented sector may be halted or even reversed. Private sector landlords are now freed from their public sector equivalents, and rents may be market determined instead of relating to the concept of "use value". Equally important is the pressure being exerted in the public sector, discussed below, which is both affecting the level of public sector rents and raising the possibility of privatization.

The public rented sector

As mentioned already, it is hardly appropriate in Sweden to speak of a social rented sector, since all housing sectors receive substantial subsidies with the aim of making them more affordable, and to a broadly similar degree. But there is a public rented sector, distinct from the private sector described above. This sector has grown from negligible proportions after the Second World War, when it accounted for only some 4% of the total stock, to 21% today. The public sector is dominated by Municipal Housing Companies, but in addition there are a few dwellings in the direct ownership of the State and municipalities, which have gradually diminished over the years and now account for only about 1% of total housing stock.

Municipal housing companies

The Municipal Housing Companies (MHCs), sometimes known as SABO companies from the association to which they belong (*Sveríges Allmännyttiga Bostedsföretag* or Swedish Association of Municipal Housing Companies), go back as far as 1935, but they grew particularly fast in the post-war period, when the State set objectives for housing standards and for costs, and wanted to secure appropriate management. Non-profit making companies were thought to be the best way of administering rented housing that was in receipt of substantial State subsidy, without running the risk of speculative profit at the taxpayer's expense. MHCs were therefore explicitly favoured by the Social Democrat government, and their growth has been encouraged, as has that of co-operatives.

There is no means test applied for tenants in MHC housing. This also accords with the Swedish policy of avoiding social segregation in housing. Allocation of tenants is either through the local authority housing exchanges or by the MHCs themselves, the latter being more common among the smaller MHCs. Criteria obviously vary with the size of MHC and the local circumstances. But need, rather than ability or lack of ability to pay, is seen as the guiding principle by most of the MHCs.

Throughout the 1950s and early 1960s, the MHCs accounted annually for at least 40% of new multi-apartment dwellings constructed. But during the "million dwelling programme" of the late 1960s and early 1970s, and even up to the early 1980s, the proportion was higher, rising as high as 68% at the peak (Lundqvist 1988b: 91). As in other countries, this massive programme created some problem estates; there have been some high vacancy rates and problems of vandalism. There is system building, which produces some unpopular house forms, and sometimes there is a lack of social amenities. But these are on a much lesser scale than in the UK or, indeed, most other European countries. Since 1980 the role of the MHCs in new construction has declined. Especially under the coalition government that was in office until 1994, opinion swung away from public enterprise in Sweden, as elsewhere, and there has been encouragement to tenants to form co-operatives to take over MHC housing.

In many respects, MHCs fulfil the role of housing associations in other countries and of local authorities in Britain. But their structure differs from both. There are 320 companies affiliated to SABO and about 400 in all. About 70% are organized as foundations, roughly equivalent to companies limited by guarantee, which have no shareholders; the remainder are normal companies, with the local authorities as shareholder. They operate on a non-profit making basis, and, as with many of the HLMs in France, they are set up on the initiative of local authorities. Unlike the HLMs, however, the local authority appoints the whole Board, which is given the same political balance as the Council itself. The MHCs vary greatly in size. At one extreme, the smallest has only 20, and the 75 smallest companies manage an average stock of fewer than 500; at the other extreme, the largest company has 50000 and the 14 largest companies manage 41% of the total stock, an average of more than 21000 (Lundqvist 1988b: 93; Lindecrona 1991: 3).

This system therefore involves much greater local authority involvement in direct housing provision than is to be found in any other country covered in this study, apart from the UK. But the system is much more arm's length than that of a British local authority housing department. MHCs are constituted as separate organizations, and they are intended to be financially viable, although in practice this has not always been the case and losses have been made good by grants from sponsoring local authorities. Although MHCs tend to 'be larger in the city areas, their size is not determined by the size of a local authority and there may be several companies operating in one local authority area. A degree of competition is therefore possible within the sector. In view of the extent of local authority involvement, it is striking to anyone accustomed to the public expenditure rules in Britain that the loans raised for investment from private institutions do not count as part of public expenditure, nor are they subject to government control.

Finance and rents

Finance for the MHCs follows the same pattern as for the other sectors. Under the old system they drew the same 70% first mortgage, but in contrast to the

133

other providers of housing they could obtain a 30% second mortgage, making 100% in all. (This compared with 99% for co-operatives and 95% for owner occupiers, private co-operatives and the private rented sector.) In 1992 interest was set at the same pegged rate as for co-operatives and the private rented sector, 3.7% for new build and 5.25 for rehabilitation, escalating by 0.375% per annum until the market rate was reached. Under the new 1993 system, they also received the same subsidy as the other two sectors, 57% of the market interest rate, which will be reduced annually for new borrowings by 4% to reach 25% by the year 2000.

Rents are determined mainly by negotiation between tenants' and landlords' associations, with recourse to the Rent Tribunal, which, in determining what is reasonable, has regard to the rents charged for other properties with similar "use value". Both the tenants' and MHCs' associations have issued guidance to encourage rent pooling, so that rents would be averaged in a way that set them above cost for older dwellings and below for new ones. However, this does not seem to have come fully into effect (Lundqvist 1988b: 70). Rents therefore still tend to be a function of the age of the dwelling, and rent averaging seems to have been abandoned for more recently built stock, where the levels charged have been high.

Despite the generous interest rate subsidies and the fact that rents tend to be higher than in the private rented sector, as well as exceeding the annual payments made by co-operative members, the public rented sector has sometimes had difficulty in covering its costs. The MHCs were in deficit throughout the years 1976–84, with particularly large losses in the early 1980s. In consequence, the State has provided subsidies to compensate for high levels of vacant stock and there have also been municipal grants to cover rent losses. State loans at market rates have been given to help with maintenance and repair in both the public and private sectors.

The future of the MHC sector

The role of the MHCs seems likely to be one of the aspects of housing policy that will undergo most change as a result of the measures introduced by the Coalition government. The freeze on local authority taxation in the early 1990s and the pressure on local authority finance generally has already resulted in a sharp reduction in direct support from authorities to the MHCs, with the result that rents have risen by about 50% over the three years to 1993. The companies are increasingly required to conform to the disciplines of the market, and whole or partial privatization is now a matter for consideration. If this were to occur, of course, it would involve a major change in board structure and in the influence local authorities could exercise over the companies. It holds out the probability that the distinction between those private landlords that are companies and some of the MHCs may gradually diminish, and that there could be a substantial transfer of stock from the public sector to the private sector.

These developments could leave Sweden in the position where housing allowances have to carry virtually the whole burden of enabling the less well off to afford an acceptable standard of housing. In future, not only may some of the MHCs become private sector landlords and give up their non-profit status, but those that remain in the public sector will, like the co-operative and private rented sectors, have their interest subsidies reduced to 25% by the year 2000. Although a shift from bricks and mortar subsidies to income support is typical of housing policy in almost all countries covered in this study, a continuing social sector is likely to remain a feature of the others. In Sweden it remains to be seen whether housing allowances will be able to provide sufficient support to maintain the wellbeing of the poorer sections of the community when the bricks and mortar subsidy is reduced.

Housing allowances

Personal housing allowances started in Sweden as early as the 1930s. They are paid to occupants in all house tenures, but hitherto they have been available under two separate schemes, one for the elderly and the other mainly for those with families. From 1991 the system was extended in connection with the major tax reform of that year and is now available to everyone with inadequate means. In May 1993, 27% of all households with children and a third of all pensioner households received an allowance (Papa 1992: 138; Petersson 1993; Westerlund 1994).

The allowance is related to income and family size as well as housing costs, and it consists of a fixed part and a variable part. Relevant housing costs include rent or mortgage interest, heating and running costs (water, sewerage, road and building maintenance, insurance and property tax), but the allowance is calculated on the basis that claimants must pay the initial or basic portion of housing costs themselves. It is therefore not intended to cover the whole costs, even for those on very low incomes or social security. For owner occupiers, account is taken of tax relief, and members of co-operatives may claim benefit to cover interest payments on their purchase of a right in a co-operative as well as their annual payments. Full allowance is paid up to an income of SKr91000 a year (£7600); thereafter it falls by 20% of the increase in income. There is a maximum level of income beyond which the allowance ceases to be payable, which depends on marital status and family size. Because of the gradual 20% taper, allowances come well up the income scale, but in 1992 about 30% of the allowances went to the 9% of households with lowest incomes and about 50% went to the lowest 19% (Petersson 1993: 6–7).

Expenditure on housing allowances more than doubled (at current prices) between 1980 and 1992, when they totalled SKr13800 million (£1200 million). The greater part of this is accounted for by allowances paid to the elderly, with less than half paid to families with children. The share of the expenditure paid to the elderly has also risen faster, by a multiple of approximately three times between 1980 and 1992, compared to a doubling for families with children. The scale of payments is, however, directly influenced by the level of social security and by housing subsidies received from other sources. The reduction in mortgage tax relief and the increases in rents of recent years will already be causing the payments of housing allowances to increase, and it can be expected that this trend will be strongly reinforced as interest subsidies are gradually phased out.

The costs of the policy

Swedish housing policy is expensive; and it is not surprising that successive governments of different political persuasions have concluded that the costs must be reduced. Table 7.2 shows that the costs in 1991 totalled about SKr56000 million (approximately £5300 million). This is more than a quarter of the cost of housing policy in the UK, although the UK's population is more than six and a half times that of Sweden. As a proportion of GDP, the cost is 4.1%, the highest percentage among the countries in this study.

Table 7.2 shows that interest subsidies account for about half the total cost for 1991, the latest year for which all items are available. In that year the remainder was split roughly equally between housing allowances and tax relief, although the cost of the latter had been substantially higher than housing allowances in earlier years. Interest subsidies have risen very much more since 1980 than either of the other two categories, reflecting the upward movement of market interest rates. From being the smallest of the three, accounting for less than a third of the total, they are now easily the largest.

Table 7.2 The cost of Swedish housing subsidies (SKr 000 million, current prices).

	1980	1985	1988	1990	1991	1992
Housing allowances	6.0	7.1	8.1	9.3	12.9	13.8
Interest subsidies	5.0	12.3	15.2	22.9	29.1	29.3
Tax relief for owner occupiers	7.9	13.0	16.5	16.2	13.9	na
Total costs	18.9	32.4	39.8	48.4	55.9	na
Property tax		−3.6	−6.0	−8.5	−15.6	na

Source: Swärd (1993).

The high cost of the policy is of course in part deliberate. Since the Second World War, successive governments have followed a non-discriminatory policy, with the aim of achieving a high standard of provision. In this objective they have succeeded. Swedish housing is generally of a high standard, better than in most if not all of the other countries covered in this study. The shortages that were evident in the post-war years have been eliminated and the amount of space per person is more generous than in other countries.

But there is also an element in these costs that was not originally intended. The rise in market interest rates has opened up a gap between these rates and the pegged interest rate on mortgages for new construction, which is certainly greater than was foreseen at the time the system was introduced, and the effect on the cost of housing policy has been dramatic. Similar considerations applied to the cost of mortgage tax relief, as not only Sweden but other countries have discovered, but at least with it the cost of higher market rates was not borne solely by the State.

Successive governments have moved to limit these costs, and the impact has been felt first on tax relief for owner occupiers and co-operative members, where the limits imposed have resulted in the cost falling (even in current prices) from its peak at the end of the 1980s to about SKr14000 million (£1200 million) in 1991. There have also been savings in the public sector as a result of the freeze on local authority tax rates, the restraint on expenditure and in consequence the sharply raised rents for MHC housing.

For the future, however, the great change will be the phased reduction of interest subsidies on new construction to zero in the owner occupied sector and 25% elsewhere. In time this will result in a higher cost for housing allowances; but since the latter are income related, which the former are not, substantial overall savings should result.

Conclusion

There is much about Swedish housing policy that is highly rational, notably the commitment to neutrality of support between the tenures and the availability across tenures of housing allowances. But it is not surprising that changes have now been made in the policy, particularly in the context of the pressures on public expenditure throughout Europe and the need to keep tax rates broadly in line with other countries.

The policy has been heavily focused on the encouragement of new housing investment and has had the character of a policy designed to overcome a housing shortage. Since this no longer applies, changes were overdue, quite apart from the financial considerations. But in view of the surplus of stock that now exists and the slow growth in demand that is forecast, the level of housebuilding activity for the rest of the century is expected to be at a lower level than at any time since the Second World War, and this will inevitably have serious implications for the construction industry.

A feature of Swedish policy that must be of particular interest to the other countries, including Britain, is the part played by the co-operatives. This form of co-ownership is much more fully developed in Scandinavia than elsewhere in Europe, although it has similarities to the condominiums in Germany. It could have attractions in Britain, as a means of introducing a substantial element of ownership into multi-apartment housing, while retaining the benefits of common management of the external fabric. In this way it could provide a solution for some local authority housing blocks, where full transfer to owner occupation raises difficulties and where the private rented sector, being so small, provides little alternative. But it is important to recognize that this sector is only as large as it is in Sweden because normal owner occupation of multi-apartment housing is not possible under Swedish law, and also because co-operatives are given comparable subsidies and fiscal incentives to other sectors.

A further distinctive aspect of Swedish housing policy is that there is no separately identifiable social sector, as there is in other countries, since all sectors have been supported in approximately equal degree. The substantial changes now introduced to reduce the cost of the policy are intended to retain the principle of tenure neutrality, which Sweden has pursued further than other countries. This has had beneficial effects in helping to avoid social segregation and producing a quality of housing overall that is better than in other countries. But the price is a high one, since support is much less targeted on those who really need it.

For the future, the changes now under way will have an impact on all housing sectors as reduction in interest rate subsidies cause the costs of borrowing for new construction to increase. It will take time for this to affect the market as a whole, but eventually it will raise the cost of existing dwellings as well.

The question that this raises is whether it will be possible for Sweden to continue without an explicit social sector. The official line is that the principle of tenure neutrality will not change, but that will mean putting more weight on the system of housing allowances, if the less well off are to be decently accommodated at a price they can afford. Although in principle this should be possible, in practice no other country covered in this study has so far found it possible to do without a social sector, although the debt/subsidy swap being considered in the Netherlands could in the end have something of the same effect (see Ch. 5). This is partly because housing allowances tend not to be sufficiently comprehensive to cater for everyone in need and partly because of the poverty trap problem they tend to create. It may also prove difficult politically to raise rents by so much for the less well off, although rents have already risen much faster than the consumer price index in recent years, not only in Sweden but in other countries.

It will therefore be interesting to see how this works out in Sweden. If in the end the present approach proves untenable, the likely outcome would be some kind of split in the MHC sector, with some of the companies being privatized and joining the private rented sector, and the rump being subsidized by local authorities to provide housing at lower rents. But that would destroy the principle of tenure neutrality, and the resistance to such a move is likely to be strong in a country that has prided itself on a policy designed to avoid social segregation in housing.

CHAPTER 8

Housing policy in Britain

Over the past half century the UK has faced broadly the same housing problems as other European countries. But the policies adopted have been substantially different. There has never been any attempt at tenure neutrality in policy; with the exception of Spain, rent control and rent regulation were tighter and lasted longer than elsewhere; the social rented sector has been dominated by direct local authority ownership; and governments, particularly since 1979, have given more encouragement than their counterparts in other countries to the growth of owner occupation. At the same time, policy has almost certainly been more ideologically driven and more contentious than elsewhere; and, whereas in other countries it has generally undergone a process of change by evolution, in Britain there has been a continual stream of major legislation and some abrupt changes in direction.[1]

Housing policy in the UK is a matter for central government, with only modest and diminishing scope for local authorities to vary its application. There is no equivalent to the position of the *Länder* in Germany, which can vary policy and introduce modifications. But neither does the UK have a completely unitary policy. Until the early 1970s, Northern Ireland had its own government and its own parliament. It still has its own legislation and the measures adopted differ considerably from the rest of the UK. The Northern Ireland situation is therefore not considered in this chapter. The position in Wales, on the other hand, although having some distinctive features, differs relatively little from England and it is therefore not given separate consideration in this chapter either. Scotland, however, although also without a separate legislature and administered by the Scottish Office (which is part of the UK's unitary system of government) has in most cases its own legislation enacted at Westminster. Although in general this is similar to the legislation for England and Wales, both the Scottish housing situation and the policy measures differ in some important respects from the rest of Great Britain and they provide some interesting points of comparison. Finally, although British local authorities have an executive role in the provision of social housing that is more direct than in the other European countries, their powers

---

1. For a description of the historical background to British policy, see A. E. Holmans (1987: 272), Malpas (1990) and Hills (1991)

are not constitutionally entrenched. They can therefore be made to act in accordance with the wishes of central government to a degree that would be difficult if not impossible elsewhere.

Britain emerged from the Second World War with a housing shortage on a scale similar to that of other countries, apart from Germany. Unlike France, there was no serious pre-war shortage, but during the War supply failed to keep pace with demand, as there had been very little new construction, and maintenance had been neglected; in addition, over 200000 dwellings had been destroyed and a further 250000 damaged to the point of being uninhabitable. This resulted in an overall shortage of some two million dwellings (A. E. Holmans 1987: 93). Furthermore, because of Britain's early urbanization, much of the building in cities and towns was old and seriously substandard. There was, therefore, an exceptionally large slum clearance problem, which added substantially to the construction effort required to make good the physical shortage. On the other hand, as was seen in Chapter 2, despite substantial immigration from former British overseas territories in the 1950s and 1960s, the proportionate population increase between 1945 and 1990 was only 16%, compared with over 40% in France, Germany and Spain, and over 60% in the Netherlands. And the fact that the population was already highly urbanized meant that the movement from the rural areas to the towns was much less important than in the other countries, particularly in France, Spain or Sweden.

The construction programme moved into its stride quickly, and the local authorities were given the principal role in new building for rent by both Labour and Conservative governments. The disappearance of material shortages, coupled with the ending of the post-war system of building licences, permitted the owner occupied sector to play an increasingly important part from the 1950s onwards. The peak levels of construction were achieved in the late 1960s, earlier than in France or Germany, but at a somewhat lower level, when for a few years over 400000 dwellings a year were built (see Fig. 8.1).

In Scotland, continuing net emigration to the rest of Britain and overseas resulted in a 1991 population that was actually slightly less than in 1945. It is remarkable that the housebuilding effort in Scotland has been greater than in Great Britain as a whole, 59% of the 1991 stock having been built since 1945, compared with 54%.[2] As with the rest of Britain, the housebuilding programme got under way more quickly and reached its peak earlier than in other countries. The reason for this substantial construction effort was the importance attached to slum clearance and particularly the notoriously poor housing conditions in Glasgow.

The result of this was that by the 1970s considerable progress had been made both in Scotland and in Great Britain as a whole. The crude housing shortage was eliminated, although some regional imbalances remained (Secretary of State for the Environment & Secretary of State for Wales 1977). Overcrowding and

---

2. Secretary of State for Scotland, *Scottish housing* Cmnd 6852 1977: 5; DOE et al. *Housing and construction statistics* 1994; *Scottish Office Statistical Bulletin, housing series* 1994.

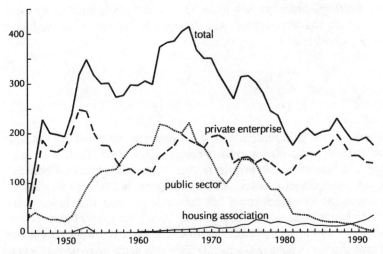

Figure 8.1 Annual completions in Great Britain, 1945–91 (*Source:* DoE, Scottish Office, Welsh Office, *Housing and construction statistics*).

the slum problem were largely overcome. The standard of housing was generally good in terms of space, and basic amenities were probably better than in many other European countries. Nevertheless, there was growing dissatisfaction with the policy: it was seen as expensive and not well targeted. The social sector was large and the low rents were thought to benefit many who did not need them. The rent levels contributed to the low level of maintenance undertaken by many local authorities, and, particularly in some of the large cities, the scale to which the operation had grown made effective management difficult (Grieve Report 1986). Novel building methods in the 1960s and early 1970s had given rise to structural problems in some estates, as they had done elsewhere in Europe; and, particularly in the Scottish climate, problems of damp penetration, combined with inadequate insulation and costly heating, led to very bad conditions that had adverse effects on health. As in some other parts of Europe, estates in the social rented sector were frequently on a very large scale, the peripheral estates of Glasgow being among the clearest examples. There was no mix of social class in such areas and they were often lacking social amenities. As unemployment rose with the closure of traditional industries, poverty and social problems, such as rising crime and the spread of drugs, contributed to an increasingly serious situation.

By 1979 a change of direction was certainly needed. The incoming Conservative government took the view that the local authority sector, which comprised the bulk of social rented housing, was too large. The new policies therefore aimed to increase owner occupation, to provide greater choice of landlord in the social rented sector, while diminishing the part played by local authorities as direct providers, and to revive the private rented sector (DoE 1987: 1, 3; Scottish Development Department 1987b: 1–5). The result was that new construction as a whole declined, mainly as a result of the sharp reduction in building by local authorities, which was already well past its peak, but the emphasis on house improvement was increased.

Tenure

A consequence of the policies followed is not only that the pattern of housing tenure has changed more than in other countries since 1979 (Table 8.1), but, despite some efforts to revive private renting, it remains polarized between owner occupation and social renting. In 1992, England had 67% of its stock in the owner occupied sector; the sector had increased by some 10% in ten years and was large by the standards of the European Union, exceptionally so if compared with other northern European countries. The share of owner occupation had also risen sharply in Scotland, which at 54% was much more normal by EU standards, but surprisingly different from the rest of Britain, considering that broadly the same policies had been followed. The social rented sector grew steadily up to the end of the 1970s, but the policies since 1979 have brought about both absolute and relative decline. At 23% in England, it is nevertheless still larger than in France or Germany; and in Scotland, at 40%, it is still exceptionally large, comparable only with the Netherlands. In both countries the private rented sector has been in long and steady decline, but there has been some modest recovery, especially in England, in the late 1980s and early 1990s. It is too soon to say whether this is more than a temporary phenomenon. At 10% in England and 6% in Scotland in 1992, it is smaller than in any of the other countries, even smaller than it was in Eastern Germany under Communist rule.

Table 8.1 Housing tenure in the UK.

	Owner occupied		Private rented		Housing assoc.		Local authority[a]	
	1981	1992	1981	1992	1981	1992	1981	1992
England	57.7	67.3	11.4	9.9	2.3	3.4	28.6	19.4
Scotland	35.6	53.6	10.1	6.4	1.7	3.1	52.6	36.9
Wales	61.8	71.4	9.7	7.9	1.0	2.7	27.5	18.1
Northern Ireland	53.1	67.0	7.9	3.8	0.4	1.7	38.6	27.5
United Kingdom	55.7	66.3	11.0	9.3	2.1	3.3	31.2	21.1
Total stock (UK)		15829		2228		790		5033

a. Includes New Town Corporations and SSHA/Scottish Homes.
Source: Housing and construction statistics, Scottish Office Statistical Bulletin: housing series.

As with the international comparisons in Chapter 2, the striking difference between Scotland and the rest of the UK cannot be ascribed to differences in living standards.[3] Scottish GDP per head is only very slightly below the UK average (see Fig. 2.1), is similar to Wales and is above the level in Northern Ireland. In part, the explanation is historical, relating to the priority given to slum clearance, especially in Glasgow, since much of the slum housing was privately rented and it was replaced by local authority housing. But it may be that the difference in dominant house form also offers some explanation. The tenement, a housing form largely absent in England, except in some parts of London, has always played a large part in Scottish cities, as it has in other European countries. Such dwellings, along with the more modern high-rise apartments that are also quite numerous, lend themselves much less readily to transfer into owner occupation than do the terrace houses that are the traditional house form in many English cities.

The owner occupied sector

The substantial size of the owner occupied sector owes nothing to the type of measures that have been principally used in other countries to assist less well off households into this form of house tenure. As other chapters show, most other countries have schemes for new housing offering concessionary low interest loans for households whose incomes fall below a particular level. France, Germany and Sweden also have housing allowances available to owner occupiers. Such measures do not apply in Britain.

Nevertheless, the situation in Britain has consistently favoured owner occupation. Rent control, security of tenure and lack of parity of fiscal treatment between owner occupation and renting have all contributed to boosting demand for the owner occupied sector. Houses or flats with vacant possession have in consequence fetched far higher prices than those that are sold tenanted. This has induced landlords to sell their dwellings throughout most of the past half century either to sitting tenants or, when they could get vacant possession, on the open market. In the 1980s a rather similar transfer has been taking place in the social rented sector as a result of deliberate government policy. The result was that those looking for accommodation found their options limited and people who in other countries would have chosen another tenure increasingly turned to owner occupation.

Finance for owner occupation

Owner occupation in Britain is greatly encouraged by the efficiency and simplicity of the arrangements for providing finance. The transaction cost of house

---

3. See also *Scottish Economic Bulletin* **49** (Summer 1994), where GDP figures for Scotland are given.

purchase is low by the standards of other European countries, and taxation on such transactions amounts only to VAT on conveyancing fees and stamp duty (Stephens 1993: 163; see Ch. 11 for a comparison of these costs between countries).

The building societies – mutual societies whose origins can be traced back to 1775 – still dominate the supply of finance for house purchase. They provide an extremely efficient and flexible mechanism for translating personal savings into loans for investment in housing. Their funds are based mainly on retail finance, although competition has brought about increasing use of wholesale finance in recent years. Originally priority in the provision of loans was given to depositors and, had tax incentives on savings been available as they are in Germany, the system might very easily have developed into a closed-circuit contract savings scheme, similar to that managed by the *Bausparkassen*.

However, the way in which the British market for housing finance has developed is completely different from the segregated and highly regulated German system. Before deregulation in the early 1980s, the building societies did have the housing finance field largely to themselves; and, although they were always in competition with the banks for retail deposits, the composite rate of tax to which they were then subject gave them an advantage in attracting funds. At that time, substantial mortgage lending by the banks was restricted by quantitative controls (known as the "corset"), and building societies operated a lending cartel that tried to keep interest rates down, with the result that queuing for funding was sometimes necessary. But since 1980, when the controls on bank lending were brought to an end, the commercial banks, the centralized lenders (many of which are subsidiaries of overseas banks) and some insurance companies all moved into the mortgage market. The banks now compete strongly against the traditional lenders.

In contrast to other countries, the system of variable rate mortgages became the dominant form of housing finance in Britain. There has been a sharply increased use of fixed rate mortgages for new lending in the special circumstances of the early 1990s, to the extent that they accounted for 60% of new borrowing in late 1993. This was in response to inflation and rates of interest on loans being lower than for many years; borrowers had also become alert to the dangers of variable rates as a result of the very high interest rates in 1990 and 1991. But such fixed rate loans are generally for much shorter periods than is common in other European countries. Although a fixed rate loan for ten years is possible, they carry much higher interest rates than loans fixed for shorter periods. Consequently, interest rates on the vast majority of fixed rate mortgages are reviewed after one, two or sometimes five years.

Fixed rate loans still comprise a small part of the outstanding housing debt and it remains to be seen whether they will remain an important part of new lending. So far, building societies have been able to use retail deposits to fund fixed rate mortgages through derivative instruments, principally interest rate swaps.[4] However, it may be necessary to make greater use of longer-term finance if the duration of fixed rate mortgages were to be lengthened, in which case banks are likely to have a competitive advantage over the building societies, because the latter have restricted access to wholesale funds.

Deregulation has not only brought about some important changes to the market, but increased competition has also speeded up the evolution of the institutions that was already taking place. The number of building societies has reduced from 2286 at the turn of the century to 87 in 1993, and some of those in the industry think it likely that the continuing process of amalgamation will lead to less than half this number by the year 2000.[5] The five largest societies hold 56% of the total assets, and the number of borrowers has risen steadily from 1.5 million in 1950 to 7.3 million in 1988. The Abbey National has since ceased to be a building society and has become a bank. At the time of writing, the outcome of a proposed take-over of the Cheltenham & Gloucester Building Society (C&G) by Lloyds Bank depends on a favourable vote by C&G's members in 1995 (see Ch. 10). Similarly, the proposed merger of the Halifax and Leeds Permanent building societies also requires the approval of its members, as will the proposed conversion of the successor society to bank status. Some others may follow these examples, although the continual easing of restrictions on building society activities, such as access to wholesale funds, is designed to make conversion less necessary.

An important consequence of the greatly heightened competition is that both societies and banks market their business intensively. As a result, in the absence of any statutory limit, business has been conducted on ratios of loan to property value that are much higher than previously and which in the boom of the late 1980s often reached 100% or even higher. This contrasts with the limits imposed either by statute or by decision of the institutions on loan to value ratios in some other countries in this study, notably France and Germany. It has been made possible by indemnity insurance covering the risks of the lending institutions and taken out by them rather than by the individual borrower. The risks inherent in such arrangements, both to borrowers and to the insurance companies, have become only too obvious with the onset of the recession and the fall in house prices that took place in the early 1990s.

Fiscal incentives

The most important incentives available to British owner occupiers are those relating to tax. These comprise mortgage interest tax relief, the absence of tax

---

4. "Derivative instruments" are products *derived* from standard products. In an interest rate swap, the lender raises funds by the normal means (e.g. from savers' deposits at variable rates), but then exchanges (hence *swaps*) the variable interest liability for a fixed interest liability with another party. This enables the lender to lend at fixed interest rates without risking making losses if interest rates on savings rise. It is normal for lenders to arrange for a swap on a certain amount of money before funds are lent at fixed rates. See Coles (1993).

5. Discussions by the authors with banks and building societies.

on imputed rent for owner occupiers (since the abolition of Schedule A income tax in 1963), and exemption from capital gains tax on an individual's main residence, although not on second homes or on any part of a principal residence used for business purposes. VAT is not levied on new construction, as it is in many other countries, although it is paid on alterations and repairs. The ending of property rates in Scotland in 1989 and in England and Wales in 1990, and their replacement by the community charge (poll tax), also removed another housing-related tax. This situation was restored with the new council tax introduced in April 1993, which is partially based on property values. Like its predecessors, the rate of tax is set by local authorities, but the new tax finances a lower proportion of local authority revenue than the old property rates. The average burden is therefore lower than it would have been had property rates continued.

Mortgage interest tax relief (MITR) is not a tax credit, as in some other countries, but it permits mortgage interest costs to be deducted from pre-tax income. Since the early 1970s, when MITR was available without restriction, the open-ended nature of the relief has been progressively reduced. First, in 1974 a ceiling of £25000 was set on the maximum mortgage sum on which interest could be deducted for tax relief. This was raised to £30000 in 1983, which was insufficient to compensate for inflation in the intervening years, and it has remained unaltered since (A. E. Holmans 1987: 272; Hills 1991b: 195). £25000 in 1974 would cover the greater part of the purchase price of all but the most expensive houses and would have been the equivalent of £119000 at 1991 prices; £30000 in 1983, if indexed, would be £57000 (HRH the Duke of Edinburgh 1991: 36). In 1993 the average house price was £59000 in Scotland, £65025 in the UK as a whole and £86818 in Greater London.[6] In 1988 MITR was further restricted by limiting the relief to £30000 *per dwelling*, thereby ending the arrangement where people owning mortgaged dwellings jointly, including unmarried couples (but not married couples), could each claim MITR on the same dwelling. The tax rates against which MITR could be claimed were also reduced: in 1992 to the basic 25% rate, and with effect from April 1994 to the lower 20% rate. A further reduction to 15% is to take effect from April 1995.

As a result of these changes and the large fall in interest rates, the cost of MITR has come down from £7700 million in 1990/1 to an estimated £4300 million in 1993/4 (Wilcox 1993: 165). However, it remains substantial and highly volatile, depending not only on activity in the housing market but on the prevailing levels of interest rates.

An important feature of the British system, which does not apply in France or Germany where the tax incentive is of limited duration, is the encouragement it gives to house owners to keep their mortgage borrowing up to the maximum allowed for MITR for as long as possible, even when they could afford to increase their personal equity. This has contributed to the use of mortgages backed by life assurance, in place of the normal annuity system. Whereas the latter results in

---

6. Halifax Building Society house price index.

the outstanding capital sum diminishing over time, the former involves payment of interest only, until the maturing insurance policy pays off the capital at the end of 25 years, or such other period as may be arranged. The additional tax relief that may be obtained in this way is of course substantial, but it has little to do with the objectives of housing policy. However, there has been some shift back to traditional repayment mortgages as public awareness of the disadvantages of endowment mortgages grows. The tax advantages are not now as great as they were and, if borrowers surrender policies before maturity, the value is comparatively low. The popularity of endowment mortgages may decline further as a result of the requirement for the value of commissions to be disclosed to customers from January 1995.

A factor that became increasingly important in the second half of the 1980s was the dramatic rise in equity withdrawal, from £540 million a year in 1980 to £21556 million in 1988 (Wilcox 1993: 26, table 2). This process enables house owners to increase their borrowing, usually as a result of moving house, to give them resources to spend on other things (the implications of equity withdrawal for the economy are discussed more fully in Ch. 12). A survey of 10000 households for the Joseph Rowntree Foundation found that two-thirds of those with mortgages in 1982 borrowed additional money in the period up to 1989. On average they borrowed an additional £10000 in 1991 prices, and 60% of this was not made necessary by higher housing costs but was equity withdrawal (HRH the Duke of Edinburgh 1991: 32). Clearly, where tax relief is obtained on such borrowing, it cannot be justified on the grounds of making housing more affordable or improving house conditions; indeed, tax relief will, at least in some measure, be capitalized into higher prices.

Grants to owner occupiers

Britain has no general scheme of low interest loans or grants to assist owner occupiers. In Scotland the central government housing agency, Scottish Homes, has powers to grant aid to both owner occupied and privately rented housing, but in the former case has mainly used them where such housing has formed part of a wider scheme of urban renewal. Other central government agencies concerned with economic regeneration likewise have powers to assist new construction or reconversion of existing buildings to provide owner occupied housing where it is part of a scheme of urban renewal and where, in consequence, importance is attached to attracting private investment.

In addition, schemes of low-cost home ownership (LCHO) and equity sharing have played a modest but useful part. These are normally offered by the housing associations, which provide dwellings for owner occupiers as well as tenants and can use Housing Association Grant (HAG) to subsidize their schemes. This grant, which is described in the section on social rented housing, is normally at a much lower rate than is applied to rented housing; and as a result of the maximum

147

limits now set on HAG by government as a percentage of total funding, there has been an incentive for associations to increase the element of LCHO in order to reduce average HAG rates. Local authorities are also encouraged to develop grant-aid schemes to assist those of their tenants who are in a position to purchase a house of their own in order to free rented accommodation for applicants on their waiting list. These schemes, although much more modest in scale, can be seen as the only British counterpart of the more general assistance to owner occupiers, sometimes called "social ownership", which is available in France, Germany and the Netherlands.

Of greater importance are the grants for house improvement that are administered by local authorities. Scottish Homes also has a power to provide such grants, but would not normally do so in circumstances where the responsibility properly falls to a local authority. The grants may be either mandatory (that is, the local authority has to provide them) or discretionary, depending on the work to be carried out. The former applies generally where the work involves installation of missing standard amenities or other work to bring the dwelling up to the English "fitness" standard or the "tolerable" standard in Scotland; they may also apply to expenditure on loft insulation to conserve energy or the removal of lead piping from domestic water supply.[7] Grants are also mandatory where a local authority has served notice for repair work to be carried out. For other repairs the availability of grant will depend on the attitude of the authority and the resources it has available. Rates of grant have varied between 50% and 90%, depending on the work to be undertaken, the date of the application, the kind of property and on whether it is in a designated Housing Action Area.

Legislation in 1989 reformed the system of improvement grants in England in ways that do not so far apply to Scotland. The most important change was the introduction of a means test, which has the effect of making grants available up to 100%, but depending upon the applicant's resources. The system resembles the arrangements for Housing Benefit, which are described below, and suffers from the same problems. It means that, in England, grants will not now be available except to those on limited incomes. The principle that has governed these grants in the past – that their purpose was to help ensure the maintenance of the nation's housing stock, regardless of the circumstances of the owner – has now been replaced by one that sees them as a form of aid to individuals of limited means.

Schemes to promote transfer of tenure

Since 1979 some incentives have been developed to encourage increased home ownership on the basis of transfer from the social rented sector. These include

---

7. The "fitness" standard is defined in the Housing Act 1985 and the Scottish "tolerable" standard in the Housing (Scotland) Act 1987.

Right to Buy (RTB), Rent to Mortgage (RTM), and various schemes for low-cost home ownership and equity sharing.

Before 1980, sales of publicly owned houses at a discount to sitting tenants occurred, but were at the discretion of the landlord and therefore limited in number. The change introduced by the 1980 Housing Act was that Right to Buy became a tenant's statutory right that landlords could not refuse. It applied to all housing owned by local authorities and New Towns and, in Scotland, by the Scottish Special Housing Association (a government agency) and its successor Scottish Homes, but only to those housing associations that were not registered as charities. Discounts on the estimated vacant possession price are substantial, but depend on the length of the tenancy. The minimum for houses is now 32%, rising to a maximum of 60% for those who have held the tenancy for 30 years, and a minimum of 44% rising to 70% for flats for those who have 15 years as tenants. However, discounts are restricted to prevent the net sales price falling below what has been spent on the building in the previous eight years, and there is a maximum discount of £50000 (Hills 1991b: 143).

Not surprisingly, this scheme has been popular. It amounts to a major transfer of wealth from the community to tenants and has had a significant effect on housing tenure. Since the scheme began, over 1.2 million houses have been transferred in England and some 220000 in Scotland, amounting to 23% and 21% of the 1979 publicly owned stock respectively.[8] The scheme has resulted in the transfer of some of the best local authority housing stock out of the social rented sector and has had much less success in problem areas or in high-rise and apartment blocks.

The Rent to Mortgage scheme started in Scotland, where it was operated at first on a non-statutory basis by Scottish Homes. Legislation has now extended the scheme to the whole of Great Britain, covering the same landlords as RTB. The scheme was intended to build upon the success of Right to Buy, by offering a stage by stage conversion of rental payments into mortgage for those tenants who could not afford outright purchase, even under RTB. Overall, the terms are less generous than RTB and, only 848 tenants in Scotland had taken it up by the end of 1993 (Scottish Office 1993b). With RTB offering such very attractive terms, perhaps relatively few of those unable to afford purchase by that route find that they are in a position to assume the financial burdens of ownership by the less generous but more gradual RTM route.

The trend in British house prices

In addition to the various policy measures to encourage it, the growth of home ownership in Britain, has owed much to a strongly held belief that ownership of

---

8. See DoE et al. (1994), *Housing and construction statistics,* and Scottish Office's *Statistical bulletin, housing series*, where the latest figures are regularly published.

a house is the best investment that can be made. This is because many people assume that, over the long term, house prices will rise at least as fast and probably faster than general inflation. In their view, it is better to pay mortgage interest on a loan of fixed capital value that results in the acquisition of an asset at diminishing real cost than to pay rent, probably at similar levels, but escalating over time and with no asset to show for it.

To some extent this may have been a self-fulfilling prophecy, as more and more people moving into home ownership encouraged prices to rise, particularly where there were supply constraints. Until the early 1990s, when house prices fell not only in real terms but for the first time for many years in nominal terms as well, this view seemed correct. Chapter 4 has already shown that experience in Germany was very different. There, as research by Holmans has shown, house prices did not rise in real terms by nearly as much as in Britain (0.4% a year over 17 years, compared with a long-term annual rate of 2.2% in Britain), and housing was not therefore seen as a particularly advantageous investment (A. E. Holmans 1991b: para. 16).

Problems arising from British policy for home ownership

British policy has undoubtedly been successful in promoting owner occupation. Yet by stimulating demand in such a general way, the tax reliefs are not only unnecessarily expensive for any housing policy objectives that can be defined but also to some degree self-frustrating, since some of the effect feeds through into higher house prices, with consequences for everyone, including those at the margin of owner occupation who most need help. In 1993, when MITR was already greatly reduced, this price effect was estimated at 4% after four years by the National Institute for Economic & Social Research (Westaway & Pain 1993: 16)

Fluctuations in the housing market occur in all countries and sometimes they are severe. But, following deregulation, the greatly increased competition among lenders resulted in some cases in the offer of funds at very high loan to value ratios. Combined with the government's general encouragement of home ownership, this gave encouragement to the housing boom and the rapid house price inflation of the late 1980s. When the government raised interest rates sharply to control inflation, the effect was severe, particularly on those with high mortgages, which were almost universally at variable rates. Rising unemployment with the onset of recession also made it difficult for those at the margin of affordability to meet their commitments. The result was 350000 householders in 1992 who were in mortgage arrears in excess of six months, 75000 repossessions in 1991 and 68000 in 1992, and an estimated 1.8 million who found themselves with houses that had fallen in value below their outstanding loan, the situation known as "negative equity" (Bank of England 1992, 1993; Dorling et al. 1992; Wilcox 1993: 104–5).

The problems that can be created by the housing market for macroeconomic management are dealt with in Chapter 12, but the British situation in the late 1980s and early 1990s would appear to illustrate them in an extreme form (Muellbauer 1990). The very high levels of equity withdrawal in the late 1980s, followed by negative equity, arrears and repossessions when the boom collapsed, had a major impact on consumers' expenditure and were therefore seriously destabilizing for the economy. Although different criticisms can be made of the operation of housing markets in France and Germany, owner occupation there is a lower percentage of the total stock, a substantial part of housing finance is provided by contract savings schemes and fixed rate mortgages, and the maximum loan to value ratios are well below 100%. They are therefore much less liable to distress caused by housing market volatility, nor does it have such damaging effects on the economy.

The private rented sector

Before the First World War the private rented sector accounted for some 90% of the housing stock in Britain. Since that time, the sector has undergone a process of virtually uninterrupted decline. In 1950 the sector was still the majority housing tenure, with just over half of the total stock; but by the early 1990s it had fallen to only 10% of the total stock in England and 6% in Scotland.

Decline of this sector is of course a feature of the housing situation in most European countries, Germany being the main exception. In large measure this has been inevitable, even where policies do not discriminate against it, because owner occupation has become easier to afford as incomes rose, systems of mortgage finance became more widespread, and the social rented sector has developed. But rent control and the absence of neutrality in fiscal treatment undoubtedly played a major part in the decline of the sector in Britain, as did slum clearance, since the bulk of slum housing was privately rented.

Rent control

Like France and Germany, Britain first adopted rent control as a temporary measure because of the exceptional circumstances of the First World War. In fact it continued in some form for the next 50 years, until it was partly replaced in the 1960s by a system of rent regulation. It was only in 1988 that this latter system was in turn replaced by a regime of market-related rents for new tenancies. Rent control in various guises has therefore bedevilled the market for private rented housing in Britain for the greater part of the present century. Particularly after the Second World War it was applied more rigidly and for longer than in France and Germany, and it produced all the classic effects associated with this form of intervention: deterioration of stock, bad landlord practices, misallocation, and continual transfer out of the sector as opportunity arose.

In the interwar period, the effects were not so very damaging, considerably less so than in France. Rents were raised by 40% in 1920, which, although not compensating fully, went a considerable way towards adjusting for wartime inflation. Thereafter, until 1933, the general price level in Britain fell gradually, thereby improving the position of the private landlord in real terms.

But the 1939 Rent Restriction Act, at the outbreak of the Second World War, froze rents at the levels then applying and extended the control to almost all unfurnished lettings. Unlike the situation in 1920, and despite a doubling of prices between 1939 and the early 1950s, there was no adjustment of rent levels for almost 20 years, until the Rent Act of 1957. This Act, which was the first attempt at decontrol, lifted restrictions on the top 10% of the stock, gave power to the government to extend decontrol by reducing the rateable value limit to which it applied, and provided for all rented dwellings to be eventually decontrolled, as regards both rent and security of tenure, when vacancy enabled them to be relet. In the meantime, controlled rents were raised substantially, to twice rateable value or about double 1939 rents. The effect of this reform was that by 1964 1.5 million dwellings were decontrolled, as compared with 1.8 million still subject to control (A. E. Holmans 1987: 412). However, the result was considerable hardship on the part of some tenants, and some notorious cases of harassment and exploitation. This led to widespread opposition to further decontrol, in both Parliament and the country at large. It may be argued that this reform failed for two reasons: first because decontrol and rent adjustment were carried out in the absence of a scheme of personal housing allowances, which, for example, existed in France from 1948 onwards, but did not generally extend to this sector in Britain until 1972; and, secondly, because the lifting of rent restrictions was coupled with loss of security of tenure in circumstances where there was still a shortage of supply.

The rent regulation system introduced by the Labour government in 1965, which formed the basis of the system in Britain until the reforms of the Thatcher government in the 1980s, restored security of tenure to the decontrolled dwellings and made them subject to a regime of "fair rents", while leaving the remaining controlled sector unaffected. Fair rents, which were set by Rent Officers, seem to have been in some respects a copy of the regime operating in Sweden, but the arrangements for rent setting were different. Rent Officers were required to set the rent at what the market level was estimated to be *in the absence of scarcity*. Disputed cases could be referred to Rent Assessment Committees. Inevitably this was difficult to interpret and it gave no incentive for supply to adjust to demand. Not surprisingly, rents were increasingly set on some kind of comparability basis, which imported a strong conservative bias into the system, especially in the inflationary conditions of the 1970s, and no effort was made, as it was in Germany, to try to correct for this. The extension in 1974 of security of tenure to the furnished sector, which was hitherto largely outside the scope of control, further reduced the attractions of being a private sector landlord.

152

Since its election in 1979, the Conservative government has repeatedly stressed the importance of the private rented sector and the contribution it expects it to make to the housing market. A start was made in 1980 with reforming the system in so far as it applied to new or renovated dwellings, when the new concepts of "assured" and "shorthold" tenancies (or "short assured" in Scotland) were introduced. The English and Scottish Housing Acts of 1988 extended this reform to all new lettings, apart from specified exceptions (DoE 1987: 9f; Scottish Development Department 1987b: 16f).

Under these arrangements landlords may choose between:

- letting on an assured tenancy basis, with rents freely negotiated between landlord and tenant, but with security of tenure protected; or
- letting on a short tenancy basis ("shorthold" or "short assured"), with no security beyond the period of the tenancy, but with the right of either party to seek determination of the rent in cases of difficulty by the Rent Assessment Committee.

To safeguard the interests of tenants and to make security of tenure meaningful under assured tenancies, tenants have the right to seek the help of the Rent Assessment Committee in determining the rent level on *renewal* of a tenancy, just as they may do initially for a short assured or shorthold tenancy. But in all cases the rent is intended to be a market rent rather than a "fair" rent. The provisions of the Rent Acts, which protect tenants from harassment, remain; and no change was made to existing tenancies, which would become subject to the new arrangements only on reletting.

This system at last gave Britain arrangements for rent setting that were reasonably fair as between tenant and landlord, and were not dissimilar from the arrangements applying in other European countries. The new regime could be expected to produce rents that approximate to free-market levels, but with safeguards for tenants, including security of tenure. The introduction of housing allowances for this sector in 1972, now known as Housing Benefit, also avoided the more serious cases of hardship that resulted from the attempt to decontrol in 1957.

Taxation and fiscal measures

The tax regime applied to private landlords puts them at a disadvantage compared not only with British owner occupiers but with their counterparts in the private rented sector in all of the other countries in this study, except Spain. Rented dwellings are subject to capital gains tax, from which owner occupiers are exempt for a principal residence, and from which rented dwellings are exempt or largely exempt in France, Germany and the Netherlands. Income from rents is taxed at the landlord's marginal tax rate, whereas owner occupiers have no tax on imputed rent. Landlords may deduct interest charges on loans and other expenses from their taxable income, but, unlike Germany, Sweden and the

Netherlands, this is restricted to their income from letting. Perhaps the most important omission, and the most anomalous, is the absence of any provision for depreciation. Depreciation allowances are available in Britain for investment in other productive assets, including commercial property, and in the other countries they are available on rented dwellings, with an accelerated rate of depreciation applying in Germany.

However, there is no VAT payable on rent, and council tax is the responsibility of tenants, falling to landlords only where rented dwellings are vacant or used for short holiday lets. For other aspects of taxation, the private rented sector is in the same position as owner occupation.

The difficulty of getting worthwhile benefit from tax relief on loan interest becomes more apparent when one considers the problems of using variable rate mortgages in the rented sector, the most common instrument for financing private housing in Britain. In the circumstances that have prevailed in recent years, short-term interest rates have varied widely, roughly between 5% and 15%. Even if rents rise over time, they remain relatively steady. With the variation in mortgage costs potentially so large in the face of revenue that has much less scope for adjustment, no landlord could afford the commercial risk of financing private rented accommodation with a high loan-to-value variable rate mortgage. Some form of long-term fixed interest funding is therefore necessary for the viability of the operation and if the tax benefit of interest relief is to be secured. Such funding was not attractive when inflation was high and has been unusual until very recently. Private renting has therefore only been a practicable proposition if a substantial part of the financing was done by equity. This excludes many individuals as potential landlords. And for those who could afford it, or for companies, the advantage of deducting interest charges from taxable income disappears with equity finance.

The only major fiscal incentive directed specifically at investment in this sector was the extension of the Business Expansion Scheme (BES) to rented housing from 1988 until its expiry in 1993. Individuals could invest up to £40000 a year in BES companies from pre-tax income and were free of capital gains tax on the proceeds if the investment was left in place for five years. The scheme had a significant impact in encouraging both refurbishment and new-build. Some £2100 million was invested during the period of the scheme, much of which was in furnished accommodation, frequently for students. But the costs in tax revenue forgone were high, amounting to about £20000–£30000 per dwelling. (The average price of all dwellings in the UK was £60800 in 1992.) And the structure of the scheme was designed more to encourage a short-term five-year investment for tax relief and capital gain, with many of the buildings being resold into owner occupation at the end of this time, than to provide the basis for a long-term revival of investment in the sector. Research showed that in the absence of the tax relief the investors would not have put their funds into rented accommodation at all (Crook et al. 1991b).

Grants

Britain has no general system of grants or subsidized loans to encourage investment in the private rented sector comparable with the schemes that operate in the other European countries. In Scotland, however, Scottish Homes has power under the 1988 Act to give grants to the private sector, both to landlords and to owner occupiers. So far, this has not been given very wide application, no doubt because of the limited resources in Scottish Homes' budget; and the grants, known as GRO-grants (Grants for Rent and Ownership) have been used mainly as leverage to attract private housing investment in areas where it is particularly needed, such as urban renewal areas. But the statute would permit the scheme to be developed in a more general way, like PLA or PLI in France, or the schemes in Germany and the Netherlands, if ministers so decided.

The introduction of a means test to house improvement grants in England and Wales under the 1989 Act weakens further the position of landlords (apart as yet from those in Scotland). This requires an assessment of the landlords' resources, which is likely to rule out all landlords except individuals of relatively slender means.

The social rented sector

It is in the social rented sector that the differences between British housing policy and that of other European countries are greatest. The landlord structure is substantially different, and the sector is large by comparison with the other countries, especially in Scotland. It has also been reducing steadily in size from its peak in the late 1970s. In this too it is unusual; only Western Germany (for rather special reasons) has had a similar decline in this sector.

Another feature of the sector in Britain, and one that goes some way towards explaining its size, is its early development. By 1939 1.18 million houses had been constructed, some 10.3% of the total stock. This was at least twice the size of the non-profit rented sector in Germany at this time, and in pre-war France the role of the sector was still minuscule (Hallett 1977: 65; Duclaud-Williams 1978; A. E. Holmans 1987: 169).[27]

It was also in the interwar period that the role of local authorities as direct providers of social housing became established. In the early 1920s, alternative solutions might well have been developed; and, in the context of the situation in Britain today, it is perhaps worth noting that it was mainly decisions taken by Conservative ministers that gave local authorities their pre-eminent role. The very widespread concern at the deplorable state of urban living conditions, especially the slums, which were mainly privately rented dwellings, was obviously a factor; and the democratically accountable local authorities, which were of course non-profit making and therefore not open to accusations of profiteering at tenants' or taxpayers' expense, were seen as suitable bodies to assume this role. They also had the advantage that, as tax-raising authorities, they could share the financial burden with central government.

The landlords

Today there are five types of social landlord in Britain: the local authorities, New Town corporations, housing associations and co-operatives, Housing Action Trusts in England, and Scottish Homes, which took over the stock of the former Scottish Special Housing Association, similarly an agency of central government in Scotland.[9]

Local authorities

The local authorities own housing stock directly and manage it through their housing departments. In this respect they are quite distinct from the municipal housing companies in Germany, the Netherlands or Sweden, which, although responsible to a local authority, are separate corporate entities. Since the reorganization of local government in the mid-1970s, responsibility has rested with district councils, the lower tier of local government, and in Scotland also with the three islands councils: Orkney, Shetland and the Western Isles, which are all-purpose unitary authorities. In the further reorganization now proposed by government, unitary councils will become the general rule in Scotland and the predominant form throughout Great Britain; these would be fewer in number and for the most part larger than existing Districts.

Districts vary greatly in size and they also differ in the proportion of their total stock that is social rented housing. In England the largest housing authority, the City of Birmingham, has 106900 dwellings, Manchester follows with 88000 and Leeds with 79000; at the other extreme 18 councils have now divested themselves entirely of their rented stock, several others have been left with only a remnant and, of the remainder, West Devon with 1600 is among the smallest. The average number for those still holding stock works out at 11413.[10] In England the proportion of stock in local authority ownership varies between 58% in the London Borough of Tower Hamlets and 2.8% in Christchurch. The proportion in Manchester is 38%. In Scotland, by far the largest housing authority is Glasgow District Council with 140000 dwellings, followed by Edinburgh with 38000; the two smallest, Skye & Lochalsh and Badenoch & Strathspey, have fewer than 1000 dwellings each. The average in Scotland is 12464.[11] The pro-

---

9. The institutional arrangements for the ownership of social rented housing are the aspect of housing policy that differs most in Northern Ireland from the rest of the UK. There, a central government agency – the Northern Ireland Housing Executive – owns 153000 dwellings, the bulk of the social rented stock, making it the largest housing landlord in the UK.
10. CIPFA, HRA Accounts Statistics.
11. *Scottish Office Statistical Bulletin*, Housing Series.

portion of the total stock of dwellings that local authorities own varies in Scotland from 82% in Monklands to 7% in Eastwood. In the cities of Glasgow and Edinburgh, the proportions are 48% and 21% respectively.

Although local authorities are still by a long way the dominant social landlords in Great Britain (Northern Ireland has no local authorities as landlords), their role has been sharply diminished since 1980 as a result of deliberate government policy. This has occurred mainly through stock transfer to tenants under Right to Buy, but also by transfers to housing associations, and by sales of stock to private developers and other landlords. This has resulted in the transfer of some 1.6 million dwellings in England between 1980 and 1992, of which 1.3 million were sold to tenants, including RTB, and 292 000 in Scotland, of which 282 000 were sold to tenants including RTB.[12] Where RTB has been exercised, the purchasers have generally been among the local authority's better-off tenants and, not surprisingly, there is a greater demand for houses than for flats, despite the potentially higher discount on the latter. Other transfers are more commonly at the lower end of the quality scale, either because dissatisfaction with quality of accommodation or service is a factor in encouraging tenants to want the stock transferred to an association or co-operative, or because local authorities themselves decide to part with what has for them been problem stock.

New Town Development Corporations

The New Town Development Corporations were set up in Britain in the 25 years or so after the Second World War. Their purpose was to provide new centres of development as part of the policy of relieving overcrowding in the cities. They were originally seen as part of urban redevelopment policy, but became important in the attraction of new economic growth as well. There were 20 in England (and 2 in Wales), but since 1979 they have been wound up. The five Scottish ones still exist, although they are also to be wound up in due course. The Corporations are agencies of central government, with nominated boards and a wide range of economic and physical development functions, including housing. As social housing landlords, they have operated in the same way as local authorities, although rents generally tended to be slightly higher. They have had rather less problem stock than the larger local authorities and also the reputation for providing a higher quality of service.

Over half of the Scottish New Towns' stock has been sold since 1980, mostly to tenants under Right to Buy, but in some cases also to housing associations. In 1993 this left the five Scottish New Towns with a total of 35 000 dwellings in their direct ownership, still a substantial amount of stock in the context of Scottish housing (Scottish Office, Annual Report 1993). But, since the New Town Corporations are to disappear, their landlord functions will come to an end and the future ownership of this stock is therefore an important issue. More tenants are expected to exercise RTB or to acquire stock through Rent to Mortgage; but

---

12. DOE and Scottish Office Annual Reports; *Housing and Construction Statistics*.

for the remainder the choice will lie between acquisition by housing associations, transfer to local authority ownership (which is an option less favoured by ministers), or Scottish Homes, which is by statute the landlord of last resort and will therefore automatically assume ownership if the other options are not exercised.

Housing associations

As in other countries, housing associations in Britain had their origins in the social conditions of the nineteenth century and in the setting up of charitable organizations to provide housing cheaply. By 1914 some 50000 houses had been built by them, mostly in London (A. E. Holmans 1987: 206; Harrison 1992). But in the interwar period, and especially after the Second World War, the movement did not develop as it did in other countries, because of the lead role that government gave to local authorities in the development of social rented housing.

The main legislative steps that have enabled housing associations to increase their role in British housing were the Housing Acts of 1964 and 1974. The former created the Housing Corporation, a public body sponsored by central government with responsibility to supervise the associations, with power to lend to them and through which, following the 1974 Act, grant aid was increasingly channelled. This was the first time that a comprehensive scheme had been provided by central government to enable associations to meet the generality of needs in the social sector at rents that were affordable, and it was therefore a key step in enabling the movement to expand. The way in which this central government support, known as Housing Association Grant (HAG), operated and the revised arrangements following the 1988 Act, are described below.

In 1992 there were 2300 registered housing associations in England and a further 249 in Scotland (Scottish Homes 1991/2; DOE Annual Report 1993). The former had a total stock of 679000 dwellings and the latter 67000, 3.4% and 3.1% respectively of the total stock. The average stock held by an association is therefore under 300 in both countries, a much smaller amount than in most other European countries. But associations vary greatly in their size and character. There are associations catering for special needs, such as the elderly and disabled, which operate across a large part of Britain, and also some large general-needs associations. At the other extreme, and especially in Scotland, there are many small community-based associations with a substantial amount of tenant involvement in management. The so-called "par value" co-operatives, which have been a form of association much favoured in Scotland by both government and local authorities, carry the community-based principle to its logical conclusion. In the co-operatives, all tenants are members and all members are tenants with a say in how the organization is run. A management committee is chosen from their number.

An important difference between these forms of association is in their accountability. All are non-profit making bodies without shareholders; but, whereas larger associations are accountable to a board that may seem at least as remote from tenants as a local authority, and in some cases more so, the smaller ones, especially co-operatives, require and generally achieve considerable tenant involvement in decision-making. There are many instances where this scope for self-help has been highly beneficial to tenants' morale, has resulted in the development of unexpected skills, and has contributed to more effective long-run maintenance of the property.

In both countries, the share of total stock, although still small, has ceased to be a guide to the importance of the sector, since associations have increasingly emerged as the Conservative government's preferred instrument for new social rented housing. They have therefore been favoured in the allocation of finance in the exceptionally tight financial climate of the 1980s and 1990s.[13]

In addition, there has been an increasing flow of stock transferred from local authorities to housing associations. Many community-based associations and co-operatives took over parts of local authority estates in Scotland; and in England 18 authorities, with the agreement of tenants expressed in a ballot, transferred their whole stock of 94000 dwellings to associations (DoE 1992: 3–4). The attraction of these transfers was both that they offered some financial advantages to the authorities from the sale, and that they gave the tenants the prospect that housing associations could more readily obtain resources for early upgrading of the stock. On this basis, such transfers might well accelerate, opening the possibility that housing associations could even emerge as the majority form of tenure in the social rented sector. In particular, if ministers permitted local authorities to retain an interest in the new landlords, by sponsoring them and appointing some of the board members, the misgivings of some authorities over such transfers would be likely to be considerably reduced.

But although transfer fits well with the government's approach to the sector, ministers are anxious to see greater diversity of ownership than occurred with the 18 authorities, where each authority transferred its stock to one association, usually set up for the purpose and comprising personnel of the former local authority housing department. Future arrangements are therefore likely to favour sale to a mix of landlords in an area, including existing associations. Concern in the Treasury at the financial implications of transfer, particularly the increased cost in Housing Benefit (which is explained below), and constraints on the budget of the Housing Corporation, have also caused a reappraisal. As a result, statutory controls have been introduced in England to restrict the number of transfers in any one year and to provide for a levy to be charged on the proceeds as a contribution to Housing Benefit costs.

Scottish Homes

Scottish Homes, a public body funded by the Secretary of State for Scotland and accountable to him, was set up under the Housing (Scotland) Act of 1988 to take

13. In the mid-1990s (at the time of writing), their programme of new construction exceeded that of local authorities in both countries (See DoE and Scottish Office Annual Reports, where financial allocations and construction programmes are given).

over the activities of the Housing Corporation in Scotland in respect of housing associations and of the Scottish Special Housing Association (SSHA), a direct landlord agency responsible to central government that had been in existence since 1938 (Begg 1987; Scottish Development Department 1987a). It has somewhat wider powers than either of its two predecessor bodies, including, as has been seen already, the ability to give grants to the private sector. Tai Cymru, a similar body, but lacking the former SSHA role, was set up at the same time in Wales to take over the activities of the Housing Corporation there. It is funded by and responsible to the Secretary of State for Wales.

SSHA was originally founded to supplement the efforts of Scottish local authorities in the provision of public sector rented housing. Its nearest counterpart in the other countries was probably SCIC in France (see Ch. 3), although that body was not a direct agency of central government. SSHA operated throughout Scotland, tending to concentrate on meeting housing needs for incoming industry, for example as a result of the development of North Sea oil, and on urban renewal. In some cases, by mutual agreement, it took over local authority stock. SSHA houses were generally very similar to those of local authorities, although rents tended to be slightly higher, and the Association endeavoured to set an example in effective management.

Under Scottish Homes this tradition has continued, but, in line with the government's policy for local authorities, there has been very little new building. Right to Buy has been encouraged and some 36000 dwellings had been sold to tenants up to 1992; some stock has been transferred to other landlords, including housing associations and a private non-profit making trust, and the government's intention is that eventually Scottish Homes' stock should be sold off completely. However, since the Secretary of State has made it plain that transfers will take place only if they are approved by a majority of tenants voting in a ballot, it is by no means clear that Scottish Homes will be able to divest themselves of the whole of their stock, which in 1993 still amounted to 59000 dwellings (Scottish Office, *Statistical Bulletin, housing series* 1994). In any event, whether or not Scottish Homes retains a direct landlord function, it will remain responsible for funding, regulating and promoting housing associations in Scotland.

Housing Action Trusts

The 1988 Housing Act made provision for Housing Action Trusts (HATS) to be set up in England to take over sections of council housing stock designated by the Secretary of State as being in exceptional need of renovation and beyond the capacity of local authorities to handle. The scheme was not a success initially, since it failed to get the necessary support of tenants to enable HATS to come into being. By 1993, however, with the support of tenants and the agreement of local authorities two schemes, at Hull and Waltham Forest (London), had come into existence and a further four were in preparation in Birmingham, Brent, Liverpool and Tower Hamlets (DOE *Annual report* 1992).

The main attraction for tenants in these arrangements is not simply the change of management, although that could be important, but the expectation that more funds for renovation will be available than under continuing local authority ownership. This could give rise to major demands on public expenditure, as well as difficult problems of management. In 1993, for example, Liverpool was proposing to transfer 68 of its 72 high-rise blocks throughout the city to the new HAT. Whether this will prove acceptable when the potential rehabilitation cost to government is assessed, and whether the HATS can make a better job of running these difficult estates, remains to be seen.

The government has not taken powers to set up HATS in Scotland, and Scottish ministers have so far followed the principle that schemes for the recovery of particularly difficult problem estates are better done with the co-operation of local authorities than by trying to force transfer to a new body. This is the philosophy underlying the many initiatives for urban renewal in Scotland. In particular it has been applied to four Urban Renewal Partnerships set up by the Secretary of State for Scotland involving the participation of central government officials, local authorities and other public agencies, including Scottish Homes. The purpose of these partnerships is to bring about economic and physical regeneration in four particularly disadvantaged housing estates in Glasgow, Edinburgh, Dundee and Paisley (Scottish Office 1988). However, transfers of stock by agreement can be made to Scottish Homes, as was done with part of the Glasgow Castlemilk estate, one of the four partnership areas; and this is a course that, although not used since 1988, remains open, if ministers, local authorities and tenants see advantages in it.

The financing of social housing

The financial arrangements for social rented housing in Britain differ fundamentally from those used in other countries, both as regards revenue and capital expenditure. There is also a major difference between the two major providers, local authorities and housing associations, which are supported under completely different systems and legislation. The key distinction is that local authorities are subject to direct control of capital expenditure, but receive no capital subsidy, assistance taking the form of a recurrent revenue grant. On the other hand, housing associations receive a capital grant but no direct revenue support.

Capital expenditure: local authorities
Because all the British social housing landlords (apart from housing associations) are public sector bodies, their expenditure is treated as falling within the total that goes to make up government public expenditure. Local authority borrowing to finance housing investment is therefore subject to central government control, and particularly over the past 15 years, when vigorous efforts were made by government to cut public expenditure, this control has been very tightly imposed (Malpass & Murie 1990: 83–6; Hills 1991b: 80–81). In so far as other items of

161

public expenditure unavoidably increase, such as health or social security, the pressure to reduce housing capital expenditure therefore becomes all the more intense.

The mechanism by which this control has been exercised in England and Wales since 1977 is the Housing Investment Programme (HIP). Individual authorities make bids to the Department of the Environment, reflecting their assessment of the need for housing investment, and, in the light of this and its own assessments, the Department sets "credit approvals" for each authority. This determines the amount they are permitted to borrow in any one year. Since 1990, these approvals have been set to take into account each authority's anticipated receipts from sales of housing and the proportion of them that may be spent on new investment.

These receipts have, of course, made government control of local authority capital spending more complex. They arise from Right to Buy (RTB) and other sales, including large-scale voluntary transfers (LSVT), all of which have been encouraged since 1980 and which have generated a total of £27000 million in Great Britain as a whole, far more than any of the other privatization programmes (Wilcox et al. 1993b: 8–9). Once again there is a substantial difference between the way in which this has been handled in England and Wales and in Scotland.

In England and Wales an authority can spend only a proportion of its receipts on new capital investment. In the past this led to a considerable accumulation of the unused portion of receipts, but since 1990 the proportion of receipts that may be spent in any one year is 25%, and the remaining 75% has to be used to redeem outstanding debt, either on housing or, if that is paid off, on the local authority general funds. However, where bulk transfers are involved, there may also be a restraint on the rate at which new housing expenditure funded from the 25% may be undertaken.

In Scotland the system has been simpler from the start. In determining the capital allocations for individual authorities over the coming year, the Scottish Office Environment Department estimates not only the likely level of receipts in aggregate but also the receipts that each authority may be expected to generate, based largely on its past record. Authorities then get an allocation that consists of two elements: anticipated receipts and consent for new borrowing. The total allocation will vary, depending not on the receipts but on the Scottish Office assessment of each authority's needs, taking account of such factors as age and condition of stock (including the amount of high-rise, "below tolerable standard" and other problematic stock), demographic trends, vacancies, homelessness, and so on. In some cases the consent for new borrowing may be the major part of the allocation, in others it may be very small, and in the extreme case negative, implying a requirement to pay off outstanding housing debt with part of the receipts. Except in this extreme case, which has arisen in only a few instances, this system has never prevented authorities from spending all of their receipts on new housing investment; and it has avoided the accumulation of past receipts that arose in England prior to 1990. Furthermore, since authorities can spend directly any additional receipts they raise over and above the Scottish Office estimate (so long as it is undertaken within the same financial year), they are encouraged to generate the maximum revenue from increased sales.

Before leaving local authority capital expenditure, it is necessary to comment briefly on the prices at which RTB and LSVT are conducted. On one view, these are asset strips at the expense of the authority concerned or the community it represents. RTB sales are obligatory, if the tenant wants to buy, and are conducted at large discounts on their vacant possession value: up to 60% for houses and 70% for flats. LSVTs, on the other hand, are at the landlord's discretion, but where the dwellings are tenanted they may be sold at even lower prices, usually based on the District Valuers' valuation. In most other countries in this study, a policy of compulsory sales forced on social landlords by central government would be constitutionally *ultra vires*;[14] but social landlords in other countries can sell stock to other owners, if they themselves choose to do so, and in most circumstances the tenanted value at social rents would fall below the unrestricted vacant possession price. In Britain it should be noted that the sale of such a large amount of social rented stock has probably been financially manageable only because inflation in the 1970s and early 1980s had so eroded the outstanding loan debt. Under the English system since 1990, although local authorities may retain 25% of receipts, the remainder is used to pay off debt, and in most cases, even at these low prices from RTB and LSVT, it will do so, largely if not completely. In Scotland, where authorities retain their receipts for new housing expenditure, they also indirectly reduce debt, even when the proceeds are not set aside to pay it off, because the need for new capital funding is reduced.

As to the prices at which the sales and transfers are conducted, it has to be borne in mind that, although these are substantially below vacant-possession prices, the houses and flats are not sold with vacant possession. What they are worth to a landlord can be considered to be the discounted flow of income they would produce, less management and maintenance costs, if they remained as social rented housing. The RTB price, including discounts, will in most cases exceed the discounted value of income foregone by the local authority; and it is approximately on this latter basis that the District Valuers determine an acceptable LSVT price, although where there is competition from several interested parties the final price may be above the minimum acceptable to the Valuer. However, this price depends on what the rent happens to be, the terms agreed for rent levels in future and the condition of the houses, with an estimate for the cost of their refurbishment. It is normally a condition of sale that it is not open to the landlord to re-sell the houses with vacant possession, even at some future date.

The process should be neutral in the short term, so far as housing shortage is concerned, since the tenants transfer into the new tenure with the houses. In the longer term, the consequences may be more serious, if funds that might have been spent on new housing investment are used to purchase existing public sector

---

14. *Ultra vires*: beyond their powers.

stock. But regardless of the effect on housing supply, such sales and transfers are very unwelcome to some local authorities. This is particularly the case with RTB, which tends to result in the authority losing its best stock, and because even if the stock is sold for more than discounted future income, it is still less than its replacement cost. A serious issue with LSVT, and one that seems so far to have been inadequately addressed, is that the sale price will tend to perpetuate any anomaly that may have existed in the rent level. It is not uncommon to find two authorities side by side, one with rent levels some 50% or more above the other, for housing that is approximately identical. On the assumption (frequently made in such transactions) that future rents will start from whatever the level happened to be under local authority ownership, however anomalous, and will then be permitted to rise by inflation plus 1%, this will translate into very different transfer-price levels for the authorities concerned. Even if new lets are on a more market-related basis than for existing tenants, they are still likely to be affected by existing rent levels, and the turnover will be slow. Anomalies may therefore be perpetuated for a very long time.

Revenue expenditure, subsidies and rents: local authorities

The arrangements for assisting local authorities' revenue or current expenditure have been revised repeatedly over the years. Originally, local authority housing started with a fixed subsidy, made up of contributions both from central government and the local authority rate fund. The amounts provided by central government were laid down by statute, but in the 1960s rising inflation made these fixed amounts no longer tenable. The arrangement was then changed to the equivalent of a pegged rate of interest, charged at 4% on borrowing, with the difference between that rate and market rates met by subsidy. This arrangement had similarities to the system that operated until recently in Sweden (Ch. 7).

In the 1980s, Conservative governments were clearly unwilling to contemplate any form of open-ended arrangement and also took the view that local authority rents, which had not kept pace with inflation in the 1970s, were too low. A system was therefore adopted that involved government setting a guideline to determine the amount by which it was considered reasonable for rents to rise, taking account of estimated expenditure on management and maintenance. Housing subsidy was then provided accordingly and, although local authorities might not put up rents by precisely the amount estimated by government, they had little choice but to raise the level of rents very sharply, well above the rate of inflation, especially in the first half of the 1980s (Table 8.2).

As a result, Housing Subsidy (England) and Housing Support Grant (Scotland) both fell, and expenditure on personal housing allowances sharply increased. The combined effect of higher rents, the inflation that had eroded outstanding housing debt, and the constraints on new capital spending made it unnecessary for the majority of authorities to continue to receive direct revenue subsidy. By 1990, less than a third of housing authorities in England, and less than half in Scotland, were receiving housing subsidy.

Table 8.2 English and Scottish local authority rents (£ per week).

	1980	1981	1982	1983	1984	1985	1986	1987	1988	1989	1990	1991	1992
England [1]													
Rent	7.71	11.43	13.52	14.05	14.75	15.63	16.45	17.24	18.88	20.76	23.79	27.26	30.65
as % male arnings	6.9	9.4	10.1	9.8	9.7	9.5	9.4	9.3	7.9	9.5	10.0	10.7	11.4
Rent at 1992 prices	15.7	21.2	23.4	23.1	23.0	23.6	23.7	23.6	24.2	24.8	26.2	29.5	30.7
Scotland													
Rent	5.88	7.69	9.01	9.86	10.47	11.53	12.99	14.59	16.29	18.76	20.91	23.13	24.4
% of male earnings	5.3	6.1	6.6	6.8	6.7	7.0	7.5	8.1	8.4	8.4	9.0	9.2	9.1
Rent at 1992 prices	12.0	14.2	15.6	16.2	16.4	17.1	18.7	20.0	21.0	22.4	23.1	25.0	24.4

Note: Rent at 1992 prices adjusted by GDP deflator.
Source: Wilcox (1993).

Many housing authorities in both England and Scotland sought to reduce the impact on rents of falling subsidy from central government by increasing the support from their general funds to their Housing Revenue Account (HRA). In effect, this transferred some of the burden of housing subsidy from the taxpayer to the ratepayer. This practice conflicted with the government's objective of pushing rents up and it was ended in Scotland in 1984, when the government exerted pressure on local authorities to control rate fund contributions (RFCs) prior to legislating. It continued in England for longer, until such transfers were stopped by the Local Government and Housing Act of 1989.

The 1989 Act did not apply in Scotland, and another of its provisions marks an important difference between present practice in the two countries. The government's power to push up rents by reducing housing subsidy was lost for all those authorities where subsidy was no longer received, but the cost of support was still very high, as a result of increased expenditure on personal housing allowances (Housing Benefit). The 1989 Act therefore amalgamated the central government payments to local authorities for Housing Subsidy and Housing Benefit into a single contribution to the HRA. Under the new arrangements, authorities are not reimbursed for the full cost of increased Housing Benefit payments, and apart from drawing on any HRA surplus the effect is to force authorities to put up rents to cover the remainder. The effect of this can only be described as vicious. Since some 60% of tenants are on Housing Benefit, this has resulted in relatively few rent-paying tenants (most of whom are of very modest means) being made to meet the housing costs of the pensioner and the unemployed in place of the general taxpayer. In some cases, the effect of the rent increase will be to bring back into the poverty trap those who had escaped from it. This arrangement does not apply to housing associations (or so far in Scotland), where the full Housing Benefit costs are still met by the Department of Social Security.

However, it is important to recognize that, even where bricks and mortar subsidy has been reduced to zero (as it has for the majority of authorities), this does not mean that rents are either at free-market levels or at an economic level in the sense of covering maintenance and replacement costs. Free-market rents depend on local market conditions and, in the short term, need not bear much relation to costs. They would generally be higher, but in some cases, where housing is particularly unattractive and in hard-to-let areas, may even be lower than the social rents charged. Rents based on a replacement cost are likely to exceed the actual unsubsidized rents, because in most cases, as a result of inflation, it is possible to cover interest charges, as well as management and maintenance, with rent levels well below their level in real terms had no inflation occurred.

Nor is the effect of this is evenly spread. Another consequence of inflation is that the outstanding loan debt per dwelling varies greatly from one housing authority to another, depending not so much on the quality or present value of the housing stock as on when it was built or subject to capital expenditure on refurbishment. Thus, although the average outstanding debt per dwelling in Scotland is £5600, in some authorities it is under £3000, and in the Shetland Islands, where construction costs are exceptionally high and there was a large programme of construction in the 1970s to cater for North Sea oil developments, it is as high as £21 800 (*Scottish Office Statistical Bulletin, Housing Series* 1994). Whether or not housing authorities still receive housing subsidy therefore depends to a considerable degree on the age of the stock and the amount of loan debt outstanding per house; and these factors also go far to explain the differences in rent levels between authorities.

Rent pooling has been used by British housing authorities since 1935, but has been the norm since the mid-1950s, when it was encouraged by government as a way of reducing the amount of subsidy required (Malpass 1990). Here again, there is a sharp difference between Britain and Continental countries, especially France and Germany, where the way in which loans are contracted to a particular development at agreed rent levels largely prevents pooling. In Britain, as a result of the inflation since the early 1960s, a non-pooling system would mean large differences in rent levels, depending more on the age of dwelling than its market value or condition. New development would have to be more heavily subsidized than it is now, unless rents were to be much higher. Indeed, under present arrangements, with new building at a very low level, pooling makes it unnecessary in most cases for central government to pay a subsidy either to new development or refurbishment. But pooling creates serious anomalies too. It has tended to result in authorities charging the same or similar rents on dwellings of equivalent size, regardless of their condition, their location, or the demand for them. The result is that rents vary much more *between* authorities, reflecting their financial circumstances, than they do *within* a single local authority area to reflect market conditions. In such circumstances it will be impossible to satisfy the demand for an authority's more desirable houses, whereas at the other extreme, unless there is an overall shortage, there will be stock lying empty because it is hard to let at the price it is offered.

Capital and revenue expenditure: housing associations

Housing associations are subject to fewer constraints than local authorities; and RTB, which is limited to those associations that are not registered charities, has affected only 3% of the stock.

From 1974 until 1988 the associations, although always seen as independent bodies, obtained the bulk of their loan finance for investment as well as grant from the Housing Corporation, which at that time covered the whole of Great Britain. In some cases they were also funded by local authorities. As with local authorities, all of their investment expenditure was therefore regarded as public expenditure and they were bound by the constraints which that implied. However, since the 1988 Housing Acts, they have been encouraged to borrow from private sector institutions instead of from the Housing Corporation in England, Scottish Homes, or, in Wales, Tai Cymru; and in this situation only Housing Association Grant (HAG), scores as public expenditure.

This grant, which was reformed in 1988, is a once-for-all capital grant paid at the outset of a project, rather than a recurrent revenue grant or a low interest loan (the forms of assistance more common in other European countries). The ability they now have to borrow from the private sector puts the associations in a position similar to most other social landlords in Europe. It undoubtedly gives them more scope than when they were wholly dependent on public expenditure, as well as enabling public sector funds to secure a larger total amount of investment through the leverage effect on private finance. But the effect should not be exaggerated. With existing levels of rent, HAG payments cover to up to 75% of capital expenditure in England, and rather more in Scotland. Without additional HAG, therefore, associations cannot contemplate a significant expansion of their programme, even if private funding is available, unless they feel able to raise rents.

HAG makes rents affordable by reducing the amount that has to be borrowed and thereby the burden of interest and repayment charges. But the difficulty with all systems of this kind in conditions of inflation, as the Dutch found to their cost with their "dynamic cost" rent system (see Ch. 5), is to set the subsidy at a level appropriate to ensure a reasonable level of rent during the life of the project, without generating surpluses or deficits. If inflation is higher than predicted, thereby eroding the real value of the outstanding capital debt, a surplus will be generated, unless the real value of rents falls, and, if lower, rents will have to rise in real terms if a deficit is to be avoided.

This problem arose with the HAG system that operated prior to its reform in the Housing Act (1988). Under the pre-1988 system housing associations borrowed from the Housing Corporation to cover the cost of their developments, rents were "fair rents" set as for the private rented sector by Rent Officers, and HAG was used to pay off the loan to whatever level could be serviced by the "fair rent", after management and maintenance were provided for. This system was successful in stimulating a major growth of housing associations, but it imposed very little discipline on costs, since HAG was determined at the stage when a development was complete and at whatever level was necessary to meet "fair rents". Moreover, since the rents were determined by the Rent Officer rather than the landlord, they were not related to the financial circumstances of the association. Arrangements were therefore made to pay back any surpluses and to fund deficits, through Grant Redemption Funds and Revenue Deficit Grants.

The post-1988 system, which was applied to all new tenancies but not to those already existing, involves agreement at the start on the level of HAG to be paid; "fair rents" do not apply and lettings are on an "assured tenancy" basis. In England the maximum rate of HAG was set at 75%, and since 1988 it has been gradually reduced thereby causing rents to increase. In Scotland no maximum was set but HAG levels averaged about 80% and there is the same policy aimed at reducing it. This system differs fundamentally from its predecessor: housing associations cannot any longer expect HAG to be increased to take account of costs that turn out higher than expected; and rents effectively become the residual, being set at a level that will make the project viable. Because the system is not tied to "fair rents", and rents can therefore be adjusted to take account of financial circumstances, it was not felt necessary with post-1988 HAG to make provision either for Grant Redemption Funds or Revenue Deficit Grant.

There was concern that the increased risk to which housing associations would be exposed, and the prospect of higher rents, would cause momentum to falter when this new system was introduced. In practice this did not occur, probably because all social rents were rising and the associations were the only part of the social rented sector able to undertake expansion in the face of continuing need. It would also appear that associations in Scotland have been encouraged by Scottish Homes to put increased emphasis on schemes for low-cost home ownership, on which the rate of HAG is lower, as a means of bringing average HAG down without too drastic an effect on rents (More 1993).

In time, however, the new HAG system is likely to have far-reaching effects on the housing association movement, especially if HAG levels are steadily reduced and rents forced up. The system can be expected to make associations more competitive with each other and more reluctant to undertake expensive schemes or those where some risk is involved. This favours new building rather than renovation, because of the much greater risk that out-turn costs exceed estimates. Hitherto, associations have played a major part in restoring existing stock; and their refurbishment of stone tenements in the Scottish cities has been a major benefit to urban renewal. The new system could also have an adverse effect on quality, if it results in efforts being made to build at costs that enable rents to be kept down. There are already indications that it is precipitating some restructuring of the movement, with smaller associations amalgamating into larger groups (Harrison 1992: 21–2). Although this could have advantages in reducing cost, if it meant the loss of community-based associations and their replacement by much larger bodies, the reduction of local accountability and local involvement could be a serious loss.

Homelessness and the supply of social rented housing

The effect of the tight capital controls on new investment in the public sector, combined with RTB and other sales, has been to produce a sharp reduction in the total stock (Wilcox 1993: 51ff). In England the local authority stock fell by 1.3 million between April 1981 and the end of 1992, and in Scotland by 228000. Although there has been a substantial expansion in the activity of housing associations, this has been from a very low base, so that the total additions to their stock amount to 297000 and 34000 for England and Scotland respectively. The result is that the social rented sector as a whole has fallen by 1 million (20% of the 1981 stock) in England and 194000 (19%) in Scotland.

How large ought the sector to be? There is no clear answer, as is apparent from the comparisons in Chapter 2. Much depends on the part played by the other two sectors. It seems likely that, with the private rented sector so very small in Britain, the social rented sector would need to be larger than elsewhere.

And so far as the owner occupied sector is concerned, it should be one of the purposes of a social rented sector to avoid the hardship that arises when people who have inadequate means attempt ownership.

Various studies, notably the Report of the Duke of Edinburgh's Inquiry into British Housing, have concluded that there is now a shortage of accommodation to rent in Britain. Because of the absence of population growth and the much larger social rented sector, this is not yet a problem in Scotland, except in particular areas. But it is much more evident in England, especially in the south, and on current trends it will get worse. Total housebuilding for rent in Britain fell from about 100000 a year in 1979 to 25000 a year by the end of the 1980s. Research studies demonstrate a wide measure of agreement that the earlier figure needs to be restored if the needs of those on lower incomes are to be adequately catered for in the longer run (HRH the Duke of Edinburgh 1991: 13, 27-9).

Homelessness is one aspect of this problem. The statistics of those officially accepted as homeless by local authorities show that numbers more than doubled in Great Britain between 1979 and 1991, an increase of 165% in England, 110% in Wales and 115% in Scotland, to 152000, 10000 and 18000 respectively (Wilcox 1993: 149). Homelessness is a complex problem, relating not only to housing but quite as much to difficult social conditions such as marriage break-up, the growing number of single-parent families, teenagers leaving home without adequate means of support, and loss of employment. Sometimes, unacceptable levels of homelessness co-exist in the same housing authority area as quite high vacancy rates, although the latter are often in peripheral housing estates.

Since 1977, unlike their counterparts in other countries, local authorities in Great Britain have been under a duty to secure permanent accommodation for certain "priority" categories of homeless households, provided that they have not become homeless intentionally. It is mainly homeless families with children who are covered by the legislation, but some other homeless people, who are classed as being vulnerable, are also protected, such as the elderly and sometimes children leaving institutional care. Many, and possibly even the majority, of homeless people are single and are not protected by the legislation. In 1994 the government announced its intention to limit local authorities' duties towards the statutorily homeless to providing temporary accommodation for a limited period. The government has argued that households currently treated as homeless gain an unfair advantage in housing allocations, and that this encourages voluntary homelessness. However, there is no evidence that homeless applicants do gain an unfair advantage or make themselves homeless voluntarily, whereas the tendency for local authorities to allow homeless households fewer offers of accommodation than other applicants often causes them to be allocated the least popular housing (Fitzpatrick & Stephens 1994).

In many of the London boroughs, the number of people to be housed under the homelessness legislation exceeds the number of council houses that become available for letting. In these and other areas of acute shortage, it is clear that the problem of homelessness cannot be solved without higher rates of new building.

The present inadequate rate of new building in this sector is therefore a matter of serious and growing concern.

Housing allowances

Local authorities were first given power to grant rent rebates to tenants of their properties in the Housing Act of 1930. The power was made general in 1935, but remained at their discretion and was used by them in varying degrees, some having well developed schemes and others none at all. This remained the position until 1972, when the Housing Finance Act made rebates obligatory and extended the system in the form of rent allowances to tenants of private rented property. Unlike the position in France, Germany and Sweden, no arrangements were made then, nor have they been since, to provide support under the housing allowance scheme to owner occupiers. Those who are not in full-time employment, without any alternative source of income and with assets of less than £8000, may have interest costs of their mortgages met through Income Support, which is part of the general system of social security; but the government announced in 1994 that, as from 1 October 1995, Income Support for mortgage interest would be paid only after the first nine months on benefit.

An important difference between the British and most of the Continental systems of housing allowances is that the latter are seldom intended to meet the whole of housing costs. Systems of social security there, notably pensions and unemployment relief, are often more generously funded than in Britain and are expected to pay at least a part of housing costs. Housing allowances are therefore seen more as intended to top up on provision from other sources. Sometimes, as for example in the Netherlands, they are based on some standardized system of costs rather than the actual amount, and their aim may then be to limit the individual's housing cost to some proportion of income such as 20% or 25%.

The present housing allowance scheme in Britain (Housing Benefit) dates from 1988. It is based on actual costs and, for those on full benefit and in local authority or housing association accommodation, it meets the whole cost. For those in the private rented sector it has also met the whole cost, subject only to the accommodation being assessed by the Rent Officer as appropriate to needs and the cost as reasonable. But as from October 1995, full Housing Benefit will be restricted to accommodation where rents do not exceed the average for the area. Above this level, only 50% of the excess rent costs will be met. Compared with their Continental counterparts, British Housing Benefit payments are generally large and the cost correspondingly high. There has also been a sharp escalation in costs as a result of the rise in rents described earlier in this chapter. Indeed, Hills has estimated that half of the savings in general subsidies have been lost in higher Housing Benefit costs. As subsidy is withdrawn, rents rise, and higher rents add to Housing Benefit costs (Hills 1991b: 27). In addition, there

171

have been increased costs from the growing number of elderly people and the rise in unemployment in the early 1990s. The number of claimants increased by more than 2.5 times between 1980/81 and 1992/93, and the cost increased from about £1000 million to over £7000 million (Table 8.3). Over the same period, claimants for mortgage payments from Income Support have increased almost four times to 500000 with a cost that has risen from under £100000 to over £1000 million.

Table 8.3   Housing Benefit in Great Britain.

	Number of claimants	Council tenants (£ million)	Private tenants (£ million)	Total (£ million)
1980/1	1570	841	183	1024
1984/5	4825	2145	687	2832
1987/8	4860	2506	1030	3536
1990/1	3989	3345	1596	4941
1991/2	4028	3675	2322	5997
1992/3	4328	4347	3257	7604

Note: The above figures exclude Rates, Community Charge and Council Tax rebates.
Source: Wilcox (1993, 1994b).

Despite this high cost, the British system of Housing Benefit has some serious deficiencies. The first is the failure adequately to cover owner occupiers. If the justification of a housing allowance scheme is to relieve hardship caused by housing costs, there would seem to be no case for discriminating on the basis of tenure, especially in Britain, where owner occupation includes a much higher proportion of people on low incomes than in many other countries. It is also anomalous to have the unemployed section of the owner occupiers covered by a different system, and those on low incomes not covered at all, thereby creating an employment trap.

Secondly, the system creates an exceptionally serious poverty trap. The 1988 reform steepened the "taper"[15] from 50% to 65% of net income (Hills 1991b: 170); this compares with tapers of around 20% for the other four countries in this study that have systems of housing allowances. This change was estimated to save between £200 and 300 million for the Exchequer, but at the expense of those on low incomes. The result is that for those on the taper an additional £1 of gross income leaves only 11 pence after tax and benefit reductions (Table 8.4). For those with children, who are also on Family Credit with a 70% taper, the position is even worse. When combined with reducing Housing Benefit, an additional £1 of gross income leaves them only 3 pence net. Furthermore, with a rent of £50 per week, the effect is to give a negligible increase in retained income until weekly income exceeds £190 (just under £10000 a year; Fig. 8.2). If rents rise, as the government clearly intends that they should, this will have

---

15. The rate at which benefit falls away as income rises.

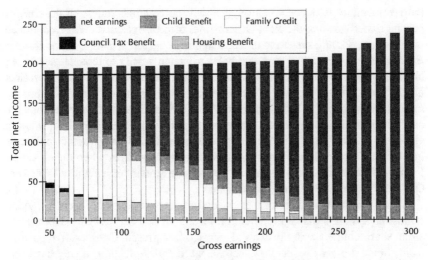

Figure 8.2 The poverty trap: £50 rent, couple and two children.

the effect of pushing the poverty trap to higher levels of income. Indeed, at a rent of £70, which in present circumstances might be regarded perhaps as approximating to an economic rent, the poverty trap would extend to an annual income of £15000. Another aspect of the same problem, which has been demonstrated by Hills, is that with benefit falling away so abruptly as income rises, the proportion of income absorbed by housing costs can rise to well over 30% for people who are still relatively poor, well above the guideline figure used in Germany and in some other Continental countries (Hills et al. 1989: 34; Hills1991b: 173).

Table 8.4 The housing poverty trap: cumulative deductions for each £1 of gross earnings.

	Single person/couple (pence)	Family (pence)
Each £ of gross earnings	100	100
less:		
Income tax at 20p	20	20
National Insurance at 9%	9	9
= Net earnings	71	71
less:		
Family Credit at 70%	0	50
Housing Benefit at 65%	46	14
Council Tax Benefit at 20%	14	4
= Net disposable income	11	3

Source: Wilcox (1993).

A further fault with the British system, and an equally serious one, is that it provides a marginal rate of increase or decrease that is 100% of the rent difference. For all those on Housing Benefit, therefore, it makes no difference what the rent actually is, since whatever it is will be covered, unless in the case of private rented housing the Rent Officer rules it to be excessive. This, combined with the rent pooling system in the local authority sector, makes it impossible for the market to operate in a way that helps to match supply to tenants' needs. As has been noted above, pooling has the effect that rents do not adequately reflect quality, condition or location of the properties; and tenants on benefit, where the marginal adjustment is 100%, have no interest in seeking anything other than the best accommodation available. This also has the perverse effect that, when a clear majority of tenants are on Housing Benefit, a landlord (whether public or independent) is much less inhibited about raising rents than when they are not. In the private sector, it means that an undesirable amount of weight falls on Rent Officers' judgement of what is reasonable.

Clearly, a substantial reform is needed to remove these deficiencies. As it stands the system's damaging effect on incentives and on fostering dependency are in sharp conflict with the avowed stance of the present Conservative government. Since those with very low incomes need full protection, a way has to be found to make the taper less severe and to alter the marginal rate of benefit, without causing hardship to the least well off. Hills, who has made a very full analysis of this problem, has suggested a reform that involves benefit meeting full housing costs for those on very low levels of income, or wholly dependent on social security, but a lower proportion and a much shallower taper as income rises (Hills 1991b: 176–7). This would have some similarities to the German system.

However it is done, any improvement that makes the poverty trap less severe will extend benefit to a higher level of income. Such a change would be expensive, as would the extension of coverage to owner occupiers. But, quite apart from the anomalies and inequity in the present system, if the government means what is says about the importance of incentives and eliminating the "dependency culture", the deficiencies in the present system should not be allowed to continue.

The costs of the policy

To compare the cost of British policy with that of other countries, it is necessary to adjust the total for public expenditure on housing to exclude the capital spending of local authorities, since this is financed by borrowing at normal market rates. To this must be added Income Support paid on behalf of home owners in respect of their mortgage costs, mortgage interest tax relief, and the cost of the BES scheme in the private rented sctor. It is particularly difficult to estimate the full costs of BES, as they depend on assumptions made about the future decisions of BES companies and their cost in tax relief, particularly exemption from capital gains tax. The Inland Revenue statistics for the years the scheme has been in operation suggest that, assuming a marginal tax rate of 60% in the first year and 40% in the remainder, the income tax benefits to those who have invested averaged about £180 million a year.

The results are shown for the UK as a whole in Table 8.5.[16] It will be seen that there are some very clear trends. The cost of Exchequer subsidy to local authority housing has come down substantially, even at current prices, and local authority current expenditure also fell following the 1989 Act. The counterpart of this is the large increase in Housing Benefit expenditure. Even without the cost of Income Support payments for owner occupiers' mortgages, Housing Benefit has become the largest item in the cost of housing policy. Subsidies to housing associations, in the form of HAG paid by the housing corporation and its counterparts in the other countries of the UK, have also risen as assistance to local authorities has declined.

Table 8.5 The costs of housing policy in the UK* (£ millions).

	1988/89	1989/90	1990/91	1991/92	1992/93
Mortgage interest tax relief	5400	6900	7700	6100	5200
BES Scheme	220	65	113	164	380
Government subsidy to LA Housing	578	699	1466	1260	1097
Other government subsidies	41	55	71	108	140
Specific capital grants	531	655	679	722	897
LA current expenditure on housing	715	697	329	336	388
Finance for public corporations	419	532	557	631	583
Housing Corporations†	738	907	1153	1638	2305
Housing Benefit	3878	4403	5675	6149	7777
Income support to mortgages	294	364	567	949	1179
	12814	15277	17710	18057	19946
As % of GDP at market prices	2.7	2.9	3.2	3.1	3.3

* Including Northern Ireland.
† Including the Housing Corporation, Scottish Homes and Tai Cymru.
Source: HM Treasury , *Public expenditure statistical supplement 1994–5*, Cm 2519 (London: HMSO, 1994); Wilcox (1994).

Mortgage interest tax relief, which for much of the period was the largest element in housing policy costs, has fallen sharply in the first half of the 1990s as a result of the limitations imposed on it by government and, more especially, the fall in interest rates. Being interest-rate related, its cost is highly volatile, reflecting not so much assistance given to housing as the state of the housing market and the general level of interest rates in the economy. Estimates for the effect of capital gains tax exemption and absence of tax on imputed rent for owner occupiers cannot reasonably be made and are not included in the table.

The total costs of British housing policy, defined in this way, came to nearly £20000 million in 1992/93; this amounts to about 3.3% of GDP. On this basis, the policy costs more than in France or Germany, 1.5% and 1.4% of GDP respec-

16. For statistical simplicity, Northern Ireland is included. It comprises roughly 2.5% of the total.

tively, but not as much as in Sweden, where it was 4.1%, and was comparable with the Netherlands, 3.2%. However, as is repeatedly argued in this book, it is a mistake to put too much emphasis on these comparative figures, because of the indistinct line between housing policy costs and the costs of social security more generally; and because, where so much of housing is financed by borrowing in a period of inflation, subsidy costs do not accurately reflect the economic costs of the policy.

Conclusion

This survey has shown that, although British housing policy undoubtedly has strengths, there are also serious weaknesses. And, although the major recasting of policy that took place in the 1980s was no doubt necessary, in getting rid of some weaknesses it gave rise to others. The polarization of British housing between the owner occupied and social rented sectors remains despite all the changes, and this reflects a continued absence of tenure neutrality in the policy.

The high percentage of stock in owner occupation is a distinctive feature of Britain, apart from Scotland, and is a consequence of several factors. It has been generally favoured by policy and its rapid growth during the 1980s owes much to RTB. The financing of owner occupation is simpler than in many of the other countries and is extremely efficient. But the lack of a competitive rented sector also means that in Britain many people take on ownership who in other countries would rent.

However the ease with which finance can be arranged, the predominance of variable rate mortgages and high loan-to-value ratios involve the purchaser in risks that he/she may not fully appreciate. These risks to the purchaser are all the greater because, unlike France, Germany and Sweden, Britain has no system of housing allowances to protect owner occupiers, apart from Income Support for payment of the mortgage interest costs of those who are not in full-time employment, which will in future be subject to nine months' delay.

The phenomenon of equity withdrawal in boom, to which the British system seems especially prone, has the effect of making housing a financial reservoir from which large volumes of savings can be withdrawn when markets are rising; but it then has to be replenished when the market falls. The ensuing negative equity, mortgage arrears and repossessions have resulted in a high level of distress in the sector in the early 1990s and they indicate the more obvious risks to individuals if the policy of continually promoting the sector is pushed too far; but there are also highly damaging effects on the stability of the economy, which are more fully examined in Chapter 12.

The private rented sector in Britain has declined to an exceptionally low level, but it still has a part to play as the tenure best able to promote labour mobility and for those who are on the margin of affording owner occupation. The 1988

Act at last established a satisfactory rental regime; but, compared with the other countries in this study, the sector in Britain is much less favoured by fiscal incentives or grants. It does not even benefit from a depreciation allowance, which applies to other forms of investment in productive assets in Britain and to rented housing in the other countries. The tenure is unlikely to revive until the incentives are at least neutral in respect of owning and renting. Some progress towards greater neutrality has been made as a result of the reduction in MITR for owner occupiers. But the depth of decline is such that it may be necessary to discriminate in the sector's favour for a time if it is to recover. The BES scheme, with its emphasis on a five-year investment, showed that a response could be achieved, but did not provide an incentive for stable and permanent investment across the sector as a whole.

The social rented sector is larger than in France, Germany or Sweden, at least in part because the private rented sector is so small, but it has declined sharply as a result of government policy since 1979. The dominance of the sector by direct local authority ownership artificially constrains investment, because all local authority spending is part of public expenditure. There is a considerable backlog of repairs and refurbishment to be undertaken, and substantial sums are required for this if poor housing conditions in this sector are to be overcome. The volume of new building in the sector, even allowing for the continued growth of housing associations, has fallen to very low levels and is well below forecast requirements. It is one of the factors, but only one, in the rise of homelessness.

The local authority dominance of British social housing has resulted in a much greater degree of local monopoly than in other countries. Combined with the absence of any corporate structure, giving a performance that could be measured, this has contributed in the past to the poor quality of management by some authorities. This quasi-monopoly situation is now changing as a result of the competition provided by the growth of housing associations.

RTB would probably be impossible constitutionally in many other countries and the discounts are only practical financially in Britain because the high inflation of the 1970s and early 1980s so eroded the underlying loan debt. The scheme has been extremely popular and it resulted in a large transfer of wealth to those who exercised it. It should not be regarded as an asset strip of the local authority, given the terms on which the dwellings would have been rented if they had not been sold. Nevertheless, it does tend to result in the authorities losing their best stock. LSVTs raise problems of the appropriate transfer price: since this is based largely on rent levels, which may themselves be anomalous, the anomalies may be projected into the future with less chance that they can be rectified.

The part played by housing associations is rapidly increasing, but is still very small compared with other countries. The associations vary greatly in size, in character and in effectiveness. Although the larger associations can offer a high degree of professionalism, they may give rise to problems of accountability. The smaller associations are coming under pressure to merge since the 1988 change in HAG and the government's policy of reducing the HAG percentage. But it would be regrettable if this put at risk the community-based associations and co-operatives, which have the advantage of direct accountability to tenants and afford considerable advantages in the scope they provide for them to be involved in the management of their own living conditions.

The Housing Benefit system requires major overhaul to reduce the exceptionally severe poverty trap and to end the 100% marginal adjustment for all rent changes. It is anomalous for the scheme to cover the rented sectors but not owner occupation, if its purpose is to reduce financial distress caused by the cost of housing; and payment of Income Support to cover the mortgage payments of the unemployed, without assisting owner occupiers who are low paid, creates a serious employment trap.

Despite the clear need for greater spending in several areas of British housing policy – particularly incentives to the private rented sector, greater investment in the social rented sector and reform of Housing Benefit – the present costs of the British policy are high. In the past, the policy of low rents in local authority housing was criticized as being indiscriminate and needlessly expensive. But MITR has been equally indiscriminate and, until the recent restrictions and fall in interest rates, it was the most expensive measure in British housing policy. The policy remains inadequately targeted and the complete absence of neutrality results in a tenure choice that is still heavily distorted. The result is that the substantial sums devoted to housing policy do not yet achieve as much as they could in improving Britain's housing conditions.

CHAPTER 9

The Single Market and European integration

The scope of the European Commission's activities is defined in the Treaty of Rome of 1958, the Single European Act of 1985 and most recently by the Treaty of Maastricht. In none of these major pieces of legislation was the Commission given competence in the field of housing policy. Only in three areas, all of which are strictly limited, is the Commission directly concerned with housing:

- for coal and steel workers (under the Treaty of Paris, which set up the Coal and Steel Community)
- for the handicapped (mostly studies and experimental projects)
- pilot projects on housing for immigrants.

Many people may regard that as the end of the matter. Since the Commission has not been given other than extremely limited powers in this field, the subject plainly remains the responsibility of national governments and such lower levels of government and administration as may be appropriate in individual countries. There is therefore no need, it may be argued, to consider any European dimension to this subject at all. The Commission should concern itself with matters for which it does have responsibility.

However, the issue is not so simple. In the first place, Resolutions have been passed by the European Parliament, calling for action on housing policy by the Council of Ministers and the Commission; and there are many others, including bodies responsible for social housing in Europe, who would like to see the Commission given a role in this area. The first part of this chapter therefore considers the arguments for a European dimension to housing policy, either as a supplement to or a replacement for national policies.

Secondly, there is European legislation not primarily concerned with housing, but which has implications for housing, just as it affects other aspects of economic and social life in member States. A wide range of legislation falls into this category, but among the Directives that have the most obvious relevance to housing are those on procurement, the construction industry and on the environment. The first two of these are primarily intended to open up the Single Market to firms in all member States, the latter to ensure some comparability in the approach to environmental issues and standards. The significance of these for housing has been dealt with by other authors and, since they do not concern the instruments of housing policy, they are not covered in this book (see especially Drake 1992).

The third category is European policies, which plainly do fall within the Commission's competence, and which are either closely related to housing or potentially affect housing markets, and will thereby have an impact on national housing policies. The second part of this chapter outlines the importance of the use of the EU's regional and social funds to assist housing-related projects. The following three chapters deal with the market for mortgage finance, with population and labour movement, and with housing and the economy, all of which are areas in which increased European integration will have implications for housing policy.

A European housing policy?

The European Parliament has passed several Resolutions calling for action by the Commission and the Council of Ministers, which, if acted upon, could amount to the start of a European dimension in housing policy (CEC 1992: 96ff.). Among other matters called for were:

- the formulation of a Community policy on housing and the residential environment (Resolution on the Rehousing of Families from the Place de la Réunion, Paris, and on the Right to Decent Housing, 12 July 1990)
- proposals as to whether and how loans may be granted from the resources of the structural funds and/or the European Investment Bank for supporting public housing programmes (Resolution on Shelter for the Homeless, 16 June 1987)
- a study on housing conditions with particular reference to the mismatch of demand and supply, the problem of under-occupation in areas of shortage, the need to re-establish the private rented sector, and the need for greater flexibility (Resolution on Shelter for the Homeless, 16 June 1987)
- that the public funds allocated to housing at the present time should be redirected to the construction of subsidized housing (Resolution on Shelter for the Homeless, 16 June 1987)
- a need to develop programmes of subsidized housing and a system of personal loans . . . to encourage flexibility in housing finance . . . to extend the use of formulae such as variable interest loans and the transfer of loans to facilitate personal mobility and, in general terms, to open up the mortgage market (Resolution on the Need for Community Action in the Construction Industry, 13 October 1988)
- an action programme in aid of the disadvantaged districts of the large European towns and cities and their suburbs (Resolution on the Violent Incidents in the French and Belgian Suburbs).

A desire to involve the Council of Ministers and the Commission in housing policy matters is also evident on the part of many of the experts who write about housing and the bodies with responsibility for housing, especially the various European associations concerned with social housing (ibid.). At a time when budgetary constraints impose clear and finite limits on what member States are able to spend on housing policy, and in many cases have resulted in cuts, it is only to be expected that those concerned should look to Europe as either a means of compelling national governments to do more or a source of additional funds. So far, such pressures for Europe-wide housing policies have been firmly resisted. Since 1989, European ministers of housing have held a series of annual informal meetings, at which common housing problems have been discussed; but they have repeatedly reaffirmed their view that housing policy remains a matter for national governments. For example, the Official Communiqué following the Lille meeting said:

> The European Economic Community does not include the issue of housing within its competences. Moreover, because of their different histories, cultures and institutions, the various European countries do not have the same approach to, or perception of, the problems of exclusion in housing. Of course the European Parliament registered, on 16 June 1987, the concern expressed on housing for the poorest population groups, but the "right to housing" to which it referred, is in practice understood differently from one country to the next. These very differences may even be a rich source of experience and opportunity for Europe. (CEC 1992: 110)

The Treaty of Maastricht set out in Article 3 the activities that fall within the field of competence of the European Union, and for the first time in the new Article 3b defined the limits of the Union's power in accordance with the principle of "subsidiarity"[1]:

> In areas which do not fall within its exclusive competence, the Community shall take action, in accordance with the principle of subsidiarity, only if and in so far as the objectives of the proposed action cannot be sufficiently achieved by the Member States and can therefore, by reason of the scale or effects of the proposed action, be better achieved by the Community. (Council of the European Communities 1992: 13, 14)

It is hard to see a basis on which these conditions would apply to housing. Common Union policies are necessary where co-ordination is required, for example to provide a fair basis for industrial competition to ensure unity when negotiating trade arrangements with third countries; or to ensure the most effective use of scarce resources, for example in agriculture or industry. There may also be a case for a common policy to provide a refinancing mechanism to reduce

---

1. According to this principle, powers should be devolved to the lowest possible level of decision-making.

the burden on the poorer member States, especially where they have a disproportionate share of the costs. This again justifies a common agricultural policy, and social and regional policies that aim to strengthen the economies of the more backward regions, thereby promoting economic and political "cohesion".

Housing does not fall into any of these categories. Certainly it is not justified on the basis of promoting fair competition. Although house prices and rental charges may differ substantially from one area to another, they do so within member States as well as between them; and where such differences reflect the realities of the market, it is right that they should be taken into account in economic decisions. A more equitable sharing of costs may, on the face of it, be a more plausible reason for Union action, but no more so in housing than in other fields of social policy, such as education, healthcare and social security.

There is a case for a much greater sharing of public expenditure costs generally, especially those on social expenditure, which was set out in the MacDougall Report of 1977 and more recently in a study by Begg & Mayes for the European Parliament (CEC 1977; Begg & Mayes 1991: especially 70ff and 95). The MacDougall Report argued that a necessary condition for a successful move to economic and monetary union was the development of the Union's role so as to bear a much larger share of total public expenditure costs. This was necessary not only to spread the burden and produce greater equality between member States, but particularly to cushion member States from the effects of external shocks that might result in a deterioration of local revenue. The report pointed out that within existing common currency areas, such as federal States, the upper level of government is normally responsible for financing at least 20% of total public expenditure. This produces budgetary transfers from richer to poorer regions and also reduces the impact of external shocks, if these affect only a part of the Union. The report estimated that the effect of centralizing responsibility for taxation and expenditure in this way was to reduce differences in per capita incomes by about 40% on average within the countries they studied.

The report for the European Parliament took the view that, although transfers on the scale advocated by MacDougall were unlikely to be politically acceptable, and probably not necessary, the aim should nevertheless be to make the Union budget responsible for expenditure totalling some 5–7% of GDP. Among other measures the report proposed an unemployment fund, a welfare fund, automatic transfers from richer to poorer regions and a Union-wide progressive tax on individuals or households.

Total expenditure by the European Union is still very small by these standards, less than 2% of Union GDP, and member State governments are still responsible for the vast bulk of public expenditure within the Union. In particular, apart from the Social Fund, no attempt has been made to centralize social expenditure; this contrasts with the position within a nation State, where, regardless of the amount of tax revenue that can be raised in individual regions, the maintenance of comparable standards of social security and expenditure on infrastructure normally provides a substantial part of interregional transfers.

The importance of these conclusions is plainly not accepted by those who drew up Maastricht Treaty, still less by the governments that signed it. All that remained of the need to promote convergence and greater equality was the recognition of the problems of the four less developed member countries in the setting up of the special Cohesion Fund to help finance their economic development (Council of the European Communities (1992), Article 130d: 54).

These arguments, which remain open to debate, are about the need to integrate public finance if monetary union is to succeed. They do not concern any one area of social policy specifically; but clearly, if a move were made in this direction, some centralization of the funding for housing policy might well be a candidate. However, it is far from obvious which member States would be the main beneficiaries if there were a Union housing policy with provision for centralized funding. Certainly the main contributors to any funding system would be likely to be the wealthier countries, although this depends on how the budget is financed. It is also the case, as Chapter 2 has shown, that housing conditions as measured by standard of amenities and numbers of dwellings in relation to population are poorest in the southern States of the Union, most of which have a GDP per head below the EU average. But the northern States have some particularly difficult housing problems at present: Germany, following reunification; France, with its developing housing shortage; Britain, France again and several other countries, where the problems of deprived inner-city areas or peripheral housing estates are most evident. All would have major claims.

Moreover, if there were a common funding mechanism, it would require some uniformity of policy if the distribution of funds was to be regarded as acceptable to all member States. This has been necessary in regional policy. But in housing, national policies differ greatly from one member State to another, as the communiqué from the meeting of housing ministers at Lille makes very clear. Some States spend much more on housing policy than others, and although this may reflect a greater housing need or greater concern to provide decent living conditions for the less well off, it is not always so. National policies reflect not only local circumstances but differences in political philosophy and traditions. With all policies, there is an interaction with social security provision, to the extent that the more generous the latter, the fewer subsidies are required for housing. It would plainly be unacceptable to the countries that were the main contributors to any European housing fund if its distribution depended more on the policies pursued by a particular member State than on some objective measure of need.

Yet a requirement to alter policies to conform to a common pattern would be most certainly resented, not because it would be more effective or more appropriate for the countries concerned, but simply to suit the requirements of common funding. It would no doubt be a convenient let-out for national governments to pass the blame to "Brussels" when, for example, mortgage interest tax relief was cut or arrangements for social housing altered. Even when it was action that was desirable in any event, it would be tempting to present it locally as unnecessary interference, if its consequences were unpopular. Such an outcome would be highly damaging to the public view of the European Union. Already in the debates following the Maastricht Treaty, and particularly as a result of the need to establish common rules in the Single Market, "Brussels" is widely blamed for what are often unfairly seen as bureaucratic directives and regulations, and the less scrupulous national politicians make the most of this. There can be few areas of policy that would lend themselves so readily to this as housing, without any obvious offsetting gain.

Moreover, involvement by the Union in taking responsibility for policy and providing funding would by no means ensure that more resources in total were provided. As the example of regional policy shows, some member States may simply try to use EU funding to replace resources they would otherwise provide themselves; furthermore they may be tempted to shift responsibility on to the Union, when the latter is not adequately resourced to handle it. As M. Roger Quilliot, a former French Minister of Housing and now President of the European Co-ordination Committee for Social Housing (CECODHAS), has pointed out:

> Une communautarization du dossier risque d'accentuer encore le désen-
> gagement des Etats. Chacun pourra croire, ou feindre de croire, que "Brux-
> elles" va aider, va financer. Or, les finances communautaires ne peuvent
> être à l'échelle des problèmes. Elles ne viennent qu'en complément des
> financements nationaux, en respect du principe d'additionnalité. Nous ne
> voulons pas prendre ce risque. (Ghékiere 1992: 18)

This is of course the classic problem of additionality. How does one know what member States might have done themselves if they were not able to draw on Community funds? But since there is no evidence that channelling funds through the Community would enable them to be more effectively deployed, there seems everything to be said for leaving the important decisions on housing policy to be taken by member States, and where appropriate by regional and local levels of government within the States, thereby enabling the shape of each country's policy to be determined in accordance with its own perceived needs. One is therefore driven to the conclusion that housing is a clear case of a policy area where the principle of subsidiarity should apply.

European funds

The European Union is primarily concerned with removing barriers to trade, so creating a single market; since the Maastricht Treaty, this includes the steps leading to the creation of a single currency. Funds available through the Coal and Steel Community(ECSC) legislation and under several special budget allocations, but principally from the four structural funds: the guidance section of the European Agricultural Guidance and Guarantee Fund, the European Social Fund

(ESF), the European Regional Development Fund (ERDF) and, since 1993, a fund for areas affected by the rundown of the fishing industry. These funds are intended to assist this process of integration, but the resources they provide are normally used in conjunction with those of national governments and are of secondary importance to them. For example, over the 1994–9 period the UK is scheduled to receive about £9000 million from the ERDF and ESF, only a fraction of what the government will itself spend on regional and social policies and which compares with the £20000 million cost of British housing policy in a single year (see Ch. 8).

EU programmes

The three small-scale programmes already mentioned at the start of this chapter are the exception to the rule that the EU does not fund housing directly. The ECSC has funded housing since 1954 through cheap long-term loans originally aimed at building new housing for workers. The programme has had a modest impact, with some 200000 houses either built or improved since 1954, mainly in Germany and France. More recently its emphasis has shifted towards providing cheap finance for individuals to renovate their houses, but in the UK local authorities have also managed to obtain some funding from this source in the recent past. Secondly, there is a fund that aims to promote physical access to housing for people with disabilities. It has supported seminars and conferences and the production of a manual on housing access. A third fund provides loans to support pilot projects in housing that aim to foster the social integration of migrant workers.

The Directorate-General for Social Affairs of the EU also runs three anti-poverty programmes. These started in 1975 and, during the most recent programme (Poverty 3), 41 projects received on average about £1 million. The projects have been divided into two categories, 29 being "model actions" and 12 "innovatory initiatives". Projects are selected in the UK by the Department of Social Security (in collaboration with the Scottish Office in Scotland). There are three model actions in the UK. These are at Greater Pilton in Edinburgh, Brownlow in Northern Ireland, and Toxteth in Liverpool. There is one innovatory initiative, the Single Parents Action Network in Bristol. These are smaller-scale projects that focus on particular groups and could include the homeless (Brietenbach 1993: 2–3).

Poverty 3 ended in June 1994 and a proposal for a successor programme (to be known as "Exclusion 1") was blocked by Germany, whose *Länder* objected to it on grounds of subsidiarity. By the end of 1994, it remained unclear whether agreement would be reached.

The structural funds

It is the European Regional Development Fund (ERDF) and the European Social Fund (ESF) that are of most significance for projects related to housing. Although it is important to recognize that these cannot be used to fund housing directly, they can help to tackle deprivation and unemployment, which lie at the core of so many of the problems in the more disadvantaged housing areas. They may therefore support some elements in an overall scheme of renewal and redevelopment, part of which also involves expenditure by the national authorities on housing improvement. In such schemes, no one element can hope to succeed without the others, and in this sense, as Madeline Drake has argued, they may greatly assist the objective of housing improvement (Drake 1992). The ERDF can contribute to the funding of infrastructure, workshops, factories and industrial premises, and service and tourism projects that create employment. The ESF can assist with the cost of training and thereby make it easier for those out of work to find employment.

The ERDF is, as one would expect, targeted on particular regions within the EU. These areas fall under Objectives 1, 2 and 5b of the structural funds. Objective 1 areas are defined as lagging regions and they receive the lion's share of the EU's ERDF budget. Until recently Northern Ireland was the only Objective 1 region in the UK, but Merseyside and the Highlands & Islands of Scotland have now also become eligible. Objective 2 areas are defined as regions suffering industrial decline, and it is money under this head that is the most important source of ERDF funding in the UK. Indeed, the UK receives more Objective 2 funding than any other member State. Many parts of the UK that suffer from industrial decline or readjustment are Objective 2 areas. They generally coincide with the areas that are given assisted status under UK regional policy. Objective 5b areas consist of those rural areas that the fund seeks to develop, but which have less severe problems of underdevelopment than Objective 1 areas. They include parts of the South West of England, as well as parts of rural Wales and Scotland.

The European Social Fund (ESF) is directed at people. It covers Objectives 3 and 4 of the structural funds. Following the revision of the structural fund regulations, Objective 3 now includes those regarded as being "socially excluded" and aims to facilitate their integration into the labour market. It includes groups such as people with physical or mental disabilities, immigrants, refugees, single parents, the homeless, prisoners and ex-offenders, and young people at high risk, such as drug users. Objective 4 is directed at the re-integration of workers into the labour market following industrial and technological change. Under the new regulations, residents of peripheral estates that suffer from deprivation are a priority group.

Applications for the ERDF and the ESF and administration of the funds provided are the responsibility of national governments.[2] Eligible projects receive

---

2. In Britain, the ERDF is now administered through regional offices.

up to 75% of costs in Objective 1 areas and up to 50% in Objective 2 areas. The ERDF is almost entirely used to fund capital projects, unlike the ESF, which provides only revenue funding. About half of the UK's allocation of ESF is spent on government training schemes.[3]

The issue of "additionality" has been a problem with both funds – whether the funding from the EU is additional to or are used as a replacement for funds available from national sources for the same projects. The EU seeks to satisfy itself that the funding is additional, but normally it is a condition of receiving EU funds that the cost should be shared with public authorities in the member State. In order to help achieve additionality[4] and also to give a more specific direction to its policies, the EU requires member States to draw up programmes, which must be agreed by the European Commission and which form a basis for the commitment of EU funding in the member State.

Community initiatives

In recent years the EU's own "Community Initiatives", which may be financed from any of the four the structural funds, have been one of the most interesting areas of EU policy. They are administered by DG XVI, although it is up to member States to propose areas that they think have a good claim. These schemes are mainly devoted to tackling sectoral industrial problems, such as reconversion of an area, and workforce retraining following coal, steel and textile closures. The schemes are a way of developing EU policies while shifting the balance of power from national governments and towards the Commission. They also have the attraction to the Commission of making it easier to insist that moneys spent comply with the principle of additionality.

In 1990 the European Commission launched the Urban Pilot Projects (UPPs) under Article 10 of the ERDF regulations. Their importance is twofold. First, the UPPs enabled areas not normally eligible to qualify for ERDF money and, secondly, they advanced the EU's urban agenda. Since 1990, 32 Urban Pilot Projects have been approved, including four in the UK. The first, in London, combined a series of infrastructure and labour projects with the overall aim of inner-city regeneration. It was completed in April 1993. There is also an Urban Pilot Project at Paisley (1992–6) that combines with domestic schemes to aid the regeneration of the Ferguslie Park housing estate. A project in progress in Stoke-on-Trent (1992–5) is an economic regeneration scheme, but is aimed at an industrial area, rather than a residential one. Finally, a project in Belfast (1991–6)

---

3. The remainder is administered through eight "sector" organizations, the most important being the further eduction sector, local authorities, Training and Enterprise Councils (in England), Local Enterprise Companies (in Scotland) and the National Council of Voluntary Organisations.
4. "Additionality" is achieved when European funds are used to increase national expenditure, rather than to replace it.

combines environmental and economic development, but is concentrated on the harbour area. Expenditure on these four projects will be some £17 million, just over half of which will be provided by the EU (ECOTEC 1993).

A new round of Community Initiatives was agreed in 1994. These include URBAN, which is intended to help find solutions to serious social problems that arise in depressed urban areas. The Initiative will support schemes for economic and social revitalization, the renovation of infrastructure and environmental improvement. Projects will be expected to run for four years and are intended to have a demonstration effect for other areas. Priority will be given to those proposals that are innovative and form part of an overall scheme of urban renewal.

The intention is that the Initiative will part-fund about 50 projects that will normally be in conurbations with a population of at least 100000 and where there are problems of unemployment, urban decay, bad housing and lack of social facilities, but expenditure directly on housing is not permitted (CEC 1994). There is a planned allocation of ECU600 million (about £500 million), of which two thirds is to be spent in Objective 1 areas, Objective 2 areas having priority among the remainder. Where possible, measures should be implemented in conjunction with other EU Initiatives. Member States are required to apply to the Commission to have projects approved.

A European network called *Quartiers en Crise* has been formed that brings together towns that suffer similar problems of urban decline and deprivation. Originally started by ten towns in five member States, it now includes 25 towns across the EU, including Manchester, Belfast and Paisley in the UK. The purpose of the network is to exchange information among professionals working in deprived areas, residents and local politicians, and to encourage an integrated approach to the problems of urban revitalization. This network is funded partly under Article 10 of the ERDF, but also under the HORIZON programme, which has a separate budget.

Conclusion

This chapter has argued that it would be mistaken to accede to pressure to give the EU competence in housing policy or to think in terms of European funding directly for housing. There are no good grounds for supposing that policy can be more effectively operated at the level of the Union than that of member States, or that the Union can achieve things that the States individually cannot achieve. There seems a clear case, therefore, for applying the principle of subsidiarity.

Nevertheless, other European policies and closer economic integration itself can have implications for housing, as subsequent chapters will show. And the structural funds, although not available to fund housing projects directly, can be applied in related areas of policy, thereby assisting urban renewal and helping to solve many of the problems of the more deprived housing areas. Indeed, the increasing emphasis on urban problems, as shown by the most recent Initiatives, *Quartiers en Crise* and the various pilot projects, demonstrates a growing concern with problems, the successful tackling of which is essential to the improvement of housing conditions.

CHAPTER 10

A single market in mortgage finance?

The European Commission has been interested in the creation of a single market in mortgage finance since the early 1970s and took it seriously enough in the 1980s to produce a draft directive on mortgage credit. This was eventually superseded by the general programme of banking liberalization as a part of the Single Market programme.

This chapter analyses critically the assumptions that lie behind the notion of a single market in mortgage credit, and presents empirical evidence gained from financial institutions that are developing European strategies. It is divided into three main parts. In the first, the key economic assumptions that predict price falls as a result of the Single Market are examined. In the second, the regulatory framework that governs the Single Market and its implications for British lenders are analysed. The third section places the European strategies of financial institutions in the context of the economic assumptions examined earlier. An assessment is made of the future extent and direction of a single market in mortgage finance.

The economics of the Single Market

The justification for financial institutions competing against one another across national boundaries rests on two economic assumptions: unequal competitiveness and economies of scale. The first of these assumptions features in the Cecchini Report, where it is argued that different levels of efficiency between financial institutions in member States will induce cross-border competition (CEC 1988a: 161). Such competition will, in turn, result in the prices of financial products converging around those found in the most efficient countries. The second assumption would justify cross-border operations only if economies of scale are maximized at a European, rather than national or subnational, level. If this is the case, prices in the most efficient countries might be expected to fall, as well as those in the less efficient countries.

These two assumptions are now examined – unequal competitiveness and economies of scale – each of which provides an economic rationale for a single market in mortgage finance.

Unequal competitiveness

The preceding chapters revealed that national mortgage markets are organized in quite different ways. Throughout the Union, the types of institutions and their ownership vary widely. Although commercial banks have entered several markets, offering a range of services savings banks are still common in continental Europe. Mortgage banks are unknown in Britain, but, within the EU, building societies are unknown outside Britain and Ireland. Some institutions are State owned, others privately owned and some are mutual. The extent to which funding is gained from retail deposits or from wholesale sources varies between institutions within countries, as well as between countries. The regulatory environment in which institutions operate also varies in several important respects, including the allocation of risk and the foreclosure process.

With such variations, it would be surprising if all mortgage markets were equally efficient. However, the central problem with the assumption that competition will reduce prices is that increased economic efficiency is not always compatible with lower prices. This problem can be illustrated by examining two reports that analyse the efficiency of mortgage finance institutions in several countries. The Cecchini Report covers Belgium, France, West Germany, Italy, the Netherlands, Spain and Britain.[1] A report for the USA housing agency, Fannie Mae, by Diamond & Lea (1992) examines Denmark, West Germany, France, the USA and Britain.

It is not possible to assess the relative efficiency of mortgage markets simply by comparing mortgage interest rates (or "prices") in different countries, because their main determinant is likely to be interest rates in the economy as a whole, unless the mortgage rate is subsidized in some way. Instead, the prevalent mortgage interest rate should be compared with a benchmark rate that a truly competitive system would charge. The more the actual interest rate exceeds the competitive rate, the less efficient the system. The excess interest rate (or interest rate spread) measures "intermediation efficiency" and it is intended to reflect several attributes of a finance system, including the cost of mortgage administration (origination and loan management) as well as the cost of raising funds.

In the Cecchini Report, the mortgage rates in each of the countries were compared with the money market rates in those countries, which produced an interest rate spread. The final report produces figures for 1986, but a background report to the study gives estimates of intermediation efficiency covering 1982–6. Here,

---

1. Figures are provided for Luxembourg, but they are meaningless since they are based on an average of other countries. Therefore, they have been omitted from this book.

more recent estimates have also been calculated for the years 1989–92. These are produced in Table 10.1, together with averages and rankings for the two periods.

The results clearly show the dangers of taking a single year as being typical, when they may be distorted by lags in mortgage rate adjustment, reflecting the funding sources. The two average figures do indicate above-average levels of intermediation efficiency in the UK, and below-average intermediation efficiency in Spain and Belgium.

However, the Cecchini methodology is deficient in several ways as a means of measuring efficiency. Three key problems arise. The first is the selection of an appropriate benchmark base rate. In many cases, the money market rate will be inappropriate as a benchmark rate. Indeed, there is a clearer rationale for using government bond rates. The government is able to borrow at the lowest rates because it offers the highest degree of security to its creditors. If funding for mortgages is short-term and at variable rates, then the short-term government bond rate is the appropriate benchmark. If, however, mortgage funding is long-term and at fixed rates, then it is more appropriate to use the long-term government bond rate as the benchmark rate. The Cecchini Report makes no such distinctions between short and long-term finance. The second problem arises from taking the interest rate spread at face value. If the mortgage rate is uninfluenced by subsidies and the choice of mortgage contract terms ("options"), then the excess over government bond yields is an appropriate measure of intermediation efficiency. If, however, subsidies and the availability of options affect the mortgage rate, then the excess interest rate measurement requires adjustment. Thirdly, the Cecchini methodology does not distinguish between the efficiency of different types of lender within countries.

Diamond & Lea attempted to take account of these factors. In their selection of an appropriate government bond rate, they adjust for the nature of funding. In Britain funds used for financing mortgages are quite market sensitive, causing the entire mortgage stock to be priced at the marginal cost of funds, whereas in France mortgage rates are less market sensitive and mortgages tend to be priced at the average cost of funds. In the first case, it is appropriate to use the bond yield at any given time, whereas in the second it is appropriate to use the average over the entire yield curve.

Diamond & Lea also adjusted the crude measurements of excess interest rates over base rates for factors, such as government subsidies, which otherwise distort the measurement of efficiency. A standard mortgage product is used, in this case an 80% mortgage (Table 10.2).

The results of the adjusted spread exercise indicate that British building societies are the most efficient institutions, showing an adjusted spread some 0.45% below a German packaged loan and 0.8% below the most efficient French product. There are also variations within systems. In particular, German mortgage banks exhibited a high level of efficiency, but the overall efficiency of German packaged loans is lowered by the higher cost of supplementary (especially

Table 10.1 Intermediation efficiency: unadjusted spreads.[a]

	1982	1983	1984	1985	1986	Average 1982–6	Rank 1982–6	1989	1990	1991	1992	Ave. 1989–92	Rank 1989–92
Belgium	3.36	4.69	3.41	3.23	1.92	3.32	6	2.05	-0.19	2.46	1.55	1.47	6
France	0.11	1.83	1.94	2.09	2.61	1.72	1	1.25	0.75	1.72	0.57	1.07	4
Germany	1.43	3.09	2.75	2.61	2.30	2.44	4	1.36	1.83	0.66	-0.42	0.86	3
Italy	2.12	2.06	1.68	2.00	1.40	1.85	2	2.14	2.71	2.79	0.11	1.94	7
Netherlands	2.97	3.85	2.57	1.50	1.37	2.45	5	0.91	0.96	0.49	-0.34	0.50	2
Spain	2.31	1.59	4.69	6.35	3.20	3.63	7	...	1.54	1.50	1.01	1.35	5
UK	1.60	1.53	4.17	2.61	1.16	2.21	3	-0.05	0.09	0.72	0.66	0.35	1

a. Intermediation efficiency is here measured by the difference between annual mortgage rates and money market rates (%).
Source: 1982–6: Price Waterhouse (1988) The 'Cost of Non-Europe' in Financial Services, Volume 9, Table 5.2.2; 1989–92: ECMF Annual Report 1991–92, Table 20, Annual Report 1992–93, Table 22, Eurostat, Money and Finance, Table 3.1.2.

Table 10.2 Intermediation efficiency: adjusted spreads.

Country	Lender	Period	Unadjusted spread[a]	Adjusted spread[b]
Denmark	Mortgage banks	1986–91	1.28	1.29
France	Depositories	1987–91	2.32	2.65
	Specialized	1986–90	2.34	2.00
Germany	Mortgage banks (first mortgage)	1982–91	1.47	1.46
	Depositories (first mortgage)	1982–91	2.15	2.07
	Bausparkassen (second mortgage)	1982–91	-2.21	1.65
	Depositories (top-up loan)	1982–91	2.76	2.76
	Packaged loan	1987–91	n.a.	1.65
UK	Building societies	1988–91	1.65	1.20
	Centralized lenders	1987–91	1.51	1.35
USA	Securities market	1988–91	2.07	1.23
	Depositories	1988–91	n.a.	1.82

Notes: Intermediation efficiency is here measured in two ways: (a) The unadjusted spread represents the difference between mortgage rates and the appropriate government bond rate. (b) The adjusted spread takes into account factors, such as government subsidy, which may have distorted the unadjusted spread.
Source: Adapted from Diamond & Lea (1992: Table 7.10).

unsecured top-up) finance, which is necessitated by low loan to value ratios (see Ch. 4). It is noticeable that wholesale lenders are generally more efficient than retail-funded institutions, except in the UK.

Although the adjusted-spread measurement of efficiency is a great improvement on the Cecchini methodology, it still does not give a definitive assessment of efficiency. The adjusted spread takes into account organizational efficiency (which includes mortgage origination, funding and management) and distortions such as subsidy. However, it fails to consider the allocation and pricing of risks that can affect the efficiency of a mortgage finance system.

For this reason, Diamond & Lea conducted a second, qualitative, exercise in which they examined relative efficiency relating not only to funding, operating costs and subsidies, but also to three types of risk: credit risk, prepayment/ interest-rate risk and liquidity risk. Credit risk arises from the possibility of default and can be allocated and priced through the interest rate, covered by third-party insurers (or the government), or minimized through lower loan to value ratio loans. Interest-rate risk arises from the uncertainty of future interest rates. An extreme example is where lenders borrow "short" and lend "long" (so creating a mismatch between the maturities of liabilities and assets), but borrowers and investors, as well as lenders, usually face degrees of interest risk that can be borne or hedged against through the purchase of options. Liquidity risk arises from the possibility that lenders may not be able to raise sufficient funds to meet future demand for loans or to refinance existing loans.

The authors stress that qualitative results are necessarily partly subjective and cannot be aggregated. Nevertheless, a clear pattern emerges from the summary of findings in Table 10.3.

Table 10.3   Six tests of mortgage finance efficiency.

Country	Funding market	Operating cost	Excess subsidy cost	Credit risk allocation	Interest risk allocation	Liquidity risk allocation
Denmark	4	1	2	2 =	4	2 =
France	5	5	5	5	5	5
Germany	3	4	3 =	4	3	2 =
UK	1	2	1	1	1	2 =
USA	2	3	3 =	2 =	2	1

Source: Diamond & Lea (1992: table 8.7)

On four of the six efficiency criteria, UK institutions are ranked as being the most efficient among the five countries examined, and second on the other two. Germany and Denmark are somewhat less efficient than Britain, but France is consistently categorized as being the least efficient, largely because of the high degree of government intervention throughout the mortgage finance system, which distorts the allocation of resources. Diamond & Lea identify inefficiency in the subsidy system (e.g. the PAP distorts purchasing decisions by being tied to the purchase of new properties), high operating costs (which they attribute to the privileged position of deposit-takers and to State ownership of some banks), and the inefficient allocation of risks (arising from a poor valuation system and difficulties in repossessing properties, a lack of options in the allocation of interest risk, and a relatively illiquid private market in mortgage bonds).

Diamond & Lea therefore concluded that there are widely differing levels of efficiency between national mortgage markets. However, the sources of inefficiency may themselves act as a powerful barrier to entry by more efficient institutions. This effect can be expected in three ways.

First, subsidies are identified as a major source of inefficiency, but such inefficiency can act as a barrier against competition from more efficient institutions. This is demonstrated in Table 10.2 by the differences between gross and adjusted spreads for French deposit-taking institutions (2.32 and 2.65) and German *Bausparkassen* (–2.21 and 1.65). An incoming institution would be competing against the unadjusted spread and might therefore find entry to the market difficult, unless it too could take advantage of subsidies.

The deregulation of the British mortgage market provides a good example of greater efficiency leading to higher prices. Although savings were not subsidized, banks were kept out of the mortgage market by government restrictions (known as the "corset") on the quantities of funds they could raise through interest-bearing current and savings accounts. These restrictions, which did not apply to building societies, allowed the societies to operate an interest rate cartel through which savings rates were kept below base rates. The building societies' position was further strengthened by rules that allowed them to pay interest to depositors net of tax calculated at a composite (or average) rate. The composite rate of interest did not apply to the banks until 1985. These advantages enabled building societies to keep the cost of mortgages below market levels. Sometimes, the mortgage rate was lower than base rates. However, when the restrictions on banks were removed, competition in the savings market increased the cost of funds, which, in turn, increased the cost of mortgages (Stephens 1993: 162–3). Secondly, market structures may also act as barriers to entry. In particular, the high degree of vertical integration in the German system makes entry difficult for incomers, a point discussed in more detail later in this chapter. Thirdly, it is impossible for incoming institutions to avoid all regulations of the host State, even though they may be a source of inefficiency. For example, the security offered by a mortgage is necessarily location-specific (houses do not move) and is dependent on the relevant national laws. Differential credit risk arising from different foreclosure processes is therefore beyond the scope of increased competition.

Economies of scale

Prices in financial services might be lowered not only by increased competition but also by increased economies of scale. However, as already mentioned, for this to apply to the mortgage market, economies of scale must be maximized at the supranational level, rather than the national or subnational level. Evidence from the USA suggests that economies of scale in banking are maximized at relatively small levels. Noulas et al. (1990) found that economies of scale were present in banks up to assets of US$3000 million. Gropper (1991) claimed to have found that economies of scale rose over time and he suggested that this might be caused by deregulation and technology. Nevertheless, according to this research, the size of banks that maximizes economies of scale in the USA is comparable with the smaller savings banks and building societies in Europe. There is even a real prospect of diseconomies of scale arising, when institutions merge or are taken over, from incompatible computer systems, costs associated with different languages, or from widely differing management cultures.

The research findings from the USA are supported by recent research into UK building society efficiency. The Drake & Weyman Jones (1993) survey, using 1988 data relating to 76 building societies of varying asset sizes, found decreasing returns to scale among eight of the nine societies in the largest asset group (over £5000 million).

Even if the Single Market is unlikely to lead to greater economies of scale within lending institutions, it may do so by creating a more unified capital market. Funds might then be raised and allocated more efficiently at the European level. The Single Market aims to create an environment more conducive to the development of European-wide of capital markets and transfers. First, exchange controls have now been abolished throughout the Union, and freedom of capital markets is established, apart from restrictions that remain in Greece. This will enable individuals and institutions to invest in whichever part of the Union returns are highest. Secondly, it aims to reduce the risk and costs associated with currency transactions through the managed Exchange Rate Mechanism (ERM), which greatly limited exchange rate movements between its members until much wider fluctuation bands were introduced following the crisis in the summer of 1993. Thirdly, the Maastricht Treaty envisaged that by the end of the century a single currency would be established, so removing exchange rate movements and the costs of currency transactions among those currencies participating in it.

Implementing the Single Market

The aim of the European Union and its predecessors has always been to create a single market, which the Single European Act (Article 8a) describes as "an area without internal frontiers in which the free movement of goods, persons, services and capital is ensured". It took ten years from the foundation of the Community in 1958 before its six original members abolished all quantitative restrictions on traded goods and tariff barriers between themselves and created a common external tariff. However, by the 1980s, it became apparent that member States were still using and in some cases increasing regulations as a means of protecting their indigenous industries. Such regulations are known as "non-tariff" barriers, and their removal was the principal objective of the Single Market programme. With its deadline for completion set at 31 December 1992 (hence its popular name in Britain, "1992"), a sense of urgency was added to the process.

Previously, progress towards the removal of non-tariff barriers was slow, because the Community had attempted to harmonize detailed regulations over all member States. Further, a single member State could often block agreement because unanimity was usually required in the Council of Ministers. With the Single Market programme, the Community adopted a new approach. In the *Cassis de Dijon* case of 1979, the European Court ruled that, if a good met the regulatory requirements of one member State, it could be sold anywhere in the Community, subject to certain exceptions. This created the possibility of establishing the Single Market on the basis of the minimum co-ordination of regulations. This idea was promoted in the Commission's White Paper, which proposed the Single Market programme (CEC 1985). Implementation was facilitated by the Single European Act, which amended the Treaty of Rome so as to extend the use of qualified majority voting in the Council of Ministers to the bulk of the Single Market programme.

In banking, the White Paper built on the First Banking Directive, which required member States to establish authorization procedures for all credit institutions under their supervision. The White Paper proposed that a single market in financial services could be established by the dual mechanisms of the "home country control" of institutions, and the "minimum harmonization" of prudential standards. These principles gave rise to the introduction of a "single passport" for credit institutions, combined with minimum capital adequacy standards, and are incorporated in three related directives, all of which were agreed in 1989. The Second Banking Directive introduces the single passport, and aspects of minimum harmonization, whereas the Own Funds Directive defines capital for use in the Solvency Ratio Directive, which establishes a minimum level of capital adequacy.

The regulatory framework of the Single Market is further strengthened by the measures taken to ensure the free movement of capital within the Union and also to reduce the risks that arise from exchange rate fluctuations. Institutions providing mortgages in the Community operate in an environment where flows of capital are commonplace and where exchange rate movements are crucial in determining risk when funds and loans are indifferent currencies. The Capital Liberalization Directive, the Exchange Rate Mechanism (ERM) and the Maastricht Treaty are intended to deal with these issues.

The European passport

The European passport is at the centre of the legislation aiming to introduce a single market in financial services, including mortgage credit, and is embodied in the Second Banking Directive. It is based on home country control of authorization and the single licence for activities. It is derived from the articles in the Treaty of Rome (52 and 59) relating to the right of establishment and the freedom to supply services. Its objective is stated clearly in the preamble to the Directive:

> [T]he approach that has been adopted is to achieve only the essential harmonization necessary and sufficient to secure the mutual recognition of authorization and of prudential supervision systems, making possible the granting of a single licence recognized throughout the Community and the application of the principle of home Member State prudential supervision.

The single passport (and indeed the whole of the Second Banking Directive) applies to credit institutions, which are defined by the First Banking Directive (Article 1) as institutions that "receive deposits or other repayable funds from the public and . . . grant credits", a definition that covers British clearing banks and building societies. These institutions also must comply with the minimum prudential standards established by the Second Banking Directive and its accompanying Directives, but the issue is further complicated by the ability of governments to restrict activities of institutions that conflict with national laws intended to promote the "general good".

Credit institutions may engage in a range of activities, which are listed in the Directive's Annex. These include the provision of mortgage credit and unsecured lending, as well as the normal banking activities of a credit institution, taking deposits and running a money transmission service. Activities not included in the list can be provided only with host State authorization. Non-listed services that contravene laws adopted in the "general good" (see below) can be excluded altogether, whereas it is only the method of provision that can be restricted for listed services (British Bankers' Association 1990: 41).

Activities can be provided in two ways, either through branches or subsidiaries (Second Banking Directive: Article 19(2)). The requirement for branches to be authorized by host member States is removed, as is their right to impose capital requirements for branches (Article 6(1) of the Second Banking Directive deletes Article 4 of the First Banking Directive).

Subsidiaries themselves must meet certain criteria to qualify for the passport. Activities that are to be exported through the subsidiary must also be conducted in the home member State. This condition conforms to the central principle of the passport. Home State authorization becomes meaningful as a guide to acceptability of an activity only if that authorization applies to home State operations. Supervision must take place on a consolidated basis, and the parent institution must guarantee the commitments of its subsidiary, in which it must have a 90% share. These last two conditions are particularly restrictive. Subsidiaries exist when a parent organization has a clear controlling interest, but the passport can be used only when the share of ownership is 90% or above. Further, parent companies may not guarantee fully a subsidiary's commitments. However, if the passport is to be used to export services, they must do so. This is to allow parent institutions to export activities that they themselves can conduct at home only through subsidiaries. The most prominent example concerned UK banks, which can conduct securities business only through subsidiaries.

The prudential supervision of credit institutions is therefore placed with the home State's supervisory authorities (Second Banking Directive: Article 13(1)) in all areas other than the supervision of branch liquidity, where the host State authorities take lead responsibility in co-operation with those of the home State (ibid.: Article 14(2)). This exception is intended to be temporary, pending further co-ordination.

Much controversy surrounds the "general good" provision that allows host member States

> to prevent or to punish irregularities committed within their territories, which are contrary to the legal rules they have adopted in the interest of the general good. This shall include the possibility of preventing offending institutions from initiating any further transactions within their territories. (ibid.: Article 21(5))

Such actions must be "properly justified" and are subject to appeal in the courts of the host member State (ibid.: Article 21(6)). There is some concern that the "general good" clause could be interpreted so as to give member States the ability to block any passported activity that threatens their indigenous institutions. If this turns out to be the case, then the advantages of the single passport would be nullified, and progress towards a single market in financial services impeded. But such cases would be open to challenge and, if carried too far, would become a matter for settlement at the European Court of Justice. Much would then depend on how the concept of the general good is to be interpreted.

A similar provision was included in the (now defunct) Draft Mortgage Directive (Draft Mortgage Credit Directive, Article 10),[2] which was examined in detail by the House of Lords Select Committee on the European Communities. In written evidence, the Building Societies Association (BSA) argued that, since *prima facie* all laws are justified on grounds of the general good, the host country would have *carte blanche* to pass any law it chose (House of Lords 1985, Memorandum from the Building Societies Association, para. 21). One witness, a member of the European Parliament's Economic Committee, went further, claiming that the "general good" provision "allows Member State governments to escape from the provisions of the treaty." (ibid.: Examination of Witnesses, para. 231).

However, these views greatly exaggerate the likely problems arising from the "general good" clause, which is subject to the jurisprudence of the European

---

2. There were two drafts, but the reference is correct for both.

Court. The then Director-General of DGXV (the part of the European Commission responsible for financial institutions) also gave oral evidence to the Committee. He agreed with the proposition that the "general good is a legal term of objective and limited application, and not just a vague phrase". He added that "it does not mean just any odd provision that the host country would like it to mean." (ibid.: paras 127–8).

The Treasury has summarized the European Court's definitions of the limits to the meaning of the "general good", suggesting that, to be valid, laws that are claimed to reflect the general good must meet three criteria: they must be non-discriminatory, they must not replicate home State requirements, and they must be proportionate in relation to their objective (HM Treasury 1992: para. 83).

The concern felt by some is nevertheless that the "general good" clause could be used to restrict competition. Legal restrictions on the variability of interest rates or the size of loans that may be granted are examples of restrictions that might be justified by the "general good". It is notable, however, that Belgium, the country that used to forbid the use of variable rate mortgages, has ended this restriction because of the Single Market. Other countries may be slower to remove restrictions. As has been noted, France still forbids the payment of interest on short-term accounts. It may be that the uncertainty surrounding the "general good" will be as damaging to cross-border competition as any real effect, but such uncertainty should not last longer than a few years, provided that the European Court takes a clear position.

The Second Banking Directive places no obligation on member States to allow institutions under their supervision to take advantage of the Single Market. In the UK, the banks are free to conduct business overseas and this enables them to utilize the European passport. However, the position of the building societies is far more complex. Before new legislation for building societies was introduced in 1987, British building societies were unable to make loans abroad, although there was nothing to prevent them from taking deposits abroad. The reason for this lay with the wording of the 1962 Building Societies Act, which restricted the purpose of a society to "granting loans on security of mortgage as freehold or leasehold estate" (Building Societies Act 1962, S1(1)). Since forms of tenure defined in this way do not exist in any European Union country other than in Britain and Ireland, on the Continent lending was effectively prohibited. The exclusion was not accidental, because an amendment to the Bill that preceded the 1962 Act, which would have enabled societies to lend abroad, was withdrawn after discussion (House of Lords 1985: pt 2, para. 27).

The review of building society legislation in the mid-1980s was able to give consideration to the foreign operation of societies, because, although the Second Banking Directive had not appeared, the Draft Mortgage Directive had been issued. The Treasury's Green Paper, which preceded new legislation, revealed a cautious attitude to the relaxation of geographical restrictions, merely requesting comments on the matter (HM Treasury 1984: paras 3.23–25). Furthermore, in evidence given to the House of Lords Select Committee, a senior Treasury official suggested that caution towards the direct operation of societies abroad arose from their mutual status and the implications of having foreigners as members! There was therefore a preference for any foreign operations to be conducted through subsidiaries constituted in those countries. The Treasury's views contrasted sharply with those of the building societies and the Building Societies Association. They wanted societies to be granted powers to lend abroad, both directly and through subsidiaries (House of Lords 1985: Memorandum from HM Treasury, para. 10).

The 1986 Building Societies Act (henceforth referred to as the 1986 Act) reflects the Treasury's cautious view. This Act grants the supervisory bodies (the Building Societies Commission and the Treasury) the ability to extend building society powers on a step-by-step basis through secondary legislation. This unfolding approach has offered societies two routes by which they can operate in the European Union, but neither allows them to take full advantage of the European passport.

The first route is through subsidiaries, the approach clearly favoured by the Treasury. Building societies are allowed to invest in or support various "qualifying bodies", which are subsidiaries often formed where co-operation between financial institutions is necessary. In this case, the relevant qualifying bodies or subsidiaries are termed "corresponding European bodies", which are,

> . . . bodies formed in another member State for the purpose of carrying on in another member State businesses that consist wholly or mainly in lending money on the security of land and do not (where that is not the whole business) include lending on land in the UK. (Building Societies Act 1986: S18(2)(b))

Building societies may invest in their European subsidiaries by acquiring sole or part share ownership and can support them through loans (with or without security), grants, guarantees of liabilities and the use of services or property (not necessarily with payment; ibid.: S18(1)b). But the extent to which building societies can invest in European subsidiaries is limited by statute. They are classified as Class 3 assets, which in total must not exceed 10% of total commercial assets of a society (ibid.: S20(3) (amended)).

The Building Societies Commission (BSC), which has supervised the societies since the implementation of the 1986 Act, has also been responsible for controlling the extension of building society powers under this section of the Act, through Designation of Qualifying Bodies Orders, which are statutory instruments. From 1987, societies with commercial assets of at least £100 million were allowed to adopt the necessary constitutional powers to establish European subsidiaries (The Building Societies (Designation of Qualifying Bodies) Order 1986).[3] In 1992, the BSC extended the range of services that building society

---

3. These powers were consolidated into The Building Societies (Designation of Qualifying Bodies) Order (No. 2) 1991.

subsidiaries could operate, to include life and general insurance (The Building Societies (Member States) Order 1992) and financial services (The Building Societies (Designation of Qualifying Bodies) Order (No. 4) 1992).

However, there is an important restriction in relation to the single passport under the UK legislation. European subsidiaries of UK building societies are explicitly prohibited from themselves either lending on land or taking deposits in the UK (Building Societies Act 1986: S18(4a and b)). This restriction, which is intended to prevent societies from evading restrictions on wholesale funding that apply to the parent organization, may itself represent a contravention of the Second Banking Directive and is certainly anomalous. Building society subsidiaries cannot operate in Europe using the single passport, because they cannot conduct business in Britain. It is questionable whether this restriction is compatible with European law, although the European Commission has taken no action to date.

The second route, which has been available to building societies since 1992, enables them to operate in other member States directly or on a branch basis. The Treasury used its powers under the 1986 Act to grant building societies "powers to make advances to members secured on land outside the UK corresponding to the powers to make advances secured on land within the UK" (ibid.: S14(1)). Only building societies with commercial assets of at least £100 million are allowed to do this (The Building Societies (Member States) Order 1992). This statutory instrument also allows building societies to raise deposits in other member States, provided that this is on a branch (or other direct) basis.

However, this does not allow societies to take full advantage of the single passport either. Building societies are confined under the 1986 Act to making loans secured on land, and cannot carry out any of the other activities, such as unsecured lending, which are covered by the Second Banking Directive and which societies offer in Britain already. There is little that the BSC or the Treasury can do about these restrictions, because the statutory instrument has gone as far as the Act permits. Primary legislation, amending the 1986 Act, would be required to bring into line the range of activities that societies are permitted to undertake in other Union countries with those that the Second Banking Directive allows to be passported and which societies already undertake in Britain. Without this, building societies are unable to take full advantage of the single passport.

Minimum harmonization of prudential standards

The single passport is complemented by the establishment of minimum prudential standards that must be followed by all institutions operating in the EU. These standards are intended to prevent competition reducing standards to unacceptably low levels that might endanger the banking system. They must be met by all credit institutions and not just those seeking to use the passport. Therefore, they affect institutions operating only within their own member State, as well as those that wish to extend their activities to other parts of the Union. Member States have the right to impose higher standards on domestic institutions, but not on those registered elsewhere in the Union, which are using the passport.

Many of the minimum prudential standards are of relatively little importance to building societies, although minor amendments to the 1986 Act have been necessary (The Banking Co-ordination (Second Council Directive) Regulations 1992). However, the Second Banking Directive also introduces some significant changes to building society prudential standards. It requires credit institutions to have a minimum capital requirement at authorization and on a continuing basis (Second Banking Directive, Articles 4(1) and 10) and this will have a restrictive effect on the setting up of new institutions. Normally, the minimum capital requirement is ECU5 million (about £4 million), but member States are allowed to apply a lower amount (ECU1 million) to some institutions (ibid.: Article 4(2)). The British government has adopted the lower amount for building societies and the 1986 Act is amended by the same statutory instrument (Regulation 9(13) of the Banking Co-ordination (Second Council Directive) Regulations 1992 amends S9(13) of the Building Societies Act 1986). This still represents a higher figure than previously required by the 1986 Act (about £800000 against £100000). This is likely to have the effect of ruling out the creation of new societies, but arguably it is their mutual status and the consequent inability to raise equity finance that limits the possibility of creating new societies, rather than the £800000 minimum capital requirement. It is notable that, even before the EU rules came into effect, only one new building society (the Ecology) has been created in recent decades.

The EU's capital adequacy provisions are by far the most important component of the minimum prudential standards that underpin the passport. They form a part of a wider movement towards harmonization among the Group of 10 (G10)[4] countries under the aegis of the Basle Committee. By and large, the capital adequacy requirements adopted by the G10 are the same as those adopted by the EU in the Solvency Ratio and Own Funds Directives. The principal importance of these directives to the UK is that they have brought about a considerable degree of convergence in the regulation of banks and building societies, although differences remain. The banks came under the G10 arrangements in the mid-1980s. The building societies retained their own distinctive capital adequacy regime until 1994. When the EU directives came into force in 1993, both regimes were applied for that year. From 1994, the previous regulatory regime was abandoned. Nevertheless, the BSC has exercised its right to apply more stringent quantitative and qualitative ratios than those required by the directives.

The capital of an organization is the difference between its assets (such as mortgages) and liabilities (such as savers' deposits). An organization that wishes to expand its asset base (by making more loans, for example) must have spare capital. Capital adequacy standards require organizations to back their assets

---

4. Belgium, Canada, France, Germany, Italy, Japan, the Netherlands, Sweden, the UK and the USA.

with a minimum level of capital. The amount may vary according to the degree of risk involved with different types of loans. For example, mortgages are regarded as a relatively safe form of lending, because they are secured by an asset as well as being backed by the borrowers' future income, whereas personal loans are more risky because they generally depend only on the borrowers' future income.

Under the British arrangements, building societies have been supervised under a separate capital adequacy regime from banks, on the ground that their asset base is much more concentrated. By law, at least 75% of building society assets must be held in the form of first mortgages secured on owner-occupied dwellings, and the proportion of mortgages to all assets is typically much higher than this. Until 1994, the Building Societies Commission's capital adequacy system for building societies was much more detailed than either that laid down by the EU Directives or that operated by the Bank of England for the banks. Assets on building societies' balance sheets were each given minimum percentage capital requirements, and distinctions were made between categories of mortgage, according to risk. These requirements were summed to give the level of "minimum acceptable capital" (MAC). An additional 0.5% of assets had to be added to the MAC to give the desired level of capital (DC) (Boléat 1988: 49–54). Since insufficient details of building society assets are given in their accounts, it is not possible to calculate MAC or DC ratios. Further, the Building Societies Commission set individual ratios for individual societies, taking into account qualitative factors. These ratios were higher than DC calculation. If a society's capital fell too close to the minimum required by the BSC, then it had to take steps to restore its position, for example by widening margins or even stopping lending for a period.

The Solvency Ratio Directive establishes the minimum ratio of capital ("own funds") to assets at 8% from 1993 (Solvency Ratio Directive: Articles 4,5 and 10). In the calculation, not all assets are treated alike, because they are weighted for risk. Although the whole value of most assets must be supported by the 8% capital ratio, lower proportions are applied to less risky assets. There are four risk categories (ibid.: Article 6). Cash and money held with governments and central banks are given a zero risk weighting, whereas loans to banks are given a 20% risk weighting. Mortgages are given a favourable risk weighting, being placed in the 50% category, virtually alone. To come into the 50% category, mortgages must be fully secured on residential property, whether owner-occupied or rented (ibid.). This means that, instead of requiring an 8% capital backing, mortgages require a 4% backing.

Ratios are to be calculated on a consolidated basis at least twice a year (ibid.: Article 3). Capital is defined by the Own Funds Directive (Own Funds Directive: Article 4) and is placed into two categories (ibid.: Article 6). The main components of Tier 1 (known as "primary" or "core") capital are equity capital and reserves (accumulated profits), less certain items, which include an institution's holdings of its own shares, intangible assets and current-year losses. Tier 2 (secondary) capital consists mainly of subordinated debt and preferential shares.

Secondary capital must not exceed 100% of primary capital, whereas subordinated debt and fixed-term preferential shares must not exceed 50% of Tier 1 capital.

Both the Bank of England and the Building Societies Commission have chosen to impose higher ratios on the institutions that they supervise than the minima required by the directives. In both cases, unpublished ratios are allotted to individual institutions. The BSC has gone further in a Prudential Note that took effect in 1994 and has imposed higher weightings to be used in the calculation of the 8% ratio (Prudential Note 1993/4: Annex B). Instead of attracting a zero weighting, investment in government securities in EU, EFTA[5] and G10 countries have been given a 10% or 20% weighting. Mortgages, too, come under closer scrutiny (as indeed they did under the previous building society regime). Only some residential mortgages are given the 50% weighting established in the directives. Higher risk mortgages have higher weightings, so require more capital. For example, those mortgages with loan to value ratios over 90% (95% if the loan pre-dates February 1994) are given a 60% weighting, and those where 5% or more of the balance is in arrears require a 75% weighting. Higher ratios are justified by the regulator "to reflect more accurately the risk structure of the business" (BSC 1992: para. 3.10). It might also be true that the greater transparency created by imposing higher weightings in the calculation of the solvency ratio allows the BSC to set lower private ratios for individual societies than would otherwise be the case.

The BSC has always been anxious to emphasize the ease with which building societies would meet the new capital adequacy requirements (e.g. BSC 1988: para. 4.8). In 1991, the Commission was able to report that all societies had met the new requirement, with 90% of all societies having solvency ratios in the 10–22% range (BSC 1992: para 2.18). The average ratio rose from 11.82% in 1991 to 12.17% in 1992 (BSC 1993: 33). In this respect, the new regime poses few problems.

The BSC has also aided building societies by giving them access to new sources of capital. In 1988 the BSC allowed societies to count subordinated debt as capital on the same basis as is acceptable to the EU (The Building Societies (Supplementary Capital) Order 1988 and Prudential Note 1988/1, revised). This had the effect of immediately improving the availability of capital for societies. Subordinated debt counts as secondary capital and consists of loans that are not secured and cannot be refunded in the event of liquidation until the claims of the depositors have first been met. The restriction on the use of secondary capital, in relation to primary capital, limits its utility.

Until recently the sole source of core capital for building societies was retained profits (reserves) because, as mutual organizations, they could not raise equity capital. This changed in 1991 when societies were allowed to raise a new

---

5. European Free Trade Association: includes the EU, Iceland and Norway. Austria, Finland and Sweden were also members of EFTA before joining the EU in 1995.

form of primary capital, called Permanent Interest Bearing Shares (PIBS), which are a form of quasi-equity that is nevertheless compatible with mutuality since they confer no control over the society (The Building Societies (Designated Capital Sources) (Permanent Interest Bearing Shares) Order 1991). As PIBS allow societies to increase their core capital, the 100% ratio (see above) permits the scope for subordinated debt also to be expanded.

From June 1991 to July 1993, twelve societies raised £720 million through PIBS. Under the EU rules, this figure would support an increase in mortgage lending of £18000 million.[6] Further, the creation of £720 million of new primary capital would allow these societies to increase their secondary capital by up to this amount (because secondary capital must not exceed 100% of primary capital). Thus, a further £720 million of capital could be raised, with the result that the issue of PIBS could lead to a total additional mortgage lending of £36000 million. Nevertheless, there is an effective market constraint placed on the amount of PIBS that can be issued, which is thought to be around 20% of primary capital.

Smaller societies might be expected to have some difficulty in taking advantage of new sources of capital, because fixed costs involved in issues can be too high in relation to their size. Private placements have been used successfully for subordinated debt, and might be possible for PIBS. Syndication for PIBS is allowed in principle, but societies have experienced difficulties in co-operation. Of course many smaller societies have been able to improve their capital position by increasing their reserves. However, issued capital is likely to play an increasingly important role in the future, and still more forms of capital are likely to become available to building societies. It is possible, for example, that building societies might be permitted to issue profit-related shares.

It is difficult to isolate the precise effects of the EU's capital adequacy requirements on UK institutions. A greater degree of regulatory convergence has been achieved between banks and building societies. Both the Building Societies Commission and the Bank of England have imposed additional requirements on the institutions they supervise, but the Building Societies Commission has continued to impose more detailed requirements to reflect both the concentration of building society assets and the less favourable circumstances prevailing in the housing market. The degree to which it is possible to attribute building societies' access to new forms of capital to greater regulatory convergence with the banks is debatable, but at the very least the two movements complement one another.

---

6. $720 \times 100/4 = 18000$. The 4 is derived from the 50% weighting given to mortgages and the solvency ratio of 8% (50% of 8 = 4). Clearly, the amount of possible new lending for mortgages that require higher weightings will be smaller for a given amount of capital.

Exchange risk and capital movements

A single market in mortgage credit requires the free movement of capital. All housing finance systems are based on recycling savings as loans, whether or not savings are organized on a retail or wholesale basis. Within countries, it is unlikely that the demand and supply of savings will be evenly spread. Regional restrictions on the operations of savings and loans institutions in the USA, combined with regional disparities in demand for and supply of savings, led to deregulation. Similarly, it is very unlikely that the demand for and supply of funds for housing is evenly spread across the EU. Thus, a single market in mortgage credit is likely to involve the transfer of funds between countries and hence currencies.

Two issues arise from this. First, whether funds can be moved from one country to another, and second, the extent to which exchange risk affects the demand for free movement. The free movement of capital has been one of the most problematic areas of the common market, because of the relationship between exchange controls, currency stability and national macroeconomic management. The Capital Liberalization Directive required exchange controls to be lifted from July 1990 in all EU countries except Spain, Portugal, Greece and Ireland. These countries were allowed to delay implementation until January 1993. However, the Directive allows member States,

> . . . to take measures to restrict . . . short-term capital movements that, even where there is no appreciable divergence in economic fundamentals, might seriously disrupt the conduct of their monetary and exchange-rate policies (Capital Liberalization Directive: preamble).

The Capital Liberalization Directive has now been overtaken by the Maastricht Treaty, which greatly reduces uncertainty over the continued liberalization of capital movements, both between member States themselves and between member States and third countries.[7]

Since mid-1992, the degree of stability offered by the ERM has been significantly reduced as speculation against some currencies has increased. Britain and Italy were forced out of the ERM in September 1992. Ireland, Portugal and Spain devalued, but were allowed to retain exchange controls temporarily in accordance with the Capital Liberalization Directive. In August 1993 speculation against the French Franc forced the adoption of wider permitted fluctuation limits in exchange rates between all currencies, except for the Dutch guilder and the Deutschmark, for which a bilateral agreement continued the previous 2.5% fluctuation band. The prospects for monetary union, which would remove exchange

---

7. The Treaty on European Union (Maastricht) deletes Articles 67–73 of the Treaty of Rome, replacing them with the new Article 73, which states, *inter alia*, "Within the framework of the provisions set out in the chapter, all restrictions on the movement of capital between member States and between member States and third countries shall be prohibited." Restrictions on capital movements between member States and third countries may be introduced in limited circumstances using specified procedures (see especially Article 73 (c)).

risk altogether, have been set back by economic recession. Certainly, monetary union involving all 15 member States now seems to be improbable in the foreseeable future.

The risks of taking out mortgages denominated in other currencies, or even in ECU, have proved to be too great, even though they were being promoted in the recent past. The movement of funds by institutions is less vulnerable to currency movements, because hedging instruments have been developed, although the cost of these may be expected to rise with the degree of uncertainty and to erode substantially any advantage from borrowing in the cheapest currency. The movement of savings from one currency to another would be expected to be less vulnerable than mortgages, since a block of savings might be raised by an institution that could use hedging instruments on the total. Nevertheless, the environment for a single market in mortgage credit is clearly less attractive than it was when the Maastricht Treaty was agreed.

The Single Market in operation

The previous two sections examined the key assumptions that lie behind the idea of a single market in mortgage finance. In this section the Single Market is examined in operation, using empirical evidence to give an indication of its likely future progress. This information partly tests the economic assumptions and the regulatory system discussed already. It also tests assumptions about the behaviour of financial institutions, such as profit maximization as the principal reason for their entering other markets.

Before the completion of the legislation underpinning the Single Market in banking, the UK had one of the most open markets in the world, which attracted a wide range of foreign institutions. UK financial institutions also began to enter other European mortgage markets from the late 1980s, and this trend is continuing. These developments allow an assessment to be made of the extent to which a single market in mortgage finance will be created. The assessment made here is based on discussions with senior managers of a range of financial institutions and the Building Societies Commission. The lenders covered were five building societies, three British banks (including a former building society) and two foreign banks operating in Britain (one on a branch basis, the other as a subsidiary). Summary information on these institutions is contained in Table 10.4.

European objectives

Of the eight British institutions interviewed, each had given consideration to the Single Market. The absence of existing European operations, or of specific plans to operate in Europe, does not preclude European involvement at some stage.

Table 10.4   Lenders selected for interview (assets in £000 millions).

Institution	Designation	Total assets[a]	Mortgage assets	Comments
Abbey National	Bank	71.8	40.1	Converted from building society in 1989
Bank of Scotland	Bank	24.7	4.5	Few branches outside Scotland; has central lending arm
Bradford & Bingley	Building society	13.0	10.0	Top ten society
Crédit Agricole	Federation of French credit co-operatives	192.0	. . .	UK branch of France's largest bank, but weak central control
Dunfermline	Building society	0.7	0.6	Largest of three Scottish societies
Halifax	Building society	58.7	47.9	Largest UK society and mortgage lender
Mortgage Trust	Centralized lender	. . .	0.9[b]	Subsidiary of Swedish bank
Nationwide	Building society	34.1	26.5	Top ten society
Royal Bank of Scotland	Bank	34.5	3.5	Branch network through-out UK
Woolwich	Building society	23.3	18.6	Top ten society

a. On group basis in 1992, except for Crédit Agricole (1991) and Halifax (financial year ending 31.1.92)
b. Of these only £100 million are held on balance sheet
Source: Annual reports and accounts (1992), except Crédit Agricole (1991), Mortgage Trust (interview), Bank of Scotland and Royal Bank of Scotland (*Mortgage Finance Gazette*, July 1993).

Indeed, change can occur quickly, as is indicated by the launching of two of the most significant European strategies (of the Halifax and the Bradford & Bingley Building Societies) in 1993 alone. Although the Nationwide is not yet active in Europe, it intends to be at some stage. The Dunfermline (the 30th largest society and much smaller than the others interviewed) does not rule out European operations in the future, although the Building Societies Commission thought it unlikely that societies outside the twenty largest would consider operating in Europe.

European operations of British lenders

Profit maximization is rarely an explicit objective of European strategies. The most common objective of European operations is some form of diversification. Clearly, extending operations to another country involves geographical diversification, which entails either expanding the customer base, or extending the availability of existing services to domestic customers when they are abroad. The expansion of the customer base through geographical diversification is also seen as a means of spreading risk and, in the case of the Woolwich, of lessening dependence on the volatile UK housing market. The Royal Bank of Scotland's principal objective has always been to extend services to domestic customers when they are abroad. The extension of the customer base has always been a secondary objective and has now been downgraded further.

There is also a defensive element in the formulation of European objectives, even among the larger lenders. Both the Abbey National and the Nationwide thought that European operations would help them to retain their positions as major national lenders. The defensive element in a smaller lender's objective is easier to understand. The Bradford & Bingley Building Society, which is highly innovative in its European operations, aims to retain its independence as a small-to-medium size institution in the context of a single market, where competition might intensify and predatory institutions might appear. However, the Royal Bank of Scotland's board specifically rejected the notion that its European objectives should include protection against take-over.

The continental operations of British lenders are summarized in Table 10.5. Until 1993, the choice of countries was confined to Italy, Spain and France, when the Bradford & Bingley became the first British institution to announce plans to enter the German market. The choice of countries is discussed in more detail below. It is noticeable that none of the British institutions interviewed has entered European markets on a branch basis. Building societies were in any case not permitted to establish branches in Europe until 1992, but subsequent operations have continued to depend on the establishment of subsidiaries or joint ventures.

Before 1993, the most common method of entry was through the acquisition of a subsidiary. Two of the Abbey National's three continental ventures have been established in this way, as has one of the Woolwich's subsidiaries. The Abbey National bought Fico France for £40 million; the Woolwich bought all of the assets (apart from the mortgage book) of the Midland Bank's subsidiary Banque Immobilier de Crédit (BIC) for £3 million. The Woolwich undertook to manage the mortgage book in return for a fee. The Bank of Scotland bought a part (50%) share of an Italian finance company (FIM). However, in 1993 the Halifax established its own subsidiary in Spain.

The principal attraction of acquiring an existing subsidiary is that evidence of its performance enables risk to be reduced. This does not always work, as the Abbey National discovered when its French subsidiary started making losses on an inherited loan book. Where existing subsidiaries cannot be acquired, joint ventures are a means of spreading risk and, to some extent, pooling expertise. Abbey National entered the Spanish market through a joint venture with two partners: a financial services company (Grupo Cor), offering some mortgage experience, and a Swiss insurance company (Winterhur), which has a Spanish subsidiary with a branch network. Abbey National is gradually gaining complete control over the subsidiary and, by 1995, is expected to own 92% of its shares.

More recent ventures have involved the establishment of subsidiaries, rather than their acquisition. The Woolwich started this trend in 1990, when it entered the Italian market; it has since been followed by the Halifax in Spain and the Bradford & Bingley in Germany. Go-it-alone subsidiaries are not necessarily the first choice of institutions wishing to operate abroad. For example, the Halifax

Table 10.5   British operations in Continental mortgage markets.

Institution	Country	Nature of operation	Began	Mortgage origination	Mortgage funding
Abbey National	Spain	Joint venture (Abbeycor Nacional	1988	2 branches & 3rd party	Wholesale
	Italy	100% ownership of subsidiary (Abbey National Mutui)	1989	10 branches & 3rd party	Wholesale: all raised from parent
	France	100% ownership of subsidiary (Fico France / Abbey National France	1990	12 branches & 3rd party	Wholesale: 45% raised in France, 55% from parent
Bank of Scotland	Italy	50% of subsidiary (FIM)	1992	10 branches & 3rd party	Wholesale
Bradford & Bingley	Germany	Established subsidiary (Bausparkasse)	1993	Marketing company & 3rd party	Retail
	Germany	Established branch	1994	1 branch &	Retail
Halifax	Spain	Established subsidiary (Banco Halifax)	1993	3rd party	Retail
Woolwich	France	100% ownership of non-commercial assets of former Midland Bank subsidiary (BIC / Banque Woolwich)	1989	17 branches & 3rd party	Wholesale: mainly raised in France, but some by parent
	Italy	100% ownership of subsidiary (Woolwich SpA)	1990	3rd party	Wholesale: mainly raised in Italy, but some by parent

had experienced difficulty in finding suitable partners for joint ventures. This has been attributed to its size in relation to potential partners. Institutions the size of the Halifax are unlikely to need partners in their domestic market, whereas smaller ones that might benefit from such an arrangement would exercise a disproportionately large influence over the operation, but would offer comparatively little in return.

A notable feature of each of the European operations of the British institutions surveyed is that only one is using the single passport established by the Second Banking Directive for its mortgage operations. Whether wholly owned by British institutions or joint ventures, these European subsidiaries operate under host State banking licences. As has been explained already, building society European subsidiaries cannot make use of the single passport because they are prohibited from operating in Britain. Nevertheless, there are advantages to holding a host-State banking licence, which are discussed below.

Before 1993, British institutions operating abroad adopted a fairly standard model of centralized lending. There are two distinguishing features of centralized lenders. The first is that they have either small or non-existent branch networks, so require some other means of finding borrowers. The origination of mortgages is therefore usually carried out by a third party that does have a branch network or a sales force. The second feature also arises from the lack of a branch network. Usually, their funding does not come from retail sources (individual savers). Instead, funds are raised on the wholesale markets, either by the subsidiary itself or by its parent organization. The Abbey National and the Woolwich mix their wholesale funding sources, increasing the proportion raised by the parent when funds are cheaper in the UK.

There is some evidence that the centralized model of operating is changing. Although the Woolwich has reduced the number of its branches in France (from 20 to 17), it wishes to increase their use for originating mortgages. The Halifax will have only one branch (in Madrid), but this will be used to raise retail deposits for mortgage lending in Spain. Similarly, the Bradford & Bingley's subsidiary in Germany is a *Bausparkasse*, by definition a retail funded operation. Without a network of branches through which to originate mortgages, the Bradford & Bingley has established a second subsidiary, a marketing company. This will specialize in identifying third-party outlets (brokers, sales companies and independent insurance and investment houses) for the *Bausparkasse*'s products. However, in 1994 the Bradford & Bingley also announced its intention to open a branch in Germany under the Second Banking Directive, so further mirroring the typical structure of the German market, which is discussed below.

The method of operation of UK institutions in other EU countries is therefore quite different from their traditional mode of operation in the UK. It is true that British institutions operating in their domestic market do use third-party agents and operate extensively in wholesale markets. Some banks and building societies even have central lending arms. Nevertheless, their strength still lies in retail funding with large branch networks that are also used to originate mortgages. That UK institutions, and in particular building societies with their comparative advantage in intermediation efficiency, should operate in other European markets is to be expected if the Single Market is to operate as is intended. Their operation without using the single passport is a secondary issue. Therefore, the relevant questions are the extent of their operations abroad, and the extent to which they are "exporting" their efficiency. The former is still very limited indeed and shows no sign of rapid growth in the future; as for the latter, not only are British institutions not exporting their traditional strengths, but in the case of the Bradford & Bingley's *Bausparkasse*, the British institution is taking advantage of German regulations that guarantee a particular rate of return from the intermediation process. This is not a good example of how the Single Market is supposed to increase price competition! Yet an examination of the selection of markets by British institutions, and the problems that they either anticipated or have since discovered, points to the possible limits of the single passport as a means of creating a single market in mortgage finance.

The perceived inefficiency of mortgage markets is a key factor in making them attractive to external competition. This is seen most clearly in the cases of Italy and Spain. The changes in the Spanish market, in particular, suggest that the Single Market is having its desired effect, with external competition, or at least its threat, playing a role in deregulation and increased price competition (see Ch. 8).

The experiences in France and Germany tell different stories. France was earlier identified as being an inefficient market, so should be a target for competition from more competitive institutions, especially since institutions have found it relatively easy to gain a banking licence, even before the Single Market. Yet the same inefficiencies act as effective barriers to entry for foreign institutions. Much of the problem arises from the effective prohibition on the payment of interest on short-term retail accounts (of under three months). This makes it impossible to compete for savings on these accounts, while also giving French institutions a source of cheap funds for lending that outside institutions cannot match. This has impeded the progress of foreign banks, notably Barclays, that wish to establish a presence in the retail market by competing for savings, but it also affects foreign centralized lenders and French finance companies that at present have to rely solely on relatively expensive wholesale funds. Put simply, it is this source of inefficiency that limits competition.

The French courts have so far upheld the prohibition on interest-bearing short-term accounts, but it is conceivable that the French regulations will be changed as a result of action in the European courts, or just possibly from the pressure of international competition in the savings market. In contrast, the problems that institutions have faced in the German market have arisen largely from the peculiar structure of that mortgage market. Many British institutions believed the German market to be attractive, but, until the Bradford & Bingley, none succeeded in entering it. Several decided that it was unviable because of the market structure. Others abandoned their attempt when they were unable to find a suitable partner.

The Royal Bank of Scotland is unusual in that it and its partner, Banco Santander, had gone so far as to acquire joint ownership of a German retail bank with the objective of entering the mortgage market. However, they soon concluded that the regulatory privileges conferred on some institutions made successful entry impossible. The possibility of challenging German regulations on housing finance in the courts was abandoned, because the market for consumer lending following unification was more attractive.

The difficulty in entering the German mortgage market arises from its high degree of vertical integration, which arises from the regulatory privileges conferred on *Bausparkassen* (which have a monopoly over the State-subsidized contract savings scheme) and the mortgage banks (which have a monopoly over the issue of mortgage bonds). The mortgage products that these institutions can offer are also regulated (with restrictions on the amount that can be lent, for example) and this creates a need to package loans (to increase the total amount that can be lent). The combination of regulatory privilege with the need to package loans causes the high degree of vertical integration, through ownership, takeover, control or co-operation, in Germany.

Some British institutions have considered establishing *Bausparkassen* under

213

German law, but in 1993 the Bradford & Bingley was the first foreign institution to gain a licence to operate one. As was noted above, the Bradford & Bingley can hardly contribute to price competition in the German mortgage market, since the margins of *Bausparkassen* are regulated by the State. However, the regulatory framework in Germany is not suited to single passport style competition, and foreign institutions can be successful only by playing to host-State rules. The move into Germany may pave the way for the sale of insurance products when the Single Market is extended to cover these in 1994. However, it is also true that the Bradford & Bingley's entry into the German market is a relatively low risk one, because of the highly regulated environment in which it will operate. Although the Bradford & Bingley has announced that it will open a branch in Germany, this could be seen as part of a vertical ownership structure that incorporates a *Bausaparkasse* and a marketing company.

Institutions operating in other countries have found that even supposedly uncompetitive markets can be risky. Abbey National France required an injection of £36 million from its parent in 1993. This loss was blamed on the commercial property loan book that the British institution inherited but which fell victim to the sharp downturn in this market. Abbey National is taking on no more commercial property business in France, but claims that the residential mortgage book performs as well as its British counterpart. The Royal Bank of Scotland's experience of the Spanish mortgage market was as brief as it was disastrous. The Royal Bank's attempt to enter the mortgage market with a Gibraltar-based company (Alomar) in 1990 ended in losses of about £1 million on fewer than a hundred loans in less than a year. The link with Alomar had been made in an attempt to enable borrowers to avoid the capital gains tax that is levied on domestic property in Spain, but the two organizations' business practices were incompatible.

Since then the Royal Bank's European strategy has focused on extending services to domestic customers when they are abroad. It joined the Inter-Bank On-Line System (IBOS) Association, which is a European Economic Interest Grouping (EEIG). These organizations are established under a European Directive to help small-to-medium size organizations to take advantage of the Single Market, through co-operation with similar organizations in other member States. They are intended to facilitate the pooling of expertise and distribution networks and to allow smaller institutions to gain economies of scale in other areas, such as product development and marketing. There is nothing to stop institutions from co-operating in these matters outside an EEIG, but they offer legal neutrality between partners and guarantee their autonomy. This is intended to remove any disadvantage one member may experience through a restrictive national legal system. The IBOS Association has three other members (including Banco Santander) in Spain and Portugal. Although the membership of the IBOS Association is still quite small, it has already established an international money-transmission service.

The Bradford & Bingley is also a member of an EEIG, the European Group of Financial Institutions (EGFI), which was established in 1990. It has a membership of ten, in nine countries. The members are mainly savings banks and co-operatives and, although some of them are publicly owned, none is quoted on any stock exchange. The EGFI aims to promote co-operation among its members, for example by cross-selling products through each other's branches.

In 1993 the Bradford & Bingley used its link with the Belgian EGFI member, the Antwerp Savings Bank (HBK), to raise retail funds in Belgium which were then converted into sterling for mortgage lending in Britain. The scheme was based on tight competition in the British savings market and surplus funds in Belgium, which were available at a lower interest rate than in Britain. The HBK launched a fixed-rate savings account (called "Euro-fix") with terms of 14 days to a year. Funds were raised in blocks (the first was for BFr100 million) that were then packaged into sterling for use by the Bradford & Bingley, with an equivalent swap in Belgian Francs to remove the exchange risk. The funds had to be structured in such a way as to ensure that they could still be classified as retail funds, because the amount of wholesale funds that a building society can raise is limited. This scheme gives some idea of the possibility of creating a single market in savings, even without a single currency. In turn, this may be the route through which mortgage markets, which are dependent on uncompetitive savings market, are deregulated. It also gives an idea of the complexities that arise from these arrangements, which might limit their use.

European operations in Britain

In the 1980s, Britain had one of the most open mortgage markets in Europe. The boom in the housing market attracted foreign banks to enter the British market as centralized lenders. It will be recalled that centralized lending relies solely on wholesale funds, with borrowers usually found by third-party agents, typically insurance companies or salesmen. By separating the origination process from the funding and management of loans, centralized lending dispenses with the need for a branch network, and this reduces the costs of entry into a new market. Some of the centralized lenders were also able to enter the British market with relatively little capital. This they did by importing a technique commonly used in the USA, known as securitization. Securitization involves the packaging of loans into pools, reflecting a mix of maturities and other loan characteristics. These pools of loans are credit-rated and held by a subsidiary (or "vehicle") company until tradable bonds are issued. These mortgage backed securities (MBS) have the effect of removing the loans from the balance sheet of the centralized lender, so less capital is required. The centralized lender manages the loans, collects payments from borrowers and makes payments to the holders of the securities. Payments to the holders of mortgage backed securities are usually fixed in relation to the LIBOR (the short-term wholesale interest rate used between banks).[8]

---

8. For an account of securitization in the UK, see Pryke & Whitehead (1991).

The initial success of the centralized lenders in the mid-1980s was based on an expanding market and on the competitiveness of wholesale funds in relation to retail rates. The interest-rate cycle is matched by a funding cycle, because changes in retail interest rates tend to lag behind changes in wholesale rates. So, when interest rates are falling, wholesale funds tend to be more competitive than retail funds, and *vice versa*. Building societies also suffered from the statutory limits placed on their access to wholesale funds. However, retail rates began to regain their competitiveness after the 1987 stock market crash, when funds returned to low-risk society accounts. The subsequent rises in interest rates placed the centralized lenders in an uncompetitive position and, by 1991, many were making losses. The position of lenders that securitized loans was made worse by their lack of control over their payments to the holders of MBS. If they raised the mortgage rate to match these payments, they found that they lost borrowers who found it worthwhile to repay their mortgages prematurely. This tended to lead to the loss of lower-risk borrowers, leaving a poorer-quality loan book behind. If they kept rates down to retain borrowers, then they made losses.

The problems of centralized lenders were compounded by the continued competitiveness of retail funds in the early 1990s, despite falling interest rates. It is widely believed that this may have been attributable to aggressive pricing by building societies attempting to regain market share. Some centralized lenders have experienced difficulty in retaining access to third-party distributors who are no longer willing to refer clients to them. This is because of the bad experiences of those clients (with no prepayment option) whose interest rates fell far more slowly than those using mainstream lenders. To some extent this problem might be overcome by the high turnover of personnel in financial service sales forces.

Both Crédit Agricole and Mortgage Trust are centralized lenders operating in the UK. The former's branch in London is controlled by its parent, its operations are currently funded by its parent, and the London branch does not appear to have an independent strategy. The Crédit Agricole has a world strategy, but has decided to concentrate on Europe because it is easier to control geographically proximate branches, and Europe is seen as offering relative cultural homogeneity.

Mortgage Trust is a stand-alone subsidiary that changed hands in 1990 (from a consortium of Swedish banks, to another Swedish Bank, Skandinaviska Enskilda Banken). It is funded independently of its parent and is staffed by British personnel. In a sense, it is the product of its parent's European objective, but is more or less a free-standing institution, and, in the light of the troubles of the Swedish banking system, its future ownership must be in some doubt. To the extent that Mortgage Trust has a European objective, it is to offer its expertise in securitization to continental institutions wishing to experiment with such techniques, or, following further investment, it might form the UK direct banking arm of a pan-European institution.

Both Mortgage Trust and Crédit Agricole have suffered losses attributable to the downturn in the housing market and lack of access to cheap retail finance when rates rose. Mortgage Trust, although inevitably affected by the problems of the funding cycle, has maintained market presence by acting as an intermediary distribution channel for a group of building societies. Over the longer term the likely restoration of wholesale funding competitiveness will enable Mortgage Trust once again to offer its own products alongside those of its building society associates. However, it is difficult to see how centralized lenders can maintain an active presence in the mortgage market throughout the funding cycle without access to retail funds.

Crédit Agricole has reached similar conclusions to its British counterparts operating in Europe. Longer-term viability depends on establishing a retail base in the UK, either through a strategic alliance or a joint venture. This is not only to gain access to retail funds and gain control over a distribution network, but also to establish a direct link with its customers. The latter objective is intended to gain customer loyalty and an opportunity to sell them other financial services, such as insurance products.

If foreign lenders wish to enter the UK mortgage market with the support of a retail base, then there is a possibility that some may wish to acquire a British lender. However, there are regulatory barriers to the take-over of banks and building societies. UK banks have already been targets for take-overs, although not for the specific purpose of entering the mortgage market. Hong Kong & Shanghai's take-over of Royal Bank of Scotland in the early 1980s was blocked by the Monopolies and Mergers Commission (MMC), although it successfully acquired Midland Bank, once Lloyds Bank's attempted take-over had itself been blocked by the MMC in 1992.

Building societies cannot be taken over in the same way as can a company, because they are owned by their members. Membership is made up of depositors with shareholder accounts and borrowers. It is up to a society's directors to decide whether details of a bid should be passed on to members, so a bank wishing to take over a building society cannot put its proposals directly to the society's members. Although it is possible that 50 members could move a resolution at a general meeting, which would force the board to release the terms of a bid to members, the credibility of the take-over, and indeed its value to the potential acquirer, would be severely undermined (Boléat 1989: 29–30). Hostile take-overs of building societies are therefore virtually impossible.

Take-overs that enjoy the support of the board are possible, but they require the support of a majority of borrowers who vote, as well as a majority of qualifying shareholders or the voting equivalent of 90% of the total value of the society's shares. A potential acquirer (or successor company) may offer financial inducements to the society's members, but only if they have been members for at least two years. This measure is intended to prevent potentially destabilizing speculative shifts of deposits between societies. However, a significant proportion of a society's membership may have joined too recently to qualify for the inducement, but they would still be entitled to vote. They might place the take-over in jeopardy, since they have no direct incentive to vote for it.

This consideration troubled Lloyds Bank and Cheltenham & Gloucester

Building Society (C&G), which agreed to a take-over in 1994, and an attempt was made to extend financial inducements to recent members, who made up more than one-quarter of shareholders entitled to vote. Lloyds Bank proposed that the ownership of C&G should be transferred to a wholly owned subsidiary of another company in the Lloyds Bank group, Lloyds Bank Financial Services (Holdings) Limited. This would allow payments to C&G's members to be made by the parent of the successor company (Lloyds Bank Financial Services (Holdings) Limited), rather than by the successor company itself. The Building Societies Commission took the take-over to court over this technicality. The vice-chancellor ruled that "On a proper reading of the Act this proposal is outside what is authorized by the Act just as much as if the payment were made by the successor company itself".[9] A restructured proposal followed, which offered higher cash payments to qualifying members (and other investors who were not members), but excluded recently joined members from the payment.

It seems likely that this procedure will have to be followed by other banks wishing to acquire building societies, since the legal ruling was on the basis of the intention of the legislation, rather than its letter. Nevertheless, it is possible that smaller building societies would prefer to be taken over by foreign banks, rather than be merged into larger building societies. This is because building society mergers are no longer needed for larger ones to complete their national branch network. Instead, they allow asset growth, but often branch networks are duplicated. Merger can lead to the effective closure of a smaller society's branch network. In contrast, a foreign bank would be taking over a building society to gain access to its branch network. The board of the society, as well as its staff, could face a rosier future under the ownership of a foreign bank.

Conclusions

The rationale for a single market in mortgage finance rests on two economic assumptions. First, that a single market will lead to price reductions in inefficient markets and, secondly, that economies of scale will be realized by operating at a European, rather than national, level.

In this chapter these economic assumptions have been questioned in two respects. First, it is accepted that efficiency varies between institutions and countries, but the sources of inefficiency, such as subsidized or regulated savings markets, can lower the "price" of mortgages below the competitive level. If a single market in mortgage finance were created, the costs of mortgages might be expected to rise in some countries, just as deregulation, through ending the protection of building societies, raised their cost in Britain. Price rises will not necessarily occur, but they are possible and there is precedent. Secondly, the prospect of general price reductions resulting from economies of scale appears

9. Quoted in *Mortgage Finance Gazette*, July 1994.

to be inapplicable to banking. Empirical evidence suggests that scale economies in banking are maximized at a subnational level. Economies of scale may be more relevant to a single market in capital, but this is likely to be hindered by exchange-rate instability and the absence of a single currency.

This chapter also examined the regulatory framework on which the Single Market is based. British legislation limits the ability of building societies to take full advantage of the single passport, which is meant to allow institutions to operate throughout the EU on the basis of their home country's banking licence. Those building societies that operate abroad through subsidiaries have been subject to the regulatory authorities in the host country. They cannot use the passport because these subsidiaries are not allowed to operate in Britain, whereas those that operate abroad directly, through a branch utilizing the passport, cannot offer the full range of services of a credit institution. The inability to use the single passport may be inconvenient, but is less restrictive than the limit under British legislation to the services that can be offered directly through a European bank. This provides a partial explanation for building societies' continued use of subsidiaries for lending in Europe.

The single passport is supported by minimum prudential standards that must be met by all European credit institutions, regardless of whether they operate in other countries. These standards have led to a considerable degree of convergence in the regulation of British banks and building societies. Further convergence has occurred as the scope for the building societies to raise capital externally has been widened greatly.

Several British lenders are operating in Europe. Initially, most established themselves as centralized lenders, using wholesale funds and operating without a branch network. This has not always proved to be satisfactory, partly because retail funds are sometimes cheaper. More recently, there has been a shift towards gaining access to retail funds and making greater use of branches. European banks operating in Britain on the centralized model have also found it to be unsatisfactory and some may attempt to establish a branch network through acquisition. They will face regulatory barriers, should they attempt to do so. The Monopolies and Mergers Commission may block take-overs of banks, and building societies are effectively immune from hostile take-overs. Even those that enjoy the support of the society's board face a ballot of members, not all of whom can be offered financial inducements.

The establishment of branches is a slow process, which may be done by acquisition, but it increases entry costs and it is one reason why the extension of mortgage operations to the European level is likely to be a slow process. Further, more cross-national operations of lenders do not necessarily increase mortgage market efficiency if the structural rigidities are allowed to remain. For example, if entry into the German market continues to require the establishment of lenders on the German model, under which margins are regulated by the State, there will be few benefits.

The European Union's support for a single market in mortgage finance, as outlined in the Cecchini Report, was based on a flawed analysis, which has been shown to equate efficiency with low prices. There are nevertheless wide differences in the efficiency of national mortgage markets, and considerable gains could be secured if intermediation efficiency could be raised to the standards of those countries where it is highest. But the differences are as much the result of institutional, legal and cultural factors as stemming from any lack of competition. Indeed, the lessons from those banks and lending institutions that have started operations in other countries is that the going is tough; there are no easy profits to be made and it is often necessary to conform to the institutional structures of the country concerned. A gradual increase in cross-border lending can be expected, but a single market in mortgage finance is clearly a very long way away.

CHAPTER 11
Housing and labour mobility

One of the most obvious ways in which the housing market may affect the smooth and effective operation of the economy is through facilitating necessary population movement. Any economy requires its labour force to be able to move. This may be no more than people moving to better jobs as they gain in skill and experience, a normal and essential process if the labour resource is to be used to best advantage. But, as some industries grow and others decline, there may also be a change in the geographical balance of economic activity. This process has occurred not only in Britain but in most European countries over the past 50 years; and in the normal course of events it results in labour shortages in some areas, combined with unacceptably high levels of unemployment in others.

A whole variety of factors, quite apart from the prospect of better employment opportunities, influence people's willingness to move. The vast majority of house moves are the result of changes in family size or increased incomes, and they take place within the same area without involving intercity or interregional migration. But for such interregional flows to take place, the availability of housing and the cost of moving are clearly important considerations. Apart from movement within each country, the European Union now raises the possibility of greatly increased movement across national boundaries between member States: the Treaty of Maastricht provides for unrestricted movement of EU citizens, where those involved are students, retired or have a job to go to, and the Single European Act aims to ensure interchangeability of qualifications. And there is also the continuing prospect of substantial immigration to States within the Union from countries outside.

The effective functioning of the housing market is therefore important for the economy, and more so within the integrated Union. Member States are in competition with each other in attracting the industrial and commercial investment that is the basis of economic growth, and the removal of barriers as a consequence of the Single European Act makes that competition more intense than before. Increasingly it becomes possible to choose which member State offers the most attractive location from which to do business throughout the Union. The housing market is only one factor in such decisions and, from the point of view of the typical business, is not the most important one. But if people cannot move to take up job opportunities, shortages of labour will develop in some areas, so that economic growth will be frustrated; wage rates will be raised as a result of competitive bidding, and inflation will result. Because labour shortage has a much stronger effect in raising inflation than labour surplus does in reducing it, and also because, within most European nation-States, comparability prevents wage differentials between regions from opening up to more than a very limited extent, the effect of overheating in one area, especially if it is a major region such as the South East of England, is generally to produce inflation that affects the whole of that country.

The British housing market and population movement

If one compares Britain's housing market with that of other countries, one can see both advantages and disadvantages. In the first place, there is an obvious (but not always recognized) disadvantage in the geographical balance of Britain's economic activity. Along with the Netherlands, Belgium and parts of the Ruhr, the South of England, and particularly the South East, is one of Europe's most densely populated areas. It is where much of Britain's economic growth is concentrated, yet it is an area where supply constraints are greatest, particularly as regards housing and land, and where demand is therefore most likely to have an inflationary impact. This may well have been a factor in Britain's greater tendency towards inflation than some of the other countries in the Union over the past quarter of a century.

Britain also has a very unusual tenure pattern and the characteristics of each of the tenures are rather different from elsewhere. In particular, owner occupation is much more flexible and is the main tenure of mobility. In France and Germany owner occupation would not be thought of as a flexible tenure that facilitated population movement. Whereas in Britain the average age of first-time buyers is between 25 and 30, and many owners trade up several times, in France, Spain and the Netherlands it is over 30 and in Germany between 35 and 40. Movement in the German owner occupied sector is rare, the average length of stay being 28 years, compared with only 7 years in Britain, and many people having bought a house stay in it for the rest of their lives. In France an owner occupied house tends to be seen as an inheritance that may be passed from one generation to another, the average length of stay therefore also being long (Woolwich Building Society 1990).

The relatively low cost of house purchase transactions in Britain is an important factor, in so far as it makes it easier for home owners to contemplate buying and selling houses more frequently. According to figures produced by the Woolwich Building Society, the transaction cost of buying a typical £80000 house in Britain is £1580, compared with £5650 in Germany, £8280 in Spain and as much as £11000 in France (Fig. 11.1). The largest part of this difference is accounted for by taxation on the transaction, which in France is ten times what it would be in Britain, but there are also higher legal fees, and fees to estate agents. In addition, as the country chapters of this book have shown, there is the ease with which mortgage finance can be arranged in Britain, without bringing together funds from different sources or waiting for savings to accumulate in a contract savings scheme. These factors make owner occupation in Britain a much more flexible tenure than it is in most other countries of the EU. They make possible an early start to home ownership for first-time buyers, permit upward and downward trading within the sector to an extent uncommon elsewhere, and also mean that the tenure is the one most frequently used by those whose work requires them to move.

Although the flexibility of this tenure in Britain is clearly an advantage, experience over the past ten years has shown that there are problems in relying on owner occupation as the main tenure of mobility. Widening differentials in house prices between regions, which tend to be a feature of the economic cycle, were particularly marked in the 1980s and there is much evidence that they impeded population movement. Those in the North were reluctant to move to the South, because the price they would receive for their old house would not be enough to afford a house of acceptable quality in the South. And those who owned property in the South were also reluctant to move, for fear that, if they sold, house prices in other regions would not appreciate so fast and they would therefore not be able to afford to return. Only those who wished to retire elsewhere, or had no thought of returning, saw advantage in moving. In fact, the experience after 1988 was

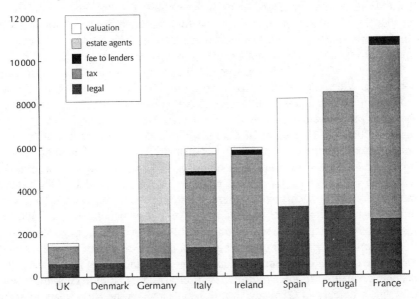

Figure 11.1 The cost of house purchase (£ sterling). Legal costs include Land Registry (UK, G), search fees (UK), registration fee (P), mortgage registration fee (F); tax includes stamp duty (DK), registration and mortgage tax (I), vat or transfer tax and mortgage tax (*Source:* Woolwich Building Society *Survey* 1993 (January).)

223

that house prices in the South East *fell* more steeply than elsewhere, and particularly in contrast to Scotland where they continued to rise, so that a move out of
the South East in 1988 would have been a good investment decision. But that was
not how it was perceived at the time. The fall in house prices also demonstrated
the shortcomings of relying on owner occupation as the tenure of mobility.
Those with negative equity were prevented from selling, and others found that
the market had collapsed to an extent that made it almost impossible to sell at
any price they considered reasonable.

As in other countries, the social rented sector, with rents below market levels,
tends to be subject to waiting lists. Prospective tenants wishing to move are usually unable to find accommodation at short notice; and, if they do, it may not be
of a quality or in a neighbourhood that they find acceptable. This problem is
endemic in the system. From time to time, efforts have been made to address it.
In Scotland one of the main functions of the former Scottish Special Housing
Association (one of the two predecessor bodies of Scottish Homes) was to provide social rented housing to meet the needs of incoming industry. New Towns
likewise gave priority to housing workers with skills required by firms moving
into their areas, and local authorities were encouraged to do the same, although
the extent to which they did so varied greatly. Several schemes have been introduced over the years to try to promote interregional movement within the social
rented sector, but surveys show that their effect has been no better than marginal
(Minford et al.: 4, 89–114). Many studies conducted over the years have shown
that this tenure is less well able to cater for mobility than the others. For example, Hughes & McCormick (1981: 934) find that their results: "dramatically
confirm our supposition that council tenants find it much more difficult to
migrate from one region to another than do owner occupiers . . . ".

Of course, where there is a substantial waiting list it is only natural that local
authorities will always tend to give priority to those who have been on the list
for some time, or for some social reason have a pressing claim, rather than meet
the needs of those moving to the area for the first time. It is perhaps not surprising therefore that Hughes & McCormick conclude that movement within the
council-owned sector is so difficult and that the low level of mobility is not
accounted for by any less of a desire on the part of tenants in this sector to move
compared with people in the other two sectors. Since they conducted their study
in the early 1980s, such scope as there was in this sector for meeting the needs
of incomers has been further reduced by the fall in new building by local authorities, mainly as a result of reduced financial allocations by central government.

The private rented sector is the tenure that, theoretically at least, is best suited
to provide the flexibility to accommodate population movement and to allow the
matching of labour to job opportunities. It clearly does so in many other countries, most notably in Germany, where people rent in the early years of their
career, partly to retain flexibility of movement. But the extent to which this sector can fulfil this role in Britain is limited. First of all, it is very small and, of
the unfurnished part, some is still housing let on "fair" rents, well below market

levels. As a result of the 1988 Act, these fair rents are ending as the tenancies fall in; but in the meantime such housing is no more available to new tenants than is council housing. And past experience suggests that, since landlords are locked in by security of tenure and have in the past found their role an unrewarding one financially, when the tenancies do end much of this property may be sold. The 1988 Act was certainly intended to make private ownership of rented accommodation more attractive again; both "assured" and "short assured" tenancies are designed to meet the needs of those who move some distance, as much as of any other tenants. But in the absence of stronger financial incentives, the new system is unlikely to have redressed the balance sufficiently, especially for those landlords who have been waiting to get out of owning property altogether. And in the absence of greater equality in fiscal treatment, given the political uncertainties it seems unlikely that the incentives are strong enough to attract new investors, whether individuals or companies, to come in.

The furnished part of the private rented sector is a more important element in Britain than in other countries, simply because for most of the past half century it escaped the more Draconian controls imposed on unfurnished rented accommodation. Rents are very much higher and are often influenced by scarcity. This part of the private rented sector is of major importance for those who move and is frequently used as temporary accommodation until something more permanent is found. Surveys have shown that, in relation to its size, it caters for a quite disproportionate number of movers, and some authors have used this as an argument to castigate the other sectors, notably the social rented sector. But the subsector is very small. Its high cost and the need to use furnishings other than one's own, which are often of poor quality, mean that it is not usually regarded as more than temporary and is unsuited to the more stable role met by the private rented sector in France or Germany. For these reasons it is hardly surprising that turnover in the sector is high and that it caters for many of those who move a significant distance.

A revived private sector could certainly play a much more substantial and valuable role; but, if it were to do so, it would have to differ considerably in character from the sector as it is at present. It would have to be more flexible than the bulk of the unfurnished part of the present sector and of better quality, and be suitable for longer tenancies than most of the furnished accommodation. Rents would also have to be attractive, when compared with the costs and benefits of ownership. It would require investment by individuals, or more likely by institutions, in a way that (apart from the BES scheme) has not occurred in Britain since 1945; and investors would commit their funds only if there were major changes that improved the attractiveness of this tenure for investment. The aim should be for the sector to be capable of meeting the needs of both those who would otherwise choose owner occupation and those who would be in the social rented sector. But, if the latter were to succeed, Housing Benefit and social security payments would also have to be reformed to reduce the effects of the poverty trap, which moves upwards to higher levels of income as the rent rises (see Ch. 8).

It is well known that interregional movement of labour and population does not respond so readily to employment opportunities in Britain as in the USA, and the same is true of other European countries, apart from Germany, where the special circumstances of the eastern *Länder* and the ethnic Germans from other countries have resulted in substantial movement. However, Hughes & McCormick (1990: 95ff.) point out that the most important difference between Britain and the USA is that there is negligible movement among the unskilled and semi-skilled workers in Britain. The professional and highly skilled move as they do elsewhere. Since their skills are more readily marketable, they also cope more easily with a change of environment and they are less likely to be affected by difficulties of obtaining accommodation in the social rented sector.

Moreover, the bulk of the existing population and labour movement in Britain is not by the unemployed, as seems sometimes to be supposed by many of those who see migration as a means of solving regional unemployment, but by those retiring or those in employment seeking a better job or being moved by their employer. Such movement is unlikely to do very much for geographical disequilibrium in the labour market and perhaps it explains the persistence of the regional unemployment problem, despite relatively high net emigration figures from some of Britain's regions. Indeed, in so far as those who move are high spenders or are from the section of the population that might provide entrepreneurs and job creators, the effect of movement may even be perverse so far as unemployment is concerned.

It is, of course, a mistake to think that the improved functioning of the labour market is simply a matter of housing policy. All manner of considerations, such as cultural attitudes, family ties, spouses with jobs and children's education, affect willingness to move. But there can be little doubt that the housing market plays an important part and that, whereas Britain scores well for the flexibility of its owner occupied sector, it comes out much less well in the other two tenures. If it were possible to revive the private rented sector to meet these needs and to make the social rented sector more sensitive to them, such changes could do much to improve the flexibility and competitiveness of the British economy within the European market. However, this would require some reversal of the policies of the past 15 years, including rather less emphasis on home ownership to the exclusion of other tenures, additional measures to make investment attractive in private rented accommodation, and appropriately targeted resources for the social rented sector.

Housing, planning and regional policy

Although changes in housing policy are certainly desirable and necessary to improve the flexibility of housing markets, such action is unlikely to be sufficient on its own to prevent economic growth from being frustrated, to reduce the danger of overheating and, in consequence, the economy's propensity to inflation in the European market. There will always tend to be problems if the strongest housing demand is concentrated in areas where the supply of available land and of housing is most inelastic.

There are those who argue that the solution to this is to be found in altering or getting rid of what they see as a bureaucratic and over-restrictive planning system (Minford et al. 1977: 3–4). But it is easy enough for this view to be taken by people who have no responsibility for environmental policy or planning. The experience of unplanned urban growth in the nineteenth century, and in some European cities quite recently, provides no assurance that scrapping planning control would not be highly damaging to the environment. The fact is that in a country as densely populated as much of Britain, especially the South of England, those who are already resident in an area become naturally protective of their environment, particularly the green belts and open space. Such environmental concerns are strongest in the northern European countries, particularly Scandinavia, Germany, the Netherlands and Britain, and they are increasing, not diminishing. Although there are always ways in which planning procedures can be improved, it is simply not politically acceptable to have a less restrictive policy. Moreover, in countries where planning controls are vigorously applied, it is far from self-evident that the effect is more damaging to the economy than in those areas, mostly in southern Europe, where they are not.

This means that if available labour resources are to be better matched to job opportunities, housing policy has to be complemented by a regional development policy. The case for such policies is that those who take the investment decisions that determine the geographical pattern of economic activity do not themselves directly bear all the social and private costs they entail. In consequence, such decisions add to congestion, the cost of which falls on society as a whole and on public authorities. Housing demand is then strongest in areas where supply is least elastic, where the cost of providing infrastructure is high and in consequence where growth is likely to be frustrated. The result is inflation, first of house prices, then spreading to wages and salaries and to other prices. Regional policy is therefore not a luxury any more than an effective policy to promote flexibility in the housing market. Nor should it be seen simply as a form of charitable hand-out for the depressed regions. Like the promotion of a more flexible housing market, it too is a means of matching demand to available resources, promoting growth and keeping inflation down, and of maintaining a country's competitive position in the European market.

Such policies encourage new investment and growth to take place in areas where surplus resources are available, especially labour. If successful, they therefore reduce the need for population movement and divert some of the demand away from areas where the supply constraints are most severe. In the modern economy, the greater part of new development is not highly location-specific, partly because of the changing nature of products and processes and partly because improved transport and communications reduce any handicaps there might have been in operating outside the main centres of growth. There is therefore considerable scope for regional policies to be effective, without imposing any significant locational disadvantage on those firms whose investment decisions are influenced by them. The advantage is that growth is less likely to be stifled by supply constraints, such as shortage of labour, housing or building land.

All countries in the European Union have had regional development policies for most of the period since 1945, although some countries have much more acute problems of geographical imbalance between demand pressure and available resources than others. Substantial funding is also available through the European Regional Development Fund to promote the economic growth of the more disadvantaged areas. Until reunification gave rise to the problems of the new eastern *Länder*, Germany had much less serious problems of regional imbalance that most of the other large member States of the EU, which was arguably a significant factor in its strong economic performance. The UK, on the other hand, has had an imbalance for most of the past half century between the prosperous and increasingly congested South and the northern regions, including Scotland, where there has been a continuing surplus labour. British regional development policy has been accorded varying degrees of priority over the past half century, but, since 1979, expenditure on regional policy measures has been sharply reduced and the impetus of policy has weakened as part of the Conservative government's general philosophy of non-intervention.[1]

The European Union and population movement

In 1991, as Table 11.1 shows, of the 15 million people registered as foreigners and holding residence permits in EU countries, only some 33% were nationals of EU States living in a country other than that of their origin, the rest being those registered as foreigners from States outside the EU. (For the working population, the comparable figure is some 2 million in EU countries other than that of which they are nationals.) This leaves some 10 million foreigners who are from States outside the EU.

The distribution of this population is very uneven. Leaving aside the rather special case of Luxembourg, the largest proportions of foreign population are in Belgium, Germany and France, followed by the Netherlands and then the UK. The long period of economic growth and prosperity, leading to the inflow of "guest workers", particularly from southern Europe and from Turkey, is clearly a major factor in the German situation, and the inflow from the former French territories of North Africa explains the high figure for France. Britain, which had a substantial inflow from the Caribbean, the Indian subcontinent and other Commonwealth States in the 1960s and early 1970s.

1. See the Department of Industry, Scottish Office and Welsh Office annual reports on the Industrial Development Act 1982, where expenditure on regional policy is given.

Table 11.1 European national population, 1991.

	(1) EU citizens from another country	(2) Non-EU citizens (000s)	(3) Total	(4) % of total population	(5) Non-EU citizens (Col. 2 as % of 3)
Belgium	551	353	904	8.8	39
Denmark	28	133	161	3.0	83
Germany	1439	3904	5343	6.7	73
Greece	54	175	229	2.2	76
Spain	273	211	484	1.1	44
France	1312	2285	3597	6.3	64
Ireland	69	19	88	2.5	22
Italy	149	632	781	1.4	81
Luxembourg	103	13	116	29.8	11
Netherlands	168	524	1092	4.6	76
Portugal	29	79	108	1.1	73
UK	781	1647	2428	4.2	68
Total	4956	9975	14931	4.3	67

Source: Eurostat, *Demographic statistics* 1993.

However, these figures do not give the complete picture. In the first place, those registered as foreigners do not include those who have assumed the nationality of the State they have entered, nor their descendants. The largest part of what was originally immigrant population in Britain is in these categories. Secondly, especially in the southern EU States, there are many illegal immigrants who are not included in the above statistics at all. According to well founded estimates, the total number of non-nationals living in the four southern States – Italy, Spain, Greece and Portugal – is at least 2.7 million, if not 3 million, compared with the 1.6 million in Table 11.1 (EU and non-EU) who are officially registered (CEC 1991b: 38–97). In Italy there are thought to be more unregistered than registered immigrants, and in Spain nearly 40% of all the non-nationals living in the country are thought to be unregistered.

Concern generally about the number of immigrants in southern EU States is growing. In the past, they used to use southern Europe as their point of entry, but move on from there to jobs in the north. But since the early 1970s, the northern countries have adopted much more restrictive immigration policies, as of course has Britain, and the long recession, with its high levels of unemployment, has made these policies ever more restrictive. The result is that, whereas in the 1950s and 1960s northern Europe provided employment for the unemployed population of southern Europe and for immigrants who came in via southern Europe, it is no longer in a position to do so. Partly because the southern States are in the front line for those wanting to come to Europe from the other States around the Mediterranean, but also because administratively they are less geared up to control it, they are especially vulnerable to this legal and illegal immigration pressure. But with the immigrants less able to move on to the north, as they used to do, they now swell levels of unemployment in the south and greatly increase the pressure on housing at the lower end of the market. Even in France, where the control on immigration is strict, the south of the country has been much affected by inflow from the former colonies in North Africa, and this puts pressure on the social rented sector in particular.

The present employment situation within the European Union is not likely to encourage population movement, at least for the time being. With labour surplus in most areas, there is no need for employers to look beyond their own region for recruitment. On the other hand, the Maastricht treaty is intended to make cross-border movement easier and to lead to the creation of a single labour market. At the same time, although member States have tightened the controls on immigration from outside the EU, the pressure from outside has intensified. How the demographic trends of the Union are likely to be affected by these conflicting forces, and where that growth is most likely to be concentrated, are therefore important questions for the future of housing markets and housing policy.

In a major report for the Council and the European Parliament, the Commission addresses these questions and attempts to indicate how the interregional balance of Europe's population may change (CEC 1991a: 14–24, 39–48). The main centre of the Union's past and present growth lies in an area stretching from the Midlands of England through the Low Countries, the north of France and the south of Germany to the north of Italy (see Fig. 11.2). But although this is expected to remain an area of major – indeed, dominant – importance, there is increasing evidence of a second newer area of growth establishing itself from southern Germany and the north of Italy westwards through the South of France to the Mediterranean coast of Spain. There are also signs that, in response to congestion, crowded living conditions and high costs, major cities throughout Europe are losing economic activity and population to smaller towns.

So far as EU nationals are concerned, it is likely that, if these trends continue, they will have a greater impact on population movement within countries than between them, at least for many years to come. Language barriers and cultural differences remain a substantial impediment to movement, to an extent that does not apply in the USA. Although there will be increasing cross-frontier movement among the highly trained professional and business management classes, this is unlikely to extend to the mass of the working population or to approach anything like the scale of labour movement that takes place in the USA. It is probably as well that this should be so, and that, by promoting growth in areas of unemployment, regional policies should be used as far as possible to make such movement unnecessary. Substantial movement of population across national frontiers, where languages and traditions differ, could very easily give rise to cultural and ethnic friction, and could foster resentment, especially where there is unemployment. All countries that have experienced substantial population inflow recognize these dangers; it is important to avoid them, if social harmony is to be preserved and the disruption caused by reactive cultural nationalism prevented.

Although there is to some extent a trade-off between regional development

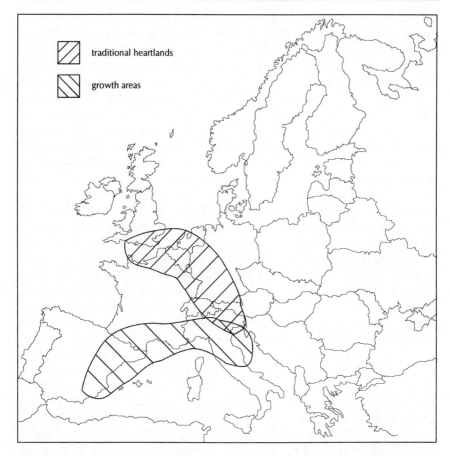

Figure 11.2 Traditional heartlands and growth regions of the European Union. (*Source:* CEC 1991a: diagram 6).

policy and population movement within the EU, immigration from outside is largely a response to factors beyond EU control. While the growth of Europe's indigenous population is expected to slow down markedly in the 1990s, as a result of the fall in birth rates, the population on the south side of the Mediterranean is rising far faster than any likely growth of employment opportunities there. In the Maghreb States[1], population is expected to double by the year 2025 (from 58 million to 103 million; CEC 1991a: 47). This brings the prospect of a potentially explosive situation in those countries, and even political breakdown, which could have serious implications for Europe, in view of the many illegal immigrants in Italy especially, and the traditional links between France and the Maghreb States.

Following the collapse of communism, the major dislocation to the economies

---

1. Tunisia, Algeria and Morocco.

of central and eastern Europe has led to high rates of unemployment and serious hardship in many of those countries, which, even in the more favourably placed, will take many years to overcome. This has already caused a substantial inflow of population to Germany and, even with greatly tightened controls, this seems likely to continue, because a significant part of those wishing to come will be able to plead some German connection. A continuing influx therefore seems likely.

It is far from easy to predict exactly what the consequences of this immigration pressure from outside the EU will be. Population movement from eastern Germany and the other former Iron Curtain countries has already caused pressure on housing markets in Germany. There is also a shortage of social rented housing in France and the flow of immigrants is one factor giving rise to this, especially in the South of France, where some housing estates have severe problems of deprivation. These pressures seem likely to continue and, in view of the nature of the immigrant population, they may be expected to impact particularly on the social housing sector. Both France and Germany have had to step up the assistance they give to this sector and to increase new construction. The indications are that a higher level of activity in this sector, amounting to a reversal of the declining trend in the 1980s, will have to continue in these countries for a considerable time. In Spain, where the social rented sector is minuscule, the present exceptionally high levels of unemployment must be a deterrent to immigrants thinking of settling there, but the unemployment is in turn a consequence of the surplus labour being no longer able to move on to jobs in other countries. Spain has a good record of economic growth over the past ten years and has a prospect of continuing to catch up on the richer countries. But, even with continuing high growth rates, it could prove difficult to absorb the immigrant population into useful employment if movement to northern Europe is denied to them. Shanty towns, largely inhabited by immigrants and gypsies, have already re-emerged in Spain, and its housing policy does not appear well equipped to cope with this problem.

In time, coupled with freedom of movement within the Community and the relatively mobile nature of much modern economic activity, these flows could result in a substantial shift in the geographical balance of Europe's economy and employment. In particular, the movement into the South of France, coupled with the attractions of the climate, could give the area stretching from northern Italy through to Spain some of the same attractive power for new investment as the Sunbelt in the USA, and make a reality of the Commission's growth pole prediction (CEC 1991a). But on the other hand, if population inflow exceeds the rate at which it can be absorbed into suitable housing or employment, it could increase deprivation, threaten the social fabric, and itself be a deterrent to investment in the creation of new economic opportunities.

Conclusion

Britain seems likely to be relatively unaffected, by either future immigration or significant population movement within the European Union. Potentially, such movements have major implications for housing policy in other countries and particularly for public expenditure on housing. Germany, France, Benelux, and perhaps Italy and Spain, seem likely to be the countries most affected.

Nevertheless, it is important that housing policy in Britain should be looked at critically to ensure that it does help the housing market to operate in a way that assists rather than impedes the growth and competitiveness of the economy. It cannot be said at present to have been framed with this as one of its objectives. Although Britain may not be in the forefront of countries likely to be affected by immigration pressure, it does suffer more than some of the others from regional imbalance, with the South East of England already among the most densely populated areas of the EU. There is therefore a danger that, as the economy recovers, pressure of demand in areas where housing supply is most inelastic will again lead to a renewal of inflationary pressure and to growth being frustrated. If so, this will only prevent Britain from realizing its growth potential. Although the owner occupied sector is generally more flexible than elsewhere, and is seen as the main tenure of mobility in a way that it is not in many other countries, the other two tenures do not adequately play their part. The private rented sector needs to be larger and of a different type, if it is to facilitate movement to the extent that it does in Germany, France or the Netherlands. And the social rented sector needs to be encouraged to give greater priority to catering for labour movement, perhaps by making explicit recognition of this through its funding. But, even if changes in housing policy were made that improved the market's response to demand, it is important to recognize that in a crowded country there will always be constraints. Regional development policy is therefore a necessary counterpart to housing policy for the country's future prosperity.

CHAPTER 12

The economics of European integration

One of the principal ways in which the operation of the housing market may affect the functioning of the economy was discussed in Chapter 11. But there are other important interrelationships between housing and the functioning of the economy. These include the effects on housing policy of pressures on public expenditure, especially in the light of European integration and the Maastricht criteria for monetary union; the implications of the structure of British housing debt, which is very different from that of most other European countries; and the consequences for macroeconomic management of the instability in the market for housing finance, which has been a pronounced feature of the British economy especially during the second half of the 1980s and early 1990s. The purpose of this chapter is to assess the importance of these issues, particularly from the standpoint of the UK, but, where appropriate, also drawing conclusions for other countries in this study.

Housing policy and public expenditure

The background

The public expenditure climate is obviously of critical importance for housing policy. Although not comparable with the costs of health, education, defence or social security, housing is a substantial item in the expenditure of most member States of the EU, and more substantial still if the cost of housing related tax reliefs are added to the total for public expenditure. Although, as argued in previous chapters, the cost of housing policy cannot be directly compared from one country to another, because it depends so much on levels of general social security provision, inflation and various other factors, it nevertheless amounts to between 1% of gross domestic product in the case of Spain to over 4% for Sweden.

All countries of the European Union have experienced severe pressure on public expenditure in recent years, and in the early 1990s the majority have substantial budget deficits (see Table 12.1). This is of course in large part a product of the recession: lower economic activity results in reduced tax revenue, whereas higher unemployment increases the cost of unemployment relief and social security. The recession boosts public expenditure on housing as well, through the need for personal housing allowances.

Table 12.1   EU convergence criteria.

	Price change, 1993 (%)	Budget deficit as % of GDP	Gross debt as % GDP
Belgium	2.8	7.0	138.4
Denmark	1.4	4.4	80.6
Germany	4.0	3.3	48.9
Greece	13.7	15.5	121.2
France	2.3	−5.5	44.1
Spain	4.7	7.2	55.9
Ireland	2.0	2.3	99.0
Italy	4.4	9.4	118.1
Luxembourg	3.6	2.5	10.0
Netherlands	2.1	4.0	81.4
Portugal	6.7	7.1	66.4
UK	3.4	7.6	48.8
EU	3.8	6.0	65.9
Sweden		14.7	67.6

Source: *European economy* (1994), OECD *Economic outlook* (December) 1993

But the pressure on public expenditure, which is a feature of all EU member States in the early 1990s, is not caused just by the recession, and it is unsafe therefore to assume that significant additional resources will be available as the recession lifts, whether for housing or other competing claims. First, it is widely accepted that a substantial part of the present unemployment is structural rather than cyclical. Although opinions differ on how much, it is most unlikely that unemployment will return in the foreseeable future to the low levels of the 1960s and early 1970s. In its White Paper for the December 1993 Brussels summit, the Commission set out action aimed at creating some 15 million new jobs by the year 2000 (CEC 1993a). Such a target is not out of scale with the average annual rate of job creation attained in the USA over the 15 years up to 1990, but it is clearly ambitious. Even if it is achieved, the continuing growth in the labour force means that it would only approximately halve the present unemployment of 17 million and bring the rate down to about 6%. This clearly implies a heavy continuing public expenditure burden, even if the policies were to succeed.

Secondly, in addition to this problem, the countries of the European Union all face growing public expenditure demands on several fronts: to meet the costs of a longer-lived population, a rapidly escalating cost of health care, and a growing demand for higher levels of skill and educational attainment in a modern economy. None of these pressures are likely to be reduced and they are largely unavoidable. They are therefore causing all governments to look ever more critically at their expenditure priorities.

235

Finally, European integration itself imposes additional constraints. First, on the revenue side, the Single Market means that there is less scope than there was previously for substantial differences in rates of both indirect and direct taxes. At the Lisbon Summit in 1993, to meet the requirement that fiscal controls at internal EU frontiers be removed, the Council of Ministers agreed on a degree of harmonization for rates of VAT and excise duty. Although personal and company taxes are not subject to such an agreement, they are exposed to the same pressures. Freedom of movement of capital and labour means that, for both investment and highly skilled individuals, choice of location within the Union can increasingly be influenced by levels of taxation. None of this means that taxation rates have to be identical. Britain's top rate of personal tax is, for example, in 1994 substantially lower than Germany's; nor does it mean that finance ministers have lost the power to raise or lower the amount of revenue taken in tax, as was shown by the two British budgets of 1993, which substantially increased revenue. But the high marginal rates of personal tax, which were a feature of Britain in the 1970s and of Sweden until more recently, would now be extremely damaging and are therefore unlikely to be within the contemplation of any government acting on it own within the Union. There can be no doubt, therefore, that, the benefits notwithstanding, the Single Market has restricted the freedom of governments in taxation policy.

Moreover, since the pressure on governments to keep taxation rates broadly in line is more the result of market competition than of Directives from Brussels, its effect is asymmetrical: it acts principally on those with higher tax rates, to avoid damage to their economies by reducing them, rather than on those with lower rates to raise them. It can therefore be expected to bear particularly hard on those countries that by tradition have had high levels of public expenditure and a high quality of service provision, financed by high levels of taxation. As the chapter on Sweden has shown, this has already had an impact on the direction of housing policy in that country, even before it was a member of the European Union. Even so, as the size of the budget deficit in Table 12.1 shows, Sweden has still a long way to go if its public finances are to be restored to health.

Secondly, the convergence criteria for economic and monetary union include reference levels for budgetary deficits and accumulated debt, the former being not more than 3% and the latter 60% of GDP (CEC 1989). After the upheavals in the Exchange Rate Mechanism in 1992 and 1993, full implementation of EMU, at least by all twelve members, seems more remote than it was two years ago, certainly from a British perspective. Nevertheless, the second stage of EMU came into operation as planned at the start of 1994, and the Single Market itself requires a degree of convergence in economic performance if it is to succeed. One way or another, convergence objectives similar to those specified are going to be required and are likely to be taken as a guide for policy, even in the absence of EMU. The budgetary policy followed in the UK in 1993 and 1994 is certainly compatible with trying to achieve them.

Table 12.1 shows that few of the countries can meet these objectives at present and the situation has actually deteriorated since they were first proposed in the Delors Report (CEC 1989). This is largely but not wholly because of the recession, which has impacted severely on government borrowing requirements, lifting even those that met the 3% target two years ago well above it in 1993. In consequence, levels of accumulated debt have also risen: they are particularly high in Ireland, Italy and Belgium, where they range from 90 to over 130% of GDP; but the 60% criterion is met in four of the six countries covered in this study, the exceptions being Sweden and the Netherlands. If these levels are allowed to rise, the servicing of debt could drive up future levels of taxation or force cuts in public expenditure. The two criteria are therefore interrelated: the target for the annual deficit is necessary to prevent the accumulated debt from rising. But the deficit target is also affected by the rate of inflation, a larger deficit being compatible with a debt level that does not rise as a proportion of GDP if inflation is high. This means that, if growth of GDP is of the order of 3% a year (an optimistic assumption on the basis of the past three years), in the absence of significant inflation a deficit target of no more than about 3% would be necessary to fulfil this condition.

The implications for housing policy

For all these reasons, the climate for public finance, not only in Britain but throughout the EU, is going to remain difficult; and it is against this background that the cost of housing policy has to be considered, in both public expenditure and tax allowances. Two conclusions can be drawn: first, it has become especially important that the resources available are properly directed to achieve the objectives of housing policy; and secondly that, where possible, maximum use should be made of private sector finance.

As earlier chapters in this book have shown, there has already been a shift in the balance of policy in all of the countries covered by this study. Public intervention in the housing market has become more selective and more sharply targeted on individuals who do not have the means to afford a satisfactory standard of housing. Eligibility for grants and low interest loans has been increasingly restricted and, over the past decade or more, all of the countries except Spain have switched the emphasis of policy from bricks and mortar subsidies to personal housing allowances; and, even in Spain, where there is no system of personal housing allowances, the policy has become more sharply focused on need.

The change has been most recent in Sweden and the Netherlands, where widespread and relatively indiscriminate subsidization of housing in all tenures had been deliberately employed to avoid the segregation of the least well off in the social rented sector, the process known as "residualization". It seems clear that in future the constraints of budgetary policy will require expenditure to be increasingly directed at those who in its absence could not afford an acceptable standard of housing.

237

If the funds available are to be used to best advantage, it is just as important to make effective use of tax reliefs as of public expenditure. Governments tend to find this more difficult politically, as the case of mortgage interest tax relief in the Netherlands demonstrates, but tax reliefs (which reduce revenue) are just as costly in terms of a fiscal deficit as is public expenditure. In a climate where resources are scarce, they should also be directed so as to have most impact on the achievement of housing policy objectives. Three principal forms of relief are involved: mortgage interest tax relief, capital-gains tax exemption, and tax exemption on income from owner occupiers' imputed rent.

Mortgage interest tax relief in France and the accelerated depreciation allowance in Germany are already aimed at the less well off and are for limited duration. In Sweden the value of mortgage interest tax relief has been sharply reduced. But in the Netherlands and in Spain, the relief is at marginal tax rates, and in the former there is no ceiling. Although the Dutch government is sharply reducing the public expenditure cost of housing policy, apparently it has no plans to alter mortgage interest tax relief. In Britain, although the value of this relief has been steadily reduced in recent budgets, and is at a flat rate of 15% from April 1995 on mortgage borrowing of up to £30000, there is still an incentive to keep its value up for the full life of the mortgage by the use of endowment-backed lump sum insurance, which in housing policy terms is not cost effective.

In most countries there is capital gains tax exemption at least on the main residence and, even if it were politically feasible to abolish it, which it clearly is not, it would be necessary to provide some form of roll-over relief if the tax was not to greatly impede population movement. The reintroduction of roll-over relief in the Swedish reform of 1993 seems to confirm this point. Only the Netherlands has a significant tax on owner occupiers' imputed rent and, as Chapter 5 has shown, it is at least in part justified there by the generous mortgage interest tax relief. But even there, it is at a low rate compared with the tax paid by landlords on rental income. For political reasons it is no more realistic to expect countries to introduce or reintroduce this tax than to remove capital gains tax exemption. The pursuit of a more targeted approach on allowances is therefore likely to be felt only on mortgage interest tax relief, if it is felt at all. In Britain there is a clear expectation now that it may be phased out altogether.

If expenditure charged to public funds is to have maximum impact in securing the objectives of housing policy, it is also important that it should be limited to investment costs that cannot be met from private sources. In the Netherlands, the system was changed in 1989, so that housing associations and municipal companies now borrow from the private market instead of being funded by local authorities. And in the other countries, even where there are municipal companies in direct local authority ownership, as is the case in Sweden and Germany, housing investment in the social sector never scored as public expenditure, apart from the element of direct subsidy. But in Britain, all housing investment by local authorities and central government agencies, which still own the major part of the social rented stock, is regarded as public expenditure, regardless of how the funding is raised and whether there is a subsidy or not. This was formerly the situation for British housing associations as well, but since the 1988 Act they have been encouraged to use private finance to meet as much of their funding requirements as possible.

This situation puts the greater part of the British social rented sector under a constraint that does not apply in any of the other five countries; it also makes British housing policy more expensive in public expenditure terms than it need be. There is little doubt that the definitions used by the British Treasury, as to what is regarded as public sector, have been more restrictive in the past than those followed by other countries. But under any accepted international definition it is hard to see how the spending of British local authority housing departments as presently constituted could be regarded as anything other than public expenditure. If the public expenditure constraint is to be relaxed, it is therefore necessary to alter the structure of British social housing ownership. As Chapter 8 has shown, a substantial amount of stock has already been transferred to housing associations, co-operatives and other social landlords, and this trend is likely to continue. But there would clearly be advantage in carrying it further.

This was the recommendation of the report by Wilcox et al. (1993b) for the Joseph Rowntree Foundation on Local Housing Companies. They proposed the setting up of local housing companies to take over local authority stock. To qualify as independent and therefore to escape the inclusion of their investment in the total for public expenditure, it is not necessary for the local authorities to sever all connection with the new landlord bodies; indeed, the process of transfer is likely to be more acceptable both to the authorities and to many of the tenants if some link is retained. The authors of the Rowntree report therefore proposed that local authorities should be able to retain a stake in such bodies, but to avoid the public expenditure constraint it should be a minority one. However, this is not a condition met by municipal housing companies in Sweden, Germany and the Netherlands, all of which raise investment funds from the market, without their inclusion in the public expenditure total, even where there is full or dominant local authority ownership of the companies.

However, the full implications of such a change on the total volume of public expenditure are not quite as straightforward as might at first appear. Some important choices would have to be made. Although comparisons are very difficult to make and rents obviously vary widely, the level of British rents in the social sector probably still tends to be lower than in the other countries, partly at least because social security payments are less generous (S. K. Holmans 1987: esp. §1). With such rent levels, the precedent of the housing associations in Britain shows that a substantial part of investment expenditure (up to 75% in England, and higher in Scotland) has had to be covered by grant, which would, of course, still count as public expenditure. The room for manoeuvre gained on this basis would therefore be fairly limited at present, although as rents rise and the level of HAG comes down (as the government apparently intends), the scope would increase. How far this process may go is at present difficult to judge. HAG rates of around 50% are spoken of as a possible objective, but much may in the end depend on the government's success in keeping down inflation and interest rates. The higher nominal interest rates are and the higher inflation is, the more the costs of housing become front-loaded and the higher subsidies have to be on new investment.

But this is not the end of the matter either. Typically, a condition of the transfer, to gain the necessary support of tenants in a ballot, is that the new landlords improve the stock. This either has to be reflected in a low transfer price for the stock, or in new HAG contributions, which at 75% makes them expensive, or, if rents are raised, in Housing Benefit. This has caused the government to have second thoughts on the financial implications of large bulk transfers. Much clearly depends on the amount of investment undertaken to upgrade the stock and on the assumptions made about rents. Indeed, the problem really arises only because undertakings to invest in what are usually much-needed improvements to the stock are generally used as a means of gaining the support of tenants for the transfer. The authors of the Rowntree report argue that these costs are more than offset by a combination of the financial benefit to the government of taking housing investment (apart from the subsidy) out of public expenditure, by the receipts from the sale of the stock that would reduce outstanding public debt, and by revenue from VAT, which does not arise on publicly owned stock. Altogether, they estimate that the transfer of stock by English local authorities alone could generate £16000 million public expenditure savings expressed at net present value when compared with a continuation of the present system (Wilcox et al. 1993b).

The structure of housing debt

The level of household debt varies considerably among the countries, and the importance of this has been analysed in a study by Rowlatt (1993). As Figure 12.1 shows, Britain has by far the largest household debt of all the major countries in the EU as a percentage of GDP and, in all of the countries, housing debt is by far the largest component of household debt. In Britain, Germany and Italy it amounts to more than half. The differences in the structure of this debt are of major importance for the management of the economy.

Britain's household debt rose sharply in the second half of the 1980s, mainly as a result of increased mortgage borrowing, following deregulation in the financial sector.[1] The issues to which this gives rise are discussed in the next section. But although the scale of the borrowing is important, the structure of the debt is also of major significance in the context of an integrated Europe, particularly if economic and monetary union is to be achieved. As the various country chapters

---

1. This process is well described by Nigel Lawson, who was Chancellor of the Exchequer during these years; see Lawson (1992: 625–36).

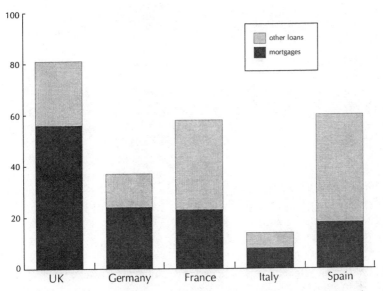

Figure 12.1 Household debt as a percentage of GDP (*Source:* A. Rowlatt, *Treasury bulletin*).

have shown, it is much more common in Continental European countries than in Britain for mortgages to be on long-term fixed interest rates. Although the special circumstances of the early 1990s have produced a rapid growth in fixed interest mortgages in Britain (see Ch. 8), the fixed term is most commonly very short by European standards. Moreover, it is by no means clear that fixed rate loans will remain a feature of the British market when interest rates rise once again. The dominance of variable rate mortgages in Britain is illustrated in Figure 12.2 and the amount of all household debt carrying short-term interest rates in Figure 12.3.

From these it can be seen that the scale and structure of UK debt causes home owners to be much more directly affected by changes in short-term interest rates than their counterparts in other countries. This was already seen in the ERM crisis of 1992. The high interest rates that were necessary to protect the sterling exchange rate had a severe and immediate impact on home owners, many of whom had borrowed to the limit to finance recent house purchases and whose incomes were not sufficient to finance the increased interest payments. When the crisis actually struck, the financial markets knew that the government's scope for defensive action was limited, because it was politically unacceptable to push interest rates any higher. In France, by contrast, although high short-term interest rates were no doubt still unwelcome and uncomfortable, they had much less impact on home owners, or on business, which also tends to use long-term finance more than in Britain. French short-term interest rates, and for that matter German, can therefore be used to protect the currency without having such an immediate or direct effect on the domestic economy.

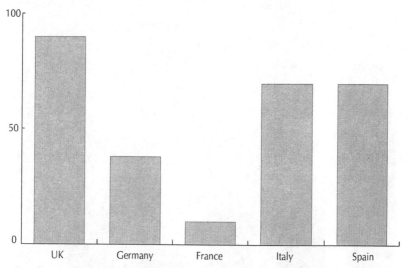

Figure 12.2   Variable rate mortgages as a percentage of total mortgages (*Source:* A. Rowlatt, *Treasury bulletin*).

In so far as short-term interest rates have to keep broadly in step across Europe, this means that the effect of interest rate movements will be very different from one country to another. By leaving the ERM, the UK gained some freedom in the setting of its interest rates; but it would be a mistake even now to suppose that British rates can be set without regard to the interest rates on other

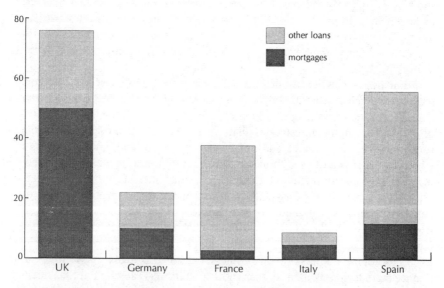

Figure 12.3   Household debt carrying short-term interest rates, as a percentage of GDP (*Source:* A. Rowlatt, *Treasury bulletin*).

242

currencies. And, as Europe becomes more integrated, even without going the full length of EMU, significant differences in rates will become even harder to sustain. Yet with the structure of British debt, and particularly housing debt, it may be very difficult to live with a monetary policy that suits the needs of the other countries. When interest rates rise, the deflationary effect in Britain is likely to be much more severe than elsewhere; and, when they fall, the stimulus is also likely to be greater, leading to a much more rapid danger of overheating. With a larger home ownership sector, a higher level of mortgage debt and a predominance of variable rate lending, measures necessary to regulate the economies of other countries will create instability in Britain. It seems unavoidable, therefore, that closer monetary integration in Europe would require Britain to reform its system of housing finance by giving greater encouragement to the use of long-term fixed interest loans and the building up of personal equity in housing.

Housing finance and macroeconomic policy

While the structure of housing debt, and indeed other debt, raises important issues for British economic management, the experience of the past decade has also shown how great can be the impact of changes in the level of debt. The work of Muellbauer and others has analysed the effects of equity withdrawal from housing and demonstrated the substantial part it played in the boom of the late 1980s (Muellbauer 1990a,b, Maclennan & Gibb 1993, Wilcox 1993). Equity withdrawal and the subsequent slump in house prices, leading to the phenomenon of negative equity, not only created much personal hardship but contributed greatly to the instability of the British economy in the late 1980s and early 1990s.

House prices are of course liable to fluctuate in all countries. Prices in Paris have been affected by the present recession and in Bonn not only by the recession but also by the decision to transfer the capital of the Federal Republic to Berlin. In the Netherlands, as was shown in Chapter 5, there was a rapid house price inflation followed by a fall in prices in the early 1980s. Of the five other countries in this study, only Spain, with its house price boom in the 1980s, and Sweden, which suffered from falling house prices as a result of a financial and credit collapse in Scandinavia, also following deregulation, had an experience that was in any way comparable to that of Britain. The distinguishing features of the British experience were the unprecedented scale of equity withdrawal in the late 1980s following deregulation (Table 12.2) and the fact that when house prices fell in the 1990s, they did so not only in real terms, which had happened before, but in nominal terms as well, leading to those with high borrowings suffering a fall in the value of their houses to below the outstanding value of their mortgage, the situation known as negative equity.

Table 12.2 Net equity withdrawal in UK housing.

	£000 million	As a % of consumer expenditure
1980	0.5	0.4
1981	2.3	1.5
1982	5.6	3.3
1983	5.6	3.1
1984	7.9	4.0
1985	9.3	4.3
1986	13.6	6.4
1987	16.1	6.0
1988	21.6	7.1
1989	14.3	4.3
1990	15.2	4.3
1991	11.8	3.2
1992	3.5	0.9

Source: Wilcox (1993).

The impact of the housing market on the British economy

The efficiency of the UK housing finance system, the much more frequent movement within the sector than in most other European countries, and the possibility of remortgaging a house (particularly for those over 60), all make it possible for owner occupiers to alter with relative ease the ratio of debt to equity in their houses. This has been a feature of the market, since deregulation in the early 1980s permitted the entry of the commercial banks into mortgage lending, caused the collapse of the building societies cartel and ended mortgage rationing. Competition resulted in higher levels of risk becoming acceptable to the lending institutions and finance being offered at much higher loan to value ratios than formerly. Housing, which had previously been regarded as a very illiquid form of investment, was transformed into a savings pool that home owners could draw on for other forms of consumption. The result was an increase in mortgage borrowing which, faced with rigidities in the housing market, led to a house price inflation and in turn through the wealth effect to further withdrawal of funds. The result was that equity withdrawal rose from relatively modest levels in the early 1980s to £21 600 million in the peak year of 1988.

Equity withdrawal on this scale is bound to have a substantial impact on the economy. Not only did house prices in London and the South East of England, the area most affected, rise by 170% between 1980 and 1989, but the leakage into other forms of expenditure was clearly substantial (Wilcox 1993). To set it roughly in context, £22 000 million of equity withdrawal in one year compares with the expected increased tax revenue in the two exceptionally tough budgets of 1993 of £17 000 million. This must have a major macroeconomic impact, and, even if some of the funds were used to finance alternative investments, as they undoubtedly were, a substantial part went into consumer expenditure. Withdrawal of equity from housing to finance consumption is a form of dis-saving. It is therefore no surprise to see from Figure 12.4 that the personal savings ratio fell sharply, reaching an extremely low level in the late 1980s, and that the financial balance became negative in 1988. The balance of payments went sharply into deficit at the same time, this also being the consequence of the surge in consumer expenditure and the counterpart of the imbalance in private sector savings and investment.

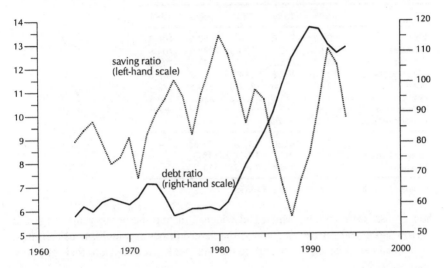

Figure 12.4 (a, above) Personal debt and savings ratios; (b, below) Personal sector financial balance. Both parts show percentages of disposable income. (*Source:* HM Treasury (1993)).

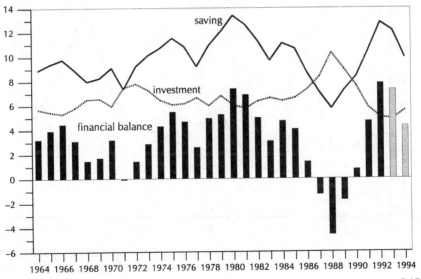

The debt-financed boom that this caused plainly could not last, and the increased interest rates that were used to check it hit precisely those who had borrowed most. The housing bubble burst and, as Table 12.3 shows, house prices fell most sharply in the area where they had risen most, so that by 1993 in the South East of England they were some 35% below their 1988 peak. Regional

Table 12.3 Regional house price indices in the UK.

	1985	1989	1991	1993	1994
UK	126.2	226.3	208.0	190.6	195.5
Scotland	124.3	152.2	179.9	198.9	204.4
Greater London	141.3	278.3	223.3	193.8	195.0
Outer South East	133.6	281.6	214.6	185.7	187.9
West Midlands	121.8	240.6	237.0	220.5	222.1
North	123.9	176.6	224.2	218.1	234.9
Inflation-adjusted rates (1983 = 100)					
UK	113.7	164.8	137.0	111.8	–
Greater London	127.3	202.7	147.1	113.7	–
Scotland	112.0	110.9	118.5	111.9	–

Source: Halifax Building Society house price index.

house price differentials, which had widened during the boom years, began to narrow again and Figure 12.5 shows that house prices as a multiple of earnings, which had been exceptionally high in the late 1980s, came back to their previous level by 1993.

The fall-out in the form of personal distress, which this situation caused, was

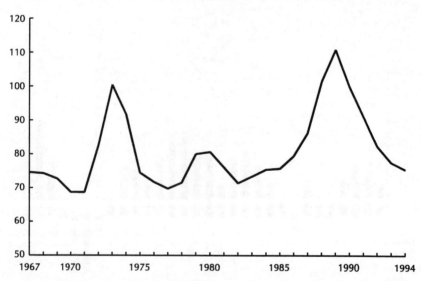

Figure 12.5 House price to earnings ratio (*Source:* Financial Statement and Budget Report, 1993–4).

considerable. Research by the Bank of England and by Dorling for the Joseph Rowntree Foundation has shown that the extent of the negative equity problem was indeed large. According to the Bank of England some 1.8 million householders were affected by 1993 and the aggregate shortfall in house values as against outstanding mortgage loans was put at £11 700 million, equivalent to £6,500 per household affected (Holmans 1991a, Bank of England 1992, 1993, Dorling 1993). Apart from those actually suffering from negative equity, many more people found that the value of their principal asset was sharply reduced and that they were not as wealthy as they had previously supposed. In addition, the combination of high interest rates and recession in the economy led to many people being unable to meet their mortgage obligations. In consequence, repossessions rose from 19000 a year in 1985 to 75500 in 1991 and 68500 in 1992 (Wilcox 1993: 103). However, in addition to the obvious personal hardship, the effect of this situation on the economy was severe. Negative equity, reduced wealth and the threat of repossessions all led to a sharp drop in consumer expenditure and a rise in personal saving, just when the economy, afflicted by recession, was in need of a stimulus and when taxes were rising to finance a growing budget deficit. Housing, having become a very liquid asset in the rising market of the 1980s, became even more illiquid than before, as the fall in prices resulted in a sharp drop in sales. Whereas equity withdrawal acted as a supercharger during the boom, so falling prices and negative equity provided an economic damper just when it was not needed.

Obviously, it is unlikely that in the absence of these effects Britain could have avoided the boom and subsequent recession in the late 1980s and early 1990s; they occurred not only here but throughout Europe and in the Western world generally. Nor is it reasonable to expect that fluctuations in house prices can be avoided. But the volatility in the housing market undoubtedly aggravated the instability in the economy and may partly account for not only sharply rising inflation during the boom but, as Table 12.4 shows, a deeper and more prolonged loss of output in the subsequent recession than in the other leading EU countries. Indeed, the National Institute of Economic and Social Research predicts a rate of growth for Britain over the period 1990–5 that is only half the rate for Germany, France and Italy.

Table 12.4   Growth of domestic product, 1990–5.

	Italy	Germany	France	UK	USA
1990	2.1	5.9	2.5	0.9	1.2
1991	1.3	4.6	0.7	−2.5	−0.7
1992	0.9	1.2	1.4	−0.5	2.6
1993	−0.4	−1.9	−0.7	1.9	3.0
1994*	2.0	1.0	1.7	2.9	3.4
1995*	2.6	1.8	2.12	2.6	2.4
Average	1.4	2.1	1.3	0.9	2.0

Source: National Institute of Economic and Social Research.
* Forecast.

247

The differing regional impact within the UK

Some idea of the importance of the behaviour of the housing market in influencing the performance of the economy as a whole can be gained from a comparison of the South East of England with Scotland since the mid-1980s. As has been seen elsewhere in this book, Scotland has a much lower proportion of owner occupied housing than England, in particular the south of England; indeed, it is more akin to the European average. The Scottish economy also had a weaker economic performance in the second half of the 1980s, and equity withdrawal was much less of a feature of the housing market. Although house prices rose, as Table 12.3 has already shown, the rise was moderate, opening up a substantial and widening gap between Scottish house prices and those in the south of England. When interest rates rose, the smaller proportion of home owners, and their much lower exposure, meant that the deflationary effect was on a much smaller scale too, with consumer spending less affected. As a result, instead of falling, Scottish house prices continued modestly to advance in the early 1990s; and just as equity withdrawal had not been a serious issue in the 1980s, so significant negative equity did not arise in the 1990s. Scottish GDP held up better than in the UK as a whole in 1991 and 1992, with the result that GDP per head rose from 92.8% of the UK average in 1989 to 98.3% in 1992 (Scottish Office 1994). Most significant of all, Scottish unemployment, which for 70 years at least had been above the average for the UK, fell below the UK level in the spring of 1992 and below the South East of England later that year.

Recent research by Maclennan & Gibb (1993) has confirmed the importance of these differences. A detailed study of the housing market in Glasgow, Bristol and Luton during the 1980s and early 1990s showed that pre-1989 equity withdrawal was much more marked in the two southern towns than in Glasgow, leaving those with mortgages (who accounted for two thirds of householders) much more exposed to interest rate increases. In the 1990s, arrears and difficulty rates varied greatly across the three cities – 20% in Luton and only 3% in Glasgow. The impact of the recession in Glasgow, where west of Scotland unemployment rates, although high, actually fell between 1989 and 1992, was undoubtedly less severe than in Luton or Bristol, where they rose from 5% to 11% and 6% to 9.5% respectively. Although it would be dangerous to ascribe all of this difference to the behaviour of the housing market, it seems highly probable that Glasgow's lower percentage of home ownership and much less significant equity withdrawal in the 1980s were major factors.

Causes and outlook

Even if it is accepted that the UK's particular economic difficulties over the past decade were largely attributable to a credit explosion and that much of that was housing related, it may still be argued that it did not require changes in housing policy to prevent it. Monetary policy is widely regarded as having been too lax in the late 1980s and, if this were avoided in future, the problems need not recur. An alternative view, argued by Lord Lawson, the Chancellor of the Exchequer at the time, is that deregulation did play an important part in the credit expansion but that this was a once for all effect (1992: 631). The experience, it is claimed, has taught both lenders and borrowers a painful lesson and they are unlikely to allow the same situation to recur.

While there is some truth in both arguments, neither is entirely convincing. Other countries which had their own monetary policies but also deregulated, notably the Scandinavian countries and Spain, had similar credit booms, and in Scandinavia the financial institutions ended up in serious difficulty. And the idea that lessons have now been learnt, which will prevent such a situation recurring, seems equally lacking in credibility. What deregulation has done is greatly to increase competition in the provision of mortgage finance. That competition has increased the risks that institutions are prepared to run in search of business and profit, risks that in the 1980s were mainly borne by the insurance companies. Certainly, the experience of default and repossessions will instil greater caution for a time. But the pressures will remain; and, in the longer run, as the traumas of the 1980s and early 1990s fade into memory, it will be surprising if a similar situation does not recur.

It may be that, if the other European countries increasingly deregulate their markets for mortgage finance, as the Single Market legislation clearly intended, they will run into some of the same problems. For example, will it prove possible against cross-border competition for the present loan to value ratios to be maintained in France and Germany, for the French to continue to prohibit the payment of interest on current and short-term savings accounts, or for the various closed circuit finance systems, notably the contract savings schemes, to survive? The conclusion of Chapter 10 was that the Single Market in mortgage finance would become a reality only very slowly, and ways will no doubt be found to preserve many of the present features of European housing markets, if member States feel their abandonment would lead to economic instability. But, even if all these features were to go, the French and German markets would remain less volatile than the British, and have a less destabilizing impact on the rest of the economy, because of the lower proportion of the housing stock in owner occupation, the lower rate of turnover in the sector, the lower level of personal debt, and the high proportion of fixed rate finance in housing loans.

It will be profoundly damaging to the British economy in an integrated Europe if its performance proves to be more unstable than that of other countries. And in so far as this is a consequence of the way in which the housing market operates, it needs to be remedied. If Britain's economic performance is really to converge with other countries in the Union, that must include rates of inflation, and long-term fixed rate borrowing should then be as viable here as elsewhere. Setting a maximum level of loan to value or, as in France, loan to income ratios may have to be considered, although this is perhaps more a matter of ensuring adequate insurance arrangements and leaving insurance companies to make a proper assessment of default. But the most important lesson is that there are dangers in the government continuing to push up levels of home ownership. A better balance between the tenures, particularly a stronger private rented sector, would help to avoid the situation of people with inadequate means taking on the burdens and risks of ownership simply because there is nowhere else to go.

Conclusion

This chapter has shown that there are some important interconnections between the operation of the housing market, housing policy and the economy. These will assume even greater importance in an increasingly integrated Europe, where the British economy is exposed to competition from other member States and has less scope to pursue its own individual economic policy.

Public expenditure will remain under severe pressure, and the cost of housing policy will continue to be put under strict scrutiny. The pressure for more selective support is likely to continue. In Britain this has implications for the continuing indiscriminate nature of mortgage interest tax relief (MITR) and particularly the use of the endowment-backed mortgage. But the most important conclusion is that public expenditure should not be used to do what private funds can be raised to do equally well. There is advantage therefore in getting social housing investment off the government books, except for the subsidy element. Quite apart from the other arguments for change that are addressed elsewhere in this book, this points to the advantage of transferring rented housing stock from local authorities to alternative social landlords such as housing associations and local or municipal housing companies, which would be independently funded but in which local authorities could continue to have a role.

Perhaps the most serious issues arise over finance for the owner occupied sector. The very high level of British housing debt, combined with its structure, makes Britain much more sensitive to movements in short-term interest rates than other countries are, with damaging effects not only for the housing market but for the economy as a whole. And the volatility of housing finance, resulting in both equity withdrawal and negative equity on a scale that does not arise in other countries, also destabilizes the economy and makes the task of economic management much more difficult. The encouragement of greater use of long-term fixed interest finance, a critical look at maximum loan to value ratios, and the promotion of alternatives to owner occupation for those who are at the margin of affordability, could all have some part to play in achieving greater stability for the economy. But the government first needs to be prepared to recognize the importance of a more stable housing market for the health of the economy as a whole and to be willing to adopt a policy aimed at a better balance between the tenures.

CHAPTER 13
The future of British housing policy

The objectives

The survey in this book has shown that an interventionist policy is common to all six countries, and although in detail it differs widely, the main objective is everywhere the same: to ensure that all sections of the community, including those economically most disadvantaged, have access to housing of a decent standard and at an affordable price.

The extent to which this objective is achieved varies. Although the major shortages that typified the two post-war decades are overcome, there are still shortages in some areas; and in some countries immigration, or too great a reduction in new construction, have caused them to increase. There is also a growing problem of homelessness throughout the European Union. This is partly, but by no means wholly, related to availability of social housing.

Qualitatively too there has been a major advance. Few houses lack basic amenities, and the slums have been replaced in most countries. But some serious problems remain. Assessment of quality involves subjective judgement, but generally the situation is regarded as being better in Germany, the Netherlands and Sweden than in Britain or France, and better in those countries than in Spain. In all countries there are problems in some inner city areas and in large, low-income housing estates on the periphery of many cities. The problems of the latter go much wider than the quality of housing, requiring solutions to be sought in social, economic and planning policies as well as housing policy. The danger of increased immigration pressure from countries outside the Union, notably from North Africa and eastern Europe as suggested in Chapter 11, could exacerbate these problems in several countries.

But if the provision of an acceptable standard of housing at affordable prices to all sections of the community is the central purpose of housing policy, it is sometimes in danger of being lost sight of, as governments focus on other subsidiary (and sometimes highly political) objectives. The British situation is a case in point. Here, the promotion of a property-owning democracy, more recently described as enabling the preferred housing tenure to be within reach of the vast majority of people, has been seen as an aim in itself. The more cynical may perhaps think that it is more straightforward than this: a tendency for governments to favour particular sections of society, whether owner occupiers or tenants, for political reasons. But whatever one thinks of such objectives, they account at least in part for the failure in many countries, not only the six in this study, to focus policy more directly on measures that will improve the living conditions of the disadvantaged sections of the community.

There are other valid objectives. Some countries set out to avoid the concentration of particular social groups in one type of housing, the process known as "residualization". Sweden provides the extreme case of this, where in the past the policy has been most nearly tenure neutral; but, until recently, support has also been very widely applied in the Netherlands. The policies of both of these countries have been marked by a particular concern for the less well off. But such policies are very expensive, because they are non-discriminatory, and the realities of pressure on public expenditure have now forced a departure from this approach in both countries. Indeed, there has been a clear tendency to move towards policies that are more sharply focused on the circumstances of the individual. This has led to the development in all of the countries, except Spain, of systems of personal housing allowances, and to a shift in the balance of housing policy expenditure in their favour. This does not necessarily lead to residualization, but there is a danger that it may, if a consequence is that social housing becomes more strictly reserved for disadvantaged groups.

There are other less well recognized but nonetheless important objectives that should be part of housing policy and which have been discussed in earlier chapters. These include both enabling housing markets to be as responsive as possible to the needs of the economy, so that growth is not frustrated or ends in inflationary pressure, and preventing volatility in the housing market from increasing the instability of the economy.

The first of these has from time to time been recognized by governments faced with acute demand pressure, although it has not recently played any part in British policy. In the context of the European Union, with a greatly enhanced degree of competition for investment between member States, the constraint of a rigid housing market could seriously damage a country's economic prospects, whereas a responsive market, and one that is complemented by an effective regional policy, will greatly benefit the economy. The second has become a potentially much more serious problem since financial deregulation, and was particularly evident in Britain, Sweden and Spain. In Britain the release of stored purchasing power from the housing market, through increased borrowing in time of boom and its replenishment in recession, has now been well documented and has clearly had a major impact on the economy. But although there has been much talk of equity withdrawal and negative equity, terms that were not heard of until recently, there has been no sign of government taking any action to prevent a recurrence of these difficulties. Rather the reverse: the pressure continues to raise home ownership to even higher levels, and the presumption in Britain seems to be that other countries, which retain much more regulated housing markets, will eventually be forced under the Single Market legislation to liberalize and come closer to the British pattern.

Despite the commonality of the main aim, this study has shown that there is widespread variation in the policies of the countries covered. However, with the exception of Spain, and apart from differences in emphasis, there is a fair amount of common ground between the policies of the Continental countries. The British situation is the one that is most out of line: an exceptionally large owner occupied sector by northern European standards, the smallest private rented sector by a clear margin, and a social rented sector that, despite the recent growth of housing associations, is still dominated by direct local authority ownership and management in a form that does not apply elsewhere. This situation is the product of policies that have never made any attempt at tenure neutrality and have in consequence resulted in extreme neglect of the private rented sector. It is also the product of the more confrontational style of British politics, leading to a more ideologically driven approach, less consensus and continuity, and a plethora of legislation by the standards of any other country.

European integration will not lead to a common European housing policy: housing is not within the competence accorded to the Commission, except in very minor respects. Nor should it be. But the process of integration will nevertheless affect housing policy: gradually, indeed only in the very long term, through the effect of financial integration on mortgage finance; more immediately through the requirements of convergence and the pressure that will be exerted on national budgets; and, in Britain's case, the destabilizing effects of a volatile mortgage market on the general economy will be increasingly hard to tolerate in a more integrated Europe. Their moderation must surely in the end become a recognized aim of policy.

The policies

The remainder of this chapter sets out proposals for the reshaping of policy in the light of these general considerations. Although the proposals take account of the measures adopted in the other countries, they refer particularly to Britain. As in the country chapters each of the main tenures is considered in turn.

Owner occupation

The aims proposed for policy in this sector can be set out broadly as follows:
- to enable people to own their own homes, so far as it is practical to do so and so long as they can assume the burdens and responsibilities involved
- to help to mitigate personal hardship and distress where this arises through unexpected changes in circumstances

- to assist the growth of the economy by making the tenure as flexible as possible and facilitating mobility
- to prevent volatility in the housing market and in the provision of mortgage finance from increasing the instability of the economy.

Although surveys show that a large majority of people aspire to be home owners, these results have to be qualified in two respects: first, they are conducted in the present state of the British market, where viable alternatives are especially limited; and, secondly, even in other countries where most people also aspire to home ownership, they see that as a long-run objective to be achieved when they are in a position to settle down. This aspiration should therefore not be interpreted as meaning that there is no place for other tenures.

As compared with the other countries, the arrangements for the owner occupied sector in Britain have obvious strengths: finance is readily available and is efficiently provided by the institutions; the transaction costs of house purchase are low; householders can move easily, and the tenure is therefore more compatible with the need for labour mobility than in many other countries. But there are also serious shortcomings. First, there is the evident personal distress caused by the volatility of the British housing market, especially over the latest cycle, as demonstrated by the high figures for mortgage arrears, repossessions, and those affected by negative equity, which were referred to in Chapter 12. Secondly, the damaging effect of the housing market on the stability of the economy has been one of the themes of this book. Although it is unrealistic to suppose that any economy will be uninfluenced by the behaviour of the housing market, in none of the other countries has the use of mortgage finance to fund general consumption been quite so apparent as in Britain.

In addition to these two major issues, it needs to be recognized that, despite the flexibility of this sector in Britain, it has limitations as the main tenure for population movement. If the share of the stock is pushed ever higher as a result of policy, this will inevitably be at the expense of other tenures, notably private renting, which could have a major part to play in mobility.

There is a potential problem of long-term maintenance in the sector, if people continue to be encouraged to buy houses who cannot adequately afford the burdens of home ownership. There is some evidence that this will be a growing problem, even with continued availability of improvement grants; and because replacement is likely to be more expensive than repair, the maintenance of the nation's stock of capital in housing should be of concern to the country as a whole, not only to those who live in the houses affected.

For all of these reasons it needs to be recognized that there are dangers in trying to push the already high share of owner occupation in Britain even higher and that a more balanced policy is required. Quite apart from those who plainly cannot afford it, many of the difficulties that have arisen are the consequence of people assuming the burden of owner occupation who would not contemplate it in other countries. Unless a better balance is achieved, therefore, there is every likelihood that the distress and instability that have typified the recent economic cycle will be even worse next time round. Although obvious enough, there is little sign that this is properly accepted by government. In England at least, where the share of the tenure is already exceptionally high by the standards of other countries, efforts to promote owner occupation further should cease. In Scotland there may still be some scope for further increase, but even there, the share of this tenure, at over half, is higher than in Germany, Sweden or the Netherlands.

Fiscal relief

Despite the reductions that have been made in mortgage interest tax relief (MITR), it remains an extremely badly targeted incentive as a means of achieving the central objective of housing policy. It also feeds through into house prices, which, according to an estimate by the National Institute of Economic & Social Research, would fall by about 4% after four years were it to be abolished (Westaway & Pain 1993). Lack of an income ceiling and a time limit for eligibility mean that many people get relief who do not need it, and may also, through the device of endowment-backed mortgages, go on claiming maximum relief long after they could afford to take a larger equity stake in their houses.

In addition, although MITR is a housing-related relief, experience has shown that people increase the borrowing on their homes for all sorts of reasons unrelated to housing. These may range from the funding of a new small business to the financing of a holiday in the Caribbean. Whatever the purpose, good or bad, the taxpayer should not be asked to fund it as part of housing policy. For all these reasons it is time for MITR to go.

It is sometimes argued, notably by the Dutch in justification of their unrestricted MITR, that housing should be regarded as an investment good and that, on this view, it is not MITR but the absence of tax on imputed rent and of capital gains tax on a principal residence that should be regarded as the subsidies. The Netherlands and Spain are the only countries among those studied where imputed rent is now taxed, albeit at an unrealistically low rate. But whatever the merits of such a tax, the reasons for its imposition would be difficult to explain publicly: it would provoke strenuous opposition, especially after the fiasco of the poll tax, and it is therefore not within the realms of political practicability in Britain. Much the same considerations would apply to the extension of capital gains tax to an owner occupier's principal residence. This would also have the severe economic disadvantage of reducing mobility. It is notable that in Sweden, probably for this reason, the rate of tax has been cut in the recent changes, and roll-over relief has been reintroduced. The fact is that housing is in a category of its own: it contains elements of a consumption good, an investment good and a portfolio investment, and what is important is to find a policy that strikes an appropriate balance between the tenures.

If MITR were to cease, is there any need for it to be replaced by any other fiscal relief in the owner occupied sector, albeit more sharply focused than MITR has been? There appears to be no need in Britain for a fiscal relief to encourage construction in this sector, which was often part of its original justification in

255

other countries; and although abolition of MITR will raise mortgage costs, a slight reduction in house prices is also to be expected as a result of reduced demand, which would go some way to compensating those at the margin of affordability. Many would therefore argue that there is no need for home owners to be given this type of fiscal incentive in addition to the other benefits they receive. Certainly, it seems unlikely that government is considering any kind of replacement if, as is widely expected, the process of reducing the value of MITR leads eventually to its abolition.

On the other hand, the exceptionally small size of the private rented sector in Britain does create a special situation. It means that, for many people, either there is no viable alternative to buying their own houses, so that making ownership less affordable will simply increase the risk of their getting into financial difficulty, or the effect will be to increase the demand for social rented accommodation. If one assumes that government wants to reduce rather than expand the social rented sector and that, even with major reforms in policy, it will take a long time to bring about a significant expansion in the private rented sector, a case may be made for continuing to assist the less well off to afford home ownership.

If tax assistance is to be applied, it should therefore be limited to first-time buyers, the expectation being that others in this sector will have had the opportunity to build up a significant amount to equity in their houses. Rather than a more restricted form of MITR, there would be advantage in the use of an annual depreciation allowance, based on the purchase value of a house, to be deducted from personal income before tax. If this followed the German model, it would be at a rate of about 5% or 6% a year, but be limited to a fixed period of between five and ten years (much shorter than the assumed life of the asset), and available only once in a purchaser's lifetime. It should also be restricted to a maximum house value. The advantages compared with MITR would be that its cost to government would not be dependent upon the level of short-term interest rates, it would be effectively targeted, and it would have less effect on general house prices. It would be available regardless of the way in which house purchase is financed. It would also have the advantage that a parallel allowance could be provided for landlords in the private rented sector, thereby achieving a greater degree of tenure neutrality and encouraging new construction in that sector.

Grants and low interest loans

There seems to be no case for introducing general grants or subsidized loans for new house construction in Britain, such as apply in several other countries, whether these are income-related or not. However, there will remain a case for giving assistance to particular projects, notably as part of urban renewal schemes, and the Scottish GRO-grants are well designed for this purpose. There is also a strong argument for continuing to provide grants for house improvement. Such grants have done much to encourage the upgrading of existing housing stock and in many cities have also played an important part in successful schemes for urban renewal. They are at least as important in maintaining and improving the quality of the nation's housing capital as in assisting individuals. In recognition of this, the grants should again be made available in England without a means test, as for the present they continue to be in Scotland.

Measures to increase market stability

In view of the extremely damaging effects that a bubble in the housing market can have on the stability of the economy, as shown by Britain's experience, it is unlikely that France or Germany will readily give up their institutional arrangements, which have given them greater stability. If such stability is to be introduced into the British system, it is necessary to consider two issues: the possible restriction of loan to value ratios (thereby reducing scope for equity withdrawal and the danger of negative equity), and the structure of housing debt, in particular whether greater use could be made of long-term fixed rate loans and whether there is a place for some form of closed-circuit funding system that would give a more stable rate of interest.

Imposing a limit on loan to value ratios would require either legislation or, at least, the setting of limits by the banks' and building societies' regulatory authorities. This would undoubtedly be seen as a retrograde step towards a more regulated market. It would also be unwelcome to potential home owners, particularly first-time buyers, who tend to have the highest loan to value ratios, since it would cause them to delay purchase until they had accumulated more savings. It would therefore have a temporary but significant impact on the housing market.

The trouble is, any measure that, in the interests of prudence, makes it more difficult for people to obtain mortgages, will to some extent reduce demand and therefore depress the housing market. In the absence of suitable alternatives in the rented market, it may also cause either hardship or a switch to the social rented sector to an extent that would not arise in other countries. One possibility might be to make personal insurance against mortgage default obligatory where loan to value ratios exceed some specified amount (say, 80%), in place of the present general indemnity arrangements that banks and building societies use. Such schemes, although involving substantial State support, operate in Sweden and the Netherlands, where, unlike France and Germany, mortgages may go up to loan to value ratios of 95% or 100%. If they were adopted in Britain without the State acting as guarantor of last resort, insurance companies would have to evaluate individual circumstances instead of providing general insurance for lenders as they do now. Such schemes appear to be worth investigation, but they would of course present difficulties to those who operated them. Without State support, the risks might be considered such as to necessitate steeply rising premiums for higher loan to value ratios, with a considerable effect on demand, especially from first-time buyers. In assessing these risks, it is likely that companies would be as concerned with security of income and employment, and the ratio of loan to income, as with loan to value. Premiums for mortgages where these ratios were high would of necessity significantly increase costs to the purchaser.

257

It would certainly both assist the stability of the owner occupied sector and benefit the economy as a whole, if purchasers in Britain, like their counterparts elsewhere, could be encouraged to make greater use of fixed rate mortgages. Although there has been some movement in this direction, rates are generally fixed for much shorter periods than is normal in other countries (Miles 1994: 38). Fixed rate loans, although accounting for some 60% of new lending in late 1993, still comprise less than 10% of total mortgage debt outstanding, and it is far from clear that they will remain attractive when interest rates begin to rise. There are difficulties in encouraging long-term fixed rate borrowing if this country cannot improve on its past inflation record. High inflation results in high interest rates, both short and long term; and in the hope that they will fall, purchasers will, at such times, prefer short or variable rates. At the time of writing (1995), although inflation and short-term rates are both low, lack of confidence in the country's future management of inflation still keeps the long-term rate higher than in Germany or France.

Other countries, even some of those with a history of inflation, have retained much greater use of long-term fixed interest borrowing, and there would be advantages if it could be encouraged in Britain. One of the lessons of the 1992 ERM crisis is that the vulnerability of British house owners to short-term interest rate movements has major implications for the management of the economy. It means that activity in the economy is much more sharply affected by interest rate changes than the economies of, for example, France and Germany, and that, if very high short-term rates are needed to support the currency, the political cost may be difficult to sustain. Apart from keeping the inflation rate down, the government therefore needs to consider ways in which long-term fixed rate borrowing can be encouraged. In Germany the mortgage bonds (*Pfandbriefe*) have established such a record for security that funds can be raised at very low rates of interest. There is perhaps a place for a similar instrument in Britain.

It may be that a low interest savings and lending system, assisted by tax relief after the fashion of that operated by the *Bausparkassen* and the *Plans d'Epargne Logement*, could also have a part to play. Although such systems may seem to British eyes unduly complicated, possibly even an anomalous inheritance from the past, they do provide not only an incentive to save for house purchase but an important source of stability in the housing market. There is no reason why they should not be operated in special accounts by banks and building societies.

The private rented sector

The objectives of this sector ought to be:
- to provide a flexible tenure, which can best cater for those who have to move in search of employment or who do not expect to be in an area or a job for more than a limited time
- to provide a decent standard of housing for those not yet able to assume

the burdens of owner occupation but not in need of the amount of State support provided by the social rented sector

- to enable elderly people of limited means to get access to their capital
- to take some of the weight off the other two sectors, particularly the subsidized social rented sector, the size of which tends to vary inversely with the size of this sector.
- to provide a vehicle for capital to be invested in housing, which might otherwise be used less productively or for less worthwhile purposes.

This sector has declined so far in Britain that it must be questionable whether it can again be restored to hold a major share of the housing market. Although it is still of much greater significance in the other countries covered in this study, the fact that it has been declining in all of them too, apart from Germany, suggests that any reversal of the downward trend would be difficult. Nevertheless, a well run good-quality private rented sector has a potentially important part to play and there would be advantages if it were stronger, providing a generally better quality of housing, and larger. However, if the sector is to recover and to play a useful part, it would have to be different in character from the run-down rented accommodation from which many of those now in the social rented sector feel glad to have escaped. The example of the Netherlands shows that investment by institutions is a much more likely way to bring this about than the return of the individual private landlord. It is also more likely to be politically acceptable. Pension funds, insurance companies and finance houses of various kinds, in which many small investors have a stake, do not evoke the same antipathy in some quarters as the landlord who is an individual, and they are in a position to benefit from economies of scale, both in raising finance and in management.

If a larger private rented sector is to be taken as an objective, how much larger is it reasonable to expect it to be? The next smallest private rented sector among the countries studied is in the Netherlands, where it is 17% of total stock. If, say, 15% were taken as an aim for the UK instead of the present 9%, that would enable it to play a much fuller part; but even that would involve an increase of some 1.4 million dwellings, something that would not be achieved easily and might take at least a decade, even with major changes in policy.

The government has repeatedly asserted the importance of the sector and expressed its desire to see it recover, but so far has not adequately willed the means. The new "assured" and "short-assured" or "short-hold" tenancies are a satisfactory solution to the longstanding and unhappy history of rent control and rent regulation, and bring the British system close to that which applies in Germany. But ministers are mistaken if they think that this is all they have to do to encourage the sector to revive. The fact that the other two tenures have been heavily supported, whereas private renting has not, means that even in a free market it is difficult to find a level of rent that landlords regard as providing an adequate return and tenants feel able to pay. The gap between rents that would provide a commercial return on investment and those in the social sector is very large, and in many circumstances the costs of a mortgage net of tax relief, especially when capital gain is assumed, make home ownership a much more attractive proposition. Moreover, confidence on the part of landlords and potential investors remains low, and such confidence is not assisted by political uncertainty, a factor that, with the British electoral system and single-party government, is more important in the UK than in many other countries. Although in the special circumstances of the housing slump in the early 1990s there was some increase in private renting, all of these factors mean that the sector is unlikely to make any permanent recovery, at least to the point of substantially enlarging its share of the total stock, unless the balance of fiscal incentives is corrected. Indeed, for a time it may well have to be skewed in the sector's favour if confidence is to be restored.

Fiscal measures

The present position is that in most of the six countries (the clear exception being Germany) this sector is still at some disadvantage, either from some degree of rent control or because incentives are less generous than for the other sectors. But Britain is the extreme case. It is the only country of the six where investment in housing is not even eligible for a depreciation allowance deductible from pre-tax income, although such allowances do apply to investment in other fixed productive assets. Most of the other countries provide significant incentives as well; Britain has not done so, apart from the temporary BES scheme. It is not surprising that a study by Coopers & Lybrand, undertaken for the Joseph Rowntree Foundation, estimated that there was at present a yield gap of 2–5% between the existing rates of return in the sector and the rate that would be necessary to attract investors (Coopers & Lybrand 1993: part 5 and appendix E).

Even if mortgage interest tax relief for owner occupiers is phased out, the balance will not be fully corrected. The owner occupied sector will still benefit from absence of tax on imputed rent and exemption of capital gains tax on a principal residence, neither of which have any parallel in the private rented sector. A neutral fiscal regime would therefore require taxation of income from rents in this sector to be lifted and some exemption from capital gains tax as well. Given the very small size of this sector, such measures would not be expensive in Britain, compared with the revenue foregone in the owner occupied sector or in comparison with the benefit they could provide.

There would seem to be a strong case for capital gains tax exemption and this might be done by excluding all dwellings valued at less than some maximum figure, rather as is done in France. If this were, say, £150000 (much lower than in France), it would exempt the bulk of rented property. There should be some regional variation, including a higher figure in London, and with adjustment made for inflation.

Freeing rental income from tax, although logical to give parity with owner occupation, might be thought objectionable, especially where commercial companies were landlords. But a depreciation allowance clearly ought to be introduced, since its absence is an anomaly, and the simplest way of providing an adequate return would be to set this at an appropriate level. This could be done either by setting it at a high level in the early years, as in Germany, or by coupling it with an initial allowance at a high rate in the first year. The level of depreciation allowance that would be necessary would of course depend on whether a comparable incentive is introduced for the owner occupied sector or MITR retained.

A certain amount of trial and error may be required before a level of incentives is found that achieves recovery in the sector. The study by Coopers & Lybrand concludes that an 8% return would be necessary, as do some others who have examined this subject, and the likelihood is that it would need to be 6% at least. This is substantially higher than the real rate of return on government bonds and is therefore heavily dependent upon the degree of perceived risk (political and otherwise) and the difficulty of getting investors to contemplate a type of investment most of them have ruled out for decades. Perhaps the main lesson of the BES scheme is that a tax incentive does work in this sector, although that scheme involved a high level of support (see Ch. 8), which has been estimated at 81% of the cost of grant aid to a typical housing association dwelling in the social rented sector (Crook et al. 1991a). It is to be expected that a scheme aimed at the sector as a whole, and at long-term investment rather than a five-year tax shelter, would give better results in relation to the amount of support provided and lead to a more permanent increase in stock. The effectiveness of any scheme would of course be increased (but so would its cost) if expenses involved in letting, including depreciation, could be deducted not simply from a taxpayer's total pre-tax income from housing but from income regardless of source, as is done in Germany.

Grants
There is a case for the use of grants in this sector, particularly if it is intended that part of the sector should meet the needs of those who would otherwise have to look for social rented accommodation. Tax relief is likely to encourage investment by institutions, especially at the more expensive end of the market, as the example of the Netherlands shows. But the subsidies available in Germany and in France have played an important part in enabling the sector to meet the needs of less well off tenants and they explain, at least in part, why it is possible for the social rented sector to be smaller in these two countries than in Britain. As has been noted in the chapter on Britain, statutory powers exist for Scottish Homes to use its GRO-grants to assist the private rented sector in Scotland. But although this has been used for individual cases, lack of funding has so far prevented it being developed into a general scheme.

The best and probably simplest approach would be a scheme of grant aid similar to the Housing Association Grant, but funding a lower percentage of costs than for non-profit making social landlords, and with the expectation that rents would be somewhat higher. This would fulfil a role similar to PLI subsidized loans in France. In Germany and the Netherlands, assistance for the private

261

rented sector has been provided on the same terms as for the social rented sector, so long as the same obligations applied with regard to rent levels. In Britain too, even if the assistance were less generous than HAG, it would be necessary for any participating landlord to reach agreement with the grant-giving body over maximum rent levels. This would apply for a given period, probably the life of a typical long-term loan; and, in such cases, tenancies should be limited to those whose financial circumstances warranted provision of assisted housing.

Such a scheme, apart from enabling the private rented sector to expand and fulfil a useful social role, could significantly increase its interest in taking over redundant or problem council-housing stock. This is already happening on a substantial scale with housing associations; and there has been considerable interest from the private sector in acquiring such stock, but so far almost exclusively for renovation and sale.

The social rented sector

The purpose of the social rented sector can be simply stated:
- to provide an adequate supply of housing of a decent standard at affordable prices for those that cannot afford the costs of accommodation in the other two sectors.

In all of the six countries (although Spain scarcely counts, because the sector is so small), the building of social rented houses pre-dated the provision of personal housing allowances; and, as earlier chapters have shown, in most of them there has been a shift in emphasis from bricks and mortar subsidies to personal support. It is therefore necessary to start consideration of this sector by asking two questions: first, whether support should now be concentrated on personal housing allowances, with subsidies to bricks and mortar gradually phased out; and secondly, if bricks and mortar subsidies do continue, whether this makes it necessary to have non-profit making social landlords.

Different views are taken of these questions in the six countries. In all of them there are still at present bricks and mortar subsidies, although in both Sweden and the Netherlands, as has been seen, there are plans to reduce them substantially. All six of the countries also have social non-profit making landlords, although in Germany since 1989 the majority of landlords in the sector have had their tax-exempt status ended and in return the limitation on profit has been lifted. For the most part, subsidies and non-profit status coincide, but they do not do so necessarily, and France, Germany and the Netherlands have all given assistance to private landlords to provide social housing.

In theoretical terms there is a case for giving all housing support in the form of personal means-related subsidies. This results in less market distortion and preserves the widest freedom of choice. But in practice there are major difficulties. The first of these is that it is difficult to devise an income-related subsidy that does not create a poverty trap and, the more reliance is put on such support, the worse the poverty trap becomes. This subject is dealt with later, but although adjustments to the system can reduce the severity, or depth, of the trap, this is at the expense of extending it to higher ranges of income. In Britain, as Chapter 8 has shown, the poverty trap is extremely severe.

Secondly, although a shift from bricks and mortar subsidies to individual subsidies in Britain would not have much immediate effect on the majority of local authorities, which have ceased to receive Housing Support Grant in Scotland or, before the 1989 changes, Housing Subsidy in England, this is only because their loan debt has been eroded by inflation. It would affect the remainder and would of course have a major impact on the rents of housing associations. In the long term, rents for all social housing would have to rise to a level that at least covered costs, if investment in refurbishment or in new building is to be maintained.

Much resistance to such a change could be expected, because of fear of inadequate increases in Housing Benefit and understandable concern in the light of recent history that the government could at any moment reduce both its level and eligibility. And because such a high proportion of tenants in Britain are on Housing Benefit already, any savings would be small. This would be particularly so if some of the shortcomings of the benefit system were tackled in the way described later in this chapter. In political terms it must therefore be doubted if such a major upheaval in the interests of what may be largely a theoretical gain would be worth the trouble. This is not to say that the present balance between bricks and mortar and personal subsidies is the right one, or that some further move towards personal allowances in Britain would be inappropriate. But there are undoubtedly disadvantages in attempting to rely entirely on income-related allowances.

Even if this case is accepted, however, it does not follow that support should be given only to a social sector comprising non-profit making landlords. Already it has been argued that there is a case for assisting the private rented sector, as in other countries, to provide housing at social or at least intermediate rents; but to go to the other extreme and rely exclusively on housing provided for profit could give rise to problems for the payment of housing allowances. Supervision would be required, as it is at present for tenants in the private rented sector who are in receipt of Housing Benefit, to ensure not only that tenants were not occupying unnecessarily spacious or luxurious accommodation but that rents were reasonable. And there would undoubtedly be concern if landlords earned what seemed to be unnecessarily large profit at the taxpayers' expense whenever there was a scarcity. The burden on Rent Officers, whose job it would be to deal with such matters, would be substantial if applied to all rented housing. Almost inevitably, concern that rents were too high, or were being unnecessarily subsidized by the taxpayer, would lead back to rent control, which has been the bane of the private rented sector in many countries, and nowhere more so than in Britain. There is therefore a strong case for non-profit landlords to avoid complete dependence on the commercial sector.

If the case for a social rented sector is accepted, it can of course still vary greatly in size. This study has shown the extreme positions of Scotland and the Netherlands on the one hand, where the sector is very large, and Spain on the other, where it is extremely small. There is no "right" size. Considerations that are relevant are the proportion of the population that has inadequate means: the number unemployed, the elderly with insufficient pensions, the low paid, and so on, and the extent to which assistance is given to other sectors to enable them to cater for these groups. The large size of the sector in Britain must reflect the absence of grants or low interest loans to the other sectors to provide low-cost housing. In France and Germany, where such schemes exist, the social rented sector is of the order of 15–20% of the total stock. It might therefore be reasonable to allow its share of the total stock to fall further in Britain, and especially in Scotland, but only if assistance to other sectors enabled them to meet similar needs.

The funding and character of landlord organizations

The character of the landlord organizations that provide social housing varies widely in the countries in this study. In the Continental countries the housing association form predominates, with municipal housing companies also playing a significant role in some countries. Britain is unique in the extent to which local authority housing departments play a direct role in both ownership and management. The recent growth of housing associations in Britain has brought considerable change to this sector, but has still raised their share of the total stock to only 3–4%. The most appropriate form of organization for the future therefore needs to be considered, and there are several factors that should have a bearing on this choice.

A central feature of the British social rented sector is that it needs investment. In some areas, especially in the southern part of Britain, there is a shortage of rented accommodation, but the need to improve quality is much more widespread, especially in the peripheral estates of cities and urban areas, and in some inner city areas. Generally, the housing is not deficient in basic amenities, but problems of outdated and inadequate heating, poor insulation, damp penetration and depressing environmental conditions are extensive. Lack of funds has made it difficult to carry out improvements that are widely acknowledged to be necessary.

The significance of this for the choice of landlord organization is (as argued in Ch. 12) that the budgetary constraints that affect all EU countries make it necessary to make use of private sector capital to the maximum possible extent. This implies that public funding should be used to provide leverage to attract private funds, rather than to meet the whole cost of the investment.

For this, the form of landlord organization is important. All funding for directly managed local authority housing is inevitably treated under any recognized definition as public expenditure, however the finance is raised; but private sector finance raised by housing associations is not so regarded in any of the countries. In other countries, even the finance raised from the private market by municipal housing companies is not regarded as public expenditure, although in

Sweden, Germany and the Netherlands these may be wholly in the ownership of a local authority.

Until now, the view of the British Treasury on this last point would have required the funding of companies owned by public authorities to be classed as public expenditure, even if the finance were raised by borrowing on the private market. It was for this reason that the report by Wilcox et al. (1993) for the Joseph Rowntree Foundation, which advocated the setting up of Local Housing Companies, proposed that local authorities should have no more than a minority stake in such organizations. But according to international usage, this is not necessary; and there is now a move on the part of the Treasury under the recent Private Sector Finance Initiative to encourage some public bodies in other sectors to raise funds privately. How far this will go and what affect it may have on housing is still not clear. The main point is that there would be advantage for Britain in moving to a structure of social landlords sufficiently detached from direct local authority management to allow maximum use to be made of private sector investment.

Other arguments point in the same direction. Housing associations and companies permit a range of choice; they provide a greater degree of competition than local authority landlords, since several of them can be operating in the same area. Their size is not determined by the size of local authority, which has resulted in some very large housing authorities, much larger than is necessary or desirable for effective and responsive management. And although many British local authority housing departments manage their housing well, not all do. There would therefore be advantage in a system that put the operation and management of housing rather more at arm's length from the day-to-day workings of the local authority and subjected it to proper management disciplines, including financial independence.

There is, of course, already a strong trend towards this more Continental type of structure in Britain as a result of the financial constraints that have been imposed on local authorities and the encouragement government has given to housing associations. It is becoming clear to local authorities that this is the only way of liberating social housing from at least some of its financial constraints. But many local authorities are, quite understandably, reluctant to abdicate from what they see as an important responsibility. If the government really wanted to speed up the process of transfer, it would do well to recognize this legitimate concern and permit local authorities to keep a stake in the successor organizations. It may be best in most cases for this to be a minority stake, as in the French HLM-OPs, to avoid giving local authorities the temptation to favour particular bodies, but in special cases a majority shareholding should not be ruled out.

This latter issue raises the question of accountability. In Britain housing associations are accountable through agencies of central government. In the case of community-based associations and co-operatives, there is also an important dimension of accountability to their members, which is valuable and of necessity much less evident in the larger bodies. Other countries tend to channel financial support for their associations through local or regional government, and in some cases they act as the regulatory body as well. It is unfortunate that, in Britain, central government antipathy to local authorities has increasingly prevented this course from being followed. Housing is essentially a local service and it seems right that, for some of the associations at least, accountability should lie through the elected local authority.

Rent policy

It seems difficult to find a rent policy for social rented housing that is not well short of satisfactory. In most of the Continental countries, where rent pooling either does not exist or is very limited, rents tend to be related to historic costs. Even where adjustments have been carried out, this often means that rents are more related to the age of a dwelling than to its condition or desirability. Tenants are then reluctant to move to a smaller dwelling when their family needs are reduced, if it has a higher rent, and the resulting mismatch leads to the stock being badly utilized.

In Britain rent pooling was introduced to reduce the subsidy required for newer dwellings, by spreading the cost over all tenants, many of whom would otherwise enjoy unrealistically low rents in real terms because of inflation since their houses were built. The trouble with this system is that it has tended to mean that, although rents vary substantially between local authorities, depending on their circumstances, there is very little variation within one local authority other than to reflect size of accommodation. For example, Eastwood District Council, which is effectively part of the Glasgow conurbation, has rents for similar houses that are not much more than half Glasgow rents, and the same is true of Midlothian and Edinburgh. On the other hand, within Glasgow a flat in a deprived and hard-to-let peripheral housing estate will have much the same rent as a local authority flat in a much sought-after area. And tenants are naturally very keen to have their houses refurbished, if they pay the same rent after refurbishment as before. As has been seen in the British chapter, the anomalies in this situation have knock-on effects for the prices at which transfers to new social landlords can be made, and which then, in turn, tend to perpetuate the rent structure under new ownership.

Obviously, it is not possible to envisage the full play of market forces in this area, but resources are unlikely to be sensibly used when market signals are distorted to this degree. Any attempt to realign rents would cause hardship to those not fully protected by Housing Benefit, and should therefore be undertaken gradually. But the general level of rents has already been raised substantially over the past 15 years, and the expectation is that it will rise further, putting more of the burden of support onto Housing Benefit. The opportunity should therefore be taken to move towards a system that relates rents, although still below free-market levels, more clearly to some proportion (say 2% or 3%) of vacant-possession capital value. This is the only value that properly reflects the market, since tenanted sale value is influenced by the level of social rents. In England a gradual move towards capital-value rents is now being undertaken, but not yet in Scotland. In the absence of a real working market, there are difficulties in establishing what capital values are and in England there seems to be a general tendency for the change to require rents to rise more in the south, where capital values are high, than in the north, where they are low (Gibb 1993). Indeed, in some northern English cities they would actually fall. But that only shows how at odds with the market the system had become, and some regional rent differential may not be unhelpful in the interests of economic development. Such a restructuring of rents should also be accompanied by a reapportionment of outstanding housing debt, which it would almost certainly make necessary.

Housing allowances

As the country chapters have shown, there are anomalies in the systems of housing allowances in most countries. In France there is the problem of two separate systems and in Germany a system that is only periodically uprated for inflation, and which for this reason does not always cover costs adequately, so that it has to be supplemented by the *Länder*.

The British system suffers from three serious defects. First, the steepness of the taper (the sharp rate of reduction in benefit as income rises) creates a much more severe poverty trap than exists in the other countries. Secondly, since the payments of benefit are directly related to actual housing costs and cover the whole of any change in costs, tenants who receive Housing Benefit are completely insulated from the market, and the actual level of rent ceases to be of concern to them. This is referred to as the "upmarketing" problem. And, thirdly, like the Dutch system but unlike the systems in the other countries, British Housing Benefit does not extend to the owner occupied sector. However, owner occupiers who are not in full-time employment, and whose assets do not exceed £8000, do qualify after nine months for Income Support, which may be paid direct to lenders to cover mortgage interest costs, although not capital repayment.

Reform of Housing Benefit is therefore clearly necessary. The difficulties arise partly from the fact that the British system of general social security is less generous than in many of the other countries. This means both that more people are on Housing Benefit than would be the case were State pensions or other social benefits more generous, and that, for those that do receive Housing Benefit, it is intended to meet the full housing costs rather than some proportion of them. For those on full social security it is inevitable that benefits of some kind, whether for housing or basic social security, meet virtually all housing costs. But the taper has to be made less steep, if the poverty trap is to be reduced and if incentives are to be provided to the low paid to take work rather than claim social security. And if the upmarketing problem is to be removed, this cannot be done with a single income-related taper, no matter how steep or shallow, which is based on covering the whole of actual housing costs.

267

A change in the system to end the upmarketing problem would give people some reason to have regard to their housing costs. This is obviously easier if other benefits are intended to cover a part of housing costs, as in several of the other countries, so that changes in the housing allowance can be less than proportional to changes in costs; or if, as in the Netherlands, housing allowances are based not on actual housing costs, but on some recognized norm. However, systems based on standardized costs could present difficulties. Although they would put more pressure on social landlords whose rents were high, they could also lead to serious hardship if they failed to cover the genuine and inescapable variations in housing costs.

Hills has made the interesting suggestion that the present system should be replaced by a dual taper, a steep one based on full housing costs at 60% of increases or decreases in income for those whose net income exceeds the Income Support rate by less than their rent, and a 20% taper based on 60% of housing costs for those above (Hills 1991b: 174). This would have relatively little effect on the least well off, who would continue to be protected by a system based on full housing costs but who would still face a sharp fall in benefit as income rose. But it would be decidedly better, in relation to both the poverty trap and the upmarketing problem for those whose incomes were sufficient to put them on the 20% taper. However, the problem extends beyond Housing Benefit to Family Credit as well. The latter is not the concern of this book; but those with families receive both benefits and, for them, little will be gained from a Housing Benefit reform if the Family Credit taper is not also changed.

The case for extending housing allowances to the owner occupied sector is that hardship can be as severe there as elsewhere, and that it makes no sense to cover one tenure but not the other. In political terms, the benefit from relief of distress would be out of proportion to the costs of a scheme. In most countries the same system of housing allowances is extended to the owner occupied sector. In Britain this would present difficulties, since the system is based on actual costs; and one could hardly expect it to be extended to cover widely differing mortgage payments. To do so would be to give owners a one-way bet when it came to trading up to a more expensive property. At the very least, much supervision of the widely differing mortgage costs would be necessary. It would therefore seem more appropriate to have a separate mortgage benefit scheme that would be based on a standardized system of costs, with some allowance for family size and for regional differences in house prices.

Financing the policy

It should not be supposed that the reform of housing policy is capable of yielding major savings for the Exchequer. However the policy is changed, its cost will remain substantial, if the central objective of ensuring a decent standard of accommodation at an affordable price for the whole of the population is to be attained. This objective is not fully achieved in Britain at present – too much accommodation, especially in the more deprived urban areas falls short in terms of quality – and it would be possible in all of the countries studied, not least in Britain, to target the policy better so that its central purpose comes nearer to being attained.

But proposals outlined in this chapter would enable much more to be achieved in Britain for the amount spent. It is not possible to be precise about what they would cost, because so much depends on how the measures are applied, at what rates and within what limits. But the following paragraphs attempt to set out some orders of magnitude.

First, on the savings side, there is the proposed ending of mortgage interest tax relief. MITR cost some £4300 million in 1993/94, but in recent years it has cost much more than this and was as much as £7700 million in 1990/91. The cost has come down as a result of the sharp fall in interest rates, the drop in the number of transactions, and restriction to the basic rate of tax. From April 1994, restriction to the lower 20% rate and from April 1995 to 15% will reduce it further, so that, assuming no change in interest rates or in the level of transactions, the cost could come down to less than £3000 million. But both of these are unlikely assumptions in the longer term: the level of transactions began to pick up in 1994 and can be expected to recover further despite continuing weak demand in 1995; and market interest rates also rose in 1994 and 1995. They too are likely to rise further, as shown by the upward movement in the bond rate during 1994 and increases in short-term rates in the USA. The expectation must therefore be that, if MITR remains at current rates, its cost could remain high, probably in excess of £3000 million and, if interest rates return to 1990 levels, as much as £4500 million.

Very substantial sums are involved in the transfer of local authority housing stock to new owners. Sales of stock under Right to Buy and through voluntary transfers have already yielded receipts of £28000 million, more than any of the major industrial privatizations. Estimating the potential effects of future transfers in public expenditure terms is extremely complex, since a wide range of assumptions and offsetting effects are involved. These have been analysed with detailed financial modelling by a team of researchers led by Wilcox for the Joseph Rowntree Foundation (Wilcox et al. 1993, Wilcox 1994). Briefly, on the benefit side are the receipts from the sale of the stock, the removal of future housing investment from public expenditure, apart from the element of grant that may be required, the levy on LSVT sales, and VAT receipts on future repair and maintenance, since VAT is not paid by the present public landlords. On the cost side is the loss of rent surpluses to part-fund Housing Benefit. This applies mainly to authorities with low debt and therefore surplus rental income. Costs will also be influenced by the rate at which new landlords undertake catch-up repairs to the stock, since these will either affect the transfer price for the stock or involve payments of HAG or its equivalent.

269

The Wilcox study found that, on balance, the public expenditure savings from transferring the remaining local authority stock could be very large. As compared with continuing the present system, the saving over a period of years was estimated at £16000 million in net present value. But individual results would vary greatly from one authority to another, some producing a saving and others a loss, depending on local circumstances. The amount of saving in any one year would of course depend on the pace at which a programme of transfers was conducted, but Wilcox's example of Newcastle, where the savings would amount to £79 million in the first year and a further £35 million over the succeeding four, shows that, if several major authorities were engaged in transferring their stock, the annual savings to the Exchequer in public expenditure could amount to several hundreds of millions of pounds.

On the cost side, much depends on whether there is any replacement for MITR, such as the proposed depreciation allowance for first-time buyers. Not only is a replacement expensive, but to achieve neutrality with the rented sector it would put up costs there as well. With the depreciation allowance, the cost depends on the rate chosen and the length of period for eligibility. Clearly, the number of transactions by first-time buyers, and hence the cost, will vary greatly from year to year. For example, transactions ranged between 619000 in 1986 and 299000 in 1992 and since 1980 the average has been 460000 (Wilcox 1993: 92). But the cost would still be lower than for MITR, a subsidy that involves a great deal of dead weight; and, unlike MITR, it would not be affected by changes in interest rates. At 5% a year and the average British house price of £48000 for first-time buyers, the annual depreciation would be £2400. If this were eligible at the standard tax rate of 25%, it would give an average relief of £600 per recipient and, if limited to the 20% rate, £480. Even at this lower rate, the benefit to a recipient would be above the average MITR relief over all the beneficiaries of £430 in 1993/4. Assuming some 460000 first-time buyers a year and a relief lasting for eight years, this would give a yearly cost at the 20% tax rate of £198 million for new first-time buyers in any one year, building up to about £1600 million for all those within the scheme in the eighth year when it is fully under way. This compares with the actual cost in West Germany of DM5000 million (£2000 million), where fewer buy their houses but average prices are very much higher and where the relief is not limited to the lowest rate of tax.

The cost of a mortgage benefit scheme would of course depend on the state of both the economy and the housing market. It is likely to fluctuate considerably with the economic cycle as unemployment rises, incomes fall, and movements in interest rates affect mortgage costs. Such a scheme was proposed in the report of the Duke of Edinburgh's Inquiry (1991), but the costs were probably underestimated and, since that time, changing economic conditions would result in a large number of applicants. The most recent estimates suggest a cost of around £800 million a year.

For private rented housing, the proposals involve capital gains tax exemption on most properties, and the initial and standard depreciation allowances. Costs

270

would depend on the response in a sector that is at present very small, building up only as the dwellings on which it is paid increase in number. To begin with, the cost would be quite modest, but after five years or so could begin to become substantial. The level of incentive would probably have to be moderated, depending on whether it was producing less response on the part of investors or more than expected. However, it is important to recognize that, if the sector expands, the dwellings provided will reduce demand in the other two sectors, both of which are at present heavily subsidized. To this extent, the net cost of any incentives introduced for this sector will be substantially (but to an unknown extent) less than the gross costs. This will be particularly so if the alternative to a private rented dwelling is a new one rented from a housing association built with 75% HAG. In their detailed study for the Joseph Rowntree Foundation, Coopers & Lybrand do not attempt to take account of this offset. But for the above package, involving a 20% initial allowance followed by 4% annual depreciation for a total of 15 years, they estimate a tax loss per unit of £3600 in net present value and, on the assumption of 400000 new dwellings over five years, an equivalent annual cost of £165 million. With an initial allowance at 40%, but the rest of the package unchanged, the cost rises to £300 million. Clearly, if the scheme were in place indefinitely, it would build up to a higher total, becoming fully mature only in the fifteenth year.

In the social rented sector the net effect should be a gain to the Exchequer, as already explained. But the financial implications are very dependent both upon the valuation at which council stock is transferred to new landlords and upon the cost of the promised modernization and refurbishment schemes usually put forward to win tenants' support for the transfer. The higher the price, the larger the receipt to the Treasury from the sale; but the lower the price, the lower the debt for the new landlord and therefore the larger the proportion of new investment that can be financed by private funds, without a need for HAG or equivalent grants to keep rents consistent with social market terms.

In the same way, the higher the level of rents, the more private funding the new landlords will be able to attract, but the higher the claims on Housing Benefit. Coupled with the loss of rental surpluses to part finance Housing Benefit, this could result in increased costs, which would be of concern to the Treasury. A principal reason for the slowing down of LSVT approvals, which has already taken place, was Treasury concern at these costs, even though in relation to the standard of housing provided there is a reduction in public expenditure costs.

However, the clearest additional cost in this sector comes from the proposed adjustments to the Housing Benefit taper to reduce the poverty trap. The dual taper scheme proposed by Hills (1991b: 178) and referred to above has been costed at an additional £200 million in 1989. On the assumption that its cost would have increased in the same proportion as the actual costs of Housing Benefit, which rose by 72%, it might cost approximately £350 million in 1992/93. This does nothing to reduce the poverty trap caused by Family Credit, which is of course not an issue for housing policy; but so long as the taper on Family

Credit is 70%, reducing the Housing Benefit taper of 65% to 20% will do relatively little for those with families who are in the poverty trap. Indeed, it would make them only about 10 pence better off for every additional £1 earned, compared with those without families, who would gain 52 pence. To adjust the Family Credit taper could probably cost about as much again as reforming Housing Benefit.

Any summary of the financial implications of these proposals must of necessity be regarded as illustrative only, since they are based on so many assumptions. But the savings from ending MITR and the sale of local authority stock to new landlords might bring a yearly total of about £3500–5000 million. This would depend on how the movement of interest rates and the level of transactions affected MITR and on reasonable assumptions about the amount of local authority stock that could be transferred to new landlords in any one year. On the cost side the principal items would be: the first-time buyers' depreciation allowance (about £1600 million), a mortgage benefit scheme (£800 million), depreciation allowances to the private rented sector (between £165 million and £300 million, depending on the rate of initial allowance), a further £350 million for reform of Housing Benefit (and a similar amount if the Family Credit taper were to be altered to reduce the poverty trap). The cost of the new measures therefore comes to a total of about £3500 million if first-time buyers' depreciation is included; if it is excluded, as being the most debatable of the proposals, and if the incentive to private renting is then taken at the lower rate, the total cost would be less than £2000 million. In either case the cost of the new measures should be covered by the savings from the changes.

Conclusion

Not all of the proposals outlined in this chapter for changes in British policy involve cost to government. The most essential step is a rebalancing of policy between the tenures, stopping the promotion of yet higher levels of owner occupation, giving more encouragement to the private rented sector, and taking steps to encourage more investment in the social rented sector.

It would be possible to make substantial improvements within the confines of the present levels of expenditure. Hardship from negative equity, repossessions and mortgage arrears in the owner occupied sector could be reduced. Greater use of long-term fixed rate finance and the discouragement of very high loan to value ratios would help to reduce the volatility of the housing market, which has had such a destabilizing effect on the economy as a whole. A meaningful start could be made with measures that stood some chance of restoring the private rented sector to a more significant role; this would have benefits for labour mobility and could at the same time reduce dependence on the social rented sector. Above all, greater progress could be made with the improvement in the quality of social housing provision for the less well off, if greater use could be made of private capital in funding investment. And the depth of the poverty trap, which is so profoundly damaging to incentives at the bottom end of the income scale, could be reduced.

These changes would enable progress to be made towards a better standard of housing at affordable costs for the nation as a whole; and they would bring into being a housing market that assisted rather than frustrated the steady growth of the economy in an increasingly integrated Europe.

Summary of proposals

- The aim of policy should be to provide a decent standard of housing for the population as a whole at affordable costs.
- A better balance is needed between the three sectors, since all three have a particular function to perform.

Owner occupation

- The sector is exceptionally large by the standards of other similar countries and should not be further promoted. To do so would add to the risk of personal hardship and leave the economy more vulnerable to the instability of the housing market.
- End mortgage tax relief and, if continued assistance to first-time buyers is judged necessary because of the small size of the private rented sector, replace with a depreciation allowance limited to a duration of eight years.
- Investigate the viability of a scheme for personal mortgage insurance for loans with LTV ratios above 80% in place of the present mortgage indemnity schemes for the lending institutions.
- Promote greater and continued use of long-term fixed interest borrowing.
- Use tax relief on savings to promote a closed-circuit housing savings scheme.

Private rented sector

- Assured and short assured tenancies to remain the basis of private renting.
- Provide an initial allowance of 20% (40% if MITR or a depreciation allowance is given in the owner occupied sector), followed by 5% annual depreciation on capital value and improvement costs.
- Permit deduction of expenses, including depreciation from landlords' total income not only income from renting.
- End CGT for dwellings under £150000 value, provided they are held in the sector for a minimum of 5 years
- Provide a grant scheme (development of GRO grants) to encourage private landlords to let property on social market terms.

Social rented sector

- To make possible greater use of private sector investment in the sector and

273

to provide other benefits, encourage transfer of local authority stock to alternative social landlords.

- To encourage this transfer and to enhance local accountability, permit local authorities to retain a substantial (but generally not majority) stake in the new landlord organizations and, where there is such a stake, enable them to act as the regulatory and funding body.
- Encourage and safeguard community-based housing associations and co-operatives against financial pressure for take-over into larger groups in recognition of their advantages for local accountability.
- Rents should be related to vacant possession values.
- A restructuring of housing debt should be carried out to permit this more rational rent structure.

Personal housing allowances
- Extend allowances to owner occupied sector, probably in the form of a mortgage benefit scheme rather than the existing Housing Benefit.
- Institute a dual taper system to reduce the poverty trap and the one-for-one ratio of benefit to housing costs (the "upmarketing" problem). Adjust the taper on Family Credit to reduce the depth of the poverty trap.

References

Alberdi, B. 1992. Financing system for the housing sector: deregulation of the banking sector. Experiences made in Spain. Paper presented at European Network for Housing Research Housing Finance Workshop, The Hague, The Netherlands. Now in *Housing finance in the 1990s*, B. Turner & C. Whitehead (eds), 67–93. Research report SB:56, National Swedish Institute for Building Research, Gälve.

Audit Commission 1992. *The development of local authority housing strategies*. London: HMSO.

Ball, M., M. Harloe, M. Martens 1988. *Housing and social change in Europe and the USA*. London: Routledge.

Banco Bilbao Vizcaya 1992. *The Spanish economy in 1991 and 1992*. Bilbao: Banco Bilbao Vizcaya.

Banco Hipotecario (various issues). *Nota*. Madrid.

Bank of England 1992. Negative equity in the housing market. *Bank of England Quarterly Bulletin* **32**, 266–8.

Barre, R. (chairman) 1976. *Rapport de la commission d'étude sur le financement du logement*. Paris: Documentation Française.

Bartlett, W. & G. Bramley (eds) 1994. *European housing finance: single market or mosaic?* Britsol: School for Advanced Urban Studies.

Begg, T. 1987. *50 special years: a study in Scottish housing*. London: Henry Melland.

Begg, I. & D. Mayes 1991. A new strategy for social and economic cohesion after 1992. Research and Documentation Papers, Regional Policy and Transport Series 19, European Parliament.

Bengtsson, B. 1994. Housing market and housing financing in Sweden. See Bartlett & Bramley (1994), 166–87.

— 1994. Swedish rental policy and the privatisation of public housing. See Swärd (1993), 220–31.

Best, R., P. Kemp, D. Coleman, S. Merrett, T. Crook 1992. *The future of private renting*. York: Joseph Rowntree Foundation.

Birchall, J. (ed.) 1992. *Housing policy in the 1990s*. London: Routledge.

Bloch-Lainé, J. M., (chairman) 1989. *Rapport de la commission de refléxion sur les aides publiques au logement*. Paris: Documentation Française.

Boelhouwer, P. & H. van der Heijden 1992. *Housing systems in Europe, part 1: a comparative study of housing policy*. Delft: Delft University Press.

Boelhouwer, P. & J. van Weesep 1988. On shaky grounds: the case for the privatisation of the public sector in the Netherlands. *The Netherlands Journal of Housing and the Built Environment* **3**, 319–33.

Boléat, M. 1988. *Building societies: the regulatory framework*, 2nd edn. London: Building Societies Association.

Boléat, M. 1989. The predator – friend or foe? *Building Societies Gazette* (December), 27–30.

Boléat, M. 1985. *National housing finance systems*. London: Croom Helm.

Boucher, F. 1988. France. See Kroes, et al. (1988), 287–349.

BOVERKET (National Board for Housing, Building and Planning in Sweden) 1991. *Housing and housing policy in Sweden* [draft information report]. Karlskrona: BOVERKET.

275

Bovy, C. 1989. *Social housing policy: Netherlands*. Brussels: Confederation of European Community Family Organisations (COFACE).

Breitenbach, E. 1993. Poverty 3: the European programme in Greater Pilton – anti-poverty strategies, participation and area renewal. Unpublished paper.

British Bankers' Association 1990. The EC banking directives of 1989: a compendium. London: British Bankers' Association.

Bruce, P. 1993. Roof falls in on Spanish union ambitions. *Financial Times*, 29 December.

Building Societies Commission 1988. *Annual report of the Building Societies Commission 1987–88*. London: HMSO.

— 1992. *Annual report of the Building Societies Commission 1991–92*. London: HMSO.

— 1993. *Annual report of the Building Societies Commission 1992–93*. London: HMSO.

Bundesministerium für Raumordnung, Bauwesen und Stadtebau 1993. *Wohngeld und Mietenbericht*. Bonn: Bundesministerium für Raumordnung, Bauwesen und Stadtebau.

Burns, T. 1993. Botin family fuels Spanish lending war. *Financial Times*, May 5.

Caminal, R., J. Gual, X. Vives 1990. Competition in Spanish banking. In *European banking in the 1990s*, J. Dermine (ed.), 261–305. Oxford: Basil Blackwell.

Cars, G. 1992. Renewal of the physical and social environment in large scale housing estates in Sweden: effects and effectiveness. Paper presented at OECD Conference, Edinburgh, Scotland.

Cecchini, P., M. Catimat, A. Jacquemin 1988. *The European challenge 1992: the benefits of the single market*. Aldershot: Gower.

CECODHAS 1993. *Le cecodhas et l'Europe du logement social*. Brussels: European Liaison Committee for Social Housing.

Central Statistics Office 1993. *National income and expenditure* ["Blue Book"], London: HMSO.

CEC 1977. *Report of the study group on the role of public finance in European integration (MacDougall Report)*. Brussels: Commission of the European Communities.

— 1985. *Completing the internal market*. White Paper from the Commission to the European Council, COM (85) 310 final, Brussels.

— 1988a. The economics of 1992 (Cecchini Report). *European Economy* **35**.

— 1988b. *1992: the European social dimension*. Brussels: CEC.

— 1989. *Report on economic and monetary union in the European Community* ["Delors Report": Report of the Committee for the Study of Economic and Monetary Union]. Luxembourg: CEC.

— 1991a. *Europe 2000, the outlook for the development of the Community's territory*. Brussels: CEC.

— 1991b. Immigration of citizens from third countries to the southern member states of the European Community. *Social Europe*, Supplement 1.

— 1992. Towards a Europe of solidarity: housing. *Social Europe*, Supplement 3.

— 1993a *Growth, competitiveness, employment* [White Paper]. Brussels: CEC.

— 1993b. *Statistics on housing in the European Community*. Brussels: CEC.

— 1994. *Official Journal of the European Communities* 94/C 180/02 **37**, 6–9.

Clapham, D. & M. Miller 1985. Housing co-operatives in Sweden. Discussion Paper 4, Centre for Housing Research, University of Glasgow.

Clapham, D. & K. Kintrea 1987. Importing housing policy: housing co-operatives in Britain and Scandinavia. *Housing Studies* **2**(3), 157–69.

Coles, A. 1993. The growth of fixed rate mortgages. *Housing Finance* **19**, 26–31.

Compagnie Bancaire 1993. *The French housing market: origin, extent and duration of the recession*. Paris: Compagnie Bancaire.

Conijn, J. 1993. Dynamic cost principle in the rented sector: the debacle with an innovative financial instrument. See Bartlett & Bramley (1994), 262–73.

276

Coopers & Lybrand 1993. *Fiscal incentives to regenerate the private rented sector* [report commissioned by the Joseph Rowntree Foundation]. London: Coopers & Lybrand.

Council of Mortgage Lenders 1990. *Housing finance in Europe*. London: Council of Mortgage Lenders.

Council of the European Communities 1992. *Treaty on European union*. Brussels: Council of the European Communities.

Crook, T., P. Kemp, I. Anderson, S. Bowman 1991a. *The Business Expansion Scheme and rented housing*. York: Joseph Rowntree Foundation.

Crook, T. (A. D. H.), P. A. Kemp, I. Anderson, S. Bowman 1991b. *Tax incentives and the revival of private renting*. New York: Cloister Press.

Cullingworth, J. B. 1969. *Housing and labour mobility*. Paris: OECD.

Davies, H. D. 1963. *The economic development of Spain: report of a mission organised by the International Bank for Reconstruction and Development at the request of the Government of Spain*. Baltimore: The John Hopkins University Press.

DoE (Department of the Environment) various years. Annual reports. London: HMSO.

— 1977. *Housing policy. Technical volume, parts I-III*. London: HMSO.

— 1987. *Housing: the Government's proposals*. Cm. 214. London: HMSO.

DoE 1992. *Local authority housing in England: voluntary transfers* [consultation paper]. London: DoE.

DoE, Scottish Office Environment Department, Welsh Office, Housing and construction statistics. Various issues. London: HMSO.

Deutsch, E. & H. Tomann 1992. Home ownership finance in Austria and Germany. Paper presented at AREUA/USC Conference, Los Angeles, USA.

Deutscher Verband für Wohnungswesen Stadtebau und Raumplanung e.V. 1985. *Terminology and definitions on housing estates in the Federal Republic of Germany*. Brochure for 38th International Congress of the International Federation for Housing and Planning, Bonn, Federal Republic of Germany.

Devlin, E. 1993. France: HLM social housing estates. Paper presented at Scottish Homes Conference on Urban Regeneration, Glasgow, Scotland.

Diamond, D. B. & M. J. Lea 1992. Housing finance in developed countries. *Journal of Housing Research* 3(1), special issue.

Dorling, D., C. Gentle, J. Cornford 1992a. Housing crisis, disaster or opportunity. Working Paper 96, Centre for Urban and Regional Development Studies, University of Newcastle upon Tyne.

— 1992b. *The extent of negative equity*. Housing Research Findings 69, Joseph Rowntree Foundation, York.

Dorling, D. 1993. *The spread of negative equity*. Housing Research Findings 101, Joseph Rowntree Foundation, York.

Drake, L. & T. Weyman Jones 1993. Measuring efficiency. *Mortgage Finance Gazette* (January), 32–4.

Drake, M. 1992. *Europe and 1992: a handbook for local housing authorities*. London: Institute of Housing.

Duclaud-Williams, R. H. 1978. *The politics of housing in Britain and France*. London: Heinemann.

Duvigneau, H. J. & L. Schönefeldt 1989. *Social housing policy: Federal Republic of Germany*. Brussels: Confederation of European Community Family Organisations (COFACE).

ECOTEC 1993. *Urban Pilot Projects: an interim report on the progress of the Urban Pilot Projects funded by the ERDF*. Brussels: DGXVI of the Commission of the European Communities.

Emms, P. 1990. *Social housing: a European dilemma?* Bristol: School for Advanced Urban Studies.

Englund, P. The collapse of the Swedish housing market. See Bartlett & Bramley (1994), 136–62.

European Community Mortgage Federation (ECMF) 1992. *Annual report 1991–92.* Brussels: ECMF.

— 1993. *Annual report 1992–93.* Brussels: ECMF

Eurostat 1993. *Basic statistics of the European Community.* Luxembourg: Eurostat.

— 1993. *Demographic statistics.* Luxembourg: Eurostat.

Fannie Mae 1991. *Proceedings: housing finance arrangements, a comparative analysis* [Research Roundtable series]. Washington: Office of Housing Policy Research.

Fitzpatrick, S. & M. Stephens 1994. Housing the homeless: policy and legal issues. Occasional Paper 2, Centre for Housing Regional and Urban Studies, University of Glasgow.

Ford, J. & S. Wilcox 1992. *Reducing mortgage arrears and possessions.* York: Joseph Rowntree Foundation.

Geindre, F. 1993. *Le logement: une priorité pour le XIe plan* [report to the Prime Minister]. Paris: Documentation Française.

Ghékiere, L. 1991. *Marchés et politiques du logement dans la CEE.* Paris: Documentation Française.

— 1992. *Les politiques du logement dans l'Europe de demain.* Paris: Documentation Française.

Gibb, K. & M. Munro 1991. *Housing finance in the UK.* London: Macmillan.

Gilbert, M. & Associates 1958. *Comparative national products and price levels.* Paris: Organisation for European Economic Co-operation.

Glasser, R. 1986. *Growing up in the Gorbals.* London: Chatto & Windus.

Greve, J. 1991. *Homelessness in Britain.* York: Joseph Rowntree Foundation.

Grieve, Sir Robert (chairman) 1986. *Inquiry into Glasgow housing.* Glasgow: Glasgow District Council.

Gropper, D. M. 1991. An empirical investigation of changes in scale economies for the commercial banking firm, 1979–86. *Journal of Money, Credit and Banking* **23**, 718–27.

Halifax Building Society House Price Index (various editions). Halifax: Halifax Building Society.

Hallett, G. 1977. *Housing and land policies in West Germany and Britain.* London: Macmillan.

— (ed.) 1988. *Land and housing policies in Europe and the USA.* London: Routledge.

— 1993. *The new housing shortage.* London: Routledge.

Harrison, J. 1993. *The Spanish economy: from the civil war to European Community.* Basingstoke: Macmillan.

— 1992. Housing associations after the 1988 Act. Working Paper 118, School for Advanced Urban Studies, University of Bristol.

Hedman, E. 1994. Housing subsidies in Sweden in the 1990s. See Swärd (1994), 106–12.

HM Treasury 1984. *Building societies: a new framework* [Cmnd 9316]. London: HMSO.

— 1992. *Implementing the Second Banking Coordination Directive in the UK: consultation document.* London: HM Treasury.

HM Treasury 1994. *Financial statement and budget report 1993-4* ["Red Book"]. London: HMSO.

Heugas-Darrspen, H. 1985. *Le logement en France et son financement.* Paris: Documentation Française.

Hills, J., R. Berthoud, P. Kemp 1989. *The future of housing allowances.* London: Policy

278

Studies Institute.

Hills, J., F. Hubert, H. Tomann, C. Whitehead 1989. Shifting subsidy from bricks and mortar to people: experience in Britain and West Germany. Discussion Paper 41, Welfare State Programme, London School of Economics.

Hills, J. 1991. *Thirty-nine steps to housing finance reform.* York: Joseph Rowntree Foundation.

Hills, J. 1991. *Unravelling housing finance.* Oxford: Oxford University Press.

HRH The Duke of Edinburgh (chairman) 1985. *Inquiry into British housing, 1st report.* London: National Federation of Housing Associations.

— 1991. *Inquiry into British housing, 2nd report.* York: Joseph Rowntree Foundation.

Hjarne, L. 1994. Mixed housing in Sweden. See Swärd (1994), 238–50.

Holmans, A. E. 1987. *Housing policy in Britain.* London: Croom Helm.

— 1991a. Estimates of housing equity withdrawal by owner occupiers in the United Kingdom 1970–1990. Working Paper 116, Government Economic Service, London.

— 1991b. House prices, land prices, the housing market, house purchase debt and personal savings in Britain and other countries. Working Paper, Department of Environment, London.

Holmans, S. K. 1987. *Social security systems in selected countries and their integration with tax systems.* London: HM Treasury.

House of Lords 1985. *A common market in mortgage credit: eleventh report of the Select Committee on the European Communities.* London: HMSO.

Hubert, F. 1992. Risk and incentives in German social housing. Discussion paper, Freie Universität, Berlin.

— 1993a. Germany's housing policy at the crossroads. Discussion Paper, Freie Universität, Berlin.

— 1993b. Private rented housing in Germany. Paper presented at Scottish Homes Conference, Edinburgh, Scotland.

Hughes, G. & B. McCormick 1981. Do council housing policies reduce migration between regions? *Economic Journal* **91**, 919–37.

— 1985. Migration intentions in the UK: which households want to migrate and which succeed? *Economic Journal* **95**, supplement, 113–23.

Hughes G. & B. McCormick 1990. Housing and labour market mobility. In *Housing and the national economy*, J. Ermisch (1990), 94–109. Aldershot: Avebury.

Institute of Housing 1987. *"Housing: the Government's proposals"* [a response of the Institute of Housing]. Coventry: Institute of Housing.

Jaedicke, W. & H. Wollmann. 1990. Federal Republic of Germany. In *International handbook of housing policies and practices*, W. van Vliet (ed.), 130–54. New York: Greenwood Press.

Kee, R. 1980. *Ireland: a history.* London: Weidenfeld & Nicholson.

Kemp, P. 1992. Housing. In *Implementing Thatcherite policies*, D. Marsh & R. A. W. Rhodes (eds), 65–80. Buckingham: Open University Press.

Kemp, P. 1984. *The cost of chaos: a survey of the housing benefit system.* London: Shelter Housing Aid Centre.

Kroes, H., F. Ymker, A. Mulder (eds) 1988. *Between owner occupation and the rented sector.* De Bilt: The Netherlands Christian Institute of Social Housing (NCIV).

Landström, I., & L. Forssén 1994. Households and tenure in Sweden 1969–91. See Swärd (1994), 208–20.

Lawson, N. 1992. *The view from no. 11: memoirs of a Tory radical.* London: Bantam.

Laxon, M. (chairman) 1987. *Rapport de la commission sur les aides à la personne en matière de logement*. Paris: Documentation Française.

Leal, J. (chairman) 1992. *Informe para una nueva política de vivienda: comité de expertos de vivienda*. Madrid: Ministry of Public Works and Transport (MOPT).

Lebègue, D. (chairman) 1991. *Financement du logement* [Rapport de la Commission, Commissariat Général du Plan]. Paris: Documentation Française.

Leutner, B. & D. Jensen 1988. German Federal Republic. See Kroes et al. (1988), 145–81.

Lindecrona, T. 1991. Non-profit housing: a fifty-year full-scale experiment in Sweden. Unpublished paper, Swedish Association of Municipal Housing Companies (SABO).

Lundqvist, L. 1988a. *Housing policy and tenures in Sweden*. Aldershot: Avebury.

— 1988b. Sweden. See Kroes et al. (1988), 55–120.

— 1994. Why different British and Swedish strategies of privatisation in the housing sector. See Swärd (1994), 192–208.

Maclennan, D. 1993. *Housing and* economic recovery. Briefing Paper 2, Joseph Rowntree Foundation, York.

— 1994. *A competitive UK economy: the challenges for housing policy*. Joseph Rowntree Foundation, York.

Maclennan, D., K. Gibb, A. More 1992. *Fairer subsidies, faster growth*. Joseph Rowntree Foundation, York.

Maclennan, D. & K. Gibb 1993. Nesting, *investing or just resting*. Briefing Paper 5, Joseph Rowntree Foundation, York.

Maclennan, D. & G. Meen 1993. Housing markets and national economic performance in OECD countries: lessons for the UK. Briefing Paper 3, Joseph Rowntree Foundation, York.

Malpass, P. 1986. *The housing crisis*. London: Croom Helm.

— 1990. *Reshaping housing policy*. London: Routledge.

Malpass, P. & R. Means (eds) 1993. *Implementing housing policy*. Buckingham: Open University Press.

Malpass, P. & A. Murie 1990. *Housing policy and practice*, 3rd edn. London: Macmillan.

Marchal, J. 1989. *Social housing policy: France*. Brussels: Confederation of European Community Family Organisations (COFACE).

Massieu, A. c. 1990. Rented housing: some thoughts. Unpublished paper.

Miles, D. 1992. Housing and the wider economy in the short and long run. *National Institute Economic Review* **139**(1), 64–78.

— 1994. Fixed and floating finance in the United Kingdom and abroad. *Bank of England Quarterly Bulletin* **34**, 34–50.

Minford, P., M. Peel, P. Ashton 1987. *The housing morass*. London: Institute of Economic Affairs.

Ministry of Finance (Sweden) 1991. *The Swedish tax reform of 1991*. Stockholm: Ministry of Finance.

Muellbauer, J. 1990a. *The Great British housing disaster and economic policy*. Economic Policy Study 5, Institute for Public Policy Research, London.

— 1990b. The housing market and the UK economy. In *Housing and the national economy*, J. Ermisch (ed.), 48–71. Aldershot: Avebury.

Murie, A. & H. Priemus 1994. Social rented housing in Britain and the Netherlands: trends, trajectories and divergence. *The Netherlands Journal of Housing and the Built Environment* **9**, 107–26.

National Institute of Economic and Social Research (various issues). *National Institute*

Economic Review.

Nesslein, T. 1982. The Swedish housing model. *Urban Studies* **19**, 235–46.

Netherlands Central Bureau of Statistics 1993. Statistics on housing and construction in the Netherlands: increases and decreases in dwelling stock since 1970. *The Netherlands Journal of Housing and the Built Environment* **8**, 237–47.

Norton, A. & K. Novy 1991. *Low income housing in Britain and Germany*. London: Anglo–German Foundation.

Noulas, A. G., C. R. Subhash, S. M. Millar 1990. Return to scale and input substitution for large us banks. *Journal of Money, Credit and Banking* **22**, 94–108.

OECD 1987. *The future of migration*. Paris: Organisation for Economic Co-operation and Development.

— 1988. *Economic surveys: Spain*. Paris: OECD.

— 1991. *Economic surveys: Spain*. Paris: OECD.

— 1992. Spain: the current situation and policy as regards housing. Unpublished paper, Project Group on Housing, Social Integration and Liveable Environments in Cities.

— (various issues). *Economic Outlook.*

Papa, O. 1992. *Housing systems in Europe, part 2: a comparative study of housing finance*. Delft: Delft University Press.

Pareja, M. & P. Riera 1993. The new housing policy programme in Spain. Paper presented at European Network for Housing Research Conference, Bristol. See also Bartlett & Bramley (1994: 165–86).

Pearce, B. & S. Wilcox. 1991. *Home ownership, taxation and the economy: the economic and social benefits of the abolition of mortgage interest tax relief*. Joseph Rowntree Foundation, York.

Petersson, A. 1993. The Swedish housing allowance system: effects and effectiveness. Unpublished paper, BOVERKET.

Power, A. 1993. *Hovels to high rise: state housing in Europe since 1850*. London: Routledge.

Price Waterhouse 1988. *The cost of non-Europe*, vol. 9: *financial services*. Luxembourg: Commission of the European Communities.

Priemus, H., The Netherlands. In *International handbook of housing policies and practices*, W. van Vliet (ed.), 155–93. New York: Greenwood Press.

Pryke, M. & C. Whitehead 1991. *Mortgage-backed securitzation in the UK: a wholesale change in housing finance?* Monograph 22, Department of Land Economy, University of Cambridge.

Rowlatt, A. 1993. UK sensitivity to short term interest rates. *Treasury Bulletin* **4**(2), 52–65.

Salmon, K. G. 1991. *The modern Spanish economy: transformation and integration into Europe*. London: Pinter.

Satsangi, M. 1993. Private rented housing in France. Unpublished paper, for Scottish Homes, Centre for Housing Research, University of Glasgow.

Schaefer, J.P. 1990. Housing finance and subsidy systems in France. In *Affordable housing in Europe*, D. Maclennan & R. Williams, 35–54. York: Joseph Rowntree Foundation.

Scottish Homes 1992. *Statistical report 1991–2*. Edinburgh: Scottish Homes.

Scottish Office 1988. *New life for urban Scotland*. Edinburgh: Scottish Office.

— 1993. *Progress in partnership. Consultation paper on the future of urban regeneration policy in Scotland*. Edinburgh: Scottish Office.

— 1993. *Serving Scotland's needs: the Government's expenditure plans* [Cm. 2214]. Edinburgh: HMSO.

— Annual reports. Various years.

— Statistical bulletin, housing series. Various issues. Edinburgh: HMSO.

Scottish Office Development Department 1987a. *Scottish Homes, a new agency for Scotland*. Edinburgh: Scottish Development Department.

— 1987b. *Housing: the Government's proposals for Scotland* [Cm. 242].Edinburgh: HMSO

Scottish Office Industry Department 1994. *Scottish Economic Bulletin, vol. 49*. HMSO: Edinburgh.

Secretary of State for the Environment & Secretary of State for Wales 1977. *Housing policy: consultative document* [Cmnd 6851]. London: HMSO.

Secretary of State for Scotland 1977. *Scottish housing: consultative document* [Cmnd 6852]. Edinburgh: HMSO.

Stephens, M. 1993. Housing finance deregulation: Britain's experience. *The Netherlands Journal of Housing and Built Environment* **8**, 159–79.

Stewart, M. & J. Carey-Wood 1992. *Mobility and housing needs in western Europe*. Bristol: School for Advanced Urban Studies.

Swärd, K. 1993. Introduction in figures to the Swedish housing market. Unpublished paper presented at the British–Swedish seminar, Gävle.

Swärd, K. (ed.) 1994. *Housing finance and tenure in Britain and Sweden*. Research Report SB:71, Stockholm Statens Institut for Byggnadsforskning, Gävle.

Tamames, R. 1986. *The Spanish economy: an introduction*. London: C. Hurst.

Tomann, H. 1990. The housing market, housing finance and housing policy in West Germany: prospects for the 1990s. *Urban Studies* **27**, 919–30.

— 1992. Towards a housing market in eastern Germany. Unpublished paper, Freie Universität, Berlin.

Turner, B. 1993. Swedish homes owners: crises and defaults. Paper presented at European Network for Housing Research conference, Budapest, Hungary.

Union Nationale des Fédérations d'Organism HLM 1993. *HLM aujourdhui, les chiffres clés du movement HLM*. Paris: Union Nationale des Fédérations d'Organism HLM.

Van Weesep, J. 1986. Dutch housing, recent developments and policy issues. *Housing Studies* **1**(1), 61–6.

VROM 1991 and 1992. *Statistics on housing in the European Community 1991 and 1992*. The Hague: The Netherlands Ministry of Housing, Physical Planning and the Environment (VROM).

— 1993. *Housing in the Netherlands: a country monograph*. The Hague: VROM.

— 1992. *Nota Volkshuisvesting in de Jaren Negentig* [English resume of Heerma Memorandum, originally published in Dutch, 1989]. The Hague: VROM.

— 1993. *Volkshuisvesting in Cijfers 1992*. The Hague: VROM.

Waldén, Lars J. 1990. What are housing policies for? The case of Sweden. Paper presented at Franco–Swedish Seminar, Investment and Utilities Assessment in the Housing Sector, Paris.

— 1994. Main features of British and Swedish housing policies. See Swärd (1994), 78–94.

Webb, S. & S. Wilcox. 1991. *Time for mortgage benefits*. Joseph Rowntree Foundation, York.

Westerlund, L. 1994. Design of income and related housing allowances. See Swärd

(1994), 112–29.

Wilcox, S. 1993. *Housing finance review 1993*. Joseph Rowntree Foundation, York.

— 1994. Making the most of council housing. *Fiscal Studies* **15**(1), 44–63.

Wilcox, S., with G. Bramley, A. Ferguson, J. Perry, C. Woods 1993. *Local housing companies: new opportunities for council housing*. Joseph Rowntree Foundation, York.

Woolwich Building Society 1990. Survey (December).

— 1993. Survey (January).

Wright, A. 1977 *The Spanish economy 1959–1976*. Basingstoke: Macmillan.

Wynn, M. (ed.) 1984. *Housing in Europe*. London: Croom Helm.

Ymkers, F. & H. Kroes. 1988. The Netherlands. See Kroes et al. (1988), 183–214.

INDEX

Abbey National 145, 209–11
accountability
of local authorities 155
of housing associations 158–9, 169, 177, 274
Act on Mortgage Regulation 1981 (Spain) 108
additionality 184, 187
Alberdi, B. 99–103, 106–10, 113–17
Alomar 214
Antwerp Savings Bank 215
apartments
as a proportion of total stock 13–14, 19, 53
legal restriction on ownership
(Sweden) 119, 126, 138
Argentaria 107–8
Association of German Mortgage Banks 54
assured tenancies 34, 44, 59, 73, 153, 168,
225, 259, 273
Austria 8, 12, 13, 18
Autonomous Communities (Spain) 97–8, 103,
112

Badenoch & Strathspey District Council 156
Banco de Crédito de la Construcción 99
Banco Hipotecario 107–9
Banco Santander 213–14
Banking Co-ordination (Second Council Direc-
tive) Regulations 1992 203
Bank of England 150, 204–06, 247
Bank of Scotland 209–11
Banque Immobilier de Crédit 210–11
banks, as a source of housing finance 19,
28–9, 33, 54–6, 80, 121, 127, 144, 244, 258
Barcelona 100
Barclays Bank 213
Barre, R. (Barre Report) 24
Basle Committee 213
Bausparkassen 55–6, 60, 72, 144, 193, 195,
212–14, 258
Begg, I. & D. Mayes 182
Begg, T. 160
Belfast 185
Belgium 8–15, 17–19, 191, 193, 215
Bengtsson, B. 125
Berlin 243

rent control in 58
Birmingham 63, 160
no. of local authority dwellings 156
BKN (Swedish National Housing Credit Guar-
antee Board) 124, 128, 130
Boelhouwer, P. & H. van der Heijden 19,
46–7, 77, 79, 83, 90, 118–19, 121
Boléat, M. 204, 217
Bonn, house prices in 243
Boyer Decree (Spain) 113–14
Boucher, F. 30–31, 35
Bourgeois Coalition 118, 132, 134
Bradford & Bingley Building Society 208–15
bricks and mortar subsidy 1, 3, 24–5, 40, 42,
45, 51, 68, 93, 95, 120, 135, 166, 237, 262–3
Bristol 185, 248
British Bankers' Association 198
Bruce, P. 98
budget deficits 118, 234–5
building regulations 16, 53
building societies 19, 93, 144–5, 209–15, 244,
258
Building Society Acts
1962 200
1986 291–3
Building Society Statutory Instruments
on European operations 201–2
on sources of capital 205–6
Building Societies Association 199–201
Building Societies Commission 201–6, 208–9,
218
Bundesministerium für Raumordnung, Bauwesen und Stadtebau 68
Burns, T. 110
Business Expansion Scheme 154, 174–5, 177,
225, 260–61

Caisse des Depôts (CDC) 37, 38, 40, 42
Caja Postal 107–8
Caminal, R. 107
capital adequacy 202–6, 219
Capital Liberalization Directive (EU) 197,
207

285

capital gains tax 2, 29–30, 34, 57, 61, 71, 82, 86, 105, 125, 127, 130, 146, 153–4, 174, 238, 255, 260, 270–71, 273
Cassis de Dijon (European Court case) 197
Catalonia 111
Cecchini, P. (Cecchini Report) 190–94, 219
CECODHAS 35, 62, 184
Central Housing Fund (Netherlands) 90
centralized lenders 143
Cheltenham & Gloucester Building Society 145, 217–18
Christchurch 156
Clapham, D. & M. Miller 127
Cohesion Fund 183
Cologne 46
Commission of the European Communities 4, 179–80, 187, 190, 197, 200, 202, 230, 232
community charge (poll tax) 146
Community Initiatives 187
Compagnie Bancaire 43
condominiums 18, 60, 83, 138
  see also co-ownership
Conijn, J. 89
construction industry 2, 98
  and level of housebuilding activity 79, 137
co-operative banks 54
Co-operative Housing Act 1972 (Sweden) 126–7
co-operative housing 4–50, 53, 62–8, 87, 98, 119–20, 126–30, 132–8, 157–60, 178, 239, 274
Coopers & Lybrand 260–61, 271
co-ownership 53, 119, 126, 138
  see also co-operative housing
"corset" 144, 195
cost of house purchase 222–3
Council of Mortgage Lenders 56
Council of the European Union 4, 197, 230
  official communiqué on housing 181
council tax 146, 154
Crédit Agricole 209, 216–17
Crédit Foncier de France 27, 32, 37
Crédit Mutuel 38
Crook, T. 154, 261

dampness in housing 14, 141, 264
Davies, H. D. 99–100
debt
  housing debt 43, 65, 162–4, 234, 240–43, 250, 257–8, 263, 267, 269, 274
  loan debt per dwelling in Britain 166, 177
  proposed debt/subsidy swap (Netherlands) 91, 95, 138

public debt as % of GDP 75, 91, 235–7
Delors, J. (Delors Report) 237
Denmark 8–15, 18, 193–4
Department of Social Security (DSS) 166
Department of the Environment (DoE) 158–9, 162
depreciation allowances 2, 33, 44, 57, 60–61, 71, 73, 86, 130, 177, 238, 256, 260, 270–73
  absence of in Britain for rented housing 154, 177, 260, 270–73
deprivation 39, 232, 266, 269
Devlin, E. 37
Diamond, D. B. & M. J. Lea 27–9, 55, 191–5
Dick, Dr E. 71
Drake, L. & T. Weyman Jones 196
Drake, M. 180, 186
Dorling, D. 150, 247
Duclaud-Williams, R. H. 23, 30, 155
Duke of Edinburgh's Inquiry 146–7, 170, 270
Dundee 161
Dunfermline Building Society 208–9
Duvigneau, H. J. & L. Schönefeldt 46, 52, 62, 71

Eastern Europe
  migration from 232, 251
Eastwood 266, 157
Ecology Building Society 203
economic and monetary union 4, 91, 234–7, 240, 243
  Maastricht criteria for 235–7
economic planning 75, 79
Edinburgh 156–7, 161, 185, 266
Emms, P. 4, 23–4, 35–6, 63–4, 71, 76, 91
employment trap 172, 178
employers' housing levy (France) 29, 38, 42
England 5–18 *passim*, 90, 139–78, 146, 151, 155, 248, 255, 257, 266–7
  south-east region of 222, 227, 233, 244, 246, 248
equity funding in housing 146, 243, 256
  equity withdrawal 72, 147, 151, 176, 243–50, 252, 257
  negative equity 43, 56, 72, 125, 150–51, 176
  private rented housing 21, 60, 67, 85
European Agricultural Guidance and Guarantee Fund 184
European Coal and Steel Community (ECSC) 179, 184–5
European Court of Justice 197, 199–200
European Economic Interest Groupings (EEIG) 214

European Exchange Rate Mechanism (ERM)
196, 207, 236, 241–2, 258
European Free Trade Association (EFTA)   205
European Group of Financial
Institutions   214–15
European Parliament   199, 230
resolutions on housing   180
European Regional Development Fund
(ERDF)   185–8, 228
European Social Fund (ESF)   182, 184, 186
Exclusion 1 programme   185

Family Credit   172, 268, 271–2, 274
Fannie Mae   53, 82, 191
Fico France   211, 214
FIM   210–11
financial sector deregulation   97, 106–10, 125,
144–5, 150, 240, 243–50 *passim*, 252
Finland   8
First Banking Directive (EU)   197–8
first-time buyers   36
average age of   16, 222
fiscal relief for   57, 256–7, 270, 272–3
Fitzpatrick, S. & M. Stephens   170
flats   *see* apartments
France   5, 8–18, 23–53, 58, 61–3, 68, 72, 76,
81, 86–7, 92, 140–47, 151–5, 160, 167, 171,
175–7, 193, 212–14, 222–51, 257–67
Franco, General F.   97, 99
Furones, L.   110

Geindre, F. (Geindre Report)   24, 34, 39–40,
43–4
Germany   5, 8–18, 34–5, 45–74, 76, 78, 81,
83, 86–7, 92, 119, 138–56 *passim*, 167, 171–7,
191, 193–5, 212–14, 222–51 *passim*, 255–61,
264–5, 267, 270
reunification of   45, 47–8, 52, 63, 70–71,
228
situation in the eastern Länder   47–8, 50,
62, 64–5, 70, 73, 142, 226, 228
Gesamtverband der Wohnungswirtschaft
(GdW)   63–4
Ghékiere, L.   26–7, 33, 38, 41, 49, 78, 80, 83,
92, 104, 106, 112–5, 184
Gibb, K.   267
see also Maclennan, D.
Gilbert, M. and associates   11
Glasgow   140–41, 143, 157, 161, 248, 266
Castlemilk housing estate 161
Glasgow District Council, no. of dwellings
owned   37, 63, 156
Glasser, R.   20

grants and loans at reduced interest for house
construction   2–3, 237, 256–7, 261–3
in France
PAP   27–32, 38, 41–2, 56, 81, 194
PC   27–9, 41, 102
PLS/I   32–3, 37–8, 42, 155, 261
PLA   32–3, 37–42, 155
in Germany   51–2, 61–2, 66
in Netherlands
BWS   81, 85, 89
BLS   81
in Sweden   *see* interest subsidies
in Spain   98–101
in Britain   143, 147–8, 155, 256–7
see also Housing Association Grant, Hous-
ing Subsidy, Housing Support Grant and
GRO grant
grants and loans for house improvement   29,
33, 37, 155, 148
France
PAH   29
ANAH   33, 41
PALULOS 37–8
Germany   51–2
Britain   148, 155, 254–7, 273
grants for mortgage and rental deposits   103–4,
115
Grant Redemption Funds   168–9
Greece   8, 10, 12, 18, 229
Grieve, Sir Robert (Grieve Report)   141
GRO grants (Scotland)   148, 155, 256, 261
Gropper, D. M.   196
Group of 10   203–5
Grupo Cor   210
guest workers (gastarbeiter)   46, 77, 228

Halifax Building Society   208–12
Hallett, G.   47, 53, 57–8, 62–3, 155
Hamburg   46
rent control in   58
SAGA municipal housing company   63
harassment, protection of tenants from   152–3
Harrison, J.   96
Harrison, Judith   158, 169
Hedman, E.   123
Heerma, E.   94
Heerma Memorandum   76, 83, 85–6, 88,
90, 95
Heugas-Darraspen, H.   23–4, 35, 41–2
Hills, J.   70, 139, 146, 149, 161, 171–4, 268,
271
HLMs   *see* housing associations
HM Treasury   200–202

Holmans, A. E.   21, 53, 139–40, 146, 150, 152, 155, 158, 247
Holmans, S. K.   239
homelessness   39, 162, 169–70, 177, 180, 186, 251
Hong Kong and Shanghai Bank   217
HORIZON   188
household size   9–11, 13
house prices   15–16, 43, 79, 110–11, 116, 125, 145, 147, 149–50, 243–50, 255, 270
  comparison of rate of increase in Britain and Germany   53
House of Lords Select Committee on the European Communities   199–201
Housing Acts 1950 & 1956 (Germany)   45, 51
Housing Act 1901 (Netherlands)   75, 86
Housing Acts
  1930   171
  1980   149
  1964 and 1974   158
  1985   14, 148
  1988   59, 158, 225, 239, 167, 177
Housing Action Areas   148
Housing Action Trusts   156, 160–61
housing allowances   1, 3, 21, 24, 33–4, 38–9, 41–2, 45, 67–70, 73–4, 76, 85, 91–3, 95, 120, 135–8, 143, 152–3, 164–6, 171–6, 235, 237, 252, 262–3, 267–8, 274
  in Britain (Housing Benefit)   148, 153, 159, 166, 171–5, 178, 225, 240, 263, 266–73
  in France
    APL   28, 29, 32–3, 38, 41, 42
    AL, ALS, ALF   41, 42
  in Germany (Wohngeld)   68–70, 73, 74
    Härteausgleich   70
    housing allowance "taper"   69–70, 73, 135, 172–4, 267–8, 271, 274
housing and management of the economy   43, 150–51, 176, 221–33 passim, 234–50, 252–3, 257–8, 273
  in the Netherlands   79
housing associations   35–44 passim, 50, 62–8, 73, 76, 87–8, 94, 133, 147–9, 157–61, 166–9, 171, 175, 177, 238–40, 253, 261, 264–6, 271, 274
  in Britain
    advantages and accountability of   265–6
    as landlords   158–9
    community based associations in Scotland   158–9, 169, 178
    HLMs in France   35–40, 44, 63, 87, 133, 265
      composition of boards   36–7

vacancies in HLM stock   39
in Germany
  removal of non-profit status   62–5, 73
  see also GdW
Housing Association Grant   90, 147–8, 158, 167–9, 175, 177, 239–40, 261–2, 269, 271
Housing Benefit   see housing allowances
housing completions   13–14, 24–5, 47, 52, 72, 76, 79, 88, 119, 140, 170
  since 1945   13–15, 24, 47, 76, 118, 140
Housing Corporation   76, 158–60, 167
housing costs   15, 53, 125
  in relation to allowances   135
Housing Distribution Act 1947 (Netherlands)   84
housing finance   54–6, 60–61, 80–82, 128, 161–9, 234, 240–50, 253
Housing Finance Act 1972   171
housing for incoming industry   160
housing investment   13, 22–4, 34, 47, 124, 137, 144, 222, 269
  rented housing as an investment   83, 94, 129, 225
  housing as an investment good   255
  need for investment in British social rented sector   264–6, 272
  private sector funds in social rented housing   264, 273
Housing Investment Programmes   162
housing policy, cost of   3–4, 42–4, 71–2, 75, 91–4, 115, 118, 136–7, 141, 174–6, 234–40, 268–74
housing policy, objectives   1–2, 6, 150, 251–5, 258–9, 262, 268–9
  regional variation in   146, 223–4, 268
  under RTB and LSVT   163–4
Housing Rent Act 1979 (Netherlands)   84
Housing Revenue Account   166
Housing (Scotland) Acts
  1987   148
  1988   167
housing shortage   251
  in France   23, 30, 35, 44
  in Germany   46–7, 58
  in Netherlands   77, 84
  in Sweden   118, 137
  in Britain   140, 152, 163
housing standards
  in East Germany   47
  in Sweden   118, 132, 137
  in Britain   140–41, 162
    "tolerable" and "fitness" standards   14, 148

housing stock   11–16, 24, 47, 49
Housing Support Grant   164, 167, 263
Housing Subsidy   164, 166–7, 263
HSB (Tenants Savings Bank and Housing
  Association)   126
Hubert, F.   49, 57–60, 66
Hughes, G. & B. McCormick   224, 226

income   7, 21, 142
Indonesia, migrants from   77
Industrial Development Act 1982 (annual
  reports)   228
imputed rental income   2, 30, 33, 57, 61, 71,
  82, 93–4, 105, 146, 153, 175, 238, 255, 260
Income Support (for mortgage interest)   171–2,
  174–6, 178, 267
inflation   144, 150, 163, 176–7, 222, 227, 233,
  240, 247, 249, 252, 258, 260, 266
    effect on rents   21, 30, 58, 66–7, 69, 131,
      152, 164, 166–7, 266
    housing as a hedge against   53, 72, 150
    in relation to housing allowances in
      Germany   69
inner city housing   251, 264
Instituto Nacional de la Vivienda   98–9
Insituto para la Promoción Publica de la
  Vivienda   98
insurance companies   121, 144
insurance for mortgage finance   29, 80, 85,
  145, 249–50, 257, 273
    guarantee arrangements in Sweden   124
Inter-Bank On-Line System   214
interest subsidies
    guaranteed or pegged rates (Sweden)   122,
      128, 130, 135–7, 164
    Spanish VPO & VPT schemes   97, 102–5,
      107, 111, 115
Ireland   6–15, 237
Italy   8, 10, 12–13, 191, 193, 210, 229–30,
  232–3, 237, 240, 247

Jaedicke, W. & H. Wollmann   46, 71
Joseph Rowntree Foundation   147, 239–40,
  247, 260, 265, 269, 271

Kee, R.   19
Kroes, H.   *see* Ymker, A.

labour mobility   4, 22, 34, 125, 176, 221–33,
  254, 272
land prices   2, 9

Länder governments, housing
  responsibilities   45–6, 52, 54–6, 63, 65, 68,
  70–71, 139, 267
landlord organizations for social
  housing   35–7, 62–5, 87–8, 132–4, 156–61,
  264–6, 273
La Rioja   111
Lawson, Lord   240, 249
Leal, J.   115, 117
Lebègue, D. (Lebègue Report)   24, 27–44
  passim, 47, 71
Leeds   156
Leeds Permanent Building Society   145
Leutner, B. & D. Jensen   46
Lindecrona, T.   133
Liverpool   160–61, 185
Livret A savings accounts   32, 38, 42
Livret Bleu savings accounts   38
Lloyds Bank   145, 217–18
loan to income ratio   257
loan to value ratio   29, 54, 56, 72, 80, 109,
  125, 145, 150–51, 154, 176, 244, 249, 257,
  272–3
local authorities   14, 24, 35–7, 39, 44, 46, 54,
  63–7, 71, 76, 78, 80–81, 85–8, 91, 94, 128,
  132–3, 135, 138, 139–42, 146, 148–9, 155–71,
  174–5, 177, 224, 238–40, 253, 264–7, 273
Local Government and Housing Act 1989   166,
  175
Loi Malandrain   31, 34, 43
London   143, 146, 158, 170
low cost home ownership schemes   147–9, 169
Lundqvist, L.   118–20, 124, 127–8, 130–34
Luton   248
Luxembourg   8, 10, 12–13, 228

Maastricht, Treaty of   4, 91, 117, 179, 181,
  183, 196–7, 207–8, 221, 230, 234
MacDougall, Sir Donald (MacDougall
  Report)   182
Maclennan, D. & K. Gibb   243, 248
Madrid   100, 110–11, 212
Maghreb States   231–2
    see also North Africa
maintenance of housing   39, 65, 126–9, 141,
  148, 163, 166, 168, 254
Malpass, P.   139, 167
    & A. Murie   161
Manchester   156, 188
Massieu, A.   113
Mayes, D.   *see* Begg, I.
Midland Bank   210, 217
Midlothian   266

migration 7–23, 46–7, 52, 73, 77, 140, 221–2, 226, 251
  from outside the EU 228–33, 96, 116
  from British Commonwealth 228
  illegal immigrants 229, 232
Miles, D. 258
Miles, Diane 102–3, 105–6, 109, 114
Minford, P., M. Peel, P. Ashton 224, 227
Monklands District, highest % social rented stock in Britain 157
More, A. 169
mortgage arrears 150–51, 176, 248, 254, 272
mortgage backed by endowment insurance 80, 146–7, 238, 250, 255
mortgage banks 54–6, 60, 72, 80
Mortgage Benefit, proposals 268, 270, 272, 274
mortgage bonds 121
  Pfandbriefe 54, 72, 258
Mortgage Credit Directive (draft) (EU) 190, 199
mortgage finance 4, 19, 21, 26–9, 32–3, 54–7, 60, 80–81, 109–10, 121–4, 127, 130, 134, 143–5, 176, 190–220, 222, 253, 257–8
mortgage interest tax relief 2, 19, 27, 29, 33–4, 57, 73, 82, 93–4, 124, 105, 116, 128, 136–7, 145–7, 174–8, 238, 250, 260–61, 269–73
  effect of abolition on house prices 255–6
Mortgage Trust 209, 216
Monopolies & Mergers Commission 217, 219
Muellbauer, J. 151, 243
Munich, rent control in 58
municipal housing companies 62, 65–8, 87, 94, 132–8, 156, 238, 264
Murie, A. & H. Priemus 78, 87–8

National Housing Council (Netherlands) 87
National Institute of Social and Economic Research 150, 247, 255
National Pension Fund (Sweden) 121
Nationwide Building Society 208–9
Netherlands 5, 7–18, 22, 35, 49, 53, 69, 75–96, 118–19, 121, 138, 140, 142, 148, 153–6, 171, 176, 191, 193, 222, 227–40 *passim*, 243, 251–2, 255–68 *passim*
Netherlands Christian Housing Institute 87
Neue Heimat 37, 63, 98
Newcastle 270
New Town Development Corporations 142, 149, 157–8
nomination rights in social housing 39, 65, 67, 132

North Africa 9, 39, 96, 116, 228–9, 231, 251
Northern Ireland 5, 139, 142–3, 156–7, 185
  Northern Ireland Housing Executive 37, 156
North-Rhine–Westphalia 70
North Sea oil 160, 167
Nota Volkshuisvesting in de jaren negentig *see* Heerma Memorandum
Noulas, A. G. 196

Oder–Neisse 46
Official Credit Institute 107, 109
"one million programme" (Sweden) 118, 133
Orgaz, L. 110, 114
Orkney 156
overcrowding in housing 20, 141, 157
Own Funds Directive (EU) 197, 203–4

Paisley 161, 187
Papa, O. 29, 42, 70–71, 80, 82, 91–2 124, 135
Pareja, M. & P. Riera 101–5
Paris, house prices in 243
  Treaty of 179
peripheral housing estates 39, 141, 170, 251, 264, 266
Permanent Interest Bearing Shares (PIBS) 205–6
Petersson, A. 135
Planificación de la Vivienda 98
planning system
  in relation to housing supply 227–8, 251
population density 9, 75, 77, 227
population growth 7–9, 23, 47, 77, 140
  explosive growth in Maghreb States 231
Portugal 8, 10, 12–13, 214, 229
Poverty 3 programme 185
poverty trap 70, 73, 138, 166, 172–4, 178, 225, 262–3, 267–8, 271–4
Power, A. 4, 62, 64
Priemus, H. *see* Murie, A.
Private Sector Finance Initiative 265
private rented sector, rates of return 31, 34, 61, 64–7, 132, 259–61
privatization, of rented housing 134, 138
  see also transfers of social rented stock and RTB
problem estates 39, 44, 63, 67, 133, 141, 160, 251, 264, 266
property and land taxes 30, 34, 42, 57, 61, 82, 86, 125, 130, 135, 146
Pryke, M. & C. Whitehead 215

public expenditure   4, 39–40, 44, 88, 90, 118, 120, 133, 137, 160–69, 174–7, 234–40, 250, 252, 264, 269–73
  government control of borrowing in UK 161
  position of British housing associations   167–8
  Swedish municipal housing companies   133

Quartiers en Crise   188–9
Quilliot, R.   184

rate fund contributions   156, 164, 166
regional policy   226–8, 230–31, 233, 252
Rent Acts (France)
  1948   24, 31
  1982, 1986, 1989   31
  see also Loi Malandrain
Rent Act 1957   152
Rent and Reconstruction Act 1950 (Netherlands)   84
Rent Assessment Committees   152–3
rent control   2–3, 20–21, 260, 263
  in France   23–4, 30–31, 34, 43
  in Germany   45, 50, 54, 58–60, 68, 72–3
  in Netherlands   76, 83–5
  in Sweden   129–32
  in Spain   97–8, 113–14, 116
  in Britain   139, 143, 151–3, 225, 259
rents, level of   3, 24, 31, 36, 38, 47, 49, 51, 58–60, 62, 65–70, 84, 92, 131–2, 134, 138, 141, 152, 157, 160, 164, 166–7, 171, 174, 177–8, 224, 239, 259, 262–3, 266–7, 271, 274
  effect of Housing Benefit upon   174
  "fair rents"   131, 152–3, 168, 224–5
  in relation to "use value" (Sweden)   131–2, 134
  points system (Netherlands)   84
  supplementary charge on social rents   68, 71, 90
Rent Negotiations Act (Sweden)   131
Rent Officers   152, 168, 171, 174, 263
rent policy for social sector   67, 89, 134, 167, 266
rent pooling   40, 67, 69, 89–91, 134, 167, 174, 266
Rent Restriction Act 1939   152
Rent Tribunal (Sweden)   131, 134
Rent to Mortgage scheme   149, 157
repossessions   56, 72, 150–51, 176, 247, 249, 254, 272
residualization   237, 252
Revenue Deficit Grants   168–9

Riera, P.   *see* Pareja, M.
Right to Buy   90, 149, 157, 160–64, 167, 169, 176–7, 269
Riksbyggen   126
roll over relief (from capital gains tax)   125, 238, 255
Rome, Treaty of   197–8
Rowlatt, A.   240–42
Royal Bank of Scotland   209–10, 213–14, 217

SABO (Swedish Assn of municipal housing companies)   132–3
SAGA (Hamburg municipal housing company)   63
Salmon, K. G.   98, 108
Satsangi, M.   24, 31–3
savings banks   32, 33, 54–6
  see also Bausparkassen
savings schemes for housing   28, 42–3, 55–6, 72, 104–5, 127, 144, 151, 223, 249, 258, 273
  in France PEL and CEL   27–8
SBAB (Swedish state mortgage agency)   121, 128, 130
Schaefer, J. P.   26
SCIC (housing landlord arm of French CDC)   37, 63, 160
Scotland   5, 8–10, 13–20, 49, 78, 94, 139–40, 142–62, 169–70, 176, 228, 246, 248, 255, 264, 267
Scottish Economic Bulletin   143
Scottish Homes   37, 76, 142, 147–9, 155, 158–61, 167, 169, 224, 261
Scottish Special Housing Association (SSHA)   37, 142, 149, 160
  see also Scottish Homes
Scottish Office   139, 141, 156–7, 159, 163, 167
  Scottish Development Dept / Scottish Office Environment Dept   141, 153, 160, 162–3
Second Banking Directive (EU)   108, 197–200, 202–3, 211–12
second homes   13, 15, 146
Secretary of State for the Environment   141
Secretary of State for Scotland   159–61
Secretary of State for Wales   141, 160
securitization   215–16
security of tenure   20, 45, 54, 59, 72–3, 83–4, 127, 143, 151–2, 225
shanty towns   2, 116
Shetland   156, 166–7
Single European Act   4, 196–7, 221, 249, 252
single passport   197–202, 211, 219
Siegfried Act 1894 (France)   35

Single Market 56
Skandiniviska Enskilda Banken 216
SKB (Stockholm Tenant Housing Assn) 126
Skye & Lochalsh District Council 156
slum clearance 140, 141, 143, 155
social exclusion 186
social rented sector
  means test in relation to 21, 38, 51, 68, 70, 121, 132
  reduction in size
    Britain 169-70
    Germany 50, 63
Social Rented Sector Guarantee Fund (Netherlands) 88
social security 68-70, 73, 91-2, 135-6, 171, 176, 239, 267
social segregation, avoidance of 120, 132, 138, 141
"social ownership" housing
  in France (PAP scheme) 27
  in Germany 51-2
  in Netherlands 81
  in Britain 147-8
Sociétés d'Economie Mixte 35, 37-8
Solvency Ratio Directive (EU) 197, 203-4
Spain 5, 7-18, 22, 72, 80, 82, 96-117, 139-40, 153, 191, 193, 210, 212, 214, 222, 230, 232-4, 237-8, 243, 249, 251-5, 262, 264
  Housing Plans 99-103, 106-7, 111, 115
  illegal immigration 229
Spanish Civil War 96, 99
standard of living 2, 7, 10-11, 16-17, 142-3
Stephens, M. 144, 195
  see also Fitzpatrick, S.
stock transfer 78
Stockholm 126
Stoke-on-Trent 187-8
subsidiarity 181, 188
Sudetenland 46
Swärd, K. 118, 125, 136
Sweden 5, 7-18, 49, 53, 75, 78, 87, 92, 94-5, 118-38, 140, 143, 154, 156, 164, 171, 176-7, 234, 235, 237, 243, 251-2, 255, 257, 262, 265
Switzerland 10, 17-18

Tai Cymru 160, 167
Tamames, R. 98-9
taxation and housing 19, 28-30, 33-4, 42, 45, 50, 55, 57, 60-61, 64, 71-2, 76, 80, 82, 86, 92, 94, 105-6, 120-22, 124-5, 127, 137, 144-7, 150, 153-4, 166, 174-6, 234, 236, 238, 255, 260-61, 273
tax reform in Sweden 120

Tenancy Protection Act (Germany) 58-9
tenemental housing 19, 128, 130, 143, 169
tenure 7, 16-22, 26, 48-51, 78-9, 97, 112, 119-20, 142-3, 171, 222, 251, 253, 268
  neutrality in policy 1, 19-20, 26, 51, 120-21, 124, 130, 137-9, 171, 176-8, 250, 252-3, 256
  tenure and mobility 222-33 passim
Tomann, H. 49, 62, 64-5, 69
Tower Hamlets 156, 160
transfers of social rented housing 134-5, 143, 148-9, 157, 159, 161, 240, 265-6, 269-71, 274
  large-scale voluntary transfers (LSVTs) 159, 162-4, 177, 270
  levy on LSVTs 159, 269
  public expenditure savings from 269-70
Turkey 9, 77, 228
Turner, B. 125

UGT 98
unemployment and the housing market 141, 150, 171, 178, 221, 226, 229-30, 232, 235, 248, 270
Ulbrich, R. & U. Wullkopf 71
UNFO-HLM 35, 36
United States 193-4, 226, 230, 232, 235, 269
"upmarketing" problem 69, 173-4, 178, 267-8, 274
URBAN 188
Urban Pilot Projects 187-8
urban renewal 57, 76, 83, 147, 155, 160-61, 169, 256
  Scottish urban renewal partnerships 161

vacancies 39, 67, 133-4, 162, 167, 170
Valenciana 111
van Weesep, J. 91
VAT 120, 144, 154, 106
  on new construction 82, 86, 125, 146, 240
  on repair and maintenance 269
VROM (Dutch Ministry of Housing) 7, 49, 75-6, 78, 80-82, 87, 89-90, 92

Wales 5, 139, 142-3, 146, 155, 157, 160
Westaway, P & N. Pain 255, 150
Westerlund, L. 135
Western Isles 156
West Devon 156
Westminster 139
Weyman Jones, T. see Drake, L.
Whitehead, C. see Pryke, M.

Wilcox, S.   15–16, 146–7, 150, 162, 169–70,
  172, 239–40, 244, 247, 265, 269
Winterhur   210
Woolwich Building Society   15, 209–12, 222
Wright, A.   98–100, 113

Ymkers, F. & H. Kroes   76–7, 84, 87